CAMBRIDGE STUDIES IN EARLY M

After the Deluge: Poland–Lithuania and the Second Northern War 1655–1660

The Swedish invasion of 1655, known to Poles ever since as the 'Swedish Deluge', provoked the political and military collapse of the Polish–Lithuanian Commonwealth, the second-largest state in Europe. Although the Swedes were ultimately driven out, the 'Swedish Deluge' proved to be a crucial turning-point in Polish history. The Commonwealth, dominant in eastern and northern Europe in the sixteenth century, never recovered from the blows inflicted during the Second Northern War (1655–1660). In the eighteenth century it was the plaything of its neighbours, and its political system was the laughing-stock of Europe. By 1795 it had been partitioned out of existence.

War has long been seen as crucial to the development of more effective systems of government in Europe during the seventeenth century, but studies usually concentrate on states which responded successfully to the challenges. Yet much can be learned from those that failed; none failed more dramatically than Poland–Lithuania. Robert Frost examines the reasons for Poland's fall and the conduct of the war by the Polish government, and addresses the crucial question of why, despite widespread recognition of the shortcomings of the political system, subsequent attempts to reform should have failed.

The paucity hitherto of English-language material on the Second Northern War means that *After the Deluge* will appeal to a broad audience among political, diplomatic and military historians of Poland, Germany, Scandinavia, Russia and early modern Europe in general.

After the Deluge: Poland–Lithuania and the Second Northern War

CAMBRIDGE STUDIES IN EARLY MODERN HISTORY

Edited by Professor J. H. Elliott, University of Oxford, Professor Olwen Hufton, Harvard University, and Professor H. G. Koenigsberger

The idea of an 'early modern' period of European history from the fifteenth to the late eighteenth century is now widely accepted among historians. The purpose of Cambridge Studies in Early Modern History is to publish monographs and studies which illuminate the character of the period as a whole, and in particular focus attention on a dominant theme within it, the interplay of continuity and change as they are presented by the continuity of medieval ideas, political and social organisation, and by the impact of new ideas, new methods and new demands on the traditional structures.

For a list of titles published in the series, please see end of book

After the Deluge

Poland–Lithuania and the
Second Northern War 1655–1660

ROBERT I. FROST
*Lecturer in the Department of History,
King's College London*

PUBLISHED BY THE PRESS SYNDICATE OF THE UNIVERSITY OF CAMBRIDGE
The Pitt Building, Trumpington Street, Cambridge, United Kingdom

CAMBRIDGE UNIVERSITY PRESS
The Edinburgh Building, Cambridge CB2 2RU, UK
40 West 20th Street, New York NY 10011–4211, USA
477 Williamstown Road, Port Melbourne, VIC 3207, Australia
Ruiz de Alarcón 13, 28014 Madrid, Spain
Dock House, The Waterfront, Cape Town 8001, South Africa

http://www.cambridge.org

© Cambridge University Press 1993

This book is in copyright. Subject to statutory exception
and to the provisions of relevant collective licensing agreements,
no reproduction of any part may take place without
the written permission of Cambridge University Press.

First published 1993
First paperback edition 2003

A catalogue record for this book is available from the British Library

Library of Congress cataloguing in publication data

Frost, Robert I.
After the Deluge: Poland and the Second Northern War, 1655–1660 /
Robert I. Frost.
p. cm. – (Cambridge studies in early modern history)
Includes bibliographical references and index.
ISBN 0 521 42008 3 (hardback)
1. Swedish–Polish War, 1655–1660. 2. Poland – Politics and
government – 1572–1763. I. Title. II. Series.
DL725.6.F76 1993
948.5´03 – dc20 92–5528 CIP

ISBN 0 521 42008 3 hardback
ISBN 0 521 54402 5 paperback

Transferred to digital printing 2003

To my parents

Contents

Preface	*page* xi
Gazeteer	xiii
Glossary	xv
Office holders	xvii
List of abbreviations	xviii
Pronunciation guide	xix
Genealogical tables	xx
Maps	xxiii
1 Introduction: Poland–Lithuania in the mid-seventeenth century	1
2 The Deluge	26
3 Recovery: July 1655 – August 1656	53
4 The widening conflict: June–December 1656	71
5 Constructing a coalition: January–December 1657	86
6 The succession and the failure of the coalition: January–July 1658	106
7 Political reform	131
8 Towards a French candidature: 1658–1660	152
9 Conclusion: the succession and the failure of reform	168
Bibliography	180
Index	203

Preface

There is no satisfactory solution to the problem of personal and place names in a work in English on east European history. I have tried to balance the conflicting claims of consistency and comprehensibility for readers unacquainted with east European languages. With regard to personal names, where an adequate English equivalent exists I have used it for the first names of ruling princes and members of royal families. Otherwise I use the Polish, German, Ukrainian, or Russian form where appropriate. I have used transliterations from Ukrainian rather than the Polish form for the names of Cossack leaders, thus Khmelnytskyi, not Chmielnicki; Vyhovskyi, not Wychowski. With regard to place names, wherever possible I have used the modern English equivalent, the seventeenth-century English equivalent for place names no longer used (for example Samogitia for Żmudź) or the form most familiar to English-speaking readers. On occasion this means preferring a Russian to a Polish, Belorussian, or Ukrainian form: thus Mogilev, not Mahiliou; Chernigov, not Chernihiv; and Brest (Litovsk) for Brześć Litewski. With regard to cities and provinces whose cultural and ethnic composition has changed radically I have preferred as far as possible the form used by the dominant linguistic group in the seventeenth century. Thus, for places in Prussia and Silesia German has been preferred: Danzig, not Gdańsk; Thorn, not Toruń; Breslau, not Wrocław. The one exception is the Catholic bishopric of Warmia (Ermland), which was held by Poles rather than Germans. Similarly I have preferred Polish, rather than Lithuanian or Belorussian forms for most places in the grand duchy of Lithuania although I have used Ukrainian forms for most places in the Ukraine. Since the Ukraine in the seventeenth century was an imprecise geographical expression, whose boundaries did not correspond with modern Ukraine, I have preferred Lwów to Lviv or Lvov. Transliterations from the Cyrillic alphabet have been carried out according to a modified version of the Library of Congress system, omitting diacritics. All dates are given in New Style. All translations from Polish, Latin, French, German and Italian are my own.

The preparation of this book would have been impossible without the help of a large number of people. I am grateful to Professor Geoffrey Parker, whose inspirational teaching at St Andrews first stimulated my interest in the problem of military change and its impact on the state in early modern Europe, and to Professor Norman Gash, who provided a wayward undergraduate with a rigorous training in

Preface

the art of writing. My greatest debt is to Professor Norman Davies, who suggested a topic and then supervised and guided me through the thesis upon which this book is based. I would like to thank him for his constant help, sympathy and encouragement. I would also like to thank Professor Józef Gierowski of the Jagiellonian University, who acted as my supervisor in Cracow, and the late Professor Adam Kersten, who made some important suggestions at an early stage of my research. Dr Frank Sysyn was kind enough to allow me to read in draft his forthcoming book on Khmelnytskyi's revolt. This work has been read in whole or in part by Professor Norman Davies, Dr Lindsey Hughes, Professor Helli Koenigsberger, Dr George Lukowski, Dr Derek McKay, Liz Rembowska, Dr Hamish Scott, Jane Sunderland, Dr Frank Sysyn and Professor Zbigniew Wójcik. Their comments and criticisms have been invaluable. All remaining mistakes are entirely my responsibility. Special thanks are due to Dr John Daly for listening and for introducing me to the world of computers; to the staff of University College London, Computing Centre, especially Dave Guppy, and the staff of King's College London, Humanities Computing Division for their continuing support. I am particularly grateful to the staff of the many libraries and archives in which I have worked, especially to Dr Adam Homecki, director of the Czartoryski Library in Cracow, who allowed me to work in his office when the building was closed for redecoration. I would like to thank my parents, who provided financial support when I was learning Polish, and the British and Polish governments for the scholarships which enabled me to undertake archival work. I have benefited greatly from the help and advice of Richard Fisher and Iris Hunter at Cambridge University Press, who have been both understanding and patient.

Gazeteer

The italicised form is the one used in the book.

The Kingdom of Poland, Royal Prussia, Silesia and Livonia

German	*Polish*	*English*
Allenstein	Olsztyn	
Breslau	Wrocław	
Braunsberg	Braniewo	
Bromberg	Bydgoszcz	
Bütow	Bytow	
Danzig	Gdańsk	
Draheim	Drawsko	
Dünaburg	Dyneburg/Dźwińsk	
Elbing	Elbląg	
Ermland	*Warmia*	
Frauenburg	Frombork	
Lauenburg	Lębork	
Lubau	Lubowla	
Marienburg	Malbork	
	Małopolska	*Little Poland*
	Mazowsze	*Mazovia*
Neisse	Nysa	
Oberglogau	Głogówek	
Oder (River)	Odra	
Oppeln	Opole	
Pommern	Pomorze	*Pomerania*
Posen	*Poznań*	
Preussisch-Holland	Pasłęk	
Prostken	Prostki	
Putzig	Puck	
Thorn	Toruń	
Wehlau	Welawa	

Gazeteer

Zielenzig	Wielkopolska			*Great Poland*
Zips	Sulęcin			
	Spiż			

Lithuania and the Ukraine

Polish	Ukrainian	Lithuanian	Russian	English
Beresteczko	*Berestechko*			
Biała Cerkiew	*Bila Tserkva*			
Bracław	*Bratslav*			
Brześć-Litewski			*Brest (Litovsk)*	
Chocim	*Khotyn*			
Czernichów	Chernihiv		*Chernigov*	
Hadiacz	*Hadiach*			
Lwów	Lviv		Lvov	
Ochmatów	*Okhmativ*			
Perejasław	*Pereiaslav*		Pereiaslavl'	
Piławce	*Pyliavtsi*			
Wierzbołów		Virbalis		
Wilno		Vilnius	Vilna	
Wolmar		Valmiera (Latvian)		
Wołyń	Volyn			*Volhynia*
Żółte Wody	*Zhovti Vody*			
Żmudź		Žemaitija		*Samogitia*

Glossary and currency

Castellan (*kasztelan*) — In origin the keeper of a royal castle. There were two kinds of castellan, both of which sat in the senate: major castellans from the chief royal town in each palatinate and minor castellans from less important towns. There were no minor castellans in Lithuania or the Ukraine.

Chamber of envoys — The lower house of the diet (*sejm*). Comprised of envoys from local dietines (*sejmiki*).

Commonwealth — *Rzeczpospolita*; a direct rendering in Polish of the Latin *res publica*. I have preferred the seventeenth-century English equivalent 'Commonwealth' rather than 'Republic' for *Rzeczpospolita*.

Confederation — A league of nobles formed for a specific political purpose, for example opposition to royal policy, in which decisions were taken by majority vote.

Crown (*Korona*) — The kingdom of Poland, as opposed to the grand duchy of Lithuania.

Czopowe — A tax on the production and sale of alcohol.

Ekonomia — A royal estate contained in the 'Lands of the Table': the directly administered royal domain, all of whose proceeds went to the upkeep of the royal household.

Equestrian order — *Ordo equestris* (Latin). Conventially used in the seventeenth century to distinguish the non-senatorial nobility.

Hetman (*hetman*) — The commanders of the armed forces. Poland and Lithuania each had a grand hetman and a field hetman.

Lan — A measure of land; most common were the lesser or Chełmno *łan*, which equalled thirty morgs or 16.7–17.5 hectares, and the greater or Franconian *łan*, which was the equivalent of forty-three morgs or 22.6–25.3 hectares.

Liberum veto — The right of individual envoys to the diet, or noblemen in their local dietine, to block proceedings by invoking the principle of unanimity (*nemine contradicente*).

Palatine (*wojewoda*) — The chief provincial official. Ranked in the senate below the bishops and above the castellans. Nominally responsible for the defence of his province.

Glossary

Piast	A native-born monarch. Named after the legendary founder of the Polish state.
Rokosz	The right of rebellion in defence of the constitution.
Ruthenians	The non Great Russian eastern Slavs: the ancestors of modern Ukrainians and Belorussians. Chancery Ruthenian was the official language of the grand duchy of Lithuania until 1697.
Sarmatism	The myth that the nobility of Poland and Lithuania were descended from the ancient Sarmatian tribe.
Senate	Both the upper chamber of the diet and the royal council, comprising Catholic bishops, palatines, castellans and government ministers. 150 strong by the mid-seventeenth century.
Starosta (*Starosta*)	There were two types of starosta: judicial and non-judicial. The former was a royal-appointed official with wide judicial and administrative powers, who presided over the local court of the first instance. A non-judicial starosta was holder of an individual royal estate. The starosta of Samogitia was equivalent to a palatine in the rest of the Commonwealth.
Starosty (*starostwo*)	Royal lands leased for life to inidvidual nobles.
Szlachta	The nobility. The translation 'gentry' is unsatisfactory for what was a legally privileged elite. Although the doctrine of noble equality meant there was no legal distinction between the great magnates and the mass of the nobility, I have used 'noble' and 'nobility' to refer to the whole class, while I have used 'magnate' and '*szlachta*' to distinguish between the wealthy and powerful elite and the mass of ordinary nobles. This is purely my own convention in the interests of clarity; in Polish the term *szlachta* would include the magnates.

The Polish złoty was adopted as money of account in 1496 and was distinguished from the so-called 'red złoty', the actual gold ducat. The Commonwealth faced serious problems during the Thirty Years War due to the devaluation of the imperial currency. The 1650 currency Ordinance attempted, without any great success, to regulate the situation, decreeing that there were henceforth to be six Polish złoties to a ducat, which was fixed at a net weight of 3,441g, the same as an imperial ducat. There were thirty silver groszy in a złoty.

Office holders

Government Ministers

Crown grand marshal	Jerzy Sebastian Lubomirski (1650–64)
Lithuanian grand marshal	Aleksander Ludwik Radziwiłł (1637–54); Krzysztof Zawisza (1654–69)
Crown grand chancellor	Jerzy Ossoliński (1643–50); Andrzej Leszczyński (1650–2); Stefan Koryczyński (1652–8) Mikołaj Prażmowski (1658–66); Jan Leszczyński (1666–77)
Lithuanian grand chancellor	Albrycht Stanisław Radziwiłł (1623–56); Krzysztof Pac (1658–84)
Crown vice-chancellor	Andrzej Leszczyński (1645–50); Hieronim Radziewjowski (1650–2); Andrzej Trzebicki (1652–8); Mikołaj Prażmowski (1658); Bogusław Leszczyński (1658–60); Jan Leszczyński (1660–6)
Lithuanian vice-chancellor	Kazimierz Leon Sapieha (1645–56); Krzysztof Pac (nominated 1656, never confirmed by diet); Aleksander Naruszewicz (1658–68)
Crown treasurer	Bogusław Leszczyński (1650–8); Jan Kazimierz Krasiński (1658–69)
Lithuanian treasurer	Wincenty Gosiewski (1652–62)
Crown marshal of the Court	Łukasz Opaliński (1650–62)
Lithuanian marshal of the Court	Krzysztof Zawisza (1649–54); Teodor Lacki (1654–83)

Military commanders

Crown grand hetman	Mikołaj Potocki (1646–51); Stanisław Potocki (1654–67)
Lithuanian grand hetman	Janusz Kiszka (1646–53); Janusz Radziwiłł (1654–5); Paweł Sapieha (1656–65); Michał Kazimierz Pac (1667–82)
Crown field hetman	Marcin Kalinowski (1646–52); Stanisław Potocki (1652–4); Stanisław Lanckoroński (1654–7); Jerzy Sebastian Lubomirski (1657–64); Stefan Czarniecki (1665)
Lithuanian field hetman	Wincenty Gosiewski (1654–62); Michał Kazimierz Pac (1663–7)

Abbreviations

AGAD	Archiwum Główne Akt Dawnych
AKW	Archiwum Koronne Warszawskie
APPot.	Archiwum Publicznych Potockich
ARadz.	Archiwum Radziwiłłów
ASang.	Archiwum Sanguszków
BJag.	Biblioteka Jagiellońska
BNAR	Biblioteka Narodowa, Warsaw
BNP	Bibliothèque Nationale, Paris
BOZ	Biblioteka Ordynacji Zamoyskich
BPANCr.	Biblioteka Polskiej Akademii Nauk, Cracow
BPAN Kórnik	Biblioteka Polskiej Akademii Nauk, Kórnik
BUW	Biblioteka Uniwersytetu Warszawskiego
CPA	Correspondance Politique: Austria
CPD	Correspondance Politique: Danzig
CPP	Correspondance Politique: Pologne
CPS	Correspondance Politique: Suède
Czart.	Biblioteka im. ks. Czartoryskich
FFr.	Fonds Français
LL	Libri Legationum
Ossol.	Biblioteka Zakładu im. Ossolińskich
PSB	*Polski Słownik Biograficzny*
PODWP	K. Lepszy (ed.) *Polska w okresie drugiej wojny północnej* (Cracow, 1957)
Sobótka	*Śląski Kwartalnik Historyczny Sobótka*
SMHSW	*Studia i Materiały do Historii Sztuki Wojennej*
SMHW	*Studia i Materiały do Historii Wojskowości*
TRz.	Teki Rzymskie
WAPCr.	Wojewódzkie Archiwum Państwowe, Cracow
WAP Wawel	Wojewódzkie Archiwum Państwowe, Cracow, Oddział na Wawelu
ZBaw.	Zbiory Baworowskich

Pronunciation guide

Polish orthography looks daunting to the untutored eye but is more regular than English spelling. The following table may help the non-specialist to cope with the many Polish names in the text. The stress in Polish falls on the penultimate syllable.

ą	A nasal 'a', usually given its full value (similar to the French *on*) at the end of words or in fine elocution. When preceding a consonant it is usually pronounced as (English) 'on'. Thus Elbląg (Elbing) is pronounced 'Elblonk'.
ch	Like the Scottish 'ch' as in 'loch'.
ci, ć	A soft 'ch' sound, as a Londoner would pronounce the 't' in 'Tube'.
cz	A hard 'ch' sound.
ę	A nasal 'e', similar to the French *en*. As with 'ą', it is usually only given its full value at the end of words or in fine elocution. When preceding a consonant, it is usually pronounced 'em' as in 'ceremony' or 'en' as in 'ten' Thus 'Lębork' (Lauenburg) is pronounced '*Lem*bork' and Wałęsa, as in Lech, is pronounced 'Vaw-*en*-sa'.
j	'y' as in 'yes'.
ł	English 'w' as in 'well'.
ń	Soft 'n', like the Spanish 'ñ'.
ó, u	'oo' as in 'good'.
rz, ż	A harsher version of the 'j' in the French *je*.
ś, si	A soft 'sh' sound.
sz	A hard 'sh' sound.
szcz	'shch', the sound which would be produced in English by saying 'wa*sh ch*air' in quick succession.
ść	A softer version of szcz.
w	'v' as in English 'vibrant'.
y	'i' as in 'bit'.
ź, zi	The softer version of 'rz/ż'; roughly equivalent to the French *je*.

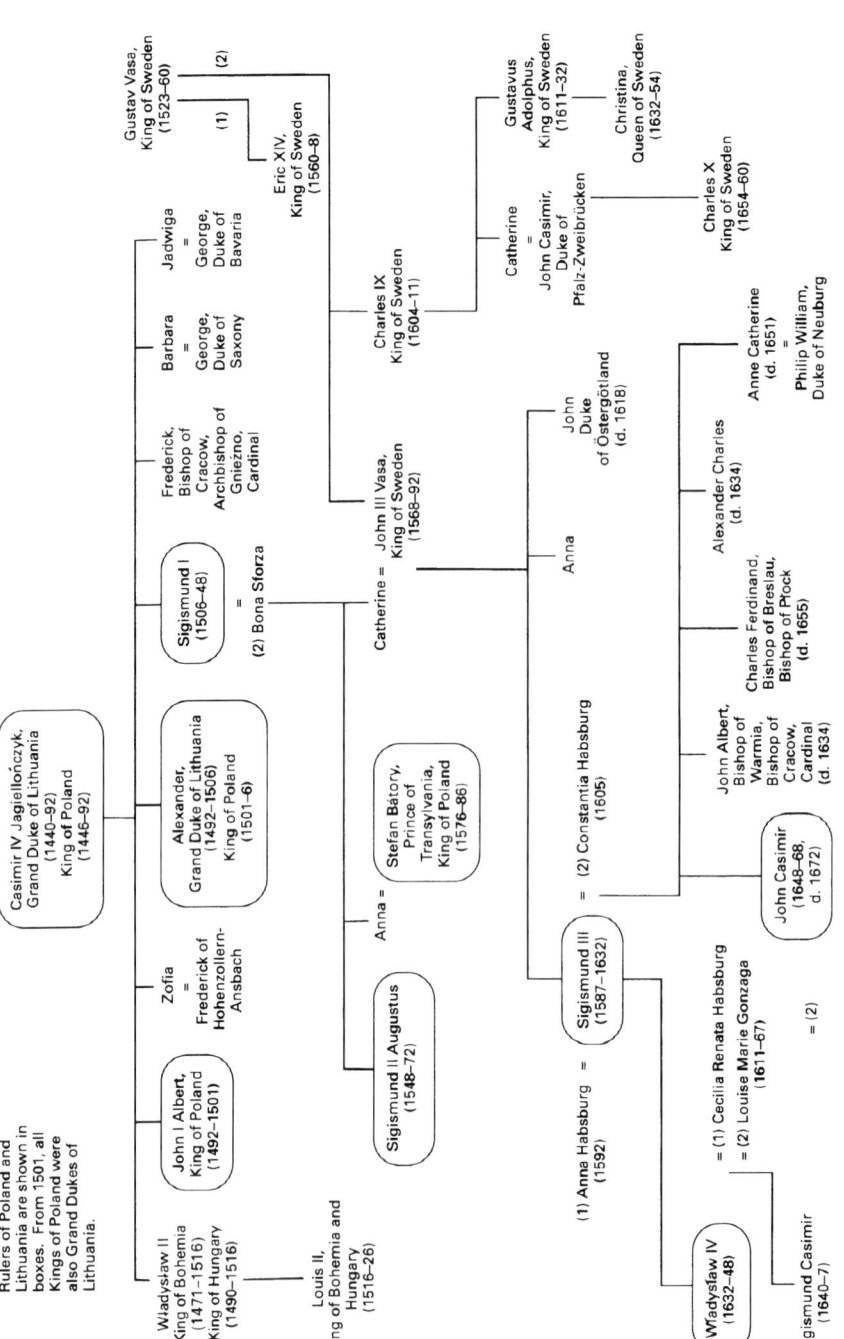

Table 1 The Jagiellonian and Vasa dynasties

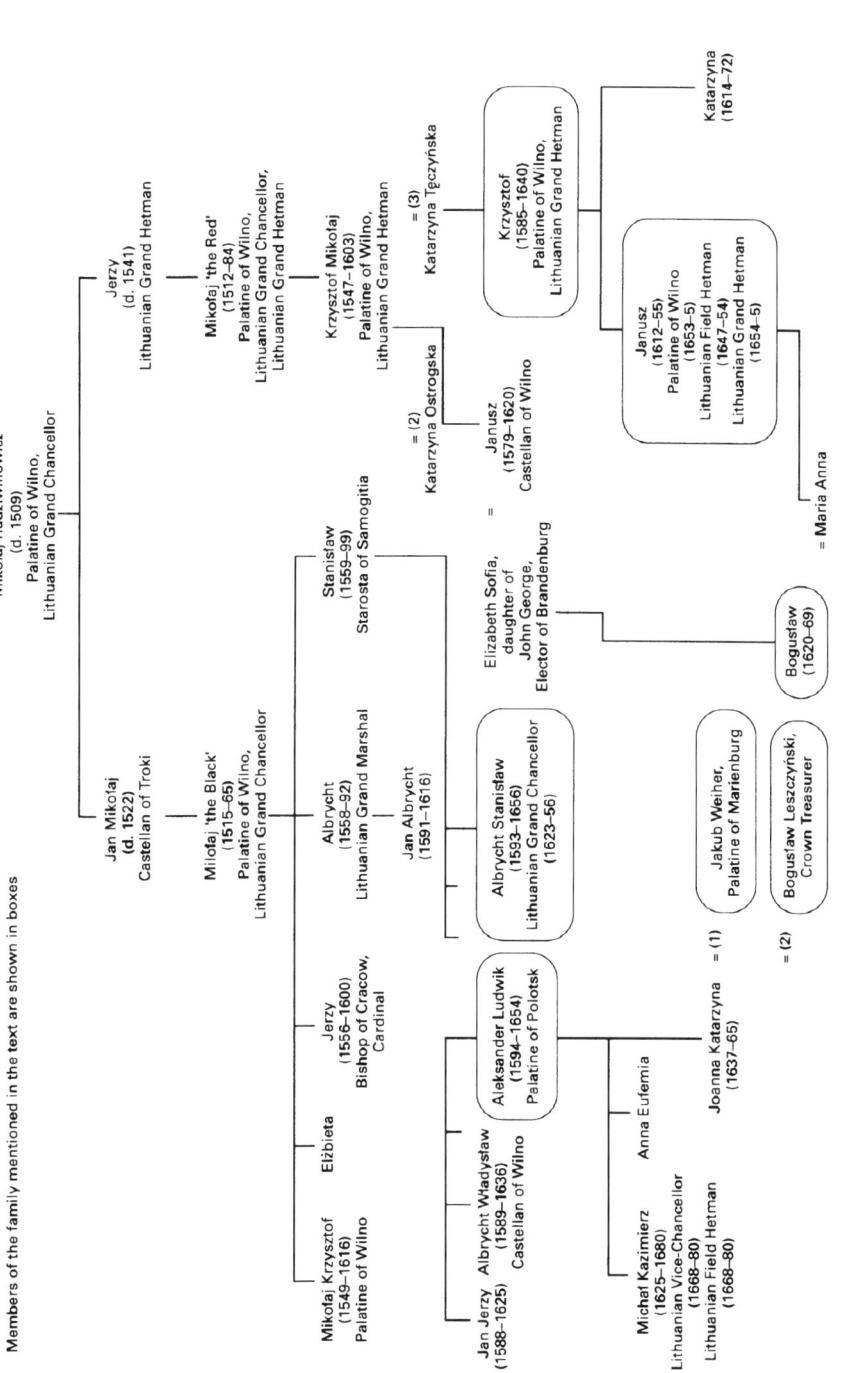

Table 2 The Radziwiłł family

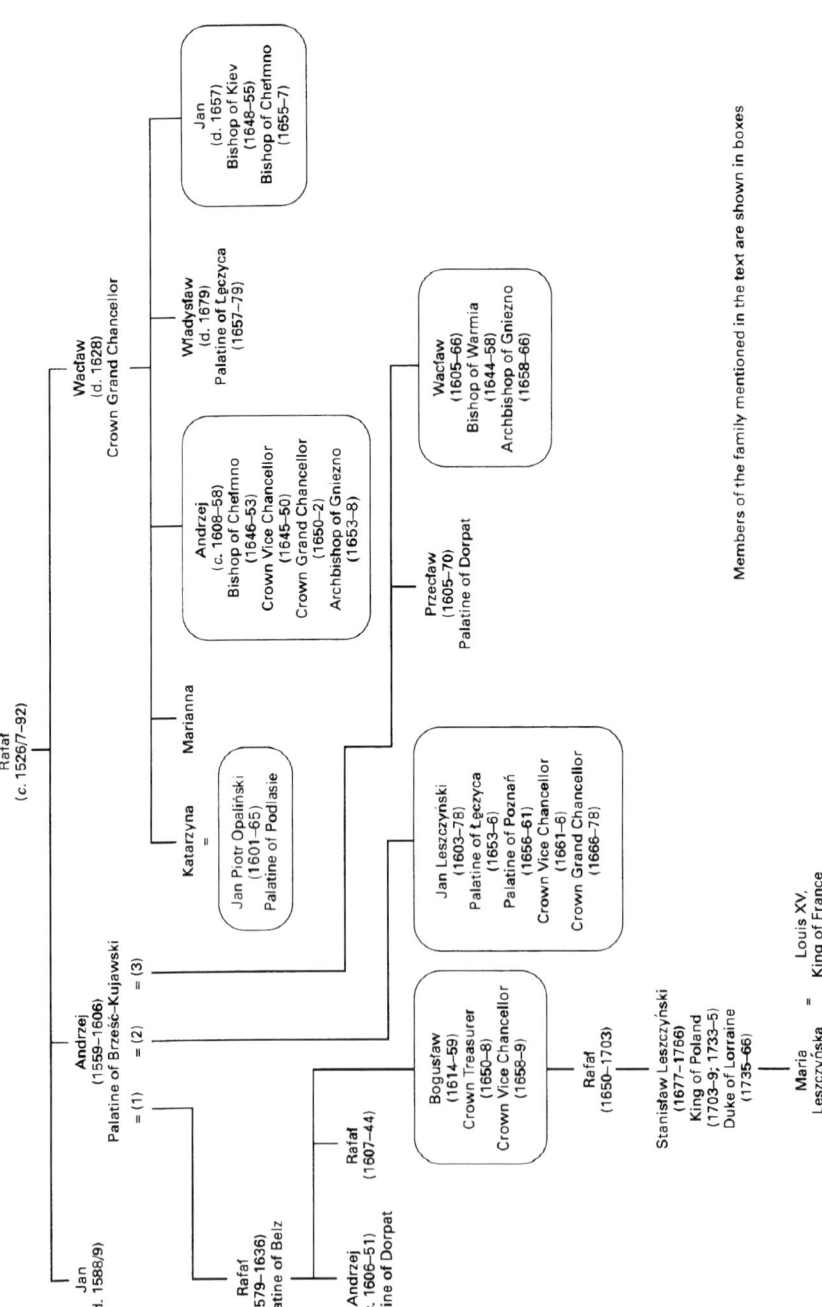

Table 3 The Leszczyński family

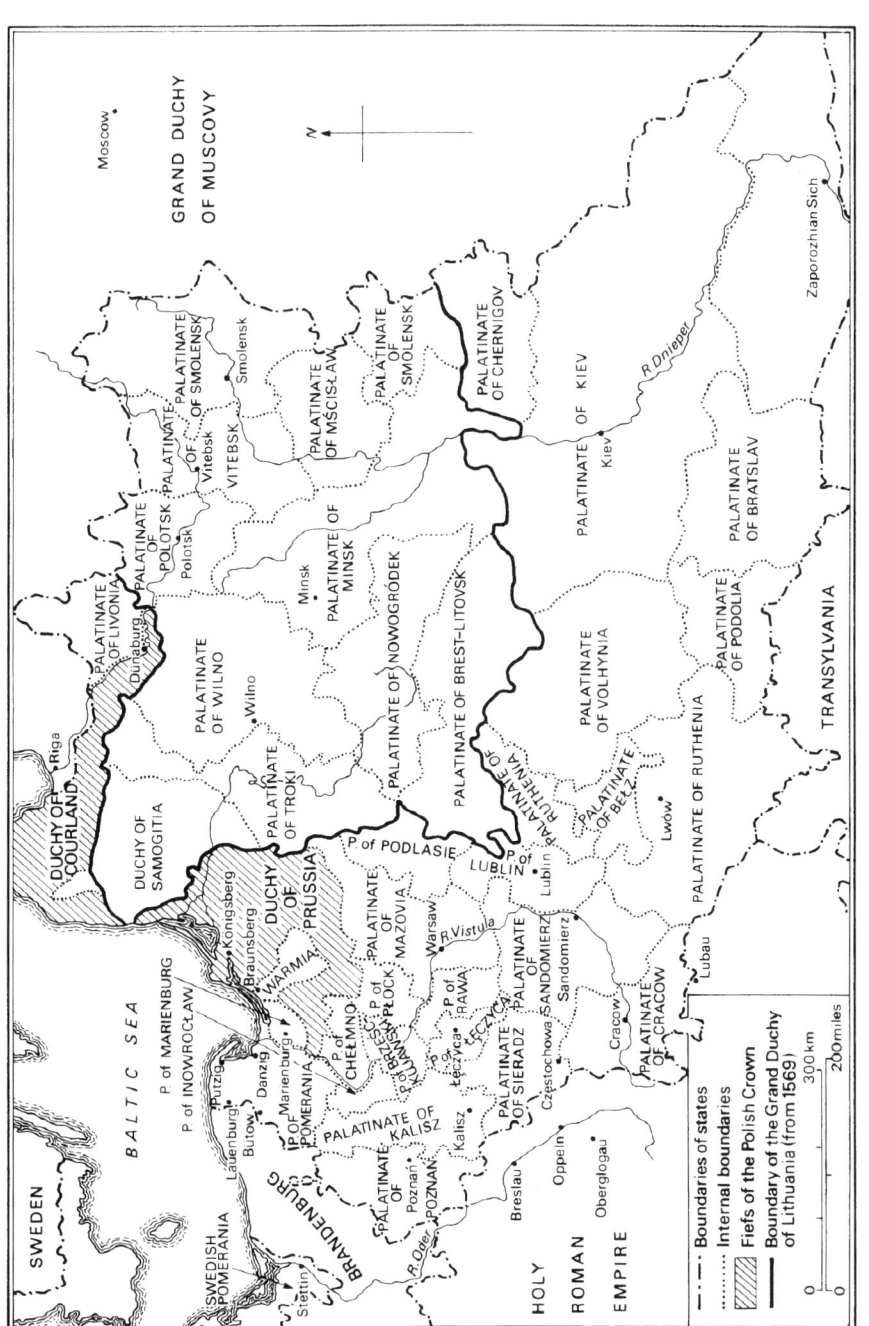

Map 1 The Commonwealth of Poland–Lithuania in the mid-seventeenth century

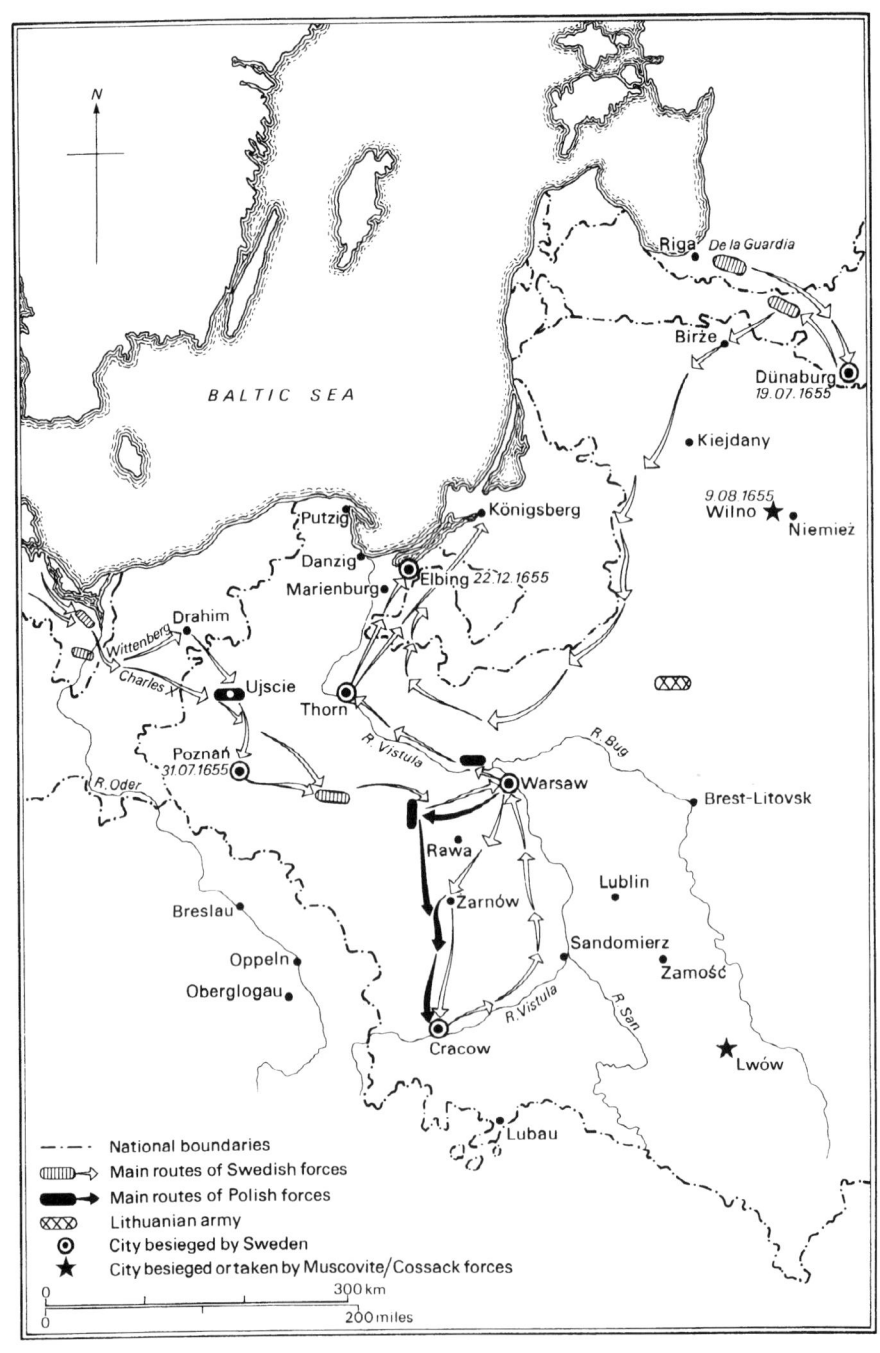

Map 2 The Swedish invasion, July–December 1655

1

Introduction: Poland–Lithuania in the mid-seventeenth century

In the summer of 1655 the second-largest state in Europe collapsed. The Commonwealth of Poland–Lithuania had struggled for seven years to contain a massive Cossack revolt led by Bohdan Khmelnytskyi which had broken out in the Ukraine in the summer of 1648. Khmelnytskyi, unable after six years of inconclusive fighting to achieve an acceptable settlement, had looked to Alexis, tsar of Muscovy (1645–76), to break the deadlock. By the treaty of Pereiaslav (18 January 1654), the Cossacks put themselves under the tsar's protection; shortly afterwards Muscovite armies swept into the Commonwealth. The military reputation of Poland–Lithuania had been shaken by the Swedish victories of the 1620s and the failure to defeat Khmelnytskyi, but nobody expected the collapse which followed: by the summer of 1655 Alexis had occupied most of Lithuania, while joint Cossack and Muscovite forces in the Ukraine had driven the Poles back to Lwów. On 9 August 1655 the tsar's triumphal entrance to Wilno, capital of Lithuania, crowned a remarkable campaign which had upset the whole balance of power in eastern Europe.

The *coup de grâce* was administered by Sweden, whose vulnerable Baltic empire was directly threatened by the Muscovite drive into Lithuania. Sweden's new status as a major power was based on slender resources; shortly after the end of the Thirty Years War in 1648, conscious of the growing cost of maintaining garrisons on the far side of the Baltic, the government in Stockholm began to consider fighting a new war to counter the domestic pressures it faced as it adjusted to the problems of defending its empire in peacetime. Queen Christina's unexpected abdication in 1654 brought to the throne her ambitious and more belligerent cousin, Charles X. The Commonwealth's apparently imminent collapse gave Charles the opportunity to forget his domestic problems by countering what appeared to be a real threat to Swedish security. In July 1655, he invaded to preempt Alexis and ensure that Sweden would enjoy its share of the spoils.

The result exceeded Charles's greatest expectations. He hoped to seize Royal Prussia and prevent Alexis, who already controlled most of Lithuania, from reaching the Baltic; instead, within three months he controlled the whole of Poland. The Polish king, John Casimir (1648–68), had attracted widespread blame for failing to defeat Khmelnytskyi and for needlessly provoking the Swedish attack by refusing to resign his claim to the Swedish throne, thereby missing an opportunity to ally with Charles against Muscovy. When two Swedish armies under Arvid

After the Deluge

Wittenberg and the king himself entered Poland in July and one under Magnus de la Gardie entered Lithuania from Livonia, John Casimir was abandoned by large numbers of nobles who saw Sweden as their potential saviour against Muscovy. At Ujście on 25 July, the Great Poland *levée-en-masse* led by Krzysztof Opaliński, palatine of Poznań, surrendered to Wittenberg. The palatinates of Poznań and Kalisz were placed under Charles's protection; he was to be accorded the loyalty and obedience due to the king of Poland. A month later, a similar treaty was signed at Kiejdany by Janusz Radziwiłł, palatine of Wilno and Lithuanian grand hetman.[1] Other palatinates swiftly followed suit as John Casimir went into exile at Oberglogau in Silesia, where he arrived on 17 October, nine days before the main Polish army surrendered to Wittenberg near Cracow. The Commonwealth had succumbed with scarcely a fight.

Charles, however, found Poland easier to conquer than to control. He showed little inclination to take the offensive against Muscovy; indeed, Swedish envoys began talks with Alexis. The necessity for Sweden to make the war pay for itself rapidly alienated the nobility, as the army levied contributions from noble and royal estates alike, demonstrating the insincerity of Charles's promises to respect noble privileges. There were not enough Protestants in the Commonwealth to provide a solid nucleus of support, and Sweden was unable to exploit religious divisions in the way it had in the Empire during the Thirty Years War; indeed, Swedish outrages perpetrated against the Catholic Church did much to turn opinion against the invader. Encouraged by the spread of resistance, John Casimir returned to Poland in early 1656; by the spring, Opaliński and Radziwiłł were dead, and most Poles had abandoned Sweden.

To defeat the Swedish army, superior in training, discipline and equipment, required more than the return of the will to fight. Although the Poles waged a daring and effective guerrilla war, it proved impossible to inflict a major defeat on the Swedish professionals in open battle, while Polish deficiencies in artillery and infantry made the reduction of occupied cities a long and slow process. From the outset, the Poles were forced to seek foreign aid; it was only after they won support from Austria, Denmark and Brandenburg that Sweden was eventually forced to make peace at Oliva in 1660. Meanwhile, the willingness of an important part of the Cossack leadership to reach an accommodation with the Commonwealth after Khmelnytskyi's death in 1657, owing to concern at Muscovite aims in the Ukraine, improved the situation on the eastern front. The treaty of Hadiach (1659) envisaged the creation of a duchy of Ruthenia as part of the Commonwealth, which guaranteed Cossack rights and decreed that the Cossack hetman would sit in the senate as palatine of Kiev. Hadiach and Oliva opened the way to the great campaign of 1660–1, in which the Muscovites were swept out of much of Lithuania. It seemed that disaster had been averted and that the crisis was over.

---

[1] 'Articuli Pacis & Conventionis inter Illustrissimis et Excellentissimis Dominum Arfid Wittemberg... & Palatinatum Posnaniensem et Calicensem' AGAD AKW, Szwedzkie, k. 11b no. 21; 'Akta ugody kiejdańskiej 1655 roku' W. Konopczyński and K. Lepszy (eds.), *Ateneum Wileńskie* X (1935) p. 3.

Introduction

It was only just beginning. The Commonwealth never really recovered from the blows inflicted during the Second Northern War (1655–60) and the Thirteen Years War with Muscovy (1654–67).[2] Despite the apparently favourable terms of Oliva, which granted Sweden nothing it had not possessed *de facto* already, and the successful campaigns of 1660–1 which drove the Muscovites out of most of Lithuania, the so-called 'Swedish Deluge' of 1655 triggered the Commonwealth's precipitate decline. The cycle of wars which had begun in 1648 did not end until 1721. Almost immediately after a disadvantageous peace had been made with Muscovy at Andrusovo in 1667,[3] resurgent Ottoman power involved the Commonwealth in a series of wars which lasted until the peace of Karlowitz in 1699, only to be followed by the Great Northern War (1700–21), largely fought on Polish territory. In 1648, as the rest of Europe emerged from the wreckage of the Thirty Years War, Poles had looked with pride on their political system and had felt secure in their boundaries; by 1721 their political system was the object of scorn throughout Europe, Russian influence was predominant and they were unable to prevent their neighbours from marching armies through their territory at will. Seventy-five years later, the Commonwealth no longer existed.

The central purpose of this study is to examine why the Commonwealth should have failed so spectacularly to overcome the political and military crisis it faced as a result of the Cossack rising and the Muscovite and Swedish invasions. Most European states struggled to adjust to the new demands of warfare in the early modern period and most underwent a comparable crisis at some point between the late sixteenth and the last quarter of the seventeenth century. All governments struggled to raise the vast sums of money required to support the new-style armies; many faced violent political upheaval, civil war, or foreign intervention in consequence, without experiencing long-term political degeneration. Indeed, comparable crises were often important for the establishment of more effective systems of government, frequently stimulating the expansion of central authority under a king who could act as a national rallying-point against internal anarchy or foreign invaders. The French Crown emerged from the wars of religion and the Frondes with its authority strengthened, as challenges to its position in the form of religious or noble rebellion failed to provide a viable alternative to a hereditary monarchy which acted as guarantor of the social and political order. The 'Time of Troubles' in Muscovy, just as traumatic as what came to be known as the Swedish Deluge in Poland–Lithuania,

---

[2] There were three periods of general warfare in the Baltic region between Ivan IV's invasion of Livonia in 1558 and the end of the Great Northern War in 1721: the First Northern War (1563–70), usually called the Seven Years War of the North in Anglo-Saxon historiography; the Second Northern War (1655–60) and the Great Northern War (1700–21). To emphasise the essential continuity between the three wars, I prefer the Polish, rather than the Anglo-German convention, in which the conflict of 1655–60 is sometimes called the First Northern War.

[3] Hadiach had proved abortive, and the Ukraine was divided along the Dnieper, with Muscovy keeping Kiev, initially for three years, in fact for good: it was surrendered *de iure* in 1686. Andrusovo also saw the loss of Smolensk and the palatinate of Chernigov.

After the Deluge

ended with the establishment of the Romanov dynasty upon the throne, while failure in war opened the way to the introduction of royal absolutism by *coup d'état* in Denmark in 1660 and with the consent of the diet in Sweden in 1680. Absolutism did not always ensure the acquisition or maintenance of great power status, or even military success; nevertheless, it could protect states from the kind of foreign interference experienced by the Commonwealth.[4] If other states, including Spain, Denmark and Sweden, experienced relative decline as bigger and more powerful neighbours proved better able to meet the challenges posed by military change, none experienced paralysis of central government on such a scale, and no other major European state disappeared from the map in the early modern period.

What was different about the Commonwealth? There appear to be no compelling socio-economic reasons why its political development should have diverged so dramatically from the central and east European norm in which central authority was extended through the development of a symbiotic relationship between ruler and nobility, and noble service in the army and the royal bureaucracy was rewarded by the extension and maintenance of peasant serfdom. If, as Anderson argues, service provided vital aristocratic unity for nobilities in eastern Europe which lacked a western-style feudal hierarchy, and if the absolute state in eastern Europe was the repressive machine of the nobility and a necessary device for the consolidation of serfdom, why did it not appear in Poland, where the legal basis of serfdom was complete by the early sixteenth century, and why did it appear in Russia, where the central components of the absolute monarchy were in place long before the final legal consolidation of serfdom took place in 1649? Poland, as much as Russia, lacked a western-style feudal hierarchy, and Anderson begs the question in the case of Russia of how the monarchy acquired sufficient power in the first place for the nobility to need any compact.[5]

The similarites in the socio-economic base of European states east of the Elbe are more striking than the differences. Production of grain, timber, hemp and other primary products was characteristic of all economies of eastern Europe in the early modern period; all suffered from the downturn in the European economy after the 1620s. Both Brandenburg–Prussia and Muscovy, like Poland–Lithuania, were economically backward, poorly urbanised and politically dominated by the nobility, yet both managed to develop successful systems of government by the early eighteenth century, in which standing armies and relatively efficient administrations were maintained with the support and cooperation of the nobility. Both emerged as significant powers in the eighteenth century despite, or perhaps because of, their serf-based economies. When Frederick William, the Great Elector of Brandenburg and the Commonwealth's vassal in Ducal (East) Prussia, created a small force of 8,000 men during the Second Northern War, there was little to suggest that

[4] J. Gierowski, 'Rzeczpospolita szlachecka wobec absolutystycznej Europy' *Pamiętnik X Powszechnego Zjazdu Historyków Polskich* III (Warsaw, 1971) p. 111.
[5] P. Anderson, *Lineages of the Absolutist State* (London, 1974) p. 195.

Introduction

Brandenburg–Prussia could ever rival its huge neighbour, despite its good showing in support of the Swedish army in the battle of Warsaw in 1656. By 1713, however, the Prussian army had grown to 40,000, small in comparison to the forces maintained by Austria (*c.* 100,000) or Russia (*c.* 200,000), but twice the size of the Polish–Lithuanian standing armies, limited from 1717 to 24,000 (18,000 for Poland, 6,000 for Lithuania), a figure which was purely notional: the actual size of the army was much smaller. By the accession of Frederick the Great in 1740, the Prussian army had grown to 83,000, dwarfing that of its erstwhile master: while eighteenth-century Prussia maintained three to four soldiers per 100 inhabitants, Poland–Lithuania supported one for every 500–600.[6] There appear to be no convincing socio-economic reasons why Poland–Lithuania should not have evolved in a similar direction to its neighbours.

It was the unique political structure of Poland–Lithuania in the early modern period which set it apart most clearly. The major structural differences stemmed essentially from the series of constitutional changes between 1569 and 1573 associated with the extinction in the male line of the Lithuanian Jagiellonian dynasty. Poland and Lithuania had been joined in a loose personal union since 1385, which had survived until the mid-sixteenth century largely due to common defence needs: both states had been threatened in the late Middle Ages by the crusading states of the Teutonic knights along the Baltic coast, while the sparsely populated grand duchy of Lithuania welcomed Polish military support in its battle with Muscovy over the remnants of Kievan Rus, shattered in the Mongol invasions of the thirteenth century. Although the Poles asserted the elective nature of their monarchy after 1385, they remained attached to the dynastic principle, electing members of the Jagiellonian house until its extinction in the male line with the death of Sigismund Augustus in 1572.

The union, reaffirmed and strengthened at Horodło in 1413, proved reasonably successful. In the fifteenth century, the challenge of the Teutonic knights had been broken, first at the battle of Grunwald (Tannenberg) in 1410, but particularly during the Thirteen Years War (1454–66) which saw the Poles recapture Danzig and Royal Prussia. The Muscovite threat proved more dangerous, however; by the end of the fifteenth century Muscovy had united the eastern Russian principalities under its rule and liberated itself from Tatar control; now the self-styled tsars of All the Russias could turn their attention to those Russias ruled by Lithuania. The Lithuanian victory at Orsza in 1514 could not compensate for Muscovy's seizure of the great fortress of Smolensk a year earlier. Fighting continued spasmodically and inconclusively until a five-year truce in 1537, later extended until 1562, which left Muscovy in control of Smolensk and Seversk.

Ivan IV's invasion of Livonia in 1558 persuaded Sigismund Augustus (1548–72)

[6] E. Rostworowski, 'War and society in the noble Republic of Poland–Lithuania in the eighteenth century' in G.E. Rothenberg, B.K. Király and P.F. Sugar (eds.), *East-central European Society and War in the Pre-Revolutionary Eighteenth Century* (Boulder, Colorado, 1982) p. 165.

to take action to establish a closer union, since the personal link between Poland and Lithuania was threatened by his lack of heirs. The support of the Polish nobility and the lesser Lithuanian nobles, who wished to share the extensive privileges enjoyed by their Polish counterparts, was sufficient to overcome the opposition of the great Lithuanian and Ruthenian magnates. The Union of Lublin (1569) created a central diet for Poland and Lithuania, although Lithuania kept its own administration, army and legal system. In the struggle to overcome magnate resistance, the Lublin diet had transferred control of Volhynia, Podlasie and the Ukraine to Poland, henceforth known as *Korona* (the Crown), to distinguish it from the grand duchy of Lithuania.

The Union of Lublin established a unique political structure. While multiple kingdoms were common in early modern Europe, they usually consisted of dynastic unions, in which the monarch provided the sole common political element between his diverse territories. The establishment of a common diet predated the Anglo-Scottish union of parliaments by 138 years and provided rulers of the Commonwealth with a series of problems not faced by any of their European contemporaries. The existence of a central diet with wide powers which met regularly made opposition to royal demands easier to coordinate and meant that the king could not play off one estates body against another, or move separately against each, as monarchs could elsewhere. Furthermore, although there was a common diet, the existence of a separate government in Lithuania, which duplicated exactly the great offices of state in Poland, made the coordination of royal policy difficult. Finally, the continuing dependence of envoys to the diet upon the instructions of the dietines, whose delegates they were, meant that the diet was limited in its ability to enforce its will.

Thus Sigismund Augustus's success in creating a more united and centralised state through the union was only partial: Lithuania was tied more closely to Poland but was not absorbed, while the issue of where power ultimately lay, with the king, the diet or the dietines, was left unresolved. The imperfect political union was matched by a similarly incomplete social and cultural union. Although the Lithuanian and much of the Ruthenian nobility underwent steady cultural polonisation after 1569, regional loyalties remained strong despite the spread of the Sarmatian myth after 1569, which claimed a common descent for the Polish and Lithuanian nobility from the ancient Sarmatian tribe.[7] The different social structure of

---

[7] For an introduction to Sarmatism, see S. Cynarski, 'The shape of Sarmatian ideology in Poland' *Acta Poloniae Historica* 19 (1969). The vital question of Lithuanian identity between 1569 and 1795 has not, on the whole, been well researched. The development of modern nationalism in the lands of the partitioned Commonwealth after 1795 and the unfortunate circumstances surrounding the creation of independent states of Poland and Lithuania in 1918 have created a legacy of bitterness above which scholars have often proved unable to rise: see, for example, the debate in *Slavic Review* 22 (1963). Polish scholars after 1945, forced to work in a Marxist framework, frequently overstressed the impact of Sarmatism, taking this ideological superstructure to reveal the existence of a genuine class-unity whose economic basis, let alone its political expression, is dubious to say the least. For a recent view of

Introduction

Lithuania and the Ukraine, where the nobility was much less numerous and its leading members, the great magnates, far wealthier than in Poland, meant that these figures exercised much greater political influence than their Polish counterparts. After the absorption of Volhynia, Podlasie and the Ukraine in 1569, the influence of Ruthenian magnates in Poland was disproportionate to their numbers, while Lithuanian magnates, still smarting over the loss of these territories, jealously defended what remained of Lithuanian autonomy. Unlike the British union, so clearly dominated after 1707 by England, the Union of Lublin was between better-matched partners, despite the transfer of such vast territories in 1569.

It was in those eastern territories that the crisis began. Although large magnate estates had been built up and colonised in Lithuania and Belorussia in the fifteenth century, and nobles had been granted extensive rights over their serfs in a series of edicts between 1387 and 1547, it was not until after 1569 that the vast lands of the Ukraine were developed on a large scale, a process stimulated by the growing demand for agricultural products and raw materials from western Europe and facilitated by the transfer of the Ukraine to Poland, which opened it up to Polish colonisation. The Ukraine, not being served by the great rivers which flowed into the Baltic, did not play a large part in the export of grain but developed as an important cattle-rearing area. The resultant development of large-scale estates and the imposition of serfdom upon the peasants reached its climax in the 1640s, by which time the battle by landlords to extend their control had tied down many who had originally fled to the Ukraine to escape the harsh conditions elsewhere.[8]

The 1648 rising received massive support from Ukrainian peasants, but it was not the direct result of peasant discontent. Peasant risings elsewhere in the Commonwealth, in protest against the harsh conditions of serfdom, were not uncommon but they tended to be highly localised and easy to control. In the Ukraine, however, it was not just the peasants who were discontented. Not every member of the Ukrainian elites benefited from the union after 1569, since not all who considered themselves noble were subsequently recognised as such. Ukrainian society came to be dominated by the increasingly polonised elite of magnate families, such as the Wiśniowieckis, Ostrogskis and Zbaraskis, and families of Polish origin such as the Potockis, Koniecpolskis, or Zamoyskis. As the estates of these families grew, largely due to their access to royal patronage, so did their power and influence over the indigenous petty and middle nobility, which provoked widespread resentment.

---

the problem, which reflects the difficulties without entirely abandoning an inappropriate nineteenth-century concept of nationhood, see J. Ochmański, 'The national idea in Lithuania from the sixteenth to the first half of the nineteenth century: the problem of cultural-linguistic differentiation' *Harvard Ukrainian Studies* 10 (1986); cf. J. Tazbir, 'Die Polonisierungprozesse in der Adelsrepublik' *Acta Poloniae Historica* 55 (1987).

[8] The scale of the expansion was staggering. In 1630, the Wiśniowiecki family estates in the Ukraine comprised 616 settlements. By 1640, this figure had risen to 7,603; in 1645, the Wiśniowieckis controlled 38,000 settlements, with some 230,000 'subjects'. Z. Wójcik, *Dzikie pola w ogniu. O kozaczyźnie w dawnej Rzeczypospolitej* 3rd edition (Warsaw, 1968) p. 140.

After the Deluge

The Zaporozhian Cossacks constituted another, more dangerous, elite which became increasingly alienated. Originally adventurers and freebooters who lived largely by mounting raids against their Tatar neighbours, the Cossacks by the seventeenth century constituted a substantial military force which was vital for the protection of the Commonwealth's south-eastern border. Although the core of Cossack society was Ruthenian, it was composed of many different ethnic and social elements. Based on their stronghold, the Zaporozhian Sich below the great rapids on the Dnieper river, the Cossacks constituted an independent force which was difficult to control.

As such, they were of constant concern to the Polish and Lithuanian nobility and especially to the magnate elite of the Ukraine. The diet attempted to control the situation from the late sixteenth century by the maintenance of an official register: only those on the register could bear arms and fight as Cossacks and enjoy the privileges of the Cossack elite. Most registered Cossacks lived in the frontier towns of the Ukraine, however, and the Zaporozhian Sich remained largely independent of control. The exclusion of many from the register increased tension, provoking discontent and periodic risings. While registered Cossacks had every incentive to support the government, the increase in their number in wartime and the reduction of the register in peacetime, or after risings, undermined the trust of all Cossacks. The cutting of the register to a mere 6,000 following the crushing of the 1638 rising caused simmering resentment in the Ukraine, which finally boiled over in 1648, when Cossacks, nobles and peasants joined in a massive revolt which the Commonwealth was wholly unable to control.[9]

Religion provided vital ideological cement for the rebels. The Union of Lublin created a state which enjoyed a religious pluralism unparalleled in early modern Europe. In sweeping up the western remnants of Kievan Rus in the thirteenth and fourteenth centuries, the pagan Lithuanian elite had come to rule over a large number of Orthodox subjects. In order to win the Polish throne in 1385, however, Władysław Jagiełło converted to Catholicism and introduced the Catholic hierarchy to his Lithuanian and Ruthenian lands. Although much of the Lithuanian nobility converted to Catholicism after 1385, many nobles and the vast majority of the peasantry remained Orthodox, especially in the Ukraine, where Orthodoxy continued to flourish, and Kiev reestablished itself as a leading centre of Orthodox learning and culture.

Apart from this large Orthodox minority, the Commonwealth also contained Armenian Christians, Jews and Moslem Tatars. The situation was further complicated by the spread of Protestantism: first Lutheranism among the German inhabitants of Royal Prussia, then Calvinism, Anabaptism and Antitrinitarianism

---

[9] For the background to the revolt see F. Sysyn, 'The problem of nobilities in the Ukrainian past: the Polish period 1569–1648' in I.L. Rudnytsky (ed.), *Rethinking Ukrainian History* (Edmonton, 1981) and T. Chynczewska-Hennel, 'The national consciousness of Ukrainian nobles and Cossacks from the end of the sixteenth to the mid-seventeenth century' *Harvard Ukrainian Studies* 10 (1986).

Introduction

among the nobility. Protestant nobles claimed that religious freedom was part of the liberties of the nobility and full religious toleration was established by the 1573 Warsaw Confederation. Nevertheless, legal toleration did not mean that relations between the confessions were harmonious and anti-Protestant feeling among the Catholic majority enabled Sigismund III (1587–1632) to launch a great Counter-Reformation offensive, spearheaded by the Jesuits. From a late-sixteenth century peak, in which over half the chamber of envoys (the lower house of the diet) had been Protestant, the number of Protestants declined rapidly, as the Court, especially under Sigismund III and John Casimir, discriminated heavily in favour of Catholics in the distribution of patronage.

It was not just Protestants who were affected. The Union of Lublin, which transferred the Ukraine to Polish control, opened it up to the forces of the Counter-Reformation. Orthodox nobles were also affected by the growing monopoly on royal patronage enjoyed by Catholics, and a number of leading Orthodox families turned Catholic. The situation was further complicated by one of the great triumphs of the Counter-Reformation, when the establishment of the Greek Catholic or Uniate Church at the Union of Brest in 1596 sought to end the schism between Orthodox and Catholic: the Commonwealth's Orthodox hierarchy agreed to accept the authority of the Pope in return for being allowed to follow the Orthodox rite. The great hopes inspired by the union were soon disappointed, however. Catholic prelates in Lithuania and the Ukraine jealously guarded their jurisdictions against their Uniate counterparts, while the state lacked the means to enforce the ban on Orthodoxy. Much of the Orthodox hierarchy became Uniate but the bulk of the parish clergy and the vast majority of the people did not. A clandestine hierarchy was soon established, and Orthodoxy continued to flourish. Few great nobles became Uniates, preferring either to turn Catholic or remain Orthodox. Although Władysław IV (1632–48) restored legal recognition to the Orthodox Church in 1632, the damage had been done. The Uniate Church remained to complicate Catholic–Orthodox relations, the gap between the Orthodox mass of the population in the Ukraine and an increasingly Catholic high nobility had widened and the Cossacks, denied recognition as part of the Commonwealth's ruling elite, could portray themselves as the defenders of Ruthenian and Orthodox culture, as well as the upholders of peasant rights against their magnate landlords.[10] Thus, while the union worked tolerably well in Lithuania, whose cultural and political autonomy was protected to an extent and where both the Uniate and Catholic Churches proved more successful in weaning the people away from Orthodoxy, it failed in those lands transferred to Polish political control in 1569, a failure whose extent only became apparent after 1648.

[10] For the religious problems of the Ukraine see F. Sysyn, *Between Poland and the Ukraine. The Dilemma of Adam Kysil, 1600–1653* (Cambridge, Mass., 1985) pp. 26–32 and H. Litwin, 'Catholicisation among the Ruthenian nobility and assimilation processes in the Ukraine during the years 1569–1648' *Acta Poloniae Historica* 55 (1987).

The Commonwealth's political system was dominated by one class: the nobility, which constituted between 6 and 8 per cent of the population.[11] Noble power had first asserted itself after the extinction of the native Piast dynasty on the death of Casimir the Great in 1370, when, like their Hungarian and Bohemian neighbours, the Poles established the elective nature of their monarchy. Henceforward, the Polish *szlachta* (nobility) demanded substantial political and social privileges as the price of royal elections or in return for permitting mobilisation of the *levée-en-masse*: at Košice (1374), where Louis of Anjou exempted the nobility from all taxation without their consent, beyond a symbolic payment of two *groszy* for every *łan*,[12] Czerwińsk (1421), Jedlno (1430), Nieszawa (1454) and Piotrków (1496).

From 1374, the need for noble consent for extraordinary taxation necessitated the assembly of local or provincial dietines (*sejmiki*) and of a central diet which soon claimed a role in safeguarding noble privileges. The Privileges of Nieszawa required the king to seek the permission of the dietines before calling out the *levée-en-masse*. The diet, composed of envoys from local dietines, met ever more frequently thereafter, usually to agree to taxation. It was finally guaranteed a central place in the political system by the statute of *Nihil Novi* (1505), which decreed that no new law could be introduced without its consent.

The diet's composition was determined with the definitive adoption of a bicameral structure at Piotrków in 1493 and with the admission of the Lithuanians in 1569. Henceforward, it was composed of three estates: the king, the senate and the chamber of envoys. The senate was based on the old royal council and, from 1635, numbered 150: the two Catholic archbishops (of Gniezno and Lwów), fifteen Catholic bishops, thirty-five palatines (provincial governors) and the starosta of Samogitia, who performed the same function, thirty-five major castellans, who exercised judicial and administrative office in the main cities of each palatinate, fifty-two minor castellans and ten government ministers (the chancellor, vice-chancellor, grand marshal, treasurer and marshal of the court, each office duplicated in Poland and Lithuania). The chamber of envoys had no fixed number of members: although most palatinates sent two envoys, some sent as many as six, while there was no limit on the number that could be sent by the palatinates of Royal Prussia. From 1635, the chamber had 172 members (118 from Poland, forty-eight from Lithuania and six

---

[11] The size of the Polish nobility is a matter of some debate. Rostworowski has recently questioned the figure of 8–10 per cent of the population which is usually given for the eighteenth century, rounding it down to some 6–6.5 per cent before the First Partition. E. Rostworowski, 'Ilu było w Rzeczypospolitej obywateli szlachty?' *Kwartalnik Historyczny* 94 (1987). The percentage was much higher in Royal Prussia and Poland proper than in Lithuania and the more sparsely populated eastern lands. The percentage of noble inhabitants for the Commonwealth as a whole was far higher than elsewhere in Europe, with the exception of Spain and Hungary.

[12] In the mid-fourteenth century, one *groszy* was the price of two chickens: H. Cywiński, *Dziesięć wieków pieniądza polskiego* (Warsaw, 1987) p. 38. The *łan* was a measure of land: for details see glossary.

from Livonia), not counting Prussian envoys, whose number varied widely, showing a steady tendency to increase after 1569.[13]

The diet's position was strengthened by the political changes following the death of Sigismund Augustus in 1572, marking the triumph of the lower and middle nobility, which had seized the political initiative in the previous decade. Henceforward, not just the diet but the whole nobility had the right to participate in royal elections, a right nobles were only too eager to exercise, turning up in their thousands. It was, however, the conditions to which the newly chosen monarch had to assent which shifted the balance of power in favour of the nobility and the diet. After the election of Sigismund Augustus in 1529, the Poles refused to permit the election of a successor *vivente rege* (in the lifetime of his predecessor), insisting on an interregnum in which the primate, the archbishop of Gniezno, acted as interrex. On the death of the king, the interrex summoned a convocation diet, which discussed arrangements for the election and conducted all the business of a normal diet, with the exception of the royal prerogatives of appointment to office and distribution of royal lands. An election diet then took place at the Wola Field outside Warsaw, which also drew up the new monarch's electoral agreement, known as the *Pacta Conventa*, to which he had to swear before his coronation.

The shift of power to the nobility was explicit and was made even more so with the deposition of the first elected monarch, Henry of Anjou, following his clandestine flight to take up the French throne in 1574. Before his election, Henry's representatives had sworn to uphold the eponymous 'Henrician Articles', which established the fundamental principles governing the new constitutional order, confirming all privileges previously granted to the nobility, including the 1573 confederation of Warsaw, establishing religious toleration, recognising the right of free election, laying down that the diet must meet for six weeks every two years and the necessity of its consent for the summoning of the *levée-en-masse* and for any new taxes or duties. Between meetings of the diet, the king was to be advised by the senate council, which was to include sixteen senators, appointed by the diet, who were to sit four at a time in rotation, changing every six months.

The Henrician Articles, which were incorporated into the coronation oath in 1576 for Stefan Batory and all his successors, laid down certain basic principles, but the personal undertakings of each new monarch, embodied in his own *Pacta Conventa*, placed further restrictions on his freedom of action: usually his predecessor's *Pacta* were incorporated into the new document with new conditions, often to counter his predecessor's perceived abuses. Taken together, the Henrician Articles and the various *Pacta Conventa* represented a growing body of constitutional law establishing the limits of royal power and defining the extent of the

---

[13] S. Kutrzeba, 'The composition of the Polish Sejm' in W. Czapliński (ed.), *The Polish Parliament at the Summit of its Development (Sixteenth-Eighteenth Centuries)* (Wrocław, 1985) p. 19.

famous *aurea libertas*, the 'Golden Freedom' which was the birthright of every nobleman.

From 1574 Polish and Lithuanian nobles were citizens of a Commonwealth, not subjects of a king; in theory they exercised a greater degree of control over their own affairs than other comparable elites. Yet, despite their apparent monopoly of political power, the nobility failed to develop an effective system: by the eighteenth century it had degenerated into an anarchic nightmare, a hideous parody of democracy symbolised by the notorious principle of the *liberum veto*, the right by which any envoy, or any nobleman attending his local dietine, could not only block individual items of legislation but could break up the whole proceedings.[14] As archdeacon William Coxe noted disapprovingly at the end of the eighteenth century: 'Anarchy ... and confusion are not only tolerated, but are even supposed by the nobles, who reap the benefit of those evils, to be absolutely necessary for the support of the constitution; so that there is a proverb, that Poland subsists by anarchy.'[15] Coxe castigated the total confusion he saw in the administration of public affairs and concluded that Polish liberty was 'the source of Polish wretchedness; and Poland appears to me ... of all countries the most distressed'.[16]

Until the mid-seventeenth century, however, there had been little to indicate that this would prove to be the case: the Commonwealth appeared to be eminently capable not just of defending itself but of expanding. Poland–Lithuania was the most dynamic state in northern and eastern Europe between 1450 and 1617, as it benefited most from the collapse of the great crusading orders along the Baltic coastline in the fifteenth and sixteenth centuries, winning control of Danzig and Royal (West) Prussia in 1466, suzerainty over Ducal (East) Prussia in 1525 and control of Livonia in 1561. It successfully defended Livonia during the First Northern War (1563–70) and repulsed Swedish attacks down to 1611. The battle of Kircholm (1605), which saw the annihilation of a superior Swedish force by the Lithuanian grand hetman (commander-in-chief) Chodkiewicz, seemed to confirm the superiority of Polish arms. Between 1558 and 1634 the Commonwealth enjoyed unprecedented success against Muscovy, pushing its border eastwards in the early seventeenth century, when it seized Smolensk and Chernigov and occupied Moscow itself between 1610 and 1612. The crushing victory at Klushino in 1610 seemed to demonstrate Polish dominance on the eastern as well as the northern front. In 1621 a great Turkish assault was halted at Khotyn, and although Sweden seized most of Livonia in the 1620s, the great Gustavus Adolphus was fought to a standstill

---

[14] This was because the acts of any diet were considered as a whole, and were agreed *en bloc* at the end of the session, with the technical requirement of unanimity: the exercise of the right of veto earlier in the proceedings meant that the diet had perforce to dissolve itself without achieving anything.
[15] W. Coxe, *Travels into Poland, Russia, Sweden and Denmark. Interspersed with Historical Relations and Political Inquiries* (London, 1784) p. 15. The saying 'Poland subsists by anarchy' (*Polska nierządem stoi*) had long been current within the Commonwealth.   [16] ibid. pp. 15, 121.

Introduction

in Prussia, where he learnt much which he was later to apply on the battlefields of Germany.

Before 1648, the Commonwealth's armies had proved perfectly capable of keeping up with the tactical changes of the sixteenth and early seventeenth centuries. Its reliance on cavalry was determined not so much by backwardness as by the nature of the enemies it fought and the terrain over which it fought them. When necessary, it was perfectly capable of raising armies as large as any of its rivals: the regular forces at Khotyn in 1621 numbered around 25,000 effectives, supplemented by 20,000 Cossacks, a battlefield force that compares favourably with contemporary figures from western Europe; in all, some 80,000 troops were mobilised in 1621.[17]

The term 'crisis' is overused by historians, but it is particularly applicable to the Commonwealth's experience in the aftermath of the Swedish deluge. Its failure to reform its political and military structures doomed it to impotence after 1668. Despite John III Sobieski's triumphs over the Turks at the second battle of Khotyn in 1673 and at Vienna in 1683, the Commonwealth's days of military glory were past: these victories were over an enemy who also failed to keep up with military change. During the Great Northern War after 1700, Polish shortcomings were revealed only too clearly. It was above all the failure immediately to reform the political system during John Casimir's reign which ensured that recovery was impossible, for it was henceforth very much in the interests of the Commonwealth's neighbours to block any political reform which might lead to its military revival: they therefore signed a series of treaties agreeing to preserve its political system.[18] Foreign ambassadors were able to form parties through persuasion or simple bribery and were frequently able to wreck the diet by persuading one of their clients to exercise his veto. The culmination of this process came in 1717, when the diet, under Russian pressure, agreed to limit the size of its army; henceforward, Poland–Lithuania was effectively a Russian satellite. When it showed signs of revival in the reign of Stanisław Augustus Poniatowski (1764–95) it was partitioned out of existence.

In 1655 Opaliński and Radziwiłł were condemned in a host of pamphlets for going over to the Swedes; in 1784 Coxe observed with surprise that: 'Many of the first nobility do not blush to receive pensions from foreign courts. One professes himself

---

[17] Regular forces of similar size were also raised in 1618 and 1633–4: J. Wimmer, 'Wojsko i skarb Rzeczypospolitej u schyłku XVI i w pierwszej połowie XVII wieku' *SMHW* 14, no. 1 (1968) pp. 39, 73. Cf. western Europe, where the first battle of Breitenfeld (1631), which saw 41,000 Swedes and Saxons fighting Tilly's 31,000, was unique until the 1660s: D. Parrott, 'Strategy and tactics in the Thirty Years War: the "Military Revolution"' *Militärgeschichtliche Mitteilungen* 38, no. 2 (1985) p. 17.

[18] Such agreements were signed by Sweden and Brandenburg (1667, 1686, 1696), Austria and Muscovy (1676), and Austria and Brandenburg (1686). K. Piwarski, 'Osłabienie znaczenia międzynarodowego Rzeczypospolitej w drugiej połowie XVII wieku' *Roczniki Historyczne* 23 (1957) pp. 240–1.

publicly an Austrian, a second a Prussian, a third a Frenchman, and a fourth a Russian.'[19] Coxe found this phenomenon astonishing but there was a simple explanation: many Poles and Lithuanians had come to regard their own king as a greater threat to their precious liberties than foreign rulers who, in their own interests, swore to uphold them. Many have found such attitudes hard to credit, in the light of the extensive restrictions on royal power: Anderson claims that the constitutional changes between 1569 and 1574 'deprived [the monarch] of virtually any substantive powers in the government of the realm', a view that has also been advanced by Polish historians.[20] This may well have been true in theory: the legal restrictions on royal power were great, especially in comparison with other monarchies in Europe. It is vital, however, not to take these restraints at face value but to examine the actual operation of the political system. Contemporary Poles did not share the belief that their monarchy was weak: the repetition of certain measures by successive diets and the attempts to strengthen sanctions against the king suggest that he was frequently able to circumvent or ignore laws supposed to limit his freedom of action.[21] The consequent breakdown in the relationship between the monarchy and the political nation lay at the heart of the crisis of government in the Commonwealth.

It was in the reign of John Casimir that the vital psychological shift took place. The political and military collapse in the face of the Muscovite and Swedish invasions shocked the Commonwealth's political leaders out of their complacency, convincing many of the most influential that reform was essential. Yet, despite widespread support for reform proposals between 1656 and 1662, not only was change definitively rejected, but in the struggle to resist royal plans in the 1660s the *liberum veto* came to be seen as a vital defence of noble liberties, and a necessary barrier against the monarchy's alleged desire for absolute power. In 1660 Andrzej Maksymilian Fredro who, as marshal of the chamber of envoys at the fateful diet of 1652, had not wished to recognise the validity of the veto lodged by Władysław Siciński, published a defence of the principle as essential for the preservation of liberty.[22] The victory of this point of view among the nobility sounded the deathknell for the diet's chances of developing into an effective parliamentary body. During the 1660s, recourse to the veto became common: it had only been used twice between 1652 and 1662; between 1664 and 1668 it was used on five occasions.

---

[19] Coxe, *Travels* p. 121.
[20] Anderson, *Lineages* p. 286; cf. A. Mączak: 'The Estates all but eliminated the king as a political factor and almost reduced him during the seventeenth century to one amongst many competing magnates.' 'The conclusive years: the end of the sixteenth century as the turning-point of Polish history.' in E.I. Kouri and T. Scott (eds.), *Politics and Society in Reformation Europe. Essays for Sir Geoffrey Elton on his Sixty-Fifth Birthday* (London, 1987) p. 517.
[21] For a discussion of contemporary views of royal power, see R.I. Frost, '*Initium Calamitatis Regni?* John Casimir and monarchical power in Poland-Lithuania, 1648–1668' *European History Quarterly* 16 (1986).
[22] A.M. Fredro, *Scriptorum seu Togae et Bellum Notationum Fragmenta. Accesserunt Peristromata Regum Symbolis Expressa* (Danzig, 1660).

Introduction

Thereafter it became a regular feature of political life. The nadir was reached in the reign of Augustus III (1733–63), when only the 1736 diet passed any laws at all.

The central political issue of John Casimir's reign was the extent and nature of royal authority, a conflict which had been intensifying since 1574. If the Henrician Articles established the theoretical limits of royal power and prescribed the parameters within which the monarch was to operate, they gave no guidance on how the system might work in practice. Despite the apparent restrictions on the king, his responsibilities were great and the scope for royal initiative was still wide. Although a diet had to be called every two years and an extraordinary diet could be called at any time, ordinary diets only lasted six weeks, while extraordinary diets were restricted to a fortnight. The diet's shortcomings were evident long before 1652. The king set the agenda through the proposals which he circulated to dietines on summoning the diet, but since much time was consumed by remonstrances or private and local matters, it was often impossible to devote enough attention to government policy. Any extension to the session beyond the prescribed span had to be agreed unanimously at the end of each day. Although diets did frequently run beyond their allotted span, envoys were usually reluctant to sanction too many extensions: a significant number of diets had ended without agreeing legislation before Siciński established the principle that the opposition of one envoy was sufficient.

The brevity of diet sessions left long periods when the king was in control of policy. The key to effective government was the monarchy's relationship with the senate council, with which he shared executive responsibility between diets. The senate possessed a dual function: apart from constituting the upper house of the diet it formed a permanent advisory body, without whose consent no royal decree could be issued. The council was seen both as an organ of the central government and a check upon it. Since the king had wide powers to send and receive ambassadors, to declare war and make treaties, and to raise troops in time of danger, the role of senators as guardians of the law was seen as vital. Nevertheless, in practice monarchs exercised far greater control over the council than they ever could over the diet. First, they had sole right of appointment to the offices which accorded senate membership. Second, while all 150 senators had the right to attend council meetings, in practice few ever did, even the senators-resident appointed by the diet. Most senators avoided their residential duties, and the nucleus of council meetings tended to be formed by government ministers and royal courtiers. Thus royal supporters usually outnumbered the opposition, giving the king substantial freedom of manœuvre.[23]

---

[23] In 1641, the number of senators resident was increased from four to seven. Under Władysław IV, four out of seven was the highest number of senators-resident which attended individual meetings of the council, a figure attained at only one in every thirty-five sessions, usually following a banquet. Czapliński, 'Senat za Władysława IV' *Studia historyczne ku czci Stanisława Kutrzeby* I (Cracow, 1938)

Moreover, although the king was technically required to seek the council's unanimous consent for his actions, in practice he did not even have to follow the majority opinion, though it was usually prudent for him to do so. For a decree to be legal, it had to bear the king's signature and the seal of one of the four chanceries; if the king could obtain the support of his chancellors, senators could do little to prevent the promulgation of a decree or the departure of an ambassador.[24] While such actions technically had to be approved by the next diet, the length of time between diets meant that the government usually held the initiative and frequently could present envoys with a *fait accompli*. The council was required to account for its activities to the diet; senators, however, tended to interpret this principle as meaning that they had a duty to inform it of their decisions, not as any expression of their responsibility to it, and they resisted attempts to give anything more than a bare summary of their deliberations.[25] While they were quick to tell the king if they felt an action was impossible without diet consent, senators denied that their own powers were subject to diet control and frequently sanctioned royal attempts to evade the restrictions placed upon the executive. Such advantages had brought an increasing reliance on the senate council by the monarchy after 1569, which was understandable but increased the suspicion with which the chamber of envoys regarded the king. Calls for fines on senators-resident who failed to fulfil their duties and for full accounts to be kept of council meetings were common.

The senate council's failure to act as an adequate supervisory body stimulated suspicion of the monarchy among the ordinary nobility, already strong owing to the preference for electing foreign candidates. This preference stemmed partly from a consciousness of the dignity of royal blood which was never wholly extinguished by noble republicanism and partly from rivalry among magnate families reluctant to countenance a native candidature which might elevate one family above its peers. There was continued respect for the dynastic principle; apart from Henry of Anjou, all monarchs until 1668 had strong links through the female line to the Jagiellons: Stefan Batory married Anna, the elderly sister of Sigismund Augustus, while Sigismund III was the son of Catherine, another sister of Sigismund Augustus, from her marriage to John III of Sweden. In 1632 Władysław IV, Sigismund's eldest son, succeeded him in what was the first uncontested election since 1573,

---

p. 38. Despite its importance, the senate council has received scant attention from historians: Czapliński's brief and outdated account is the only serious study of the council in the seventeenth century, although two recent works deal with the early eighteenth-century council: M. Markiewicz, *Rady senatorskie Augusta II (1697–1733)* (Wrocław, 1988) and 'Rady senatu za Augusta III' *Zeszyty Naukowe Uniwersytetu Jagiellońskiego* Prace Historyczne 77 (Cracow, 1985).

[24] It is true that the king sometimes had difficulty in persuading his chancellors to accept controversial decrees. A.S. Radziwiłł, Lithuanian grand chancellor, refused to put his seal to a decree in December 1649 until it accorded with Lithuanian law. A.S. Radziwiłł, *Memoriale Rerum Gestarum in Poloniae 1632–1656* ed. A. Przyboś and R. Żelewski (Wrocław, 1968–72) IV p. 150.

[25] Senators treated the requirement to keep minutes of council meetings in a cavalier fashion. At the 1649–50 diet, John Casimir explained that the minutes could not be read since they had been left in Zamość. L. Częścik, *Sejm Warszawski w 1649–50 roku* (Wrocław, 1978) p. 77.

Introduction

while the main contest in 1648 was between Władysław's two surviving brothers, John Casimir and Charles Ferdinand.

It was difficult, however, for a foreign dynasty to make the easy identification of dynastic and state interests which was possible for a native, hereditary dynasty. After Sigismund III's deposition in 1600 from the Swedish throne he had inherited from his father in 1592, the Polish Vasas stubbornly maintained their claim to their hereditary realm. Although the diet was initially prepared to offer support, albeit lukewarm, to the king's early attempts to regain his throne, the claim on Sweden was increasingly seen as a barrier to a definitive settlement of the dispute over Livonia, while Sigismund's intervention in Muscovy's Time of Troubles was seen as a private dynastic adventure detrimental to the Commonwealth's interests. Ominously, a feeling was emerging that the monarchy's concerns were different from those of the Commonwealth and that the best way of safeguarding liberty was to ensure that the king conducted a peaceful foreign policy. If the Commonwealth were attacked, the *szlachta* would defend it; they would not, however, back aggressive foreign adventures. Thus Władysław IV's attempts to intervene in the Thirty Years War were blocked, as were his grandiose schemes in the 1640s for a Turkish war. Under John Casimir, the perceived conflict between dynastic and state interests was to play a vital part in the collapse of 1655.

Nevertheless, the loss of Livonia to Sweden at Altmark in 1629, the first real setback for over a century, suggested that the *szlachta* might no longer be able to defend the Commonwealth effectively. The Swedish armies led by Gustavus Adolphus during the 1620s were very different from the disorganised rabble his father had put in the field at the start of the century: they could no longer be routed with the sort of bluff and cavalry charge that Chodkiewicz had employed at Kircholm. Most importantly, with their experienced and well-supplied infantry, they could not easily be dislodged from fortresses by the Commonwealth's cavalry-dominated armies. There were political objections, however, to the widespread employment of professional infantry. The *szlachta* preferred to keep the Commonwealth's defence in its own hands rather than risk entrusting the king with control of politically unreliable foreign mercenaries.

This attitude left the Commonwealth dangerously exposed. There was no substantial standing army: political considerations prompted the progressive reduction of the number of troops under direct government control. By 1648, these consisted of the royal guard, limited to 1,200 in 1647, a permanent force of 4,200 regulars who garrisoned the Ukraine and the registered Cossacks, reduced to 6,000 in 1638 and unavailable after Khmelnytskyi's rising began. Batory's attempt to create a permanent force of infantry, chosen by lot from peasants on royal estates, had failed.[26] The Commonwealth depended in times of need on locally raised or private forces: the *levée-en-masse*, consisting primarily of cavalry, units raised and

---

[26] J. Wimmer, *Wojsko polskie w drugiej połowie XVII wieku* (Warsaw, 1965) pp. 19, 32–5.

trained by local dietines, units raised from the great entailed estates established at the end of the sixteenth century and the private armies of magnates. Great nobles could field far more men than the king: Jarema Wiśniowiecki maintained a permanent force of 1,500–3,000; he could quickly raise 3,000 more, with a further 6,000 in an emergency. Of the 19,130 troops present at the battle of Okhmativ in 1644, there were 3,500 regulars, 4,000 registered Cossacks and 11,530 private troops.[27] Since the Commonwealth was heavily dependent upon the Cossacks and on the private armies raised in the Ukraine, when Khmelnytskyi destroyed the Polish forces at Zhovti Vody, Korsun and Pyliavtsi in 1648, he deprived it of the bulk of its army.

It was a challenge the political system was ill-prepared to meet. Poland–Lithuania, like other states, was affected by the huge increase in the cost of warfare in the preceding century, the result of military change against the background of the general inflation of the long sixteenth century. It also suffered from the economic downturn in the second quarter of the seventeenth century, when the less buoyant market for Polish grain and other raw materials, and the disruption to the Baltic trade caused by the Thirty Years War badly affected noble incomes. It was political, rather than economic reasons, however, which made it difficult for the Poles to adopt the solutions to this problem seen elsewhere in Europe. First, noble reluctance to sanction offensive war meant that the Commonwealth was unable to adopt the expedient so successfully used by Sweden in the Thirty Years War of making war largely pay for itself. Secondly, the Commonwealth was in theory a domain-state, in which the king was supposed to meet most defence costs from his own revenues but was in practice heavily dependent upon extraordinary grants of taxation from the diet.[28]

The problem of the royal domain lay at the heart of the Commonwealth's financial plight. In the first half of the sixteenth century, the monarchy had raised money to fight its increasingly expensive wars largely through raising loans on the security of royal land. By the 1550s, much royal land had been alienated, largely to the magnates who dominated the royal councils in Poland and Lithuania. Increasingly frequent demands for taxation, especially following the outbreak of war for Livonia in 1558, provoked strong calls among the Polish middle and lower nobility for a resumption of royal land, the alienation of which had been declared illegal by the diet in 1504.

In the 1560s this 'execution movement' as it was called, from its central demand for the execution of existing law, succeeded in driving through a series of statutes

---

[27] ibid. pp. 20–1, 35–6. Czapliński and Długosz doubt whether magnates maintained such large forces in practice, but it remains true that they could raise troops far more quickly than the king in an emergency. W. Czapliński and J. Długosz, *Życie codzienne magnaterii polskiej w XVIIw.* (Warsaw, 1976) p. 62.

[28] For a discussion of the problem of domain states and tax states, based on the Danish experience, see E.L. Petersen, 'From domain state to tax state' *Scandinavian Economic History Review* 23 (1975).

Introduction

which established the theoretical basis of royal finance for the next hundred years. Its prime motivation was the belief that with the privileges of Nieszawa (1454) the king had agreed to shoulder the main financial burden of defence. This was a one-sided interpretation of the statute but it stimulated strong opposition to the reform plans of Sigismund I and Sigismund Augustus, which called for general land-surveys as a basis for taxation and the foundation of a public treasury based on regular taxes.[29]

The call for the resumption of all royal land granted or alienated as security on loans since 1504 was ultimately successful. Sigismund Augustus, who desperately needed money as general war loomed in the Baltic, changed tactics at the 'execution diet' of 1562–3, joining forces with the executionists against the magnates. The diet decreed that henceforth a quarter of the income from royal estates would be assigned to defence; this represented something of a compromise with the magnates, since the executionists had called for half. The diet of 1563–4 began the lengthy process of scrutinising grants and alienations of royal lands, and the 1567 diet adjusted the way in which the proceeds from royal lands would be divided. Henceforward, although it was still known as the *kwarta* (quarter), a payment of one fifth of the income went to the so-called quarter treasury in Rawa for the upkeep of the small standing army garrisoning the south-eastern border. Another fifth was assigned to the noble leaseholder or administrator (starosta) of a particular estate, while the remaining three-fifths were to be paid into the royal treasury.[30] Henry of Anjou made a further adjustment in 1574, decreeing that judicial starostas would divide the profits of the attached estates fifty–fifty with the king after deduction of the *kwarta*; for non-judicial starostas the division was 50 per cent for the king, 30 per cent for the starosta, after deduction of the *kwarta*.

On paper, these reforms gave the monarchy a substantial income. After the Union of Lublin, royal lands in Poland and Lithuania constituted some 20 per cent of the Commonwealth's land-surface, about 815,000 km^2 before 1648; if the king had received the income that the execution movement intended, he would have been far richer than even the greatest magnate. The reforms, however, were far from perfectly executed. First, the monarchy was in no position to pay off the loans it had raised using royal land as security; indeed, with the permission of the 1565 diet, Sigismund Augustus raised another loan of 500,000 złoties to pay for the Polish involvement in the Livonian War. Until the loans were repaid, these lands paid nothing to the treasury, while in practice it was difficult to enforce their resumption, especially since the failure to carry out any thorough survey of royal estates made it hard to establish the legal position of individual pieces of land. Secondly, although the *kwarta* was collected with reasonable success, it continued to be levied at the 1560s rate in the absence of any regular auditing procedures, despite the inflation of

---

[29] W. Pałucki, *Drogi i bezdroża skarbowości polskiej XVI i pierwszej połowy XVII wieku* (Wrocław, 1974) pp. 28–9, 35, 37.
[30] ibid., p. 203; A. Filipczak-Kocur, *Skarb koronny za Zygmunta III Wazy* (Opole, 1985) p. 14.

the late sixteenth century which greatly increased the income of landed estates: although a second *kwarta* was levied at the 1560s rate from 1632, by 1765 the quarter treasury was estimated to receive only 2 or 3 per cent of the real income from royal lands.[31] Most importantly, the starostas and leaseholders of royal estates in practice kept the three-fifths of the proceeds they were supposed to pay into the royal treasury; the king was unable to enforce payment of even the lesser share he was accorded by the 1574 statute.

The execution movement sought to give the monarchy a firm financial base; in practice it promoted its financial ruin through introducing an unenforceable system, although the government had some success over the resumption of lands mortgaged up to 1565. The history of the royal lands for the whole Commonwealth has yet to be written but a recent study of Little Poland suggests that with diet backing over a long period and general inspections, most successfully carried out in 1615–20 and 1660–5, the majority of lands alienated in the first half of the sixteenth century had been reintegrated into the fiscal system by 1665 and at least paid the *kwarta*.[32]

This made little difference, however, to the overall position of royal finances, since the monarchy proved completely unable to collect the three-fifths of the income from its own lands it was supposed to enjoy. Indeed, by the reign of Sigismund III, it had effectively abandoned its claims, owing to the political tactics kings were forced to adopt to make the political system work. Their dependence on the senate council threw them into the arms of the magnates, who had most to lose if the executionist programme were realised in full. Indeed, the great patronage power afforded the king by his control of royal land through the power to grant leases on starosties was vital to his conduct of government business and to such control of the diet as he was able to achieve. In a system which insisted on the equality of all nobles and which banned the granting of titles, status was accorded by office, appointment to which was a royal monopoly, and through wealth.[33] For the ambitious nobleman, access to royal land was essential. Partitive inheritance was the norm, and only a handful of families succeeded in winning diet approval for entailing their estates at the end of the sixteenth century. A family's fortune could decline rapidly; even a nobleman of good birth might inherit only a relatively small estate: access to royal land was essential if he were to maintain his social position.[34] Few could afford to

---

[31] Pałucki, *Drogi* p. 21.
[32] K. Chłapowski, *Realizacja reform egzekucji dóbr 1563–1665. Sprawa zastawów królewszczyzn małopolskich* (Warsaw, 1984) pp. 175–8. See also A. Sucheni-Grabowska, 'Próby aukcji dochodów z dóbr domeny królewskiej w świetle lustracji z lat 1615–1620' *Przegląd Historyczny* 58, no. 2 (1967).
[33] By law, only Lithuanian and Ruthenian nobles descended from the grand ducal dynasties of Gediminas and Rurik could use the title *kniaz* or *książę* (prince). In practice, many prominent nobles acquired titles from the Holy Roman Emperor, which they insisted on using.
[34] Bogusław Leszczyński, Crown treasurer and later vice-chancellor under John Casimir, inherited six towns and seventy villages; grants of royal land added fourteen towns and 259 villages to this total. W. Dworzaczek, 'Skład społeczny wielkopolskiej reprezentacji sejmowej w latach 1572–1655' *Roczniki Historyczne* 23 (1957) p. 289.

Introduction

distance themselves too far from the Court: their own position might permit opposition but their sons' careers had to be secured.

The monarchy's increasing dependence on the senate council and its enforced reliance on patronage to achieve its political aims meant the effective abandonment of the alliance with the middle and lesser nobility which had seen the triumph of the execution movement in the 1560s. By the mid-seventeenth century, the balance of power between the rich and poor nobility had shifted dramatically. Those families who had access to the vast profits to be gained from royal land used the proceeds to build up their private estates. The demand for grain from western Europe increased the profitability of large-scale agricultural enterprises, so that the larger landed proprietors did better than the middle *szlachta*; they were also better able to absorb the effects of the downturn in the grain market after 1620. As the number of landless and impoverished noblemen increased and the average size of estates held by the middle *szlachta* declined, the importance of magnate courts as centres of employment and patronage grew. The appearance of factions based on extensive clientage networks enabled magnates to exercise greater control over provincial dietines and, indirectly, the diet.

Although Sigismund III succeeded in 1590 in converting several of the wealthiest starosties into *ekonomia*, whose proceeds were reserved for the upkeep of the royal household, the monarchy was forced to drop its claims to a direct share of the income in its other estates; by the early seventeenth century, many of the ideals of the execution movement had been forgotten, and the nobility had come to regard the revenues from the royal lands as legitimate reward for its services to the Commonwealth, even though access was reserved to a minority. Effectively, the royal lands had been removed from royal control; it was increasingly common to regard them as belonging to the Commonwealth, not the king. Given the monarchy's inability to pay its officials any kind of salary, it was not an entirely unreasonable position in principle, but no amount of sophistry could disguise the fact that the public purse had been burgled for private profit. The great magnate fortunes of the seventeenth and eighteenth centuries were built upon revenues from royal estates.[35]

The king had the right to appoint, but he could not dismiss: tenure of office was for life. Although the monarchy still favoured the promotion of individuals from the middle nobility and the core of the regalist party consisted of men ascending the social ladder, life tenure of office and starosties made control difficult. There was nowhere near enough royal patronage to go round; the noble masses were instead drawn into magnate clientage networks, which made royal control of dietines and diets more difficult, since malcontent magnates could use their local influence to frustrate royal plans. The first great confrontation came in 1606–7, when Sigismund

---

[35] By the mid-eighteenth century, the income of two individuals, M. Radziwiłł and F.S. Potocki, matched the total public revenue. J.T. Lukowski, *Liberty's Folly: The Polish–Lithuanian Commonwealth in the Eighteenth Century* (London, 1991) p. 15.

After the Deluge

III's reform plans provoked rebellion. Led by a malcontent magnate, Mikołaj Zebrzydowski, palatine of Cracow, large numbers of the lesser and middling nobility asserted their right to rebel if the king acted in breach of his coronation oath. Zebrzydowski's revolt was defeated, but although Sigismund kept his throne he had to abandon his reform plans.

Despite the increasing power of magnate factions, the magnates never formed a homogenous class, and the monarchy was able to exploit its appointment powers and the intense rivalry between individuals to exercise some degree of control. Historians, especially those influenced by Marxism, have been keen to point to the development of a 'magnate oligarchy' in the seventeenth century, in which the magnates as a social group seized control of the 'helm of state', but this is a difficult concept to sustain: the magnates never constituted a formal aristocracy within the nobility, and political rivalry, not political unity, was more characteristic of their behaviour. The problem of magnate power in the Commonwealth was not that the magnates as a group ever exercised control over the 'helm of state', but that individual magnates could frustrate central government by exploiting the decentralised political system, without themselves ever being able to seize power at the centre.[36]

There is no doubt, however, that the growing power of the magnates was making government increasingly difficult. The monarchy's weak financial position made it ever more dependent on the diet. The execution movement's success in preventing further alienations after 1565 seriously affected the king's ability to raise loans in wartime: he could no longer alienate royal land as security and the diet's control of taxation precluded the anticipation of revenues, so common elsewhere in Europe. Increasingly, loans had to be raised from magnates, with the promise of redemption at the next diet. This phenomenon, in which the king effectively borrowed money that was his by the letter of the law, merely increased his dependence on taxation, a trend the holders of royal land were only too keen to foster.[37] The main land-tax was levied at one złoty to the *łan* according to the registers of 1578, which formed the basis of the assessment until the eighteenth century, although the tariff was slightly raised in 1629.[38] In that year, a hearth tax was also introduced alongside the land-tax, in an attempt to increase revenue, particularly from the eastern and south-eastern palatinates of Ruthenia, Volhynia, Podolia and Kiev where – it was rightly suspected – many estates were not registered for the land tax.[39] The king also collected, with diet permission, the *czopowe* (a tax on the production and sale of

---

[36] The classic exposition of the theory of the magnate oligarchy is Czapliński, 'Rządy oligarchii w Polsce nowożytnej' *Przegląd Historyczny* 52 (1958), reprinted in Czapliński, *O Polsce siedemnastowiecznej* (Warsaw, 1966). See also A. Kersten, 'Les Magnats – élite de la société nobiliaire' *Acta Poloniae Historica* 36 (1977).

[37] A. Sucheni-Grabowska, 'Walka o wymiar i przeznaczenie kwarty w końcu XVI i na początku XVII wieku' *Przegląd Historyczny* 54 (1965) p. 39.

[38] In the towns, a property tax was levied. Filipczak-Kocur, *Skarb koronny* pp. 33–4.

[39] Filipczak-Kocur, *Sejm zwyczajny z roku 1629* (Warsaw, 1979) p. 81.

Introduction

alcohol), customs duties, from which nobles were exempt, poll-taxes on Jewish and Tatar communities and various levies on merchants and the Catholic clergy.

None of these taxes was permanent: consent only ran until the next diet. All attempts by Sigismund III to establish a permanent treasury, based on regular taxation, were blocked. Since the nobility resisted any proper land survey, taxation rates by the 1620s had not kept pace with inflation; to meet the escalating costs of war, multiple rates had to be agreed. A further problem was the inefficient collection of taxes. Even when the diet was in a cooperative mood, it was no more capable than the king of ensuring that its wishes were obeyed. Lacking a large central bureaucracy, the government was dependent on the dietines to implement diet decisions. It was the imperfect control of both government and diet over these dietines which was the true source of executive weakness: through deliberate obstruction, incompetence or laziness, they frequently failed to fulfil agreed quotas: of the 2,738,000 złoties voted for Poland and the 1,220,000 for Lithuania in the autumn diet of 1627, only 50 per cent had been collected by May 1628. All Sigismund III could do was to call another diet, where he faced the same problems. By December 1628, the debt to the army was 1,526,384 złoties. Diets in 1628 and 1629 did little to help. As the king remarked: 'Sufficient resources were never agreed for this war; even when funds were voted by the diet, at the dietines, everything was ruined.'[40]

The increasingly frequent demands for taxation and the increasingly frequent diets which were needed to vote it served merely to alienate *szlachta* opinion. Sigismund was forced to conclude the disadvantageous truce of Altmark in 1629 largely because the diet was no longer prepared to support the war: envoys were unwilling to continue spending money to defend the distant province of Livonia. Yet the problems faced by Sigismund in the 1620s were to return with a vengeance after 1648 when the Cossack revolt and invasion by Sweden and Muscovy destroyed the Commonwealth's ability to defend itself: the devastation caused by the invaders meant that its capacity to raise taxes was severely impaired.

John Casimir has frequently been blamed for squandering a marvellous opportunity to reform the political system. Instead of concentrating on restoring health to the diet by abolishing the *liberum veto*, for which there was substantial support after 1655, the Court concentrated on a campaign for the election of a successor to John Casimir *vivente rege* in the person of a French candidate, the duc d'Enghien. This provoked resistance which culminated in civil war and the entrenchment of Fredro's view of the veto as a necessary guarantee of liberty.[41] The French election seemed to

---

[40] Filipczak-Kocur, 'Problemy podatko-wojskowe na sejmie w roku 1628' *Zeszyty naukowe Wyższej Szkoły Pedagogicznej im. Powstańców Śląskich w Opolu* Seria A Historia 16 (Opole, 1979) pp. 23–7, 37.

[41] B. Kalicki, 'O niektórych próbach reformy sejmowej w w.XVII' *Przegląd Polski* I (1873) pp. 67–125; W. Czermak, 'Próba naprawy Rzeczypospolitej za Jana Kazimierza' *Biblioteka Warszawska* 51 (1891) pp. 519–47; H. Sawczyński, 'Sprawa reformy sejmowania za Jana Kazimierza' *Kwartalnik Historyczny* 7 (1893) pp. 240–84; W. Czapliński, 'Próby reform państwa w czasie najazdu szwedzkiego' *PODWP* I pp. 303–29; S. Ochmann, 'Plans for parliamentary reform in the Commonwealth in the middle of the seventeenth century' in Czapliński (ed.), *The Polish Parliament* pp. 163–87.

serve the interests of the dynasty rather than the Commonwealth and is usually dismissed as an inappropriate scheme dreamed up by John Casimir's French wife, Louise Marie of Gonzaga. By irresponsibly linking diet reform to the election campaign, it is argued, the Court ensured its defeat: the attempt to interfere with the right of free election, seen as the basis of noble liberty, was bound to provoke opposition, while envoys feared that if majority voting were introduced, the king's extensive powers of patronage would not only ensure victory for the election but would also allow the king to dominate the diet permanently, which might lead to the introduction of hereditary monarchy and *absolutum dominium*. Furthermore, the election campaign ensured that the Commonwealth became a battleground for foreign powers: it was inevitable that the Habsburgs and others would oppose a French election. Thus Court policy contributed directly to the domination of Polish politics by its neighbours which did so much to ensure its decline.

This study re-examines the Court's reform plans, setting them against the background of the war. It stresses the relationship between the election campaign, political reform, and the fluctuating military and diplomatic situation. When Court policy is viewed in the context of the war, it emerges that John Casimir and Louise Marie neither acted merely for private or dynastic reasons, although these certainly played their part, nor were they the passive tools of Habsburg or Bourbon diplomacy. Political reform could not be considered in isolation after 1655 while the Commonwealth was struggling for its very survival. The Commonwealth's inability to save itself by its own efforts was the fundamental reality which produced the election campaign. There has, however, been no detailed examination of the government's conduct of the war since Kubala's general narrative, written over fifty years ago, which is frequently unreliable.[42] The collective work published to mark the 300th anniversary of the war contains much useful material but is marred by its Stalinist approach; many of its contributors subsequently produced more subtle and perceptive work.[43] There have been several studies of individual problems in foreign policy but no work which evaluates government policy as a whole. Military aspects of the war have received much attention but there is no detailed account of the Thirteen Years War (1654–67), with most authors treating the Second Northern War (1655–60) and the Commonwealth's war with Muscovy (1654–67) as two separate conflicts; of the two, the former has received far more attention.

This study is based primarily on printed sources and on sources available in Polish archives. The disruption of the 1650s, when many documents were destroyed or removed by the Swedes, means that this period is less well served than others, especially with regard to Court politics. Most contemporary diaries and memoirs are concerned largely with military aspects of the war, or reflect the views of ordinary

---

[42] L. Kubala, *Wojna moskiewska r. 1654–1655* (Warsaw, Cracow, 1910); *Wojna szwecka w roku 1655 i 1656* (Lwów, 1913); *Wojna brandenburska i najazd Rakoczego w roku 1656 i 1657* (Lwów, Warsaw, 1917); *Wojny duńskie i pokój oliwijski* (Lwów, 1922).

[43] K. Lepszy (ed.), *Polska w okresie drugiej wojny północnej* 4 vols. (Warsaw, 1957).

Introduction

nobles, not senators or ministers. There is nothing to match the diary of A.S. Radziwiłł, Lithuanian grand hetman from 1623 to 1656, which is such an informative source for the reign of Władysław IV and the early years of John Casimir, but which says little after the outbreak of war in 1655. Although the diary of the queen's secretary, Pierre des Noyers, gives much useful information, he was not at the centre of politics in the same way.[44]

The relative paucity of sources for the study of Court politics has led historians to rely heavily on the reports of foreign ambassadors, especially the detailed accounts of de Lumbres and Lisola, the envoys of France and Austria respectively.[45] Yet overreliance upon these sources has reinforced tendencies to regard the Court as merely a pawn in the great battle of Habsburg and Bourbon, and its policy as subservient to foreign interests, a charge first made by opponents of the election campaign. Extensive use has therefore been made of the reports of the papal nuncio, Pietro Vidoni, who spent far more time at the Polish Court than either de Lumbres or Lisola. Vidoni's dispatches have not been used systematically hitherto, yet they cast important light on the conduct of the war and royal reform plans, and enable a more critical approach to be adopted towards the reports of de Lumbres and Lisola, demonstrating that the political situation was much more fluid and complex than has frequently been allowed and was far from the simple battle between a pro-French and a pro-Austrian party which is so often assumed.[46]

[44] E. Rykaczewski (ed.), *Lettres de Pierre des Noyers, secrétaire de la reine de Pologne Marie-Louise de Gonzague... (à Ismael Bouillaud) pour servir à l'histoire de Pologne et de Suède de 1655 à 1659* (Berlin, 1859).

[45] De Lumbres's memoirs were published by A. Lhomel (ed.), *Relations de Lumbres Antoine, ambassadeur en Pologne et en Allemagne touchant ses négotiations et ambassades* (Paris, 1912). Many of Lisola's dispatches have been published by A. Pribram, *Die Berichte des kaiserlichen Gesandten Franz von Lisola aus den Jahren 1655–1660* Archiv für österreichische Geschichte 70 (1887).

[46] Copies of Vidoni's dispatches made from the Vatican originals in the nineteenth century are in the Library of the Polish Academy of Sciences in Cracow: Teki Rzymskie 8418–8422 (1655–60). Limited extracts have been published in A. Levinson, *Die Nuntiaturberichte des Petrus Vidoni über den ersten nordischen Krieg aus den Jahren 1655–1658* Archiv für österreichische Geschichte 95 (1906) and *Zherela do Istorii Ukraini-Rusi* V Fontes Historiae Ukraino-Russicae XII, ed. M. Korduba (Lwów, 1911).

2

The Deluge

The Cossack revolt shook the Commonwealth to its foundations. Disastrous defeats at Zhovti Vody (11–16 May 1648) and Korsun (26 May), where the Polish grand hetman Mikołaj Potocki and field hetman Marcin Kalinowski were captured, were followed by the humiliating rout at Pyliavtsi (23 September), when the *levée-en-masse* once more demonstrated its worthlessness by simply running away. The death of Władysław IV on 20 May, by plunging the Commonwealth into the uncertainties of an interregnum, greatly hindered the political and military response. It was not until 17 November that John Casimir was chosen to succeed him.

The election of John Casimir, born in 1609 to Sigismund III's second wife Constance of Austria, was something of a surprise, for he had not started as favourite despite being the elder of Władysław's surviving brothers. He had done little so far to endear himself to the nobility. As a younger son of an impoverished dynasty which lacked an independent financial base after Sigismund's deposition in Sweden, John Casimir's political and financial position had been uncertain. Such resources as the family possessed were devoted to maintaining Władysław in the style befitting the heir presumptive. Three of his brothers joined the Church, simply to enjoy a career and an income: John Albert (1612–34) was successively bishop of Warmia and bishop of Cracow, the richest see in the Commonwealth; he also became a cardinal, while Sigismund succeeded in having Charles Ferdinand (1613–55) elected to the lucrative bishopric of Breslau; he was also bishop of Płock. John Casimir, as the second son, had better prospects of the throne but, despite several appeals to the diet, he was never granted an adequate income. Left to his own scanty resources, he drifted aimlessly until he became heir presumptive on the death of Władysław's only legitimate son in 1647, fighting briefly for the Habsburgs in 1635, before accepting a post in 1638 as admiral in the Spanish fleet, only to be arrested and imprisoned by the French when he inadvisedly landed in Marseilles en route. On his release, after clashes with the diet over his income, he again left the Commonwealth amid mutual recriminations. He joined the Jesuit Order in 1644, before becoming a cardinal, a position which he renounced as soon as he heard of his nephew's death.

Charles Ferdinand, who had remained in the Commonwealth, initially enjoyed the support of most of the nobility and many influential senators, although some favoured the candidature of Sigismund Rákóczi, younger son of George I Rákóczi,

The Deluge

prince of Transylvania. Gradually, however, John Casimir attracted support, particularly from those, led by Crown grand chancellor Jerzy Ossoliński, who wanted an agreement with Khmelnytskyi, which seemed after the Cossack victories to be the only practical policy. Rákóczi's candidature collapsed after the unexpected death of his father, but it was Khmelnytskyi's declaration that he would only reach an agreement if John Casimir were elected which tipped the balance against Charles Ferdinand, who withdrew his candidature.

John Casimir was crowned on 17 January 1649; the following May he married his brother's widow, Louise Marie of Gonzaga, who was to play an important political role in the years to follow. Born in 1611, the daughter of Charles, duke of Nevers and duke of Mantua from 1627, she had been brought up at the French Court. She married Władysław IV in 1645 when the latter rejected his previously pro-Habsburg policy in favour of a rapprochement with France. An intelligent and ambitious woman, Louise Marie was frustrated by Władysław's personal indifference to her and his refusal to allow her any significant role. On his death, she supported the candidature of John Casimir, who promised to marry her in an effort to win French backing to set against Habsburg support for Charles Ferdinand.

Louise Marie has long been portrayed as the driving force behind Court policy under John Casimir, who is usually depicted as weak, indecisive and inconstant but with a stubborn streak and an unfortunate temper. Contemporaries were swift to suggest that the queen dominated her husband, ruling him 'like a small Ethiopian rules his elephant' in Rudawski's colourful phrase.[1] The consequences, it is suggested, were unfortunate: as a foreigner, Louise Marie did not understand the Polish political system, disregarded its central principles and was guided by dangerous and inappropriate absolutist ideas she had learnt at the Court of Louis XIII. Moreover, as an obedient servant of France, she put French interests above those of the Commonwealth and forced John Casimir to abandon his natural inclination for his Habsburg relations. Ultimately, it is argued, it was Louise Marie who was responsible for the ill-advised French election campaign which was to have such unfortunate consequences.[2]

While there is no doubt that Louise Marie was an energetic and ambitious woman

---

[1] W. Rudawski, *Historiarum Poloniae ab excessu Vladislai IV ad pacem Olivensem* (Warsaw, Leipzig, 1755) IX p. 398.

[2] Few historians have represented John Casimir in a favourable light. The most prominent was the pro-Austrian A. Walewski, *Historia wyzwolenia Polski za panowania Jana Kazimierza, 1655–1660* (Cracow, 1866–8) and *Historia wyzwolonej Rzeczypospolitej wpadającej pod jarzmo domowe za panowania Jana Kazimierza (1655–1660)* (Cracow, 1870). More typical were the contemptuous assessments of J.K. Plebański, *Jan Kazimierz Waza, Maria Ludwika Gonzaga. Dwa obrazy historyczne* (Warsaw, 1862) and W. Czermak, 'Jan Kazimierz, próba charakterystyki' *Kwartalnik Historyczny* 3 (1889). Although military historians have stressed that John Casimir had some talent as a soldier, assessments of his character and political ability remain negative. His latest biographer is less damning than Plebański and Czermak, but does not challenge the basic view of a feeble and irresolute monarch dominated by his wife: T. Wasilewski, *Ostatni Waza na polskim tronie* (Katowice, 1984) and *Jan Kazimierz* (Warsaw, 1985). See also W. Czapliński, 'Jan Kazimierz' *PSB* X pp. 410–13.

who had great influence over her husband and played an important political role, the picture of her as all-powerful is overdrawn. Too much credence is sometimes given to the hostile pamphleteers and satirists, of which there were many in such a controversial reign, who are quoted as if they were objective sources. Rudawski, for example, was strongly pro-Habsburg and a bitter opponent of the queen. Pierre des Noyers, the queen's secretary, wrote that John Casimir was incapable of application, had never read a complete book in his life and liked to pass his time among his favourites, 'who were all of his nature; that is to say people without spirit'.[3] Des Noyers's view is frequently cited, but he too was not unbiased: he was fiercely loyal to the queen and took her side in her frequent disputes with her husband. John Casimir may not have been bookish but he was by no means stupid and was a better linguist than his wife, knowing Polish, German, Latin, French and Italian: Louise Marie never mastered more than simple Polish and knew only French and Italian.

John Casimir's relationship with Louise Marie was more complex than the simple stereotype of a hen-pecked husband ruled by a domineering wife. There appears to have been a real basis of affection: they had first met in 1640 after John Casimir's release from French captivity, when he was a regular visitor to Louise Marie's castle at Nevers, and his letters to her show respect and genuine sentiment. If he frequently deferred to his wife, John Casimir was perfectly capable of defying her, especially on political matters, and he never lost his taste for womanising, despite the queen's hot temper and sensitivity to her husband's affairs. There are more positive assessments of John Casimir's character by those who served him as soldiers.[4]

The queen's attachment to France is frequently overstated. While she never lost her regard for the land where she grew up, she was above all a Gonzaga. Her father's successful acquisition of Mantua enhanced the dynasty's status, and Louise Marie was always proud of her Italian roots: her hostility to the Habsburgs owed as much to the fact that the third wife of Emperor Ferdinand III was Eleanora Gonzaga, from the rival branch of the family, as to any loyalty to France. Mazarin encouraged her to learn Italian properly when she left France in 1645, insisting on writing to her in Italian, and it was in Italian that she conversed with John Casimir. Nevertheless, her heavily Italianate written French suggests that she learnt to write Italian first.[5]

---

[3] Des Noyers, 1.X.1658; *Lettres* p. 446.

[4] Pasek refers to him as a good master and tells of the occasion when a child found wandering wild in the forest threw some pear-peel which hit Louise Marie between the eyes. John Casimir laughed uproariously; when the queen left in rage, he ordered everyone to drink to her fury: J.C. Pasek, *Memoirs of the Polish Baroque* tr. C.S. Leach (Berkeley, 1976) pp. 155, 158. John Casimir's affairs were the subject of a racy contemporary novel, clearly written by someone with personal knowledge of his Court: M. Rousseau de la Valette, *Casimir Roy de Pologne* (Paris, 1679). Des Noyers sneered that John Casimir was 'quasi impotent' but had to admit that he enjoyed considerable success with women: *Lettres* p. 446.

[5] Her spelling in French was strongly influenced by Italian: e.g. *giaure* for *j'aurai*; Louise Marie to Mme de Choisy, 12.IX.1656, BNP FFr. 3859 f. 11.

The Deluge

Also open to question is the closeness of her relationship to Mazarin: she had been brought up by the duchesse de Longueville after the death of her mother and was very close to the *frondeur* circles of the Longuevilles and the Condés.[6]

Whoever was the driving force, the Court from the outset was determined to assert its control. This was essential, since political divisions seriously undermined the war-effort. Despite having been elected as the candidate of the peace party, John Casimir was unable to reach a lasting agreement with Khmelnytskyi, whose demands were vigorously opposed by those with estates and interests in the Ukraine, especially Jarema Wiśniowiecki, palatine of Ruthenia, leader of the war party. Yet the Commonwealth was in no state to wage war. The political system, based on constant consultation, with the discussion of royal proposals at dietines, followed by the diet, in turn followed by special dietines which assembled to scrutinise and implement diet decisions (*sejmiki relacyjne*), was dangerously cumbersome in an emergency and discouraged decisive action. Moreover, the diet was no more capable than the king of ensuring that its wishes were obeyed: in 1649, the government asked for 30,000 troops; the diet accepted 19,042 but only voted enough money for 10,000. The 32,700 men raised in 1652 may have been the largest army fielded by Poland up to that point but the diet had called for 50,000.[7] Even when taxes were agreed, dietines regularly failed to collect their allotted sums.

In this situation, the government was unable to satisfy either the hardliners, who urged that the revolt must be crushed, or the moderates, who desired a negotiated settlement. While the Commonwealth was capable of defeating the Cossacks and their Tatar allies in battle, most notably at Berestechko in 1651, it lacked the ability to win the war. The result was a series of campaigns ending in unsatisfactory compromises which soon broke down: at Zboriv (1649) and Bila Tserkva (1651). The government was caught in a vicious circle: political strife constantly hampered the military effort, while military failure merely exacerbated political strife.

Reform was clearly necessary, yet it could not be achieved without provoking further opposition. For it was inevitable that the central problem of royal authority – the independent power of the magnates – would have to be tackled if the king were to regain control. The battle over the royal lands had been lost long before 1648, but the Court, unable to enforce its rights under the law, began a vigorous campaign to increase its revenue by compelling holders of starosties to uphold the letter of their contracts on individual estates or leases, matters to which Władysław IV had frequently turned a blind eye, and by increasing such payments wherever possible when vacancies arose. This policy was unpopular but the nobility could hardly complain too much: the king could legitimately have asked for much more. It was, however, the practice of demanding payment for the granting of leases and starosties

---

[6] Her sister, Anne, played an important part in the negotiations to free Condé, Conti and Longueville in 1651: L. Raffin, *Anne de Gonzague, Princesse Palatine 1616–1684* (Paris, 1935) chapter 4.

[7] Częścik, *Sejm Warszawski* p. 27; Wimmer, *Wojsko polskie* p. 77.

which caused the greatest uproar. The Court enjoyed a monopoly in a seller's market, and the proceeds from these sales were an important source of income, though such tactics may well have been politically unwise.

If he could not fully control his own estates, the king might yet control his servants. The main, if not the only, weapon at his disposal was his power of appointment. The diet had long insisted that tenure of starosties and offices should be for life and that the king should fill vacancies at the earliest opportunity. Only a verdict of banishment and dishonour could remove an officeholder from his post. Since the judicial system was in the hands of the nobility, who elected the members of the supreme appellate tribunals of Poland and Lithuania, such verdicts were difficult for the king to obtain. Nevertheless, he had a certain amount of room for manœuvre. Although he could not dismiss his officials and ministers, the ten government ministers were last in the senate order of precedence; since pluralism was banned, they could sometimes be persuaded to resign in return for a more prestigious, if less powerful, position.

Since office was granted for life, monarchs inherited the team of ministers assembled by their predecessor. John Casimir was lucky in that several important offices became vacant through death or resignation in the first years of his reign. The king did not, however, have a completely free hand in appointments. Ministerial office was sought-after and certain expectations had to be fulfilled: when Ossoliński, the Polish grand chancellor, died in 1650, it was expected that he would be succeeded by the vice-chancellor, Andrzej Leszczyński, bishop of Chełmno. Leszczyński, however, had been a leading supporter of Charles Ferdinand in 1648, and John Casimir was reluctant to promote him.

The Court's solution to this problem was to extract secret agreements from appointees in which they pledged to resign their office if required in return for being granted another, more prestigious post. In some such documents, the powers of the office were limited: when Krzysztof Zawisza was appointed Lithuanian marshal of the Court in 1649, he agreed not to collect sales taxes from the citizens of Wilno, on the grounds that they wished to keep the proceeds for themselves.[8] Leszczyński signed such a pledge when he was appointed grand chancellor in 1650; two years later he duly resigned when requested in exchange for the archbishopric of Gniezno.

Such policies were controversial, as was the practice of selling offices, which reached unprecedented levels under John Casimir. Hieronim Radziejowski unsuccessfully offered the huge sum of 100,000 złoties for the post of Polish marshal of the Court in 1649 and paid 60,000 for the vice-chancellorship in 1650; the same position cost Stefan Koryciński 100,000 in 1651, although Andrzej Trzebicki paid substantially less a year later.[9] The general intention was clear, however: to appoint men

---

[8] ibid. p. 113. For examples of such contracts see K. Waliszewski, *Polsko-francuskie stosunki w XVII wieku* (Cracow, 1889) pp. 220–1.
[9] A. Kersten, *Hieronim Radziejowski. Studium władzy i opozycji* (Warsaw, 1988) pp. 213, 235; Wasilewski, *Ostatni Waza* p. 112. Trzebicki paid 10,000 złoties: A. Przyboś and M. Rożek, *Biskup*

who owed their career to the Court and who, by paying for their offices and signing such contracts, had potentially compromised themselves in *szlachta* eyes. Such men might prove more obedient than their predecessors, especially since so many of those promoted in the early years of John Casimir's reign, including Koryciński, Radziejowski and Trzebicki, came from relatively humble families and would be dependent on receiving further royal patronage in order to establish their position among the social and political elite.

Despite the controversy these policies undoubtedly aroused, the Court was reasonably successful in asserting its authority in difficult circumstances. Even a magnate like Jerzy Sebastian Lubomirski (1616–67) was forced to swallow his pride and sign such a contract, which included certain restrictions on his powers, to obtain the position of Polish grand marshal in 1650. Although he initially refused to fulfil his duties after obtaining the nomination, he was forced into a reluctant rapprochement after compromising himself by insulting and physically attacking Crown prosecutor Daniel Żytkiewicz and after being suspected in 1651 of dubious dealings with Sigismund Rákóczi.[10]

The risks run by lesser figures defying the Court were clearly shown in the case of Hieronim Radziejowski, who quickly forgot to whom he owed his career after obtaining the vice-chancellorship. When he inadvisedly lost the favour of both John Casimir, whom he suspected of having an affair with his wife, and Louise Marie, he was successfully stripped of office and honours after becoming involved in a brawl in Warsaw with the relatives of his estranged wife, an offence subject to royal jurisdiction. Despite receiving much sympathy from the ordinary nobility, Radziejowski had few influential friends, since most magnates saw him as a *parvenu*, and he was forced to flee the country before the second diet of 1652 confirmed the original sentence of death, infamy and confiscation of all property. It was a useful demonstration of the monarchy's power to discipline its ministers.

John Casimir's attempt to assert his control over the armed forces was, however, less successful. After the rebels captured the two Crown hetmans, Mikołaj Potocki and Marcin Kalinowski in 1648, John Casimir sought to keep the direction of the Polish army in his own hands and to exclude the popular Jarema Wiśniowiecki, a supporter of Charles Ferdinand in 1648. At the coronation diet in 1649, government supporters unsuccessfully attempted to end life tenure for the grand hetmans of Poland and Lithuania. Following the deaths of Mikołaj Potocki in 1651 and Lithuanian grand hetman Janusz Kiszka in 1653, John Casimir refused to appoint successors, citing precedents under Sigismund III. It was a bold attempt to assert royal control, understandable given the wide military, diplomatic and even fiscal

---

krakowski Andrzej Trzebicki. Z dziejów kultury politycznej i artystycznej w XVII stuleciu (Cracow, 1989) p. 19.

[10] Lubomirski was the son of Sebastian, palatine of Cracow, one of the most powerful magnates in Little Poland. Żytkiewicz was attacked when leading a commission investigating Lubomirski's right to exploit the Kunegunda salt-mine next to the royal mines at Wieliczka.

powers of the hetmans.[11] John Casimir was technically commander-in-chief and claimed that he was not obliged to appoint a hetman; nevertheless, his refusal aroused fierce opposition.

The king was reluctant to appoint a successor to Kiszka because the Lithuanian field hetman, who would normally expect promotion, was the Commonwealth's leading Calvinist, Janusz Radziwiłł, one of Lithuania's greatest magnates and John Casimir's bitterest opponent, who was widely suspected of engineering the *liberum veto* of 1652.[12] By retaining command of the armies himself, however, John Casimir attracted blame for the military failures in the years following his victory at Berestechko and provoked widespread suspicion. Diets and dietines refused to vote taxes until he agreed to appoint new hetmans, with condemnation reaching such a pitch at the diet of March 1654 that he sanctioned a second invocation of the right of veto by the royal supporter Paweł Białobłocki. The deteriorating military situation, however, forced capitulation at the second diet of 1654, when Radziwiłł and Stanisław Potocki were appointed grand hetmans of Lithuania and Poland respectively.

Mounting political discord meant that the Commonwealth was in no condition to resist the Muscovite assault in 1654. Although Alexis had entered the war in support of the Cossacks, he saw it as an opportunity to recover Muscovy's foothold on the Baltic coast, lost by Ivan IV. Lithuania therefore bore the brunt of the Muscovite onslaught. The Commonwealth was facing armies which had changed considerably since the Smolensk War in the 1630s. Under Alexis, large numbers of muskets, both matchlocks and more modern flintlocks, had been manufactured and imported. Unlike the Commonwealth, Muscovy had prepared for war by recruiting large numbers of foreign mercenaries thrown out of work at the end of the Thirty Years War, especially officers and NCOs, who were given command of new-formation regiments.[13] Thus, modern military expertise was added to Muscovy's traditionally massive numerical superiority. If the situation in the Ukraine, where Potocki faced the Cossacks and Buturlin's Muscovite army of 40,000 with only 22,000–23,000, was bad enough, in Lithuania it was catastrophic. After manning garrisons scattered across the grand duchy's vast expanses, Janusz Radziwiłł faced three Muscovite armies and Zolotarenko's Cossacks, some 80,000 men, with 8,000.[14] He was pushed back relentlessly as the Muscovites took Smolensk, Polotsk, Vitebsk and Mogilev.

The defence of Lithuania was hampered by the political conflict between

---

[11] J. Leszczyński, 'Projekty reformy państwa polskiego na sejmie koronacyjnym Jana Kazimierza w 1649 roku' in J. Gierowski (ed.), *O naprawę Rzeczypospolitej XVII–XVIII w. Pracy ofiarowane Władysławowi Czaplińskiemu w 60 rocznice urodzin* (Warsaw, 1965) pp. 91–5.

[12] Radziwiłł (1612–55) was the son of the Calvinist Krzysztof Radziwiłł, palatine of Wilno and Lithuanian grand hetman, who had been a leading malcontent under Sigismund III. He inherited vast estates on his father's death in 1640, which were supplemented by extensive holdings of royal land granted by the religiously tolerant Władysław IV, who appointed him field hetman in 1646.

[13] R. Hellie, *Enserfment and Military Change in Muscovy* (Chicago, 1971) pp. 185, 191–2.

[14] Wimmer, *Wojsko polskie* pp. 82–3.

The Deluge

Radziwiłł and the king. Although John Casimir appointed Radziwiłł grand hetman in June 1654, he did what he could to limit his power, transferring part of the grand hetman's competence to the general of Artillery and appointing Gosiewski, Radziwiłł's bitter rival, to succeed him as field hetman. The field hetman's autonomy was increased and, as Lithuanian treasurer, Gosiewski could ensure his own units were paid first.[15] John Casimir was following the time-honoured royal tactic of playing the Lithuanian factions off against one another but disputes between Gosiewski and Radziwiłł seriously hindered the war-effort.[16]

Lithuania's plight, however, was ultimately due to lack of preparation and the overwhelming superiority of the Muscovite forces, not the dispute between the hetmans. The June diet of 1654 voted 18,000 men for the Lithuanian army, but in July Radziwiłł had a nominal 11,261, in reality no more than 4,000; it was impossible to raise more amidst the chaos of the campaign. When John Casimir met Lithuanian senators at Grodno in October 1654, Radziwiłł attacked him for failing to settle with Khmelnytskyi when he had the chance, while John Casimir blamed Radziwiłł for inadequate defensive preparations.[17]

It was impossible to crush Radziwiłł in the way that the Court had dealt with Radziejowski. His extensive clientage network gave him an important power-base which, in addition to his military power as hetman, enabled him to frustrate royal plans. The decentralised political system ensured such figures great scope for obstruction through their influence over the local dietines which played such an important administrative and political role. Krzysztof Opaliński (1609–55), palatine of Poznań, was another malcontent, alienated after his failure to win one of the chancellorships in the early 1650s. He withdrew in high dudgeon to his estates, where he employed his waspish pen in attacks on the Court and used his position as starosta general of Great Poland to stir up the local dietines against Court policy.

The problem for opponents of the Court like Radziwiłł or Opaliński was that, although they had great scope for obstructing royal policy, they could offer no positive alternative. Even where they succeeded in being appointed to important offices, they could achieve little. Since senate council meetings were dominated by royal supporters, there was little point in turning up: after his appointment as Crown grand marshal, Lubomirski made little effort to fulfil his duties and was almost permanently absent from Court. The result was stalemate: opposition magnates could defy and obstruct the king; so long as they avoided the sort of indiscretions which landed Radziejowski in trouble, their position was secure. They could not, however, force any significant change in government policy.

All that malcontents could do was dream of a change of monarch, which might

---

[15] H. Wisner, 'Działalność wojskowa Janusza Radziwiłła 1648–1655' *Rocznik Białostocki* 13 (1976) pp. 95–6.
[16] Fragstein to Dietrichstein, 30.VIII.1654; J. Leszczyński, 'Dwa ostatnie sejmy przed potopem szwedzkim w oczach dyplomaty cesarskiego' *Sobótka* 30 (1975) p. 293, n. 24.
[17] Wisner, 'Działalność wojskowa' pp. 93, 97; A.S. Radziwiłł, *Memoriale* IV p. 319.

give them the position of supreme influence only someone who enjoyed royal favour could occupy. The elective nature of the monarchy afforded hope that such a change might be effected without waiting for the king to die, if a monarch should break his election agreement. The right of *rokosz* (rebellion in defence of the constitution) had already been invoked by Zebrzydowski and his supporters in 1606–7, who had declared the deposition of Sigismund III. The defeat of Zebrzydowski's *rokosz* demonstrated the dangers of such a step but did not overturn the view that the Commonwealth had the right to depose its monarch if he broke his contract; several malcontents later plotted to overthrow Sigismund, including Radziwiłł's father Krzysztof, who sought in the 1620s to interest the French Court in placing the duc d'Orléans on the Polish throne.[18]

The heightened political tension after 1648 and John Casimir's attempts to assert control stimulated such plots. George I Rákóczi's death in 1648 had ended the candidature of his son Sigismund, but Transylvanian interest in the internal politics of its northern neighbour remained high.[19] George II Rákóczi (1648–60), Sigismund's elder brother, was worried as a Calvinist by John Casimir's Catholic and pro-Habsburg sympathies. Since Transylvania was the one power to have shown a real interest in the Polish throne in 1648, some malcontents, including Radziwiłł and Lubomirski, kept in contact: Ferdinand III warned John Casimir in 1650 of a plot to depose him in favour of Sigismund; there are strong indications that Lubomirski was involved.[20] In 1654, Radziwiłł sent Rákóczi a detailed set of proposals, in which he did not conceal his contempt for what he called a 'preposterous regime' which, he claimed, had earned the hatred of all estates of the realm. He asserted that discontent with John Casimir was so great that some senators were considering deposition and a new election.[21] Nothing had come of these approaches by early 1655, however, when Radziwiłł was in contact with Sweden through the duke of Courland, stating to one of his agents that the election of a new king was 'in our own hands' and that Charles X should be approached.[22]

The capitulation of so many nobles to Sweden in 1655 suggests that the efforts of the malcontents were successful. The leading role at Ujście was played by Krzysztof Opaliński, the most prominent opposition figure in Great Poland, while Radziwiłł was the mastermind behind Kiejdany. It has long been suggested that the capitulation of 1655 was the result of a coordinated plan and represented the triumph of the

---

[18] U. Augustyniak and W. Sokołowski, '*Spisek orleański*' *w latach 1626–1628* (Warsaw, 1990).
[19] Transylvania, once part of the medieval kingdom of Hungary, enjoyed a precarious autonomy under Ottoman suzerainty. Rulers of Transylvania had long taken a close interest in Polish politics, seeking support against their Ottoman overlords or the Habsburgs, who aspired to extend their control beyond the narrow strip of Hungary which they ruled. Links with Poland had been closest under Stefan Batory, prince of Transylvania and king of Poland (1576–86).
[20] This was at the height of Lubomirski's estrangement from the Court. Wasilewski, *Ostatni Waza* p. 96; Kersten, *Na tropach Napierskiego. W kręgu mitów i faktów* (Warsaw, 1970) pp. 115–16.
[21] 'Puncta nomine ilmi. principis Radzivilli sermo Transylvaniae principi proponenda'; S. Szilágyi, *Transsylvania et bellum boreo-orientale* (Budapest, 1890) I p. 310.
[22] Radziwiłł to Stryżka, Mogilev, 20.III.1655; E. Kotłubaj, *Życie Janusza Radziwiłła* (Wilno, 1859) dodatek XIII no. 2, p. 375.

The Deluge

magnate opposition over the politically isolated king. Many historians, especially after 1945, suggested that John Casimir faced a coherent opposition based on a 'family alliance' between the Opalińskis, Radziwiłłs, Leszczyńskis and Lubomirskis, who suspected him of seeking to introduce absolutism and who wished a future monarch to base his rule more firmly on the magnates and to pursue their interests, particularly in the east, which John Casimir had proved incapable of protecting.[23] Firm evidence of the existence of an organised opposition, however, is hard to come by. Talk of the 'family alliance' is based on a report by Adersbach, the Brandenburg observer at the March diet in 1654. There is nothing in Adersbach's letter, however, to indicate that this alliance went further than opposition to the king's stand on the specific issue of control of the army; even if he stressed the unity of this group, he gave no hint of the nature of their programme, or of actual plots against John Casimir.[24]

Attempts to link Radziejowski with a concerted opposition party remain unconvincing. His appointment as vice-chancellor had been deeply resented by leading magnates, who regarded him as an upstart. Łukasz Opaliński, who presided over the marshal's court which condemned Radziejowski, had insulted him when handing over the seals of office at the diet two years earlier by openly claiming that he had bought his position.[25] Radziejowski bombarded senators with letters complaining about the injustice he had suffered and requesting support for his rehabilitation, but there is little evidence of any response, though some were sympathetic.[26] Radziejowski's contacts with the Cossacks, revealed at the second diet of 1652 through intercepted letters, brought widespread condemnation and the confirmation of his sentence. Henceforth, Radziejowski wrote as many letters to those at Court seeking rehabilitation as he did to opposition figures.[27] When he wrote to the nobility of

---

[23] T. Nowak, 'Geneza agresji szwedzkiej' *PODWP* I pp. 109, 117; Czapliński, 'Rola magnaterii i szlachty w pierwszych latach wojny szwedzkiej' ibid. pp. 151, 169.

[24] Adersbach to Frederick William, 14.III.1654; *Urkunden und Aktenstücke* VI p. 685.

[25] The insult was a trifle hypocritical, since Opaliński had paid for his own office; it was delivered by Opaliński, not Lubomirski as maintained by Szajnocha and Kubala. Kersten, *Hieronim Radziejowski* p. 233.

[26] Nowak, followed by Czapliński, cites one letter from Krzysztof Opaliński, where he 'did not conceal his contacts with Radziejowski': Nowak, 'Geneza agresji szwedzkiej' p. 111; Czapliński, 'Rola magnaterii' p. 151. The letter is published in R. Pollak (ed.), *Listy Krzysztofa Opalińskiego do brata Łukasza 1641–1653* (Warsaw, 1957) p. 501. One letter is insufficient evidence for the 'broad network of contacts' which Nowak alleges existed; furthermore, as Sajkowski has demonstrated, Opaliński was referring to Radziwiłł, not Radziejowski: A. Sajkowski, *Krzysztof Opaliński, Wojewoda Poznański* (Poznań, 1960) pp. 227, 232, n. 100. Kersten argues that Radziwiłł at least was a 'silent ally' of Radziejowski, but admits that despite Radziwiłł's hostile attitude to John Casimir, he did not openly intervene on Radziejowski's behalf; many recipients of Radziejowski's letters either destroyed them or gave them straight to the king to avoid being implicated. Kersten, *Hieronim Radziejowski* pp. 327, 333–5, 357.

[27] Radziejowski wrote to Butler, John Casimir's confidant, and Fleury, Louise Marie's confessor. Kersten suggests that there were more letters which have not survived. This seems probable, but he can find few replies and none that go beyond a certain sympathy with Radziejowski: ibid. pp. 382, 633. For a noncommittal reply, see J. Leszczyński to Radziejowski, Warsaw, 25.V.1655, Czart. 384 no. 98, f. 222, which is not as warm in its tone as Kersten implies. Leszczyński certainly expressed sympathy, but stressed the problems Radziejowski faced in winning rehabilitation.

Great Poland urging surrender in early July 1655, with the Swedish army already on the march, the reply did not respond to the political offers and made no mention of any previous contacts.[28]

The lack of response to Radziejowski's overtures demonstrates that it was one thing to express opposition to individual royal policies, quite another to consider formal deposition. Although Jan Leszczyński was in frequent contact with Opaliński, Radziwiłł and Lubomirski, the Leszczyńskis, while deeply critical of John Casimir, were not prepared to go to the same lengths as Radziwiłł and reacted with horror to rumours of plots. As Fragstein remarked, there was a lack of trust not merely between John Casimir and the Commonwealth but also between various political factions.[29] When Radziwiłł complained to Andrzej Leszczyński in September 1654 about the king's behaviour, he was rebuked for his conduct: 'I have recently heard enough alarming and pitiful accounts of the wretched state of ... Lithuania, but the worst of all must be that contained in yesterday's letters, which appal me, for I hear not only of your implacable hatred for your colleagues but also of your terrible disagreement with ... His Majesty ...' Responding to Radziwiłł's contention that Lithuania's desperate plight was due to the breaking of the diet, Leszczyński acidly pointed out that the 1652 diet had been broken by Siciński, a Lithuanian envoy, and that the issue which caused the breaking of the 1654 diet was the hetmanship of Lithuania, not the attempt to exclude the Prussian envoy Bąkowski, the ostensible reason:

> I do not blame ... Bąkowski so much, since I believe he bears less responsibility, for the diet had been divided for six weeks over the issue of the Lithuanian hetmanship and it would certainly have broken up over the matter in any case. I pass over in silence the fact that His Majesty awarded the field hetman's baton without consulting Your Grace; in truth it is not the first occasion on which this has occurred and it would be the last only if someone were to impose a law upon His Majesty. Previous hetmans experienced such slights without taking them so amiss.[30]

Radziwiłł had to deny that he sought to break the union, or that he had done anything improper:

> It is permitted to hold sessions and councils at diets on matters of private interest; there is nothing to prevent it: ultimately every palatinate is free to provide for its security itself. Lithuania, however, is apparently not permitted to do so, out of suspicion that I counselled that it should seek its freedom. I am astounded that anyone could think of dismembering [the

---

[28] Reply to Radziejowski, 19.VII.1655; Jakub Michałowski, *Księga pamiętnicza* ed. A. Helcel (Cracow, 1864) no. 330, p. 761.

[29] Fragstein to Dietrichstein, 30.VIII.1654; Leszczyński, 'Dwa ostatnie sejmy' p. 293, n. 24. Sajkowski, who does not doubt the existence of a coherent opposition, is puzzled by Adersbach's inclusion of the Leszczyńskis in the 'family pact', since he considers them to have been supporters of the Court; Sajkowski, *Krzysztof Opaliński* p. 214.

[30] A. Leszczyński to J. Radziwiłł, 18.IX.1654; BUW 66 ff. 88–9; Trzebicki was also alarmed at rumours that Lithuanians intended to go over to the Swedes: Trzebicki to A. Leszczyński, Grodno, 11.X.1654; Czart. 384 ff. 133–4.

The Deluge

Commonwealth]; to speak or think of such a thing is forbidden by the ties of our sacred union.[31]

If Radziwiłł was plotting to depose John Casimir, he was aware that he did not enjoy widespread support. His Calvinism was an important reason for his opposition but he knew that he could not rely on Protestant support alone, as he had stressed to Rákóczi in 1654; although he stated that many leading politicians were considering deposing the king and justifed such a course of action, he stressed that it would be dangerous for him, as a Calvinist, to make a move:

> It does not behove us, who worship God under the sacred name of the pure Gospel and for whom it is seemly to turn away not only from this act, but also from the sight of all evil, to raise the standard of just rebellion for others, unless death or flight impels us, (which indeed to those concerned with the state of our fatherland seems such a close and likely prospect) and frees us from our sacred vow ... or if some violent necessity drives us to take this step.[32]

If the opposition was divided before 1655, John Casimir's attitude towards Sweden seemed to provide an issue capable of uniting it. As the Muscovite advance resumed in early 1655, the conviction spread that the Commonwealth could not save itself by its own efforts and that foreign aid was essential. Sweden was the most obvious potential ally, and many hoped for an alliance with the power which had forged such a reputation for itself during the Thirty Years War. Yet Swedish–Polish relations were poor. Although Sweden had been forced to grant concessions at Stuhmsdorf in 1635 in renewing the truce of Altmark (1629), no peace treaty had been signed. The truce was due to last until 1661, but there were worrying signs it might not.

The poor relations between the two branches of the Vasa dynasty were the biggest obstacle to a permanent settlement. John Casimir was well aware that Swedish aid might save the Commonwealth. He had approached Sweden as early as 1649, when a Muscovite invasion was already feared, but he broke off negotiations in 1651 after Berestechko. When talks resumed at Lübeck in 1652, they soon foundered over John Casimir's refusal to compromise over his claim to the Swedish throne.[33] On Christina's abdication in 1654, the king sent his secretary, Canasilles, to Stockholm to protest at Charles's accession. Nevertheless, he had already begun privately to seek a Swedish alliance through French mediation. In August 1654, he urged Piquet, the French resident in Stockholm, to do all he could to achieve peace with Sweden and an alliance against the tsar.[34] Canasilles, despite the protest at Charles's

---

[31] Radziwiłł to A. Leszczyński, Minsk, 2.XII.1654; Kotłubaj, *Życie Janusza Radziwiłła* dodatek XV, p. 397.

[32] 'Puncta nomine ilmi. principis Radzivilli'; Szilágyi, *Transsylvania* I p. 310.

[33] The Swedes were only willing to pay John Casimir a sum of money as compensation, and grant him a military alliance and 4,000 men if Poland were attacked; L.V. Zaborovskii, 'Politika Shvetsii nakanune pervoi severnoi voiny (vtoraia polovina 1654 – seredina 1655g).' *Voprosy Istoriografii i Istochnikovedeniia Slaviano-germanskikh Otnoshenii* (Moscow, 1973) p. 207.

[34] In January, Mazarin had instructed d'Avaugour, the French ambassador in Stockholm, to seek a Polish–Swedish alliance against Muscovy. Mazarin to d'Avaugour, 15.I.1655; *Lettres du Cardinal Mazarin* VI, M.A. Chéruel (ed.) (Paris, 1890) no. 276, p. 424.

accession, suggested a settlement and a defensive alliance against Muscovy, in the hope that the French might persuade Sweden to be more reasonable.[35] Canasilles was rebuffed, as was Jan Andrzej Morsztyn, who spent three fruitless months in Stockholm in early 1655. Charles insisted that the preconditions for talks were John Casimir's resignation of his claim to Sweden and recognition *de iure* of Swedish rule in Livonia.

John Casimir's attitude provoked widespread outrage. It was suspected that the deficiencies in Morsztyn's credential letters which led to Charles X refusing him an audience were a deliberate attempt to sabotage the negotiations, an impression reinforced by the moderate letter of the Swedish council to the Polish senate, sent on 13 March 1655, offering further talks without preconditions. This letter seems to have been a deliberate attempt to increase the divisions between John Casimir and his senate council, of which the Swedes were fully aware.[36] Jan Leszczyński was certainly angered by the king's apparent willingness to put his personal interests before those of the state: 'I am satisfied with His Majesty with regard to personal matters but I am not satisfied that he ruins us by his plans and ... with his lack of faith in any of his senators ... so that every piece of advice is suspect and he does nothing for the senate except in the last resort.'[37]

Leszczyński's attitude seems to confirm the view that John Casimir's policy was motivated by personal interests and was 'violently at odds with the wishes of the Polish magnates'.[38] The king certainly attempted to gain political advantage from the situation. For, however attractive the prospect of Swedish aid might be, he could not consider it in isolation. Even if the Commonwealth expelled the Muscovites with Swedish aid, its structural problems would remain. John Casimir had shown his conviction from the moment of his election that royal authority must be increased; his attempts to use his powers of appointment to assert control had provoked opposition: his hereditary claim to Sweden was one of the few bargaining-counters he still possessed. He therefore suggested to Sweden that should an anti-Muscovite alliance be formed, he should receive any lands taken from Muscovy as hereditary prince.[39] When Sweden rejected this idea, John Casimir sought political concessions from the Commonwealth in compensation.

[35] S. Pufendorf, *De rebus a Carolo Gustavo Sueciae rege gestis* (Nuremberg, 1729) I p. 31; A. Stade, 'Geneza decyzji Karola X Gustava o wojnie z Polską w 1655 r.' *SMHW* 19 (1973) p. 53; Zaborovskii, 'Politika'. p. 210; F. Grönebaum, *Frankreich in Ost- und Nordeuropa. Die französisch-russischen Beziehungen von 1648–1689* (Wiesbaden, 1968) pp. 13, 135–6; M. Roberts, 'Charles X and the great parenthesis: a reconsideration' *From Oxenstierna to Charles XII. Four Studies* (Cambridge, 1991) p. 106.

[36] That was certainly John Casimir's interpretation: John Casimir to d'Avaugour, Warsaw, 29.IV.1655; CPP XI f. 66. The letter of the Swedish senate is published in 'Akta poselstw Morstina oraz Leszczyńskiego i Naruszewicza do Szwecji w roku 1655' Wójcik (ed.), *Teki Archiwalne* 5 (1957) pp. 81–7.

[37] J. Leszczyński to A. Leszczyński, 23.IV.1655; Czart. 384 no. 94, f. 216; cf. J. Leszczyński to Krzysztof Opaliński, Warsaw, 8.III.1655; Czart. 384 no. 84, f. 192.

[38] Roberts, 'Charles X and the great parenthesis' p. 129.

[39] Canasilles had suggested in 1652 that John Casimir should receive Ducal Prussia in return for resigning his rights to Sweden and for the Commonwealth resigning its claim to Livonia. Frederick

The Deluge

His price was high. Like Władysław IV, John Casimir had sworn an oath to surrender his rights should it be necessary in the Commonwealth's interest. In the copy held in the archives, however, the phrase 'if suitable recompense is made to Our House' had been inserted.[40] When this issue was discussed in March 1655, some argued that, since the phrase had been inserted after the agreement of the *Pacta Conventa*, the Commonwealth was not bound to honour it. Nonetheless, an offer was made which the king rejected on 2 March. He revealed his price the following day. The details are unknown but they shocked Jan Leszczyński: 'my hair stood on end ... if we submitted these terms to the king of Sweden he would renounce the Swedish throne to become king of Poland.'[41]

Historians have taken Leszczyński's reaction to indicate that John Casimir was demanding absolute power, although none defines what this might mean.[42] It is clear, however, that the proposal essentially concerned the succession:

I declare that I cannot consent to such servitude. Uncertainty over the election has ensured the moderate rule of our kings, who, not having an hereditary kingdom, endeavour to gain their subjects' affection by the moderation of their rule in order to win support for the future election of their sons ... whatever abuses they perpetrate can be dealt with at the election.[43]

Leszczyński's reaction suggests that John Casimir's proposal was at least for the acceptance of Charles Ferdinand as successor *vivente rege* and at most for the establishment of hereditary rights for the Vasa dynasty. The proposals were rejected, however, and it was decided merely to send Morsztyn new plenipotentiary powers, necessary after the Swedish refusal to accept his credential letters.

Nevertheless, not everyone shared the views of Leszczyński, whose detailed correspondence has sometimes been the basis for misleading generalisations about the feelings of the whole magnate class.[44] Although Kentrshynskyj argues that Charles X was primarily concerned with the Muscovite threat and really desired an alliance with Poland which proved impossible due to John Casimir's intransigence, there is much evidence to suggest that the attack on Poland had been an option long under consideration, particularly once Charles received the reports of his agents Kock, and especially Meyer von Lilienthal in late 1654, which detailed the growing chaos in Poland.[45] Lilienthal's report emphasised divisions between John Casimir and the senate council, which Canasilles had imprudently confirmed in a letter to

---

William would be compensated by receiving Bremen from Charles X. In 1654, John Casimir proposed that Charles Ferdinand should be given part of Livonia, since he wished to marry. Kubala, *Wojna szwecka* pp. 22–3, 27–8.

[40] Copy, Czart. 402 f. 1. Printed in Kubala, *Wojna szwecka* pp. 20–1.
[41] J. Leszczyński to A. Leszczyński, 4.III.1655; Czart. 384 f. 190.
[42] Kubala, *Wojna szwecka* p. 33; Czapliński, 'Rola magnaterii' p. 150; Kersten, *Hieronim Radziejowski* p. 382.
[43] J. Leszczyński to A. Leszczyński, 4.III.1655; Czart. 384 no. 83, f. 190.
[44] e.g. Czapliński, 'Rola magnaterii', especially pp. 144–8.
[45] B. Kentrschynskyj, 'Karl X Gustav inför krisen i öster 1654–1655' *Karolinska Förbundets Årsbok* (1956), especially pp. 88–91. Roberts, 'Charles X and the great parenthesis' pp. 112, 125, 128–36; Stade, 'Geneza agresji' pp. 65, 71.

d'Avaugour, much to Morsztyn's disgust. Morsztyn's reports of the military build-up and the attitude of Charles X strongly suggested that the Swedes were decided on war whatever was offered.[46] The terms with which Morsztyn had been presented in February demanded not only the abandonment of Livonia and John Casimir's claims to the Swedish throne but also the cession of Royal Prussia, including all its ports, as satisfaction for the Swedish army and security for the future.[47]

This was a price which even supporters of a Swedish alliance might not be prepared to pay. By June, Leszczyński himself suspected that even if the Swedes wanted to avoid war, as he believed, they were not dealing in good faith and might demand humiliating conditions.[48] He might think John Casimir's attitude unreasonable but others felt that Sweden was in the wrong: the Church objected to the loss of Livonia, while there was widespread concern over the Swedish demand for the Prussian ports, or at least the right to levy tolls on them.[49] Bogusław Leszczyński disagreed with his cousin over the compensation issue, while John Casimir's proposed deal was put before the council by Trzebicki, which suggests that he supported the plan. Even Radziwiłł accepted that the king was entitled to deal privately with Sweden over his hereditary rights, but attacked him for trying to win Livonia for the Polish Vasas in compensation, since, he maintained, only the Commonwealth could treat over Livonia.[50] After the Swedish invasion, K.L. Sapieha argued that nothing could have been done to prevent it, claiming that Sweden had worked in collusion with Muscovy after rejecting talks for a permanent settlement.[51]

All parties hoped that a settlement with Sweden was possible and thought that it ought to be pursued. It was rumoured that Swedish preparations were not as advanced as some maintained; many in consequence refused to believe that Sweden was in a position to invade in 1655.[52] Dietines urged John Casimir to comply with

---

[46] Morsztyn to unknown, Stockholm, 20.III.1655: 'Tous les mouvements de la Couronne d'icy ne visent à autre bout, qu'à rompre entièrement avec la nostre, ou bien de nous offrir quelque mauvais accord, et des conditions que ne sçauroient passer qu'estants sustenues d'une puissance armée.' BNP FFr. 13040 f. 184. This letter is not included in Wójcik, 'Akta poselstw' and is unknown to Stade, 'Geneza decyzji' pp. 61–2.

[47] Kentrschynskyj, 'Karl X Gustav inför krisen i öster' p. 88; Roberts, 'Charles X and the great parenthesis' p. 130.

[48] J. Leszczyński to Trzebicki, Thorn, 12.VI.1655; Czart. 384 no. 101, f. 228.

[49] J. Leszczyński to J. Radziwiłł, Warsaw, 22.III.1655; Czart. 384 no. 88, f. 200. For Catholic objections to the cession of Livonia, which was central to the debate, see Walewski, *Historia wyzwolenia* I p. 53, Vidoni to Orsini, Warsaw, 15.III.1655; TRz. 8418 no. 7, p. 12. In general, ecclesiastical senators were more willing to consider war with Sweden, since they sensed an opportunity to recover Livonia. Pufendorf, *De rebus a Carolo Gustavo* I p. 38. The bishops of Samogitia, part of whose diocese was in Swedish hands, and of Warmia, whose diocese was in Prussia, were both present at the Warsaw meeting and were unlikely to agree to the loss of Livonia or Royal Prussia.

[50] Radziwiłł to Stryżka, Mogilev 20.III.1655; Kotłubaj, *Życie Janusza Radziwiłła* dodatek XIII, no. 2, p. 375.

[51] K.L. Sapieha to P. Sapieha, Warsaw, 14.VIII.1655; BPANCr. 354 f. 270.

[52] R. Damus, *Der erste nordische Krieg bis zur Schlacht bei Warschau, aus Danziger Quellen* (Danzig, 1884) p. 19.

the terms of his oath and refused to consider compensation.[53] The diet granted plenipotentiary powers to Jan Leszczyński and Aleksander Naruszewicz to undertake a new mission to Sweden, which sought to avoid the mistakes that had caused Morsztyn's embassy to fail. Nevertheless, it could not force John Casimir to abandon his claim; on the day the instructions were drawn up for the new embassy, the king absented himself, demonstrating that he had not yet agreed to resign his personal rights.[54] It was hoped that French pressure in Stockholm might smooth the way for Leszczyński and Naruszewicz, while the situation looked promising on the south-eastern front, where a new agreement had been reached with the Tatars and John Casimir had launched an initiative to win over the Cossacks.

Nevertheless, there was widespread recognition that war might come, and there was a readiness to face the enemy if necessary. The government had begun military preparations in March. Although a request to Ferdinand III for permission to raise troops in the Empire was rebuffed, it was reported that he might permit unofficial recruitment.[55] Crown grand chancellor Stefan Koryciński was aware of the problems of fighting a war on two fronts and suggested that an army of at least 30,000 needed to be raised, although he admitted that such a figure could only be achieved on paper. He was contemptuous of the noble levy's ability to resist Swedish firepower and feared that the Commonwealth would be unable to raise sufficient mercenaries in time; nevertheless, far from fearing further disorder, he was confident that the perilous state of the Commonwealth would ensure a cooperative mood at the diet.[56]

Historians have argued that by the time the diet assembled on 19 May, the nobility was affected by profound feelings of apathy and defeatism. Kersten suggests that John Casimir was almost completely isolated and that the few supporters he had did not dare to speak up, while Wisner argues that the low attendance at the diet demonstrated that the nobility had no understanding of the nature of the Swedish threat and felt a deep mistrust for the king: by 27 May, only two bishops, three palatines and seven castellans were present in the senate.[57] Yet this was an extraordinary diet, with dietines taking place only twenty-one days before it opened, instead of a month or so for an ordinary diet. It was common for senators not to turn up at the start of a diet, when much routine business was conducted and Wisner overlooks the presence of five ministers.[58] Considering the

---

[53] Lauda sejmiku lubelskiego: Artyculy na Sejm Anni 1655, Lublin, 28.V.1655; Czart. 394 f. 214; cf. Instructions of the General Dietine of Royal Prussia, 4.V.1655; Czart. 977 f. 327.
[54] Damus, *Der erste nordische Krieg* p. 22.
[55] Stade, 'Geneza decyzji' p. 38; Vidoni to Orsini, Warsaw, 9.V.1655; TRz. 8418 no. 10, p. 20.
[56] Koryciński to John Casimir, undated, Czart. 402 ff. 79–81.
[57] Czapliński, 'Rola magnaterii' p. 151; Kersten, *Hieronim Radziejowski* p. 383; Wisner, 'Działalność wojskowa' p. 101.
[58] 'Copia listu z Warszawy z Seymu Ostatniego przed zawierucha ta wielka od wszech Nieprzyjaciół Rzeczypospolitey, 27.V.1655'; Ossol. 3564 f. 325. In fact, the attendance of seventeen senators so early in a diet was unusual: while nineteen senators were present at the start of the 1632 diet, this figure was the highest for the reigns of Sigismund III and Władysław IV. There were only five senators at the

disruption of the war and the short notice given, it was by no means a disastrously low attendance and should not be seen as evidence of indifference or opposition.

The envoys showed no lack of urgency. Fragstein reported that they were already arriving by 25 April, with more appearing by 15 May, four days before the diet opened. When it did, Umiastowski was immediately elected marshal of the chamber of envoys without the usual problems, while envoys urged that the session be completed within a fortnight, with defence as the priority.[59] The government proposals, read by Koryciński on 22 May, were concerned solely with defence, with no mention of diplomatic initiatives: measures were proposed to liquidate arrears in the payment of the army, to fortify towns and fortresses near hostile borders and to raise new troops. At the primate's suggestion, debate was conducted in secret; despite objections to this procedural innovation, it was accepted.[60]

The prospect of war was taken seriously. If envoys supported further talks with Sweden and called for negotiations with Muscovy and the Cossacks, they were ready to fight if necessary. The problem was to raise a force capable of resisting the Swedes, especially since Potocki was calling for all available infantry for the campaign against the Cossacks. The royal instructions had castigated dietines for their slowness in implementing the decisions of the last diet. John Casimir reported that he was trying to raise mercenaries from abroad but that they would arrive late owing to shortage of money and be insufficient to match the Swedes. He therefore called for the *łanowa* infantry and warned that he might have to call out the noble levy.[61] Privately, John Casimir urged senators to ensure that dietines agreed to the *łanowa* infantry and did not rely solely on the levy; by the time the diet assembled, this force was essential, since Ferdinand III had rejected requests to permit recruitment in the Holy Roman Empire, to John Casimir's intense anger.[62]

The response was encouraging. While the Chełmno dietine rejected the call for the *łanowa* infantry, instead summoning the noble levy for 30 June, as did the general dietine of Royal Prussia, this was not through any lack of urgency: the Prussians agreed to taxes to raise mercenaries, being well acquainted with the nature

---

start of the first diet of 1629, six at the second diet of 1637, and the diets of 1638 and 1639. Between twenty-four and twenty-seven senators attended the 1655 diet; while this was some way short of the fifty-five present in 1627 and 1631, it was more than the twenty-one at the second diet of 1637 and not much below the average attendance for the peacetime diets of Władysław IV's reign, which was thirty: Czapliński and Filipczak-Kocur, 'Udział senatorów w pracach sejmowych za Zygmunta III i Władysława IV' *Przegląd Historyczny* 69 (1979) pp. 668, 671.

[59] Leszczyński, 'Dwa ostatnie sejmy' p. 293.
[60] 'Copia listu z Warszawy; Ossol. 3564 f. 326; Leszczyński, 'Dwa ostatnie sejmy' pp. 298, 300.
[61] Royal instructions to dietines of the duchies of Zator and Oświęcim; A. Przyboś (ed.) *Akta sejmikowe województwa krakowskiego* II (Cracow, 1955) p. 534. After the failure of the attempt to establish the permanent force of infantry volunteers envisaged by Batory, the Commonwealth had on occasion resorted to calling up a force of peasant infantry. Usually one soldier had to be provided by every ten *łan*. Unlike Batory's infantry, these men were untrained conscripts and did not provide their own equipment. Wimmer, *Historia piechoty polskiej do roku 1864* (Warsaw, 1978) pp. 225–6.
[62] John Casimir to Branicki, Warsaw, 5.IV.1655; Czart. 148 no. 24, f. 123; another copy: Czart. 400 f. 361; Vidoni to Orsini, Warsaw, 23.V.1655; TRz. 8418 no. 12, p. 24.

of the Swedish army. Similarly, if the general dietine of Great Poland called out the noble levy and an infantry levy of one man from every fifty households and fifteen *łan*, slightly smaller than the king had asked for, it also sanctioned the raising of 3,000 troops from abroad.[63] There was little sign that the *szlachta* felt the state was unequal to its task. Defence against Sweden was entrusted to Great Poland, while Little Poland was to aid the Lithuanians and parry any thrust from the Ukraine. An oath was taken to defend the Commonwealth, and the mood was confident: 'Zeal for the fatherland was that day most fervently displayed by all and when ... Dembinsky cried in a loud voice that whosoever wished to complicate proceedings should leave the chamber immediately, he was hailed by everyone with a loud *Amen*.'[64]

The government could be reasonably satisfied with the Polish response to the crisis. John Casimir was disappointed that the compensation issue had not been settled but although some were suspicious of his desire to recruit mercenaries, fearing that he might use them to make his rule absolute, he had avoided the sort of criticism he had faced at previous diets.[65] If no new taxes were voted for Poland, except for a levy of 20,000 złoties on the Jews, this must be seen in the context of the great efforts made over the previous four years: between June 1654 and July 1655, the nobility paid 80 per cent of the 10,000,000 złoties voted in taxation. It was the greatest financial effort since 1648; indeed, of the 30,500,000 złoties paid between 1648 and 1655, 9,300,000 had been collected in the last year. The royal proposals had not called for new taxes; it was hardly surprising that after such a great financial effort, which had in principle ensured pay for the army until the end of 1655, envoys did not vote further taxes of their own accord.[66]

The main problems at the diet came not from Poland but from Lithuania, where the military and political situation was desperate. The Muscovite war placed the most serious strain on Polish–Lithuanian relations since 1569 and highlighted the fragility of the union. Already in 1648 Radziwiłł, who wanted a vigorous war to be waged against Khmelnytskyi, fearing that the unrest would spread to Lithuania, attacked the attitude of the Poles, who were not directly threatened. Radziwiłł may also have been the author of a 1648 letter to Sweden hinting at the possibility of breaking the union.[67] In 1655 he claimed that Lithuanians could not forget that the

---

[63] Wimmer, 'Wojsko i finanse' p. 60; Laudum Contributionis in Conventu Gen. Graudentansi, 4.V.1655; Czart. 977 f. 372; Lauda sejmiku średzkiego, 28.IV.1655; Czart. 1774 ff. 299–300; Damus, *Der erste nordische Krieg* pp. 22–3. Cf. Lauda opatoviensis oblata, 28.IV.1655; Teki Pawińskiego 8338 p. 191.
[64] Hoverbeck to Frederick William, 16.VI.1655; *Urkunden und Aktenstücke* VI p. 698.
[65] Instructions of the palatinate of Sieradz, 28.IV.1655; Teki Pawińskiego 8342 pp. 623–4.
[66] Wimmer, 'Wojsko i finanse' pp. 64–5.
[67] Wisner, 'Działalność wojskowa' p. 64; Bengt Skytte mentions the approach in a letter to Per Brahe, 27.XI.1648; F. Carlson, *Geschichte Schwedens* (Gotha, 1855) IV, p. 27. There is no proof, however, that it was from Radziwiłł. Czapliński originally thought it was, but later expressed his doubts: Czapliński, 'Rola magnaterii' p. 152 and 'Parę uwag o tolerancji w okresie Kontrreformacji' *O Polsce siedemnastowiecznej* (Warsaw, 1966) p. 121. Nowak and Wasilewski are convinced that Radziwiłł was responsible: Nowak, 'Geneza agresji szwedzkiej' p. 102; Wasilewski, 'Zdrada Janusza Radziwiłła w 1655r. i jej wyznaniowe motywy' *Odrodzenie i Reformacja w Polsce* 18 (1973) p. 128.

After the Deluge

Lublin agreement had taken the Ukraine from Lithuania: they had accepted it nonetheless because they needed Polish military support. If this had largely been forthcoming in the first half of the seventeenth century, the growing control of dietines over taxation and the raising of troops meant that responsibility for defence was increasingly devolved: local nobles proved reluctant to defend more than their own region; after 1654 it appeared that Poland was no longer prepared to defend Lithuania 'with its former enthusiasm'.[68]

Radziwiłł attacked the low numbers of troops allowed Lithuania by recent diets and the lack of money voted to pay them, so that even those sent to aid Lithuania laid waste the countryside. He also feared that the Poles would ask the diet to revoke subsidies already agreed.[69] At the diet, the Court did what it could to isolate Radziwiłł. One barrier to his achieving widespread support was his Calvinism, which was an easy target. Karwat, the royal chaplain, mounted a fierce attack on dissidents at the opening Church service. Since most dietines had urged their envoys to ensure that no private matters be considered but only those relevant to the defence of the realm, when Protestants reacted angrily to Karwat's sermon, they seemed to be wasting valuable time on an unpopular private issue: the resultant criticism rebounded on Radziwiłł when he arrived in Warsaw.[70] Wisner argues that the attack was irresponsible in a situation when unity was important, but the policy seems to have been successful: Hoverbeck, the Brandenburg ambassador, was alarmed at the extent of anti-Protestant feeling, seeing the attacks on Radziwiłł as part of a Jesuit-inspired attempt to use his Protestantism to force him onto the sidelines; ultimately, Hoverbeck feared, it was hoped to drive the Protestants from the kingdom.[71] The Court's anti-Protestant campaign was not due to any lack of concern for Lithuania, as Wisner suggests: John Casimir was merely exploiting an easy target in Radziwiłł's Calvinism to isolate him even further and divide the opposition.

Radziwiłł's clients, determined on confrontation, tried to impeach the royal supporter Obuchowicz over the surrender of Smolensk. The affair wasted two valuable days, all but causing the breaking of the diet. Although Obuchowicz was prevented from taking his seat in the senate, support from the Sapiehas helped the king to block the impeachment. While Radziwiłł attracted some support in this matter, many blamed him for the loss of Smolensk. When he addressed the diet on the state of the Muscovite war, reporting the capture of fifty-six Muscovites, including four princes, and of fifty-four standards, he was poorly received: one envoy tried to prevent him speaking, there were several interruptions to his four-

---

[68] J. Radziwiłł to Slonim district, Mogilev, 7.IV.1655; Czart. 148 no. 26, f. 139.
[69] ibid. ff. 127, 136, 138.
[70] e.g. Instruction of the Sieradz dietine; Teki Pawińskiego 8342 p. 625; Instructions of the Cracow dietine, *Akta sejmikowe województwa krakowskiego* II no. 209, p. 537.
[71] Hoverbeck to Frederick William, 10.VI.1655; *Urkunden und Aktenstücke* VI p. 698; Wisner, 'Działalność wojskowa' p. 101.

The Deluge

hour speech and he was kept waiting half an hour before he was thanked by K.L. Sapieha in 'cold and ungracious terms'.[72]

Concentration on the personal clash between John Casimir and Radziwiłł obscures the extent to which Lithuanians were divided amongst themselves and to which general relations between Poland and Lithuania were deteriorating. The traditionally bitter rivalry between the great Lithuanian magnate families was intensified by the military and political crisis. While Radziwiłł was convinced that the main priority should be to resist the tsar and that an alliance with Sweden was therefore essential, Gosiewski, Sapieha and other Lithuanian magnates wanted to settle with Muscovy. Gosiewski had already sent his agent, Medeksza, to Radziwiłł in September 1654 to try and win the soldiers under his command for the king.[73] The depth of the political chasm between the two hetmans was revealed at a stormy meeting of Lithuanian envoys in mid-June, when Radziwiłł, who called for large sums of money for the Lithuanian army, was attacked by Gosiewski and others over the conduct of the Muscovite campaign.[74]

As one observer remarked, the devastated grand duchy was in no state to raise the proposed taxes; he sarcastically enquired whether the tsar would 'graciously consent to wait until we gather such prodigious sums in taxation and until we have recruited an army'.[75] Although Radziwiłł blamed the king for Lithuania's plight, the government recognised the problem, proposing that the mutinous Lithuanian army be paid by the Polish treasury. The plan was rejected, however, by Polish envoys, who followed the Lublin dietine in demanding that the Lithuanian army be paid by Lithuania.[76] While the diet voted no new taxes for Poland, Lithuania was saddled with twenty-two rates of the hearth tax, to be paid in two instalments; the alcohol tax was voted for two years and customs duties were increased.[77] Radziwiłł was perhaps justified in feeling deserted; Lithuania was, however, abandoned by the Polish nobility rather than John Casimir.

Despite the problems with regard to Lithuania, the 1655 diet was characterised neither by united opposition to John Casimir nor by defeatist sentiments, at least on the part of Poles. If there had been time to implement its decisions, the catastrophe might have been averted or at least reduced in scale. The speed of the Swedish attack, however, caught everyone by surprise: Great Poland in particular was in no position to resist an invasion. The Commonwealth was already fighting on two

---

[72] Hoverbeck to Frederick William, 9.VI.1655; *Urkunden und Aktenstücke* VI p. 699; Kubala, *Wojna Moskiewska* p. 281. *Theatrum Europeum (Ireno-polemographia, sive Theatri Europaei septenniam)* VII ed. J.G. Schledunus (Frankfurt-am-Main, 1684) p. 770; Leszczyński, 'Dwa ostatnie sejmy' p. 294; Wasilewski, 'Zdrada Janusza Radziwiłła' pp. 131–2; R. Mienicki, 'Utrata Smoleńska w r.1654 i sprawa Obuchowicza' *Kwartalnik Litewski* 1 (1910) p. 58.

[73] Medeksza, *Księga pamiętnicza* p. 1.

[74] Leszczyński, 'Dwa ostatnie sejmy' p. 296.

[75] Tyzenhaus to his brothers gathered at the dietine, 19.V.1655; Czart. 148 no. 29, f. 127. Printed in Kubala, *Wojna szwecka* p. 43.

[76] 'Articuly na Sejm Anni 1655', Lublin 28.IV.1655; Czart. 394 f. 211.

[77] *Volumina Legum* IV pp. 480–1.

fronts, while in an attempt to ensure continuing Tatar support, most of the Polish army had been committed to the Ukraine, stripping Great Poland of regular troops.[78] Krzysztof Opaliński, as General of Great Poland, was responsible for the province's defence; he was aware of the difficulties he faced and had contacted Frederick William of Brandenburg on his own initiative to ask for protection in the event of a Polish–Swedish war. The contacts were renewed after the diet, but the *szlachta* proved more suspicious than Opaliński of Frederick William's desire to occupy a series of fortresses and strongpoints; nevertheless, there was a general feeling that, in the event of an immediate attack, the province was unable to defend itself.[79]

There was good reason for these fears. John Casimir considered that Royal Prussia, not Great Poland, would be the main Swedish target. Should the Swedes take Danzig, Marienburg or Elbing, it would be difficult to dislodge them, given Polish deficiencies in artillery and infantry. Such regular troops as could be spared were therefore sent from the Ukraine to Prussia rather than Great Poland, which was to be defended by the *łanowa* infantry and the *levée-en-masse*. There was, however, little time to organise before Wittenberg crossed the Oder on 14 July. The king issued the first two calls-to-arms for the *levée* on 21 and 25 July, and the final summons only after the surrender at Ujście, for which he has been criticised.[80] In John Casimir's defence, it should be pointed out that he did not expect Frederick William to grant the Swedes free passage so quickly at a time when he was hoping for the elector's support. Furthermore, as Koryciński had argued, it was dangerous to call the levy before enemy intentions were clear, since the *szlachta* had a tendency to return home if nothing happened immediately.[81]

The course of events at Ujście suggests that the surrender was not the result of long-term planning. Contemporary accounts give an impression of confusion and uncertainty, which was to be expected since Opaliński had minimal experience as a soldier. Wittenberg, with 13,650 men, including 7,500 infantry and 72 cannon, was faced by 13,000 from the noble levy and a mere 1,400 *łanowa* infantry, of whom 400 garrisoned the strongpoint of Drahim.[82] The Poles were drawn up on the south side

---

[78] Kersten, *Chłopi polscy* p. 65; Sajkowski, *Krzysztof Opaliński* p. 218; Kubala, *Wojna szwecka* pp. 44–5. Jarochowski claims that troops were available which could have been used: *Wielkopolska w czasie pierwszej wojny szwedzkiej od roku 1655 do 1657* (Poznań, 1864) p. 23. Great Poland, unlike Royal Prussia, was short of modern fortifications: W. Majewski, 'Polska sztuka wojenna w okresie wojny polsko-szwedzkiej' *SMHW* 21 (1978) p. 335. Royal Prussia was the only province with adequate fortifications: J. Stankiewicz, 'System fortyfikacyjny Gdańska i okolicy w czasie wojny 1655–1660' *SMHW* 20 (1974) pp. 73–121.
[79] Sajkowski, *Krzysztof Opaliński* p. 218; Damus, *Der erste nordische Krieg* p. 23.
[80] Wimmer, 'Przegląd operacji w wojnie polsko-szwedzkiej 1655–1660' in *Wojna polsko-szwedzka* pp. 137–8.
[81] Koryciński to John Casimir, (April 1655); Czart. 402 ff. 80–1.
[82] Wimmer, 'Przegląd operacji' p. 138; L. Termesden, 'Karola X Gustava plan kampanii polskiej 1655 roku. Powstanie planu i jego przeprowadzenie' *SMHW* 19 (1973) p. 97 and 'Carl X Gustafs Armé 1654–1657. Styrka och dislokation' in A. Stade (ed.), *Carl X Gustafs Armé* Carl X Gustaf-Studier VIII (Stockholm, 1979) p. 192.

The Deluge

of the river in a good defensive position which forced the Swedes to approach across marshy ground. Any Polish advantage was nullified, however, by the fact that their forces consisted overwhelmingly of cavalry, not best suited to defending a river crossing against seasoned infantry, especially since they had few cannon and little gunpowder. Grudziński, palatine of Kalisz, held off the Swedes for five hours at the head of the infantry until his troops ran out of ammunition. When news came that the Swedes threatened to outflank the Poles after seizing a crossing further down, neither Opaliński nor the noble levy showed any desire to fight.[83] In the circumstances, the decision to surrender almost certainly averted a rout.

In the absence of firm evidence that Opaliński or any other magnate from Great Poland was plotting with Sweden before the invasion, it is difficult to accept that the surrender was the result of deliberate, premeditated treachery.[84] If many blamed John Casimir for provoking the invasion, this view was by no means unanimous. Opaliński may never have considered mounting significant resistance and his undoubted defeatism certainly affected morale; others among both senators and *szlachta* were of a different opinion, however. Grudziński's brave, if hopeless, five-hour resistance shows that not all intended surrender from the outset. Three senators followed Opaliński's lead: Grudziński, who argued passionately against the surrender before signing with expressions of deep regret at being forced to comply with such an unpatriotic act, Maksymilian Miaskowski, castellan of Krzywiń and Paweł Gembicki, castellan of Międzyrzecz. After a heated debate, Rozrażewski, palatine of Inowrocław, who was related to Radziejowski and Krzysztof's cousin Jan Piotr Opaliński, palatine of Podlasie, both refused to sign. Such evidence supports Sajkowski's conclusion that the decision to surrender was taken only in the camp at Ujście.[85] In the end, only 800 out of 13,000 signed the capitulation.[86] Once the Swedes outflanked the Poles and the noble levy began to flee, surrender was the only realistic option. In the absence of convincing evidence to the contrary, Ujście should be seen as a military defeat caused by inadequate preparation and consequent low morale, not premeditated political treason.

The surrender at Ujście had a profound effect on events in Lithuania, seeming to vindicate Radziwiłł's view that Poland had abandoned Lithuania to its fate. With no hope of Polish reinforcements, a decision had to be taken swiftly: Lithuania faced

---

[83] Wimmer, 'Przegląd operacji' pp. 139–40. The confusion of the fighting is well described by contemporary witnesses: K. Jarochowski, 'Przejście województw wielkopolskich do Szwedów pod Ujściem w roku 1655, z współczesnego rękopisma' *Przyjaciel Ludu* 6 no. 53 (1840) p. 411; 'Causa deditionis albo sposób y przyczyny Podania się Szwedom Wielgopolanów 1655' BNAR BOZ 934 f. 273.

[84] While Wimmer agrees with Jarochowski that effective resistance was impossible, he still believes in Opaliński's contacts with Sweden: 'Przegląd operacji' p. 140; Jarochowski, 'Przejście' p. 31.

[85] 'Actum in castris sub Uscie...' AKW Szwedzkie k.11B/21; 'O Woynie Polskiey z Szwedzkim Królem Carolem Gustavem' Czart. 1657 p. 229; W. Sauter, *Krzysztof Żegocki, pierwszy partyzant Rzeczyspospolitej, 1618–1673* (Poznań, 1981) p. 35. Two other senators present, Czarnkowski and Gajewski, also did not sign; Sajkowski, *Krzysztof Opaliński* pp. 227–8, 233.

[86] W. Majewski, '1655–60: Potop' in J. Sikorski (ed.), *Polskie tradycje wojskowe* I (Warsaw, 1990) p. 315.

After the Deluge

not one enemy but two. In the spring of 1655, Alexis had resumed his offensive, crossing the Berezina with the main army on 4 July. A week later, Minsk fell to the Muscovites, who now seemed unstoppable. Although Alexis feared the arrival of a Polish army under John Casimir, the Poles showed no sign of sending aid; indeed, the few Polish troops still in the grand duchy had left to garrison Marienburg.[87]

The capture of Dünaburg by Sweden on 19 July and the fall of Wilno to Alexis on 9 August made the Lithuanian position untenable. Radziwiłł wrote of the impossibility of carrying on unaided:

> Not only do we bear the full brunt of the enemy's attack ... but we also hear disturbing reports from our Polish brothers. We are already destitute of all ordinary means of saving ourselves ... it only remains for the Commonwealth to harvest the fatal bounty ... since loyal and well-intentioned counsel for [its] pacification ... has either been ignored or wilfully misinterpreted, the unhappy and parlous state of the Fatherland has been aggravated.[88]

Since Lithuania had been abandoned by Poland, he continued, many had decided to follow the example of Ujście in order to avoid a terrible subjugation. He could even suggest that he had official backing for talking to Sweden, since John Casimir had written after Ujście giving permission for armistice talks with Muscovy, or at least with Sweden.[89]

Few regarded the prospect of Muscovite rule with anything but trepidation. Basarab is wrong to assert that Muscovy's victory was achieved with the support of many Lithuanian magnates who opposed John Casimir.[90] The strongest opponents of John Casimir in Lithuania, led by Radziwiłł, preferred a settlement with Sweden, while it was his erstwhile supporters, led by Gosiewski, who looked more to Muscovy. Mal'tsev argues that many Lithuanian nobles accepted the rule of the tsar, welcoming a strong monarch capable of dealing with anti-feudal tendencies among their serfs, but fails to offer any evidence beyond a general quote from Lenin. There was indeed widespread peasant disorder in Lithuania and some nobles, such as Konstanty Pokłoński and Samuel Drucki-Sokoliński, did accept Muscovite rule, but evidence as to their motivation is inconclusive and equally large numbers fled the approaching armies: Radziwiłł was not alone in fearing a ruler who subjected his nobles to the knout.[91] If Alexis declared his willingness to put down peasant disorder, the Cossack forces under Zolotarenko actively encouraged peasants to join their ranks, while the Muscovites not only stripped the towns of skilled artisans, they also deported thousands of peasants.[92]

For the Catholic and Uniate nobility, the Muscovite invasion was a grave threat;

---

[87] Wisner, 'Dysydenci litewscy' p. 128.
[88] Radziwiłł to Koryciński, 7.VIII.1655; Czart. 917 ff. 1371, 1373–4.
[89] K.L. Sapieha to P. Sapieha, Warsaw, 14.VIII.1655; BPANCr. 354 f. 270.
[90] J. Basarab, *Pereislav 1654: A Historiographical Survey* (Edmonton, 1982) p. 10.
[91] Radziwiłł to J. Leszczyński, 4.VIII.1655; Czart. 384 f. 282. A.N. Mal'tsev, *Rossiia i Belorussiia v seredine XVII veka* (Moscow, 1974) p. 138. J. Morzy, *Kryzys demograficzny na Białorusi w II połowie XVII wieku* (Poznań, 1965) p. 46.
[92] Morzy, *Kryzys demograficzny* pp. 51–2, 56.

The Deluge

even the Orthodox did not necessarily welcome it. As the Muscovite armies swept through Lithuania, preceded by waves of refugees, lurid and exaggerated reports of atrocities spread:

> The Muscovites are subjecting Polish [sic] cities to a tyranny the likes of which cannot be found in any story: they have put everything to the torch within seventy miles of the border and they have put everyone over sixteen to the sword, while all those under that age have been taken to Muscovy ... where they have been displayed to the Russians and pressed into perpetual slavery.[93]

In early August, Lithuanian senators complained to the Muscovite boyars about the behaviour of the tsar's armies.[94] The day before Alexis entered Wilno, he stated that if the Lithuanians wished an alliance, the whole grand duchy must submit to his rule. His proclamation following the fall of Wilno demanded that everyone 'bowed their head' to his power.[95] Alexis was interested in submission, not negotiation.

This fear of Muscovy persuaded many Lithuanian Catholics to support Radziwiłł's initial approach to Sweden: Jerzy Tyszkiewicz, bishop of Wilno, signed the conditions for accepting Swedish protection sent to de la Gardie, as Radziwiłł stressed to Jan Leszczyński.[96] Even Gosiewski, who arrived in Kiejdany in early August, was prepared to countenance talks with Sweden. Yet Radziwiłł failed in his attempt to win wide backing for his plans; de la Gardie was proved correct in his view that he would be unable to win the wide support that he had promised.[97] Tyszkiewicz and Gosiewski were willing to await the Swedish response to Radziwiłł's proposals, but they wished to explore other options and both sent letters assuring the tsar that all Lithuania wanted to discuss a settlement; Radziwiłł signed Gosiewski's letter, probably in an attempt to play for time and raise his value to the Swedes, who were known to be in touch with Muscovy themselves.[98]

The submission to Sweden, signed at Kiejdany on 17 August, was couched in moderate terms. It stated that Lithuania, oppressed by a powerful enemy and denied protection from the king of Poland, was compelled to reach agreement with Charles X.[99] The signatories swore obedience to the Swedish king, who was granted the right to distribute all royal estates in Lithuania. Noble privileges were to be respected. The exact status of the union with Poland was left unclear: Lithuania was to take part in peace talks alongside Poland, with respect given to the union, but the

---

[93] *Theatrum Europeum* VII p. 764.
[94] K.L. Sapieha to P. Sapieha, 14.VIII.1655; BPANCr. 354 f. 270. Lithuanian Catholics and Uniates faced forcible conversion to Orthodoxy: see reports of the siege of Vitebsk; WAP Wawel, A Sang. 67 f. 339.
[95] Zaborovskii, 'Russko-litovskie peregovory vo vtoroi polovine 1655g.' *Slaviane v epokhu feodalizma: k stoletiiu Akademika V.I. Pichety* (Moscow, 1978) pp. 207–8.
[96] Radziwiłł to J. Leszczyński, 4.VIII.1655; Czart. 384 f. 282.
[97] Wisner, 'Rok 1655 na Litwie: pertraktacje ze Szwecją i kwestia wyznaniowa' *Odrodzenie i Reformacja w Polsce* 16 (1981) p. 87.
[98] 'Akta ugody kiejdańskiej' pp. 199–200; Wisner, 'Rok 1655' p. 89; Wasilewski, 'Zdrada Janusza Radziwiłła' p. 137; Zaborovskii, 'Russko-litovskie peregovory' p. 207.
[99] 'Akta ugody kiejdańskiej' p. 187.

After the Deluge

possibility of a future union with Sweden as an equal partner was mooted. The Lithuanian and Swedish armies were to be united against Muscovy but Lithuanians were not to fight the king of Poland. The question of financial support for Swedish troops was to be decided by assemblies of the nobility.

Despite its moderation, Kiejdany failed to attract the wide support for which Radziwiłł had hoped. The only other senators to sign were Eustachy Kierdej and Gosiewski. Radziwiłł's cousin Bogusław, one of the authors of the original invitation of 29 July, left Kiejdany before the signing, while his brother-in-law, Jerzy Karol Hlebowicz, starosta of Samogitia, who was present, refused to sign. Radziwiłł had clearly overreached himself. Although Tyszkiewicz accepted Swedish aid in principle, he rejected the terms on offer:

I would not be adverse to your proposals, or to any means which might prevent our complete ruin. But when I consider that we are to surrender ... before we are certain of receiving any help, I fear that in trying to escape our present plight we may fall into a worse one, even though we imagine it to be better.

Tyszkiewicz regarded Radziwiłł's action as premature and was unwilling to break the union with Poland for Swedish promises alone: 'By this surrender we are dissolving the sacred union with Poland, whose inviolability was sworn by our ancestors; those of us who sign will be branded for eternity with the mark of destruction for betraying our loyalty to our king and our fatherland.'[100] He had accepted negotiations with Sweden partly because the king had sanctioned such contacts. As a Catholic bishop, however, he was concerned at the possible breaking of the union with Poland since, deprived of the powerful support of the Polish Catholic Church, Lithuanian Catholics would face serious challenges not so much from Protestantism but from Orthodoxy.

Although Gosiewski signed Kiejdany, he still put more faith in Muscovy; owing to the tsar's hardline attitude he could not afford to stand aloof from talks with Sweden. He was, nevertheless, concerned at the prospect of Radziwiłł's dominance and had his own clause included, urging the appointment of Krzysztof Pac as vice-chancellor should a vacancy occur. If Gosiewski was trying to raise his price with regard to Muscovy, he was successful: Alexis was forced to moderate his position, sending Likhariev to talk to the two hetmans at the end of August. Although Radziwiłł opposed concessions, Gosiewski suggested an immediate armistice, playing on Muscovite fears of Sweden.[101] After Likhariev's departure, Gosiewski was sufficiently confident that the Muscovites would cease operations against the Commonwealth to break with Radziwiłł, declaring to the troops: 'Brothers ... let everyone understand that my senior colleague wishes to harness you to a terrible yoke, to place you, due to the old hatred which he bears you, in the powerful hands of the Swedes, so that you, who once struck terror into the hearts of all nations, must

[100] Tyszkiewicz to J. Radziwiłł, 1655; Czart. 148 f. 1117; 'Akta ugody kiejdańskiej' pp. 186–7, pp. 198–9.
[101] Wisner, 'Rok 1655' pp. 93–4, Zaborovskii, 'Russko-litovskie peregovory' p. 211.

lay down your arms.'[102] The understandable concern of Gosiewski and other leading Lithuanian magnates about Radziwiłł's political ambitions, and the effect that Kiejdany might have on the balance of the factions in Lithuania, was heightened by Radziwiłł's proposal for the creation of duchies out of Lithuanian territory for himself and his cousin Bogusław, in which they would be granted sovereign rights under the Swedish crown similar to those enjoyed by princes of the Empire.[103]

Radziwiłł's private ambitions cost him any chance of support from his powerful magnate rivals in Lithuania, who might have been attracted in the circumstances of 1655 by Lithuanian separatism. Although the Sapiehas had been in contact with Sweden, Paweł Sapieha protested strongly against Kiejdany and declined to accept their protection.[104] On 23 August, a group of Lithuanians signed a confederation at Wierzbołów, declaring their opposition to Kiejdany. Sapieha quickly made a truce with Muscovy and concentrated on keeping Lithuanian forces together until John Casimir should return. Radziwiłł's panic-stricken letter to his cousin, in which he berated him for disappearing, showed that he realised the extent of his failure:

On one side we face the suspicion of the Prussian *szlachta* and of [Gosiewski's] faction; on another, the Poles, who have abandoned us; on yet another, those traitors who escaped from our camp and formed a confederation, traitors who are hostile not only to our estates but also to their friends and servants and who intend to join the king.[105]

In early September, suspicious of Gosiewski's duplicity, Radziwiłł arrested him; on 20 October, he abandoned any attempt at moderation, signing a treaty of union with Sweden which was far more radical than the original agreement of 17 August: the union with Poland was effectively broken, Charles X and his descendants were recognised as grand dukes of Lithuania and de la Gardie was named viceroy, although the post would normally be reserved for a Lithuanian.[106] Although over 1,000 nobles signed the document, Radziwiłł could not disguise the lack of magnate support.

Ujście and Kiejdany were the result of the Commonwealth's military incapacity in the face of overwhelming odds, not a coordinated plot on the part of a widespread, coherent opposition. Magnates and *szlachta* alike were affected by a profound sense of disorientation following the sudden military collapse, and they were forced to take decisions which would have seemed preposterous a few weeks earlier. Ujście and Kiejdany had a catastrophic effect on morale. John Casimir had left Warsaw on 17

---

[102] Medeksza, *Księga pamiętnicza* p. 15.
[103] 'Akta ugody kiejdańskiej' p. 179. The lands claimed for Janusz were 53,455 km² in area; for Bogusław, over 91,000 km²; they were also to keep their Lithuanian offices. Wisner, 'Kiejdany' p. 181.
[104] A. Rachuba, 'Paweł Sapieha wobec Szwecji i Jana Kazimierza (IX.1655–II.1656). Przyczynek do postawy magnaterii w okresie "potopu"' *Acta Baltico-Slavica* 11 (1977) p. 83.
[105] J. Radziwiłł to B. Radziwiłł, 26.VIII.1655; Kotłubaj, *Życie Janusza Radziwiłła* dodatek XIV, no. 7, p. 387.
[106] Wisner, 'Kiejdany' p. 194.

August, the same day on which Kiejdany was signed and part of the Sieradz *szlachta* accepted Charles X's protection; by 4 September it was reported that only four palatinates remained loyal.[107] At a council meeting two days after the defeat at Żarnów on 16 September, the king was met with demands for pay from an army on the verge of mutiny.[108] On 25 September, a Cossack and Muscovite army began the siege of Lwów, while the main Crown army was defeated at Gródek at the end of the month. The decision of John Casimir and many leading senators to follow Louise Marie into exile prompted other palatinates to join Sweden:

> We have been abandoned by our ... brethren from the senate, some of whom have fled the country, while others have abandoned His Majesty, who has been escorted out of the kingdom, taking with him the *insignia regni* and priceless jewels from the Cracow treasury without informing the estates of the realm. They gave no reinforcements to the Commonwealth and have abandoned the equestrian order, their own lands, the *szlachta* and even the army; all have been left in the lurch.[109]

The fall of Cracow on 17 October and the surrender of the bulk of the Crown army a few days later seemed to end John Casimir's hopes of saving his kingdom.

---

[107] Unknown bishop to Vidoni, Wolbórz, 5.IX.1655; TRz. 8418 p. 66.
[108] 'Relation von der Königl. Pollnischen Armee', 13.IX.1655; Czart. 148 no. 112, f. 575. Lanckoroński to John Casimir, Wojnicz, 3.X.1655; Czart. 917 f. 1385.
[109] 'Manifestatia Wdwtwa Sendomierskiego' Nowe Miasto Korczyn, 5.X.1655; Czart. 1656 f. 174.

3

Recovery: July 1655–August 1656

Poland's submission to Sweden was more apparent than real. The scale of the surrender should not be exaggerated: while some leading magnates such as Radziwiłł, Opaliński, Koniecpolski and the future king, John Sobieski, went over to Sweden, the majority remained uncommitted. About thirty senators went into exile; others resisted, such as Jakub and Ludwik Weiher in Royal Prussia; many did nothing, waiting to see how the situation would develop. The Leszczyńskis, who blamed John Casimir for what they saw as a needless war and who appeared keen in July and August to secure his abdication, could not obtain satisfactory terms from Sweden. Lubomirski, long an opponent of John Casimir, also failed to reach agreement despite protracted negotiations during the siege of Cracow.[1]

Poland had been easy to conquer; with an army of 36,000 it might not prove easy to hold. The victory was by no means as complete as it seemed: Charles X had sought above all to seize Royal Prussia, but proved unable to take Putzig and Marienburg, which held out until the spring, or Danzig, which he never took. The loyalty of those who had already accepted Swedish overlordship, many of them reluctantly, depended on Charles's behaviour. Faith in Sweden was rapidly disappointed, however. Despite attempts to maintain discipline in the Swedish army, incidents such as the murder of suffragan bishop Branecki in August turned people against the invader. The supply of the Swedish army by techniques refined during the Thirty Years War brought demands on the local population which they were unwilling to meet after seven years continual warfare, and which trampled over the noble liberties that Charles had sworn to uphold. Charles, despite his earlier promises, proved reluctant to hold a diet and, as winter approached, the demands of the Swedish army grew.[2] The first signs of resistance appeared in November and spread rapidly.

---

[1] Wittenberg to Lubomirski, Cracow, 9.X.1655; Czart. 148 no. 124, f. 625; Charles X to Lubomirski, Cracow, 12.X.1655; ibid. no. 127, f. 637; Lubomirski to Wittenberg, Lubau, 30.X.1655; ibid. no. 145, f. 699; Lubomirski and Zasławski to Charles X, 10.XI.1655; ibid. no. 157, f. 731. For the efforts to secure John Casimir's abdication, see Adersbach, Warsaw, 5.VIII.1655; *Urkunden und Aktenstücke* VII p. 374.

[2] On arriving in Poznań, the Swedes murdered a priest at the Bernardine monastery and began demanding contributions for the army in the shape of money, food and grain, which the local *szlachta* found insupportable: Jarochowski, *Wielkopolska* pp. 37, 41; K.L. Sapieha to P. Sapieha, 14.VIII.1655; BPANCr. 354.

After the Deluge

Since 1654, many had been convinced that Poland could only be saved by a Swedish alliance. As it became clear that Sweden was pursuing its own aims with scant regard for Polish interests, John Casimir's position improved dramatically. There is no evidence to suggest that anything more than a tiny minority had considered his deposition before the military collapse of 1655, and many who went over to Sweden had serious misgivings. At least John Casimir had been elected in accordance with the law, by which his actions were limited. Fears increased that Charles might attempt to negotiate a partition of the Commonwealth with Muscovy, the Cossacks and other powers. By mid-November, the mood among the exiles had changed dramatically from the defeatism of a few weeks earlier, as news arrived in Silesia of growing resistance. John Casimir, with the backing of the senate council, issued a call-to-arms and began to plan his return. Much of the Polish army returned to loyalty in the Confederation of Tyszowce, signed at the end of December. While a few lingered in Swedish service until the spring of 1656, most returned to loyalty at the end of 1655.

Charles's behaviour seemed to demonstrate that John Casimir had been right to be suspicious of Sweden, while the military collapse of July and August had proved that he had been right to insist that the Commonwealth's political and military system needed to be reformed if it were to be capable of resisting its enemies. Whatever the reasons for Ujście and Kiejdany, their constitutional significance was unmistakable: in both cases integral parts of the Commonwealth signed treaties with a foreign power without reference to the king and senate council, the diet or local dietines. Such action was clearly illegal and was widely condemned, and Opaliński and Radziwiłł were vilified as traitors. As Condé had discovered in France, a powerful magnate could only take opposition so far, and association with a foreign power was dangerous. The attempts of Opaliński and Radziwiłł to find a legal basis for their actions ended in failure, and the discrediting of his main opponents opened the way for John Casimir to strengthen royal power. From the autumn of 1655, political reform became an urgent topic of debate.

If reform were to succeed, however, the invaders would first have to be expelled; despite the return of the will to fight, that would be no easy task. The first priority was military support. The collapse of July–August 1655 demonstrated that it was no longer possible for the Commonwealth to improvise defence after the opening of hostilities: modern warfare demanded careful preparation, as the Swedes – who had been arming since the spring of 1654 – had shown. Thus, when news of the surrender at Ujście arrived in Warsaw on 31 July, the senate council immediately decided on the absolute necessity of foreign aid. The lack of time to organise defence and the disasters at Ujście and Kiejdany effectively destroyed any hopes of raising forces capable of matching the Swedes in the short term. What was needed above all, as Polish commanders constantly urged, was regular, professional, trained infantry, to supplement the plentiful cavalry.[3] The Cossack revolt had deprived the Com-

---

[3] e.g. Stanisław Potocki to John Casimir, undated; Czart. 402 f. 256.

monwealth of its traditional source of infantry, while the disruption caused by the Swedish invasion meant that money could not be easily raised to recruit professional troops. The only realistic source of infantry in the short term was from abroad.

The diplomatic situation was, however, unpromising. The Commonwealth was at war with both Muscovy and Sweden. Its Tatar allies had returned to the Crimea and were in any case of limited value in a war with a western army. France, nominally friendly, was Sweden's ally, and many believed that it had encouraged the Swedish attack.[4] England, now at peace with the Dutch, was not as favourably disposed towards Charles as a year previously, and had a healthy concern over Swedish designs in Prussia. Nevertheless, Sweden was actively wooing England in an attempt to end its diplomatic isolation and to counteract the efforts of Nicholas de Bye, who was attempting to negotiate a naval treaty with the Dutch on John Casimir's behalf. Polish Catholicism and support for the Stuarts effectively ruled out English aid; indeed, Cromwell had already snubbed de Bye, who had arrived in England in early 1655 to seek support.[5] John Casimir hoped for more from the Danes and the Dutch. He had sent Canasilles to Frederick III in May to discuss the 'common peril', without any result.[6] The Dutch, however, were more concerned about the position of Denmark and wished to avoid provoking Cromwell into supporting Sweden by coming out on the Polish side; all de Bye's efforts in the Hague were therefore in vain.[7] The one hopeful sign was the attitude of Khmelnytskyi, who was concerned at the prospect of the complete collapse of the Commonwealth in the light of Muscovy's increasingly authoritarian attitude, which prompted him to adopt a more neutral position towards John Casimir from the autumn of 1655, hoping that the Commonwealth's plight would lead it to make concessions to the Cossacks.[8]

The best hope for immediate aid lay with Transylvania, Brandenburg and Austria. Transylvania might provide troops quickly but Rákóczi's army was largely composed of cavalry; only Brandenburg or Austria could supply the infantry which the Poles so desperately needed. Many hoped for help from Frederick William of Brandenburg, who had seen Stettin and the richer half of Pomerania go to Sweden in 1648. Nevertheless, despite being bound to help the Commonwealth as its vassal in Ducal Prussia, Frederick William had granted the Swedes free passage through Brandenburg, merely marching his small standing army to Ducal Prussia to protect Königsberg. The best hope of aid appeared to lie with Austria, which would be

---

[4] Des Noyers, Oberglogau, 27.X.1655; *Lettres* no. 3, p. 6.
[5] M. Roberts, 'Cromwell and the Baltic' *Essays in Swedish History* (London, 1967) p. 151 and *Swedish Diplomats at Cromwell's Court, 1655–1656* Camden 4th Series 36 (London, 1988) p. 11.
[6] See Barkmann's report, Damus, *Der erste nordische Krieg* p. 34. Instruction to Canasilles, 29.V.1655; *Polonicae ex Archivo Regni Daniae* VI Elementa ad Fontium Editiones XXXIII ed. C. Lanckorońska and G. Steen Jensen (Rome, 1974) no. 67, p. 89.
[7] H. Rowen, *John de Witt, Grand Pensionary of Holland, 1625–1672* (Princeton, 1978) pp. 306–7; Termesden, 'Karola X Gustawa plan kampanii' p. 95.
[8] A.B. Pernal, 'The Polish–Lithuanian Commonwealth and the Ukraine: Diplomatic relations 1648–1659' University of Ottawa Ph.D. (1977) pp. 232–42.

unlikely to welcome Swedish control of Poland and which was the Commonwealth's only Catholic neighbour. It was therefore to Austria that the senate council chose to turn: on 1 August, John Casimir wrote to Ferdinand III asking for help.[9] Austria, however, was reluctant to intervene. Ferdinand could not afford to risk reopening the Thirty Years War and was afraid that the situation might be exploited by discontented elements in the Habsburg patrimonial lands, where he did not wish to risk squandering the gains his father had made in the 1620s. Moreover, he was in poor health and faced a succession crisis after the death of his son, Ferdinand IV, in 1654, which left him with the problem of securing the acceptance of his next son, Leopold, as king of the Romans. Sweden's new influence in the Empire meant that any intervention in Poland would carry the grave risk of political problems over the election, especially since Austria would have to shoulder the main burden of the fighting.[10]

In the circumstances there was only one offer the Poles could make which might tempt Ferdinand to intervene. After Charles Ferdinand's death on 9 May, there was no legitimate Vasa heir to the throne, which made possible an offer of the succession to Austria in return for military aid. The council sent Adriano with a document signed by the king, Andrzej Leszczyński, Lubomirski, Koryciński, Trzebicki and others, which offered Ferdinand the thrones of Poland and Sweden for a member of the house of Habsburg.[11] After Adriano had left, the emperor's envoy, Schönhoff, arrived in Warsaw, with expressions of encouragement and sympathy, whereupon the council granted plenipotentiary powers on 13 August to Jan Leszczyński, bishop nominate of Chełmno, to discuss the terms of the offer.[12]

Historians have traditionally seen the offer to Vienna as a Court initiative.[13] It is true that the Court had always supported the idea of an election *vivente rege* and had made the first approach to Vienna after Charles Ferdinand's death, sounding out archduke Ferdinand Charles on the possibility of the candidature of his brother, Sigismund Francis.[14] It was on the initiative of the senate council, however, that

---

[9] John Casimir to Ferdinand III, Warsaw, 1.VIII.1655; Walewski, *Geschichte der hl. Ligue und Leopolds I. vom Umschwung im Gleichgewichtssystem des Westens durch den schwedisch-polnisch-österreichischen Krieg, bis zur Verwicklung der orientalischen Frage durch August II 1657–1700* (Cracow, 1857–61) II, abt.1, no. XXIX, p. xlvi.

[10] 'Relatione de sensi della Corte Imperiale circa le cose di Polonia, e solutione di tutti le difficolta nel'Negotiar con essa gl'aiuti' Czart. 2576 f. 335; this account was probably by Visconti, the Polish resident in Vienna: K. Targosz, *Hieronim Pinocci; studium z dziejów kultury naukowej w Polsce w XVII wieku* (Wrocław, Warsaw, Cracow, 1967) p. 36, n. 1.

[11] Vidoni, 9.VIII.1655; TRz. 8418 p. 6. Lisola was shown a copy in October, signed by twenty-three senators. Lisola, Stettin, 6.X.1655: *Berichte* no. 11, p. 111.

[12] W. Seredyński, 'Sprawa obioru następcy na tron za panowania Jana Kazimierza' *Rocznik Ces. Krol. Towarzystwa Naukowego Krakowskiego* 32 (1864) p. 20; Walewski, *Historia wyzwolenia* I, document XIII, p. xiii. Leszczyński, a relative of Jan Leszczyński, the palatine of Łęczyca, left for Vienna on 15.VIII.1655: Vidoni, Warsaw, 16.VIII.1655; TRz. 8418 p. 8.

[13] K. Piwarski, 'Rywalizacja francusko-austriacka o wpływy w Rzeczypospolitej w latach 1655–1660' *PODWP* I p. 409; Kubala, *Wojna szwecka* p. 94; Seredyński, 'Sprawa obioru' p. 206.

[14] Nani to Signori, Pressburg, 17.VI.1655; *Zherela* p. 349.

Recovery

Adriano and Leszczyński were sent to Vienna. For although the initial plan was to suggest the election of a Habsburg to succeed on John Casimir's death, the Commonwealth's desperate military situation had led some to consider asking John Casimir to abdicate. Before John Casimir's arrival in Cracow, Vidoni worked hard to combat defeatist sentiments, condemning Andrzej Leszczyński's willingness to consider talks with Sweden.[15] Leszczyński, however, along with other bishops, was considering the possibility of appealing to Ferdinand III over John Casimir's head to accept the throne immediately. It was the ecclesiastical senators, led by Leszczyński, Trzebicki and Czartoryski, bishop of Cujavia, who took the initiative in promoting the Habsburgs as the most suitable Catholic candidates and were prepared to sacrifice John Casimir if necessary.[16] Trzebicki sent a passionate plea to Auersberg, urging him not to forget the vital interests of the Habsburgs: 'His Imperial Majesty and his August House should not suffer this neighbouring kingdom to be torn from their hands...'[17]

Until there was a positive response from Vienna, however, it was important for supporters of a Habsburg succession to stay loyal to John Casimir. As it became clear that Ferdinand was not prepared to send immediate aid or accept the offer of the throne, the king's position improved. The official reply of the secret council was not given until 8 November. The Austrians refused reinforcements, offering only mediation; as for the succession, they neither rejected nor accepted it, merely thanking the Poles for the offer.[18] This noncommital response hid a definite private rejection: Auersberg was strongly against accepting, while Lisola drily remarked that the Poles had failed to maintain their present king on the throne; what made them think they could make it safe for a new one?[19]

Vienna's failure to respond ended talk of deposition or abdication and enabled John Casimir gradually to reestablish his position. The evening of his arrival in Cracow on 19 September, there had been a dramatic council meeting, attended by about forty senators.[20] It is unclear whether news of the Vienna decision had

---

[15] Vidoni to Orsini, Cracow, 19.IX.1655; TRz. 8418, p. 71.
[16] A. Leszczyński to Ferdinand III, Neisse, 5.XI.55; Walewski, *Geschichte der hl. Ligue* II, abt.1 no. xxxvii, pp. l-li; Czartoryski to Ferdinand III, Neisse, 29.X.1655; ibid no. xxxvi, p. l. Krebs stresses the influence of the Austrian party, especially the episcopate, on John Casimir; O. Krebs, 'Vorgeschichte und Ausgang der polnischen Königswahl im Jahre 1669. Nach den Berichten der pfalzgräffisch-neuburgischen Gesandten im kgl. Bayer. Geh. Staatsarchiv zu München' *Zeitschrift der Historischen Gesellschaft für die Provinz Posen* 3 (1888) p. 155.
[17] Trzebicki to Auersberg, Warsaw, 1.VIII.1655; Walewski, *Geschichte der hl. Ligue* II, abt.1 no. XXX, p. xlvi. He later stressed the threat to Silesia posed by Sweden's possession of Cracow and gave assurances that the nobility would rally to Austria: Visconti to Ferdinand, 19.XI.1655; Walewski, *Historia wyzwolenia* I document XVII, pp. xv-xvi.
[18] Minutes of the Secret Council, 8.IX.1655; Walewski, *Geschichte der hl. Ligue* II, abt.1 no. xxxiii, p. xlviii.
[19] Vidoni, 27.X.1655. TRz. 8418 p. 29; Lisola, Stettin, 6.X.1655. *Berichte* no. 11, p. 110.
[20] W. Kochowski, *Annalium Poloniae Climacter Secundus Bella Sueticum, Transylvanicum, Moschoviticum, Aliasque Res Gestas ab Anno 1655 ad Annum 1661 Inclusive Continens* (Cracow, 1688) I p. 33. 'Relacja Wojny Szwedzkiej' Czart. 425 f. 10.

arrived: Leszczyński had not reached Cracow by 22 September.[21] The council decided unanimously to confirm the succession offer with a new embassy to be undertaken by Lubomirski and swore not to abandon the king.[22] There was no talk now of an immediate assumption of the throne. Lubomirski was to assure Ferdinand of the intention of both king and Commonwealth to arrange for the election of one of his sons, his brother Leopold, or some other member of the Habsburg family, as king of Poland and grand duke of Lithuania; he was then to discuss the time and place of this election. The conditions on which the crown was to be offered, however, demonstrate the Court's improved position: the elected or crowned king was to enjoy none of the rights, powers or privileges of his position during the lifetime of John Casimir, under whose direction and tutelage he was to be placed.[23]

Despite the Commonwealth's desperate position, many felt that a Habsburg succession was too great a price to pay for Austrian aid. Traditionally, the Habsburgs had been unpopular candidates among the nobility, who still recalled 1587 when archduke Maximilian had used force in an attempt to secure his election. More recently, the Habsburgs' destruction of political liberties in their patrimonial lands in the 1620s served as a grim warning of what might lie in store for the Commonwealth under a Habsburg monarch. Finally, Poles were aware of the dangers of a French reaction if a Habsburg were elected.[24] Even among the episcopate, often portrayed as the blind tools of Vienna and Rome, support for the Austrian policy was by no means solid: Piotr Gembicki, bishop of Cracow, told Vidoni that he did not agree with the appeal to Ferdinand III made after a meeting of senators called by Andrzej Leszczyński in Cracow on 28 August, and would not have signed it had it not been for the urgings of Leszczyński and Trzebicki, adding that others were of his opinion.[25]

More fundamental opposition came from Lubomirski, who was still in contact with Sweden. Although he signed the new appeal to Vienna, he told Vidoni bluntly that John Casimir had been to blame for the outbreak of war and that opinion in the Cracow dietine was highly favourable to Sweden.[26] He refused to go to Vienna, stating that there was no real hope of Austrian support and that he did not see that his proposed mission would achieve any more; indeed it might be counter-productive. He suggested a meeting with the king at Czorstyn, where John Casimir had arrived on 5 October, to discuss changes to the instructions. It had been

---

[21] Vidoni, Cracow, 22.IX.1655; TRz. 8418 p. 20.
[22] 'Instructio ad Aulam Caesaream Illrmo. Supremo Marschallo nomine SRM,' Nowy Sącz, 30.IX.1655'. AGAD, LL33 f. 91; 'Instructio a Senatu Legato ad Aulam Caesaream data ut supra'; AGAD LL33 f. 92; extracts printed in *Zherela* pp. 352, 354. Plenipotentiary powers from king and senate, (copies) dated November, AGAD AKW Cesarskie, k. 25a, fasc I no. 3.
[23] 'Instructio ad Aulam Caesaream'; AGAD LL33 ff. 91–2; *Zherela* pp. 352–3.
[24] cf. letter from Munich, December 1655; Czart. 2576 f. 399.
[25] Vidoni, Cracow, 29.VIII.1655; TRz. 8418 pp. 9–10. According to Vidoni, the letter was signed by the two archbishops, four bishops and twenty others. For the letter see Walewski, *Historia wyzwolenia* I document XIV, p. xiv.
[26] Vidoni, Cracow, 29.VIII.1655; TRz. 8418 p. 9.

proposed that a son of the emperor be elected and that anyone in line for the imperial dignity be excluded. Lubomirski accepted the second point: 'But the first will never receive my assent by any means; here I abandon my character of ambassador and adopt that of senator. For I cannot permit that I should see a boy king dependent on the rule of the father and, most likely, fathers.'[27]

Lubomirski's remarks indicate that the domestic implications of the succession plan were already emerging. His opposition to a Habsburg election was motivated by his own political ambitions, not by any desire to defend the principle of free election. He refused to go to Vienna, partly because he was still awaiting the outcome of his contacts with Sweden, partly because he was thinking of running his own candidate: George Rákóczi with whom he had already been in contact during his bitter dispute with John Casimir in the early 1650s. He refused to attend the important council which met at Oppeln in mid-November, where Habsburg supporters were dominant.[28] While the council decided to suspend all talks with other powers until the Habsburg position was known, Lubomirski held his own council in Zips, just over the Hungarian border, where a large group of senators was gathered.[29] On 17 November, Władysław Lubieniecki, Lubomirski's private envoy, wrote to Rákóczi, claiming that all the ecclesiastical and the majority of lay senators in Silesia and Hungary now despaired of keeping John Casimir on his throne 'because of his incapacity', and that the senate had sent a letter to the king with a unanimous request for his abdication. Lubieniecki, in the name of the senators in Zips, invited Rákóczi to the Polish throne and to send an envoy for talks.[30]

Lubieniecki's assurances were premature. Although John Casimir's deposition had certainly been considered, the senators in Silesia supported an Austrian candidature and recognised that, for the moment at least, he was indispensable. Furthermore, the improvement in the military situation, as the first signs of resistance appeared, worked to the benefit of the Court. The political battle over the succession now gathered momentum. The victorious party had much to gain: if political reform were achieved, the monarchy promised to emerge from the war with its position further strengthened. The Vasas had always seen reform of the election as the key to increasing royal power; all previous attempts, however, had ended in failure. Now, for the first time since 1569, there was substantial senate support for setting aside the normal succession procedure. In March, when John Casimir had suggested the idea, it had been met with hostility from the senate council; the

---

[27] Lubomirski to Koryciński, 6.X.1655; Czart. 917 ff. 1379–80.
[28] Lubomirski to John Casimir, 9.XI.1655; Czart. 148 no. 153, f. 717.
[29] Among those present were Piotr Gembicki, bishop of Cracow; Jan Gembicki, bishop nominate of Płock; Władysław Dominik Zasławski, palatine of Cracow; Jan Tarło, palatine of Lublin; M.K. Czartoryski, palatine of Volhynia; Jan Wielopolski, castellan of Wojnicz; Jan Boguski, castellan of Czechów, and Jan Zamoyski. A. Leszczyński to John Casimir, Neisse, 20.I.1655, A. Grabowski (ed.), *Ojczyste spominki w pismach do dziejów dawnej Polski* (Cracow, 1845) II no. 57, p. 91; *Zherela* p. 365; Wielopolski to Rákóczi, 16.XI.1655. AGAD, APPot. 45 f. 41.
[30] Lubieniecki to Rákóczi, 17.XI.1655; Szilágyi, *Transsylvania* I pp. 493–4.

Swedish invasion, however, had caused many to change their minds, to the extent that, according to Rudawski, the Oppeln council decided unanimously to offer the throne to the Habsburgs as hereditary, not elective monarchs.[31] As Andrzej Leszczyński pointed out, if John Casimir were to die during the war without a nominated successor, the Commonwealth could be plunged into even greater disorder, as domestic factions and foreign powers vied for the throne.[32] The best way to avoid such an outcome would be to elect or appoint a successor under the supervision of the king and the senate council, which would ensure respect for the Commonwealth's constitution.

As Leszczyński observed, the factions were already beginning to form. It was not just the Court which might profit from an election *vivente rege*. Not since the election of Sigismund III in 1587 had such an opportunity presented itself for a politician to emulate the achievements of Jan Zamoyski (1542–1605), who had risen from the ranks of the middle nobility to become grand chancellor and grand hetman, and to enjoy fabulous wealth, through masterminding the elections of Stefan Batory and Sigismund III. Lubomirski's support for Rákóczi was clearly motivated by such considerations. Already one of the most powerful magnates in Poland, should Lubomirski repeat Zamoyski's role as kingmaker, his political power would be great indeed.

He might do even better. The senate council had already discussed the possibility of a native or 'Piast' candidate and, as Trzebicki told Vidoni: 'There are many senators who have discussed the matter among themselves and consider that it would be good to elect [Lubomirski] as successor. He is a Pole and is capable of ruling and of safeguarding liberty. Nobody is better qualified than a citizen of the Commonwealth to preserve freedom.'[33] Even if Lubomirski were attracted by such a prospect, however, for the moment it would be unwise to pursue it. Although a Piast candidature was traditionally popular, Lubomirski would face serious opposition from John Casimir, as Trzebicki stressed, and, more importantly, from other magnates, especially the Leszczyńskis. Nevertheless, whether as candidate or as kingmaker, Lubomirski was determined to use the election to improve his political position.

The main objection to a Piast candidature was that it would not bring the foreign aid which the Commonwealth so desperately needed. Once Lubomirski had decided that Sweden had little to offer him, he advanced Rákóczi's candidature, leaving others to speculate on a Piast election. By November, however, it was clear that he could no longer act unilaterally with the support only of the handful of senators which had followed him into exile in Hungary. It was necessary to reconsider his plans and try to win wider support, if not of the Court, then at least of the senators in Silesia, especially Andrzej Leszczyński, who would act as interrex on John Casimir's

---

[31] Rudawski, *Historiarum* VI p. 206.
[32] A. Leszczyński to John Casimir, 20.I.1656; Grabowski, *Oyczyste spominki* II p. 93.
[33] Vidoni, Podoliniec, 1.I.1656; TRz. 8419 p. 3.

death. The vilification of Opaliński and Radziwiłł, who both died in December, was a terrible warning of the possible consequences of independent action.

Vienna's rejection of the offer of the throne improved the chances of Rákóczi's candidature. In September, John Casimir sent Szumowski to Transylvania. Although the king later denied that Szumowski had discussed the succession, Andrzej Leszczyński maintained that an offer had been made – 'if I remember correctly'.[34] Whatever the truth of the matter, Szumowski's mission raised Lubomirski's hopes that he might be able to win support among the Silesian exiles for a Rákóczi candidature. He now stressed the importance of winning over the Court. Lubieniecki assured Rákóczi that the king, and especially the queen, supported his candidature.[35] Des Noyers claimed to have seen letters in which Rákóczi offered to become a Catholic and to send all his forces to support the Commonwealth if John Casimir adopted his son and had him elected successor, but these assurances, as Vidoni's more sceptical report makes clear, were from Lubomirski, who recalled the successful reign of Stefan Batory, Rákóczi's compatriot and pointed out that Rákóczi had a large army.[36] It was Lubomirski who encouraged the hope that Rákóczi or his son would convert to Catholicism and would be content to wait until John Casimir's death before succeeding. John Casimir's response to this initiative is unknown, though the possibility of a Transylvanian candidature was not ruled out: in the same dispatch, Vidoni reports Koryciński as saying that now Austria had rejected the Polish offer, there could be no other candidate but Frederick William or Rákóczi, if they agreed to become Catholics.[37]

Rákóczi soon made it clear that he was not prepared to convert. On 16 December, his envoy Mikes arrived at Lubau for talks. The next day, he had a private meeting with Lubomirski, who assured him that the Poles were ready to grant the throne to Rákóczi. Since John Casimir was still alive, however, Lubomirski stressed that a way must be found to satisfy Rákóczi, without prejudicing John Casimir's rights to govern. Mikes replied that his master had no wish to be a 'painted puppet', Lubomirski drew his attention to the many examples of adoption with a view to succeeding and asked if Rákóczi would accept if John Casimir named him co-ruler (*consortem regiminis*). Mikes replied that he did not know, but suspected not. The

---

[34] John Casimir to A. Leszczyński, 4.II.1656; S. Temberski, *Roczniki, 1647–1656* Scriptores Rerum Polonicarum 16 ed. W. Czermak (Cracow, 1897) p. 338. A. Leszczyński to John Casimir, Neisse, 20.I.1656; Grabowski, *Oyczyste spominki* II no. 57, p. 93; S. Zarzycki, *Stosunek księcia siedmiogrodzkiego Jerzego Rakoczego II do Rzeczypospolitej polskiej od początku wojny szwedzkiej do wyprawy tegoż na Polskę w roku 1657* (Kołomija, 1889) p. 32.

[35] Lubieniecki to Rákóczi, 3.XII.1655; Szilágyi, *Transsylvania* I p. 496.

[36] Des Noyers, Oppeln, 23.XI.1655; *Lettres* no. 7, p. 18; Vidoni, Oppeln, 22.XI.1655; TRz. 8418 pp. 40–1. Des Noyers's version is accepted uncritically by I. Hudita, *Relations diplomatiques entre la France et la Transylvanie au XVIIe siècle (1635–1683)* (Paris, 1927) p. 159. Vidoni's report justifies Zarzycki's scepticism about the rumour reported by des Noyers; Zarzycki, *Stosunek* p. 54, n. 5. Lubomirski wrote again, a few days before Mikes arrived for talks: Lubomirski to Louise Marie, Lubau, 12.XII.1655; Des Noyers, *Lettres* no. 17, p. 45.

[37] Vidoni, Oppeln, 22.XI.1655; TRz. 8418 p. 42.

next day Mikes attended a general meeting of the Lubau exiles. When asked directly whether Rákóczi would convert to Catholicism, Mikes, while stressing the toleration extended towards Catholics in Transylvania, again said he suspected not. It was decided, nevertheless, that if Rákóczi would accept 'common government', the Poles were prepared to agree to all his terms.[38]

This outcome was a serious blow for Lubomirski. It was unlikely either that John Casimir would agree to common government, or that the Rákóczi candidature would receive the backing of other senators without that of the king. The most important setback, however, was Rákóczi's refusal to change religion, which meant the certain opposition of the ecclesiastical senators at least. Confrontation soon followed the king's arrival in Sobota on 29 December on his way back to Poland. John Casimir immediately expressed his displeasure at the dealings with Rákóczi, making it clear that Lubomirski's talks with Mikes had no official backing.[39] The king was worried that the Transylvanian negotiations might prejudice chances of reaching an agreement with Austria. He resented attempts to persuade him to adopt Rákóczi's son and agree to him as co-ruler before Jan Leszczyński returned from his new mission to Vienna.[40] For such a step, he wrote, the unanimous consent of the senate council would be necessary.

Circumstances were nevertheless pushing John Casimir towards acceptance of a Transylvanian candidature. The Court had pinned its hopes on Frederick William as an alternative who might provide military reinforcements and, more importantly, who might be popular: according to des Noyers, the royal couple would have Frederick William elected if only he would become a Catholic, or give his son to be raised at the Polish Court, since there was much support for him among the nobility.[41] A further approach was made in October, when the elector was offered sovereignty in Ducal Prussia and the cession of John Casimir's rights over Sweden and Livonia in return for military aid.[42]

It looked for a time as if Frederick William might respond. On 12th November, he signed the treaty of Rinsk with the estates of Royal Prussia, offering them his protection.[43] It was the first sign of foreign willingness to help the Commonwealth but any hopes that the elector would offer substantial aid were soon dashed; Frederick William was by no means powerful enough to confront Sweden and showed no interest in the succession. He abandoned any thought of helping John Casimir when Charles X threatened to invade Ducal Prussia, hastily agreeing to the

---

[38] Kubala, *Wojna szwecka* p. 245. Based on Mikes's account; Szilágyi, *Transsylvania* I pp. 511–17.
[39] Vidoni to Orsini, Podoliniec, 1.I.1656; TRz. 8419 no. 4, p. 148; Vidoni, Podoliniec, 1.I.1656; TRz. 8419 p. 4.
[40] John Casimir to A. Leszczyński, Krosno, 8.I.1656; Grabowski, *Oyczyste spominki* II pp. 87–8.
[41] Des Noyers, 27.X.1655 and 12.XI.1655; *Lettres* no. 3, p. 5, no. 6, p. 13.
[42] Instructions for Jan Tański to the estates of Royal Prussia, 21.X.1655; Czart. 927 pp. 408–9. There is no reference to the succession, but Andrzej Leszczyński mentioned the offer in January: A. Leszczyński to John Casimir, Neisse, 20.I.1655; Grabowski, *Oyczyste spominki* II p. 94.
[43] T. Moerner (ed.), *Kurbrandenburgs Staatsverträge. v.1600–1700* (Berlin, 1867) no. 104, pp. 192–4.

Recovery

treaty of Königsberg (17 January 1656) in which he accepted Charles as his feudal suzerain in Ducal Prussia and agreed to remain neutral in the war.[44] This blow was followed by Austria's rejection of the new terms brought by Jan Leszczyński. Rákóczi now seemed the only possible source of aid for the spring campaign.

The continuing need to win foreign support thus forced the Court to consider a Transylvanian candidature. With so much at stake, however, it was determined to keep control of the election campaign and prevent ambitious magnates such as Lubomirski from manipulating the situation to their own advantage. It was this consideration, not John Casimir's supposed preference for a Habsburg, which explains his reluctance to accept a Transylvanian candidature: from the outset, the Court was more flexible in its approach than is usually allowed. The traditional picture of a simple division between a pro-Habsburg group led by the king and a pro-French group led by the queen is seriously distorting. It was not John Casimir but a small group of ecclesiastical senators, led by Andrzej Leszczyński, Trzebicki and Czartoryski, which proved to be the Habsburgs' most loyal supporters. The Court, in contrast, was keen to consider a wide range of candidates. In August 1655, when the plan was first discussed, several possibilities were suggested, including Mattia de' Medici, younger brother of duke Ferdinand II of Tuscany, the elector of Bavaria and Philip William, duke of Neuburg.[45] Each had strong points in his favour. They were all Catholics; Ferdinand-Maria of Bavaria was young and unmarried, while Philip William of Neuburg had been married to John Casimir's late sister, Anne Catherine, and had been suggested by none other than Władysław IV as a potential candidate for the throne.[46] Mattia had won quite a military reputation during the Thirty Years War and was commander of the forces of the grand duchy of Tuscany and a successful governor of Siena.

John Casimir's favourite candidate, far from being a Habsburg, seems from an early date to have been Mattia, with whom he had fought in the Thirty Years War. He had met Mattia again during a brief visit to Florence in 1643 and had spent several months at the Medici Court, where he was received with honour, in 1645.[47] In October 1655, the queen said that since Ferdinand III had not suggested a Habsburg, John Casimir was considering Mattia, to whom he had always inclined, only approaching Austria first because the emperor was more likely to provide support. She told Vidoni that John Casimir wished him to suggest the idea in

---

[44] ibid. nos. 105–7, pp. 195–200.
[45] Vidoni, 9.VIII.1655, TRz. 8418 p. 6. For a long and well-argued case supporting the elector of Bavaria, see the anonymous letter from Munich, possibly from Nowiejski to Jan Leszczyński, dated 23.XII.1655; Czart. 2576 ff. 395–6.
[46] H. Schmidt, *Philipp Wilhelm von Pfalz-Neuburg (1615–1690) als Gestalt der deutschen und europäischen Politik des 17. Jahrhunderts* I (Düsseldorf, 1973) pp. 39–40.
[47] G. Castellani, 'Giovanni Casimiro di Polonia. Tra la porpora e la corona' *La Civiltà Cattolica* 102 (1951) Vol. 3 p. 182. For the 1643 meeting, see *Carta de un Cortesano de Roma para un correspondiente suyo, en que le dà cuenta del fin de los successos de Prencipe Casimiro, hermano del Rey de Polonia, primo de nostro Rey Phelipe III, que viniendo à la guerra de Portugal fue preso en Francia, y de su entrada en la Compaña de Iesus* (1643).

Florence. Vidoni refused, saying he had no orders on this point; the queen pressed him, however, asking if John Casimir had spoken to him about it. Vidoni said not but revealed in his dispatch that this was because the king had indeed spoken to him but had asked him to mention it to nobody, not least the queen. Louise Marie concluded by stating that Mattia would have a good chance of being elected, since he was a Catholic prince, as well respected as any other and especially since the king would consent and help.[48]

John Casimir's reluctance to tell the queen may have stemmed from fears that she was too attached to the idea of a French candidature: in December 1655, Andrzej Leszczyński accused her of trying to promote French interests.[49] Yet there is no evidence at this stage that Louise Marie was committed to a French candidate and her reaction to Mattia showed that she was prepared to consider other possibilities. For the queen, as for John Casimir, it was the achievement of an election which was vital; the identity of the candidate was of secondary importance. Mattia was attractive because he would be less controversial than a Habsburg, yet he might appeal to those senators who favoured an Austrian. At the end of October, John Casimir sounded out the views of bishop Jan Leszczyński, who had responded favourably to the idea. The king later informed Vidoni he was thinking of sending to the Italian princes for aid; the nuncio replied that most were too absorbed in their own affairs and that Ferdinand II would not make a move on his brother's behalf without some positive token of interest.[50]

Contacts with Florence continued, however, until the summer of 1656, with Louise Marie by now involved. In December, des Noyers asked Bouillaud to send him details of Mattia's nativity, saying that he could not say why.[51] In April 1656, Vidoni reported that John Casimir's greatest preference was still for Mattia, 'if Mattia could be persuaded to make up his mind'.[52] Shortly afterwards, in rejecting Rákóczi's pretensions, John Casimir again expressed his interest in Mattia. He was annoyed at the delays and problems which bedevilled contacts with Florence, but his hopes were raised once more in August when Mattia decided to send an envoy to discuss the succession.[53]

Vidoni's role as intermediary in these negotiations demonstrates that the papacy was prepared actively to support any suitable Catholic candidate and was not merely a blind tool of the Habsburgs, as is sometimes suggested. It was keen that the

---

[48] Vidoni, 5.X.1655; TRz. 8418 p. 23.
[49] A. Leszczyński to Grzymułtowski, 18.XII.1655; Czart. 148 no. 182, p. 824; cf. Vidoni, Oppeln, 22.XI.1655; TRz 8418 p. 41.
[50] Vidoni, 27.X.1655; TRz. 8418 p. 30; Mattia was interested, but doubted that anyone apart from the king 'and one or two others' had much enthusiasm for him. Vidoni, 2.XI.1655; TRz 8418 p. 34.
[51] Des Noyers, Oberglogau, 28.XII.1655. BNP FFr. 13019 f. 21. This paragraph is omitted in the published edition: *Lettres* no. 12, pp. 38–40.
[52] Vidoni, 5.IV.1656; TRz. 8419 p. 30.
[53] Vidoni, 24.IV.1656; TRz. 8419 p. 35. Vidoni, 12.VIII.1656; TRz. 8419 p. 67; cf. 'Notitia historiche della Polonia'; BNAR ZBaw. 261 f. 7.

election should succeed but it sought only that a good Catholic be chosen, as Vidoni's instructions following the death of Charles Ferdinand made clear.[54] Vidoni himself considered that the Austrians offered the best hope of aid but this did not mean he opposed other candidates.[55] This attitude did not change. In June 1656 Vidoni, when asked the Pope's view, said he was indifferent so long as the new king were pious and zealous in promoting public order and the interests of the Catholic Church.[56] The Pope was prepared to accept either Neuburg or Mattia, whose 'great merit and valour enable one to hope for the public benefit of that kingdom and of the Catholic religion'.[57]

It was dissension among the Poles themselves which blocked agreement on a suitable Catholic alternative to the Habsburgs. The elector of Bavaria was swiftly ruled out, since it was felt that his candidature would be opposed by Vienna. From the outset, advocates of Mattia and of Neuburg were unable to agree. While the king was strongly inclined to Mattia, he was equally strongly opposed by Andrzej Leszczyński. Vidoni was told in confidence by bishop Jan Leszczyński in October 1655 that Andrzej Leszczyński would not accept Mattia but rather favoured Neuburg who might provide aid and was popular and well-known in the Commonwealth because of his marriage to John Casimir's late sister.[58]

The reasons for this disagreement remain obscure. Although he declared his interest in Neuburg, Andrzej Leszczyński's general attitude suggests that he consistently supported a Habsburg, despite Vienna's reluctance to respond to the succession offers, and that he was unwilling to consider alternatives. The Court, on the other hand, was not keen on Neuburg: as an ally of France, his selection might upset the Austrians and jeopardise chances of Austrian aid. Furthermore, he had family connections with Charles X, who had supported his candidature in the past.[59] Finally, the long-running dispute between Neuburg and Brandenburg over the Cleves-Jülich succession was another complicating factor. John Casimir, despite Frederick William's support of Sweden, still hoped to persuade him to change sides, which might be hindered by a Neuburg candidature; indeed rumours of a planned attack by Neuburg on the elector reached the Polish camp in July 1656, when the king was making a last, desperate appeal to Frederick William to abandon the Swedes.[60] When two Neuburg envoys discussed the possibility of a grand anti-Swedish alliance of Poland, Neuburg, Austria, Denmark and the United Provinces at Krosno in December 1656, Vidoni reported that although the proposal was acceptable to the Catholic Church, it was opposed by Poles who favoured Brandenburg.[61]

---

[54] Instructions to Vidoni, Rome, 19.VI.1655; TRz. 8418 p. 51.
[55] Vidoni, 5.X.1655; TRz. 8418 p. 23; 22.III.1656; TRz. 8419 p. 25.
[56] Vidoni, 27.VI.1656; TRz. 8419 p. 49.
[57] Instructions to Vidoni, Rome, 23.X.1655; TRz. 8418 p. 57.
[58] Vidoni, 27.X.1655; TRz. 8418p. 29–30.
[59] J. Leszczyński to Louise Marie, 24.IV.1656; Czart. 384 ff. 439–40.
[60] Vidoni, 11.VII.1656; TRz. 8419 pp. 55–6.   [61] Vidoni, 23.II.1657; TRz. 8420 p. 12.

After the Deluge

John Casimir's lack of enthusiasm for Rákóczi, therefore, was not primarily motivated by any desire to promote a Habsburg. Indeed, he was still bitter about Vienna's failure to aid the Commonwealth. He rejected a proposal by the Spanish ambassador in Vienna for the candidature of archduke Leopold of Innsbruck, stating that the proposal was only made to hinder other negotiations and should be ignored.[62] Political realities had, nevertheless, to be faced; despite the improved military position it was necessary to choose a candidate who would be able to provide military aid. Mattia might be an attractive figure as far as the Court's political plans were concerned, and he might have good military credentials, but it was unlikely that Tuscany would be able or willing to offer aid on a scale sufficient to expel the Swedes: indeed, in April 1656, des Noyers reported that Mattia's reluctance to commit himself was due to the Polish demand for a large loan as the price of being recognised as John Casimir's successor.[63]

By early 1656, therefore, it looked as if Rákóczi represented the only realistic source of aid, even if John Casimir was unwilling to sanction a candidate supported so enthusiastically by Lubomirski. In his perplexity, he turned to Andrzej Leszczyński for advice. After suggesting that the long delay in the king's return had led Lubomirski's group to appeal to Rákóczi out of desperation, the primate admitted that he found it extremely difficult to decide on the matter. Nevertheless, in the light of the failure of his cousin's mission, which showed that reinforcements were unlikely not only at present but also in the spring, since the imperial forces on the border had gone elsewhere, Leszczyński confronted the reality of Poland's position:

Let nobody imagine that we can revive our fortunes without foreign aid. The Tatars are unreliable: they merely attack, lay waste the land and then return home... Although we now have a firm peace with the Cossacks, we still cannot much trust them. From these sources, however, we would not receive such aid as is necessary for such an enemy, who allows himself to be chased easily enough out of some palatinates, only to transfer the whole weight of war to Prussia and Great Poland, shutting himself up in fortresses to prolong the war. I do not know whom we should approach: I see no aid coming from the Empire and even if it were found, it would come with its usual delay. The king of France, being an ally of the Swedes, cannot rescue us from them, unless by mediation and peace talks, for which we would have to pay with enormous damage to the Commonwealth.

He bluntly stated the position: since Frederick William himself needed reinforcements, it was unlikely he would be able to assist the Poles. There was no quicker or more certain aid than that offered by Rákóczi, who was promising both men and money. While Leszczyński made it plain that he did not like the situation, he suggested that the religious problem should not deter the king:

Religion creates all kinds of obstacles but when all we receive from Catholics are commiserations in place of assistance, we need to seek aid without scruple wherever we can, whence not

---

[62] Vidoni, 25.II.1656; TRz. 8419 p. 17; cf. Vidoni, 16.II.1656, ibid. p. 13; Des Noyers, Oberglogau, 17.II.1656; *Lettres* no. 27, p. 83.
[63] Des Noyers, 13.IV.1656; *Lettres* no. 46, p. 138.

only our political status but our religion can be saved, whence not by oppression but by election we, or our children, will have a king following Your Majesty's death.

He urged John Casimir to consider the dangers if the election and signature of the *Pacta Conventa* were not carried out during his lifetime. His final message was unambiguous: 'If you wish a speedy pacification for yourself and for the Commonwealth do not miss this opportunity and do not withdraw from this adoption.'[64]

Leszczyński was referring not to the candidature of Rákóczi himself but of his son. John Casimir told Vidoni that he would not consider Rákóczi and that if he had to consent to a heretic he would prefer Charles X, who was at least his relation.[65] In his reply to Leszczyński, he expressed his preference for the adoption of Frederick William's son, due to his ties of blood to the Polish people. He proposed that Rákóczi be offered a rich starosty, not the throne, in return for aid, remarking that it was difficult for an old man to change his religion. He expressed his readiness to do anything to save the kingdom, so long as religion was conserved, and emphasised his opposition to any scheme for joint rule. Two kings at once, in his view, could not be tolerated: he was ready to agree to any successor designated with the consent of the estates but was not prepared to allow common rule. Finally, he doubted the ability of Rákóczi to save the Commonwealth. Hungarian troops, in his opinion, were ignorant of modern warfare and therefore of little use: 'If Poles and Tatars fear the crash of firearms, the Hungarians are equally seized with this dread.'[66]

The clash between Lubomirski and the Court was not over the principle of an election but over control of the future king-elect. John Casimir was determined to prevent Rákóczi's election, for he would then face the prospect of a reversionary interest led by a man with whom he had never enjoyed good relations. The king's mistrust of Lubomirski led to his blatant preference for Stefan Czarniecki, the defender of Cracow, as a military leader in 1655–6. Lubomirski, himself a talented soldier, resented such favouritism, but Vidoni considered that the Rákóczi issue was the main cause of ill-feeling.[67] In March Rákóczi's agent reported a violent scene between the king and Wielopolski, one of Lubomirski's closest associates, in which John Casimir angrily declared that he considered as his enemy anybody who offered his crown to anyone, be it Charles X or Rákóczi.[68]

Despite John Casimir's reluctance to accept a Transylvanian candidature, Crown grand secretary Mikołaj Prażmowski was sent to Rákóczi in the spring of 1656, empowered to discuss the succession. His instructions reveal the Court's strong desire to keep control and represent an important step in the development of the election campaign. Prażmowski was to ask for military and financial aid; if Rákóczi

---

[64] A. Leszczyński to John Casimir, 20.I.1656; Grabowski, *Oyczyste spominki* II pp. 91–3.
[65] Leszczyński later asserted that everything he had said in his previous letter had been meant to refer to the son, not the father; A. Leszczyński to John Casimir, 19.II.1656; Temberski, *Roczniki* p. 338; Vidoni, Łańcut, 24.I.1656; TRz. 8419 p. 8.
[66] John Casimir to A. Leszczyński, Sambórz, 4.II.1656; Temberski, *Roczniki* p. 337.
[67] Vidoni, Oppeln, 22.XI.1655; TRz. 8418 p. 8. [68] Zarzycki, *Stosunek* p. 41.

wished anything in return, Prażmowski was to propose the adoption of his son by John Casimir with the hope of the succession. If this was unacceptable, he was to propose the election of the son. Prażmowski was instructed, however, not to agree easily to this. If, nonetheless, he could not avoid it, stringent conditions were to be laid down: the future king was always to live at John Casimir's side, he was to be raised as a Catholic and was to be educated in the laws and customs of the realm. The major officials of his court were to be Poles, appointed by John Casimir, although he could bring his own servants with him. If Rákóczi's candidature were insisted upon, Prażmowski was only to accept as a last resort; this, too, was to be surrounded by conditions so severe that Rákóczi was unlikely to agree: as a Protestant, even if elected, he could not be crowned, he was not to be allowed to come to Poland while John Casimir lived, the estates and citizens of the Commonwealth were to have no dealings with him in the meantime, (a condition plainly directed against Lubomirski), the Transylvanian army could only enter Poland if specifically requested by John Casimir and, finally, Rákóczi could only use the title *Electus Poloniae Rex*.[69]

It was Lubomirski who had first suggested Rákóczi's son as a means of winning support for a Transylvanian candidature. Prażmowski's instructions demonstrate that the Court recognised that this plan offered it a chance of retaining control; indeed, the prospect of an infant candidate might facilitate the achievement of an election *vivente rege*, always the Court's main political goal. The idea would appeal to the Catholic Church more than the candidature of Rákóczi himself, since the child would be brought up as a Catholic, and to senators in general, for he could be educated in the Commonwealth's political traditions. As far as the Court was concerned, however, the important thing was that the king-elect should be subject to its influence: this, indeed, was the main idea behind the scheme, first suggested in connection with the proposed adoption of Rákóczi's son, possibly by Jan Leszczyński, to marry the heir to Louise Marie's niece Anne Henriette, daughter of the queen's sister Anne of Gonzaga and of Edward, son of Frederick V, elector of the Palatinate.[70] This plan, usually seen as proof of selfish concern with dynastic politics on the part of the Court, should be viewed in the context of the factional struggle to control the future king-elect. Henceforth, the Court sought an unmarried candidate, preferably a minor, who could be adopted and married in due course to Anne Henriette. If a minor could not be found, the marriage plan might still provide a means of tying an adult candidate to the Court. It was important, therefore, that an adult candidate should be a bachelor: this was another reason for preferring the unmarried Mattia over the married Neuburg.

For Lubomirski, however, such an outcome would be disastrous. Should Rákóczi's son come directly under Court influence, he could expect no political advantages whatsoever. He rapidly abandoned his support for Rákóczi's son: in January he rejected the adoption idea, arguing instead for the election of Rákóczi

---

[69] Instructions, 10.IV.1656; *Zherela* p. 373.
[70] 'Relacja wojny Szwedzkiej'; Czart. 425 f. 12; printed in Kubala, *Wojna Brandenburska* p. 325, n. 7.

himself, claiming that the Austrian refusal left the Poles with little choice and that it was better to have an elected king who would swear to uphold his subjects' liberties than one who was imposed by conquest, who would make laws as he pleased. He stated that Rákóczi was not prepared to allow his son to be adopted by John Casimir with a view to succeeding. He later expressed outright hostility to the candidature of Rákóczi's son, stating that the Commonwealth ought not to be governed by *un Putto*.[71]

The deep divisions over the Transylvanian candidature made it extremely unlikely that Rákóczi would accept the offer. Prażmowski was pessimistic about his chances of success, only agreeing to go with extreme reluctance. Foreseeing the difficulties he would face he told Vidoni that his instructions were too strict, owing to disagreements between Koryciński and Lubomirski.[72] Prażmowski was right to be pessimistic: he was condemned to a long, frustrating, fruitless stay in Transylvania.

The Court recognised that the time was not yet ripe to implement its election plans and that the Transylvanian candidature was not ideal. Nevertheless, the battle over this issue did much to crystallise Court thinking: henceforward the ideas of adoption and of the Palatinate marriage were central to its strategy. For the moment, however, internal manœuvrings over the succession had once more to take second place to the need to win foreign aid. In the first half of 1656, the Commonwealth's military position had improved, which encouraged hopes that the war might soon be over. By April 1656, the vast majority of Poles had abandoned Charles X, who narrowly avoided a catastrophic defeat when trapped by the Polish and Lithuanian armies in the confluence of the rivers Vistula and San. Czarniecki and Lubomirski defeated Charles's brother, John Adolf, at the battle of Warka on 5 April, while in June the spring campaign was triumphantly crowned by the recapture of Warsaw. Nevertheless, any optimism aroused by these successes was premature. The change in his fortunes merely persuaded Charles to modify his aims and adapt his tactics. Unable to hold the whole of Poland, he now sought to secure control of Livonia and Royal Prussia, thereby returning to the more traditional Swedish policy of seeking to dominate the Baltic coast. Although he had failed to take Danzig, his control of so many important Polish cities, including Cracow, Elbing, Poznań and Thorn, meant that he possessed important bargaining-counters which the Poles were unable to retake owing to their deficiencies in artillery and infantry.

Moreover, Charles was himself using diplomacy to try and force a quick end to the war. In June he finally persuaded Frederick William to support him openly. At the treaty of Marienburg, the elector promised to aid Sweden with all his forces in return for four palatinates in Great Poland, which he was to be granted as sovereign, although he was to remain a Swedish vassal in Ducal Prussia.[73] Shortly afterwards,

---

[71] Vidoni, Lwów, 25.I.1656; TRz. 8419 pp. 16 7; Vidoni, 27.VI.1656; ibid. pp. 49–50.
[72] Vidoni, 25.II.1656; TRz. 8419 p. 17; cf. Vidoni, 16.II.1656; ibid. p. 13.
[73] Moerner, *Kurbrandenburgs Staatsverträge* nos. 109 13, pp. 201 9.

at the battle of Warsaw (28–30 July) the new allies defeated a large force of Poles, Lithuanians and Tatars. John Casimir was forced to abandon his capital once again and withdraw to Lublin. Any thoughts that the Commonwealth might be capable of defeating Sweden unaided had been dispelled by the superiority of the Swedish army displayed at Warsaw. Once again, foreign aid was vital if a quick end to the war were to be achieved. Once again, the succession became an important bargaining-counter. For the next year, thoughts of domestic political advantage had to take second place to diplomatic negotiations; nevertheless, the changing diplomatic situation had important implications for the succession question.

4

The widening conflict: June–December 1656

The second half of 1656 was marked by increased foreign interest in the Polish–Swedish war. French concern was growing at the involvement of Sweden, their most important ally in Germany and the Baltic. Mazarin wished Charles X to play a more active part in imperial politics as an election loomed, and he feared that the Austrian Habsburgs would intensify support for Spain while Sweden was distracted. In the summer of 1656, Antoine de Lumbres was sent to Poland to persuade John Casimir to settle with Sweden; meanwhile d'Avaugour, the French ambassador to Sweden, sought to moderate Charles's demands. De Lumbres was given a frosty reception when he arrived in Warsaw on the eve of the battle; nevertheless, John Casimir told Vidoni that there was a feeling Charles might prove conciliatory and be content with a few Prussian towns, although the attitude of Andrzej Leszczyński and Trzebicki did not lead the nuncio to suppose that the idea had much chance of success.[1]

Some, however, were prepared to listen: de Lumbres suggested that Poland should cede Samogitia to Sweden in exchange for Prussia, which, he reported, was not badly received in some quarters. Immediately after the battle, Charles offered an agreement in order to turn on the Muscovites. Although John Casimir and his ministers initially raised hopes of a settlement by agreeing to talks without mediators, majority opinion was strongly anti-Swedish.[2] Feelings ran high against Charles after the capture of Warsaw and the revelation of the extent of damage and looting carried out by the Swedes during their occupation: '[De Lumbres] constantly pesters us to agree to talks with Sweden but nothing will come of it because they have destroyed everything here: all the palaces, including the royal palace, have been stripped bare; the royal gateway has been razed to the ground and they even wanted to take the statue of Sigismund III'.[3]

Nevertheless, the Commonwealth's military situation was by no means as bad as it had seemed in the immediate aftermath of defeat at Warsaw. The Dutch, worried about the implications of possible Swedish control of Royal Prussia, had sent a fleet to protect Danzig, while John Casimir was able to withdraw to Lublin with his army

[1] Vidoni, 28.VII.1656; TRz. 8419 p. 61.
[2] De Lumbres, 17.XI.1656; CPD I p. 245; Trzebicki to Wilno commissioners, Lublin, 22.VIII.1656; Czart. 386 f. 179; De Lumbres and d'Avaugour to Brienne, Frauenburg, 28.VIII.1656; CPS XXI f. 136.   [3] Letter to Koniecpolski, Częstochowa (1656) AGAD ARadz. II, 21 f. 201.

intact, since Frederick William's refusal to support an offensive into central or eastern Poland and the return of his army to Ducal Prussia frustrated Charles's hopes of forcing a swift military solution. After taking Radom, the Swedish army withdrew to Prussia, giving the Poles time to regroup. In the autumn, John Casimir launched a new campaign, moving north to Danzig to take advantage of the Dutch presence and to put direct pressure on the Swedes. Meanwhile, Gosiewski marched on Ducal Prussia with the main Lithuanian army and a force of Tatars, aiming to force Frederick William to abandon Sweden. It was hoped that this twin strike might bring success, especially since at last there were signs that Austria might be prepared to offer support: reports of the emperor's willingness to consider an alliance reached Lublin on 19 August. Instructions were immediately drawn up for Jan Andrzej Morsztyn for preliminary talks, while a full-scale embassy was planned, to be undertaken by Jan Leszczyński, now palatine of Poznań, and Jan Wielopolski.[4] As it became clear that Charles was unable to follow up his victory at Warsaw, the Polish government rejected talks without Austrian mediation. De Lumbres reacted angrily, threatening that if the plan were not accepted, Sweden would cede Livonia to the tsar to win Muscovite support.[5]

This was an empty threat. By the end of July, John Casimir knew that the Muscovite ambassador to Charles had left Thorn empty-handed: the Swedish successes in 1655–6 had worried Alexis, and although Charles tried not to offend him, relations deteriorated rapidly. In December 1655, the Swedish envoy to Muscovy was told of Alexis's displeasure at Charles's invasion of Poland, and in August 1656, the tsar invaded Swedish-held Livonia and laid siege to Riga. If Muscovy should launch an all-out attack on Sweden, it would reduce a great deal of the pressure on the Commonwealth. De Lumbres admitted that since his first proposals had received a sympathetic hearing, the Poles had received certain news of the rupture between Alexis and Charles, who would now be reduced to a simple defensive campaign; consequently they refused to consider concessions.[6]

These apparently favourable developments brought the Commonwealth little concrete advantage, however. Ferdinand was not concerned enough to send aid immediately: Leszczyński and Wielopolski had to bargain for reinforcements sufficient to defeat Sweden. Moreover, despite the outbreak of hostilities between Sweden and Muscovy, the Muscovite successes of 1654–5 masked the real problems they had faced after the fall of Wilno: plague, which had broken out in 1654, ravaged the country into 1656 and beyond, while hunger and war-weariness threatened a repeat of the serious popular unrest seen in 1648. Galiński, in Moscow in April 1656, reported:

A terrible and considerable devastation ... there is a lawless desert in the towns and villages and especially in the capital itself. The Muscovite waged war on the Commonwealth and the

---

[4] Instructions for Morsztyn to the Emperor, 1656; AGAD, LL33 f. 101 (27.VIII.1656).
[5] J. Leszczyński to Schönhoff, Częstochowa, 9.VIII.1656; Czart. 384 f. 447. Leszczyński replied that the Poles preferred Muscovy to Sweden.   [6] De Lumbres, 17.XI.1656; CPD I f. 245.

The widening conflict

Lord waged war on him in the form of a terrible plague. Food is expensive, especially bread; with the men away at war, the fields were not sown and famine is to be expected in Moscow. The people are strongly opposed to going to war; they have to be driven to it by force, leaving few people in Moscow.[7]

Under such circumstances, Muscovy was in no position to launch a major strike against Sweden. Nevertheless, although the king and the majority on the senate council would have preferred to rely on Austria, Vienna's dilatory approach meant that consideration had to be given to a Muscovite alliance.

Galiński had originally been sent to Muscovy by Paweł Sapieha in the autumn of 1655. On his return, he was sent back, this time on behalf of the government. Leaving Lwów in February 1656, he arrived in Moscow in late April.[8] The optimism aroused by the apparent improvement in Poland's position in the spring of 1656 ensured that a firm line was adopted in his instructions:

We believe that the use of arms is unjustified only in your case and that we bear the scars for our defence of liberty; [your use of arms] is in breach of treaties, is against all considerations of justice and has caused the shedding of Christian blood, for which crime God will be the judge ... The whole world bears witness to our innocence; we insist that we have violated nothing and have broken no agreement.[9]

According to Kubala and Wójcik, Galiński's talks with the Muscovites took place in a friendly atmosphere.[10] Galiński's diary of the expedition, however, paints a different picture: his herald was arrested in Smolensk and only released on the personal intervention of the tsar; Galiński himself was held for two days when six miles from Moscow, only being released on signing a testimony that he was from the king and the senate. When talks finally began, the Muscovites demanded the retraction of Polish complaints at the shedding of blood and burning of churches and the claim that Muscovy was solely responsible for the outbreak of war. They attacked the Poles for not using the tsar's correct titles, which must have seemed strange, considering that Alexis had unilaterally adopted the title of grand duke of Lithuania in 1655. The Muscovites also demanded Wilno, on the grounds that the Poles had lost it as a divine punishment for their sins, a point Galiński was reluctant to concede. Finally, Galiński was prevented from seeing the imperial ambassadors, Lorbach and Allegretti, who were supposed to be mediators.[11]

---

[7] Galiński, 'Transactia ostatniego Rozgoworu z Boiarami Dumnymi, Panem Bohdanem Mateeiewiczem Chytrym [B.M.Khitrovo] ... y Panem Almazem Iwanowiczem [Almaz Ivanov] Canclerzem Przykazu Poselskiego, y ze dwiema Tłumaczami y dwiema Dyakami, w stolicy Aprilla 30 Dnia' Czart. 2103 ff. 139–40.

[8] John Casimir to Alexis, 10.I.1656; Copy, Czart. 384 ff. 429 30; Galiński, 'Transactia ostatniego Rozgoworu' Czart. 2103 f. 137.

[9] 'Summa literarum regiarum ad Magnum Ducem Moschoviae, quibus Senatus suas quoque ad Senatores Moschoviae adiecit' Rudawski, *Historiarum* VI p. 229.

[10] Wójcik, 'Polska i Rosja wobec wspólnego niebezpieczeństwa szwedzkiego' *PODWP* I p. 348; Kubala, *Wojna brandenburska* p. 30.

[11] Galiński, 'Transactia ostatniego Rozgoworu' Czart. 2103 ff. 137–40; Gawlik, 'Projekt unii rosyjsko-polskiej w drugiej połowie XVIIw.' *Kwartalnik Historyczny* 23 (1909) p. 78.

The Muscovites did, however, agree to formal talks, which were to start on the last day of July. Galiński returned with this answer to the royal camp at Warsaw in early June. Instructions were drawn up for the Polish and Lithuanian commissioners in early July, before the battle of Warsaw; they therefore adopted a hard line: a long preamble contained bitter complaints about Muscovite behaviour, while the commissioners were urged to obtain a military alliance against the Swedes as the main priority, with the minimum of territorial concessions.[12] Alexis, however, wanted more than territory in return for an alliance: in August he refused to evacuate any of the occupied lands and demanded his election to the Polish throne in return for an anti-Swedish league. The Poles must have expected such an approach. Alexis had already expressed his interest in April, while there was constant talk in Moscow, where it was expected that Galiński would bring an official offer.[13]

Alexis's interest was by no means welcome; over the next two years, it was seriously to complicate the Court's efforts to use the succession as a means of strengthening royal power. Opinion in the Commonwealth was immediately and bitterly divided over the issue. Many Lithuanians were prepared to support the idea, if only as the quickest means to secure a return to their estates, now under Muscovite occupation. Many Poles, however, led by Koryciński, were horrified at the prospect, feeling that the tsar's election would threaten Polish liberties: 'For although the emperor has done nothing for us to date, it is one thing to ask someone to rescue me and restore me to my former state, another to proclaim as Lord him who invades me...'[14] Koryciński feared for the Polish constitution should the tsar, with his despotic inclinations, be elected. Furthermore, his election would bring the Commonwealth new enemies:

Muscovy has demanded the harsh condition of the election of the tsar himself and of his son after His Majesty's death, or the cession of whole provinces, which we shall be unable to avoid unless [the emperor] sends aid, and quickly at that. Then we should soon deal with Sweden, and Muscovy would be more tractable; otherwise, if we settle with Muscovy and concede the succession, we would have their help against Sweden but in that case the Cossacks, Tatars and Rákóczi with the hospodars [of Moldavia and Wallachia] would certainly declare war on us; this is the reason that Khmelnytskyi will conclude nothing with us; he will only enter a new alliance if we break with Muscovy.[15]

Fear that Alexis might become king convinced Koryciński that it was better to pursue the option of peace with Sweden through French mediation. In common with his colleagues, immediately after the battle of Warsaw he had supported a

---

[12] 'Instrukcya od króla JM komisarzom do traktowania na dnia 10.VIII.1656 z posłami cara mosk. wyznaczonym'. Warsaw, 7.VII.1656; Czart. 386 no. 1, f. 1.
[13] Ex literis Nissa, 18.VI.1656; E. Rykaczewski (ed.), *Relacje Nuncyuszów Apostolskich i innych osób o Polsce od roku 1548 do 1690* (Paris, 1864) II p. 297; Kubala, *Wojna brandenburska* p. 30.
[14] Koryciński to Brzostowski, Lublin, 14.X.1656; Czart. 386 no. 33, f. 140. Printed in part by Kubala, *Wojna brandenburska* dodatek I pp. 392–4.
[15] Koryciński to Pinocci, 14.X.1656; BPANCr. 426 f. 127.

Muscovite peace and opposed talks with Sweden. He wrote to Jerzy Zawisza, the new bishop of Wilno, denying that anything had been agreed with de Lumbres and calling for a quick agreement and an alliance against Sweden. Two days later, he adopted a similar tone, expressing his great joy at the good news contained in the commissioners' first letter (dated 14 August), angrily reporting that the Swedes and Brandenburgers were burning their way to Radom, and stating that the Court was in great suspense waiting for news of the Muscovite talks.[16]

Once the tsar's demands became known, however, Koryciński immediately expressed opposition. The Wilno commissioners received conflicting instructions during August, from Koryciński, Trzebicki and John Casimir. Trzebicki and the king urged the commissioners to make a military alliance their first priority, while Koryciński played down this aspect:

The emperor is still wondering what to do. The king of Sweden has dismissed the Austrian ambassador, saying that he did not want him as a mediator. When the French came to us in Warsaw ... we declared that we were not opposed to peace and that we were willing to have the emperor, the king of France, the Danes and the Dutch as mediators ... We will be able to make of this what we choose.[17]

He sought to avoid any commitment to an attack on Sweden, hoping to keep open as many options as possible by adopting a cautious approach. He urged the commissioners to play for time, claiming optimistically that Austria would invade Brandenburg and Pomerania by early October at the latest and that mutual interest would ensure an agreement with Vienna, in which the emperor would not concern himself with the succession, 'for he sees that it would harm him rather than help him'.[18] He denied that talks were proceeding with the Swedes and urged the commissioners to treat in accordance with their instructions, drawing their attention to the Dutch fleet protecting Danzig.

Nevertheless, Koryciński was already advocating peace with Sweden. Those who supported the offer of the throne to Alexis, such as the Leszczyńskis and Trzebicki, shared Koryciński's doubts about his suitability but were prepared to agree to his candidature as a tactical ploy.[19] Andrzej Leszczyński was angered by Koryciński's proposal for talks with Sweden: 'I do not know that you could find anyone who wishes his country well who would advise Your Majesty to enter [talks with Sweden], considering the inconvenience, danger and downright ruin of the Commonwealth which would ensue'. He saw little chance of any territorial restitutions, 'but rather a ruin of abomination and desolation which the Swedes have created everywhere', arguing that the Commonwealth could not expect reinforcements

---

[16] Koryciński to Zawisza, Lublin, 18.VIII.1656; Czart. 386 no. 26, f. 113; Koryciński to commissioners, 20.VIII.1656; ibid. no. 27, f. 115.
[17] Koryciński to Pinocci, 14.X.1656; BPANCr. 426, p. 127; Kubala, *Wojna brandenburska* pp. 33–4.
[18] Koryciński to Brzostowski, Lublin, 14.X.1656; Czart. 386 no. 33, ff. 140–1.
[19] See B. Leszczyński's long letter to Koryciński, 12.X.1656; AGAD Zbiór Anny z Potockich Branickiej; V, 10, ff. 458–6. Printed with mistakes: Plebański, *Jan Kazimierz Waza* pp. 330–48.

After the Deluge

from the Swedes for any campaign against Muscovy, since they had other interests and could only preserve their international position by waging war.[20]

The Leszczyńskis felt that once a treaty of military cooperation was signed with Muscovy, Austria would join the war as promised on the Polish side; this alliance, it was thought, would be too powerful for the Swedes to resist: they would quickly sue for peace on more reasonable terms and, it was hoped, withdraw from Prussia.[21] If the promise of the succession was necessary to achieve an agreement, then it should be made. In contrast to the offer made to the Habsburgs in 1655, however, when the senate council had been prepared to grant the succession outright, the offer to Muscovy was to be dependent on the calling of a diet, which was to be held as soon as possible. Such a condition at least gave the Poles the chance to play for time: as Jan Leszczyński argued, it would later be possible to withdraw from the election on the grounds that it was illegal and since the Muscovites had done the same when they rejected Władysław IV after having accepted him as tsar in 1610.[22] Meanwhile, the alternative to accepting the Muscovite terms was even worse:

As I understand it to be inevitable that if we do not achieve peace the Commonwealth will be torn apart ... it is better to keep the state together under one lord, even if chosen in a premature election, since an elected king is better than a conqueror and although we would appear to breach ancient custom with regard to elections, the important compensation is not only the restoration of occupied territories but also the conservation of the whole state, so long as we are careful always to conserve the right of free election in the future.[23]

There was another reason for this tactical support for a Muscovite election. Habsburg supporters hoped that acceptance of the Muscovite terms might encourage the Austrians to respond to the Polish offer of the throne in order to prevent the tsar's election, to which Vienna was certainly opposed. It was repeatedly stressed that the Austrian failure to send aid left the Poles no choice but to agree to the Muscovite conditions. There were hopeful signs that Vienna was finally about to respond. In September, after a discussion of the merits of Alexis and Mattia de' Medici as potential candidates, John Casimir told Vidoni that Ferdinand was close to agreeing to a Habsburg candidature and that aid would therefore soon be forthcoming. He felt that a decision was vital for the Austrians, for it did not make sense for Ferdinand to keep his army idle at such great expense.[24]

John Casimir was determined to block any talks with Sweden; accordingly, when de Lumbres arrived in Danzig in mid-November with a new peace offer in which Charles X proposed to exchange Cracow and Thorn for Elbing and Marienburg, he

---

[20] A. Leszczyński to John Casimir, Częstochowa, 18.IX.1656; Czart. 149 no. 117, ff. 377–80.
[21] J. Leszczyński to A. Leszczyński, Breslau, 22.IX.1656; Czart. 384 f. 478.
[22] Vidoni, Wolbórz, 11.X.1656; TRz. 8419 pp. 79–80. Jan Leszczyński made the same point: J. Leszczyński to A. Leszczyński, Breslau, 3.X.1656; Czart. 384 ff. 485–6. Władysław had surrendered his claim at the peace of Polianovka in 1634.
[23] J. Leszczyński to A. Leszczyński, Breslau, 22.IX.1656; Czart. 384 ff. 477–8.
[24] Vidoni, 27.IX.1656 and 4.X.1656; TRz. 8419 pp. 75, 77.

The widening conflict

was accorded a poor welcome by the king, complaining to Mazarin that nobody seemed interested and that he was kept waiting for an audience. John Casimir wished to hear from both Vienna and Wilno before he would even see de Lumbres, who reported that the majority of senators, and especially the Lithuanians, desired peace with Muscovy rather than Sweden. Although Koryciński seemed to prefer the Swedes, he had thereby acquired several enemies, who accused him of having been corrupted by the French.[25] For John Casimir and his supporters, de Lumbres's suggestion that Poland should cede Prussia to Sweden was unacceptable: it was hoped that once the Muscovite treaty was achieved, Sweden would prove unable to resist two such great powers. De Lumbres reported that the Poles did not trust the Swedes, whom they hated so violently that they not only preferred peace with Muscovy but were even ready to elect Alexis or his son.[26]

Nevertheless, de Lumbres's prospects were better than they at first appeared. The key factor was the state of morale in the army, which had been marched north to put pressure on Sweden and Brandenburg. Despite retaking Łęczyca, Kalisz and Chojnice, after its triumphal reception in Danzig on 12 November it showed little desire to fight until it was paid. John Casimir's consequent inability to put pressure on Charles X meant that Gosiewski could not force Frederick William to abandon Sweden, despite his victory at Prostken on 8 October, where he captured Bogusław Radziwiłł, who had thrown in his lot with his cousin Frederick William in 1655. In the absence of military backing from John Casimir, Gosiewski departed from his instructions by ceasing hostilities and opening talks with Frederick William.[27]

John Casimir was concerned that Gosiewski might concede too much to win Frederick William's support and ordered him to follow the instructions sent after his departure from Lublin, which had forbidden the suspension of hostilities until Frederick William abandoned Sweden.[28] Gosiewski, however, was concerned at the possibility of a Muscovite alliance with Brandenburg after Alexis and Frederick William signed a non-aggression pact on 22 September, which he thought would cost Lithuania dear.[29] He wanted peace with Muscovy and a military alliance above all, and was worried by reports that John Casimir was about to settle with the Swedes in Prussia.[30] To prevent this, Gosiewski sought to detach Frederick William from Sweden as quickly as possible, which meant that he was willing to concede far more than John Casimir to obtain an agreement. This was his policy even before his

---

[25] De Lumbres to Mazarin, Danzig, 17.XI.1656; CPD I f. 243; John Casimir to A. Leszczyński, Lublin, 12.IX.1656; Czart. 149 no. 110, ff. 357–8; Masini to Vidoni, Borucin, 13.X.1656; TRz. 8419 p. 122.
[26] De Lumbres to Mazarin, Danzig, 17.XI.1656; CPD I f. 245.
[27] Majewski, 'Bitwa pod Prostkami' *SMHSW* 3 (1956) p. 326; Gosiewski wrote on 16 October informing John Casimir of Frederick William's inclination to negotiate: John Casimir to Gosiewski, 6.XI.1656; BPANCr. 363 f. 233. Worried by Gosiewski's long silence, the king commanded him to carry out his orders.
[28] John Casimir to Gosiewski, 11.XI.1656; BPANCr. 363 f. 231.
[29] Moerner, *Kurbrandenburgs Staatsverträge* no. 114, p. 209.
[30] Gosiewski to unknown, 19.X.1656; BJag. 6357 f. 237.

defeat at Philipowo on 22 October, which made it more likely that major concessions would have to be made to tempt Frederick William away from Sweden. After Philipowo, Gosiewski further dashed royal hopes of forcing Frederick William to abandon Sweden by concluding a three-month armistice at Wierzbołów.[31] This enabled the elector to transfer troops to the Danzig front, further weakening John Casimir's position.

The Court's initial reaction to Wierzbołów was hostile. Louise Marie attacked Gosiewski for the defeat and for allowing Bogusław Radziwiłł to escape instead of executing him as he had been ordered. John Casimir blamed Gosiewski for squandering a magnificent opportunity to force Frederick William to settle on favourable terms and attacked him for not having followed up his victory, for abusing his plenipotentiary powers, for sparing Radziwiłł when he had him in his hands and for the way in which he had conducted the talks with Brandenburg.[32] The king was in no mood to be conciliatory: Gosiewski was to demand that Frederick William should abandon the Swedes immediately and join his forces with those of the Commonwealth, and to insist that the elector accepted his vassal status in Ducal Prussia. In return, all that the king offered was a pardon for having abandoned the Commonwealth.[33]

This hard line was unlikely to succeed. Piwarski suggests that the Polish desire to draw closer to Frederick William was due to pressure from Vienna, which was trying to detach the elector from Sweden, in order to use him to further Austrian policy in the Empire. In this, he alleges, the Court defied public opinion, which called for Frederick William's treason to be punished.[34] In fact, the decision to talk to Brandenburg had been taken before the Austrian ambassador Lisola arrived in Danzig at the end of January, when Austrian delays in coming to Poland's aid made it unpopular. It was military incapacity, not pressure from Austria, which decided Polish foreign policy. Gosiewski did not have sufficient military force to inflict a major defeat on Frederick William, especially after the departure of the Tatars. He had completed his mission of keeping the elector's forces busy and away from Danzig as long as he had been able. If anything further were to be achieved, the main army would have to take a more active role; by the end of October, this seemed increasingly unlikely. Gosiewski was forced to withdraw over the border, where he

---

[31] A. Neuber, *Der schwedisch-polnische Krieg und die österreichische Politik (1655–60)* (Prague, 1915) p. 42; cf. The Prussian *Oberräthe* to the elector, Königsberg, 15.VIII.1656; *Urkunden und Aktenstücke* VIII p. 195.

[32] John Casimir's confessor to Vidoni, 14.XI.1656; TRz. 8419 pp. 103–4; Vidoni, Wolbórz, 11.XI.1656 and 18.XI.1656; TRz. 8419 pp. 90, 93, 96–7; Krzysztof Pac, seeing an opportunity of destroying Radziwiłł power in Lithuania, had urged John Casimir to poison Radziwiłł, or have him killed; John Casimir seems to have agreed, wanting at least to intern Radziwiłł for life. B. Radziwiłł, *Autobiografia* ed. T. Wasilewski (Warsaw, 1979) p. 70.

[33] K. Pac to Gosiewski (undated), *Urkunden und Aktenstücke* VIII p. 196; John Casimir to Gosiewski, Danzig, 22.XI.1656; BPANCr. 363 f. 235.

[34] Piwarski, 'Rywalizacja francusko-austriacka' p. 393 and 'Stosunki szwedzko-brandenburskie a sprawa polska w czasie pierwszej wojny północnej' *PODWP* I p. 446.

The widening conflict

anxiously tried to persuade the Muscovites to send him reinforcements, especially infantry and artillery, since only a third of his force remained, the others having returned home with their booty, and there was no sign of the Tatars, who had promised to return with 7,000 men.[35]

John Casimir was forced to admit that without military aid, Gosiewski could achieve little and had to tell him to keep the armistice for the moment.[36] He told Frederick III of Denmark of his hopes of detaching Frederick William from Sweden but ordered Gosiewski to prepare for the continuation of hostilities on the expiry of the armistice.[37] A few days later, he urged that if Frederick William did not move against Sweden very quickly the armistice should be abandoned as soon as possible:

> Although we have word from that quarter that this armistice is only for show, and that the elector is sending his regiments to help the Swedes against us, we have nevertheless held back our forces on your word from invading [Brandenburg], although they were willing and ready; we will order them to wait a while yet, so that the elector might see that we do not wish to shed blood or see his destruction but we will only do this if ... he settles with us.[38]

He complained at the elector's slowness in sending ambassadors and urged Gosiewski to prepare for military action as soon as the armistice expired, expressing his hope for Muscovite support.[39]

Nevertheless, pressure on Frederick William to desert the Swedes was increasing: from his wife, from a majority of his councillors, and from the Dutch; furthermore, Muscovy threatened that he would no longer be considered neutral if he did not do so.[40] Despite signing the treaty of Labiau with Sweden on 20 November, in which Charles recognised Frederick William as sovereign in Ducal Prussia, the elector did little to fulfil his obligations.[41] Having obtained recognition of sovereignty from Sweden, there was little reason for him to support Charles further, especially since Swedish designs in Royal Prussia constituted a direct threat to his own interests. Frederick William was now more interested in gaining recognition from his true feudal superior, John Casimir. The pro-Swedish Waldeck was dropped from the elector's council in favour of Schwerin and immediately after Labiau Hoverbeck wrote to Jan Leszczyński, who had always seen Brandenburg as a potential saviour of the Commonwealth, to explore the possibility of a settlement.[42]

Pressure was growing in Danzig for peace with Sweden, however. If the Court

---

[35] Gosiewski to unknown, 19.X.1656; BJag. 6357 f. 237.
[36] Vidoni, Wolbórz, 7.XII.1656; TRz. 8419 p. 105. John Casimir to Gosiewski, Danzig, 24.XI.1656 and 1.XII.1656; BPANCr. 363 ff. 237, 239.
[37] John Casimir to Frederick III, 29.XI.1656; *Polonicae ex Archivo Regni Daniae* III Elementa ad Fontium Editiones XX, ed. C. Lanckorońska and G. Steen Jensen (Rome, 1969) p. 198; John Casimir to Gosiewski, 1.XII.1656; BPANCr. 363 f. 239.
[38] John Casimir to Gosiewski, Danzig, 4.XII.1656; BPANCr. 363 f. 241.
[39] John Casimir to Gosiewski, 20.XII.1656; BPANCr. 363 f. 244.
[40] De Lumbres and d'Avaugour to Mazarin, Danzig, 2.XII.1656; CPD I f. 253.
[41] Moerner, *Kurbrandenburgs Staatsverträge* no.115a, p. 211.
[42] Hoverbeck to J. Leszczyński, 21.XI.1656; Czart. 388 f. 5.

was still fully committed to war, Koryciński was by no means isolated in his support for peace talks, as is sometimes argued; indeed he claimed that most Poles supported him.[43] It was reported from Danzig that a major split was emerging between Lithuanians, who wanted to settle with Alexis, and Poles, a large number of whom wished peace with Sweden. Support for peace with Sweden was motivated by more than simple fear of a Muscovite election: while all were agreed on fighting the Swedes if the emperor should join the coalition, reports from Jan Leszczyński in Vienna suggested that there was little hope of an agreement.[44]

The army remained the most important source of support for peace with Sweden. Its leaders and a large number of others urged John Casimir to settle. More alarmingly, Austrian unpopularity was so intense that some even talked of joining Sweden in an anti-Habsburg league:

> It does not seem that anything more than promises can be expected from the Pope and even if his intentions and efforts are still good, nevertheless, in the council summoned by the king, His Majesty had to defend the Pope since opinion in the army suggests that he does not care for the interests of the Catholic Church.[45]

The efforts of the Court, Andrzej Leszczyński, Lubomirski and Trzebicki to counter proposals for peace with Sweden were in vain: the army commanders were ready to settle whatever the cost, talking of an anti-Austrian league comprising Poland, Sweden, Brandenburg and Rákóczi. Confederation was in the air and Vidoni was worried that Poland might see a second Cromwell or Khmelnytskyi.[46] There were attacks on Austrian supporters, including Andrzej Leszczyński, and Vidoni despairingly remarked that 'things are going from bad to worse, as crimes remain unpunished, while neither merit nor virtue is rewarded and ... there are more rebels than loyal subjects'.[47]

The problem was that John Casimir and Trzebicki were isolated in Danzig, since the queen had returned to Silesia following the army's departure from Lublin. Although Pac opposed peace with Sweden, there were too few Lithuanians in Danzig to counteract its supporters: Pac complained that the three Lithuanians present were always outvoted by the six Poles on the council, led by Koryciński, who were even ready to cede Lithuanian territory to Alexis to avoid a Muscovite succession.[48] Potential supporters of peace with Muscovy were absent: Jan Leszczyński was in Vienna, and although Louise Marie and Andrzej Leszczyński were on their way to join the king, the presence of Swedish troops in the vicinity meant that

---

[43] Koryciński to unknown, 1656; Czart. 149 no. 185, f. 671; cf. Wójcik, 'Polska i Rosja wobec wspólnego niebezpieczeństwa szwedzkiego' *PODWP* I p. 361.
[44] Unknown to Orsini *Collectanea* XIV p. 47. The letter is undated, but is clearly written in the autumn of 1656; de Lumbres and d'Avaugour to Mazarin, Danzig, 24.XI.1656; CPD I f. 249.
[45] Unknown to Orsini, 1656; *Collectanea* XIV p. 48.
[46] Vidoni, Wolbórz, 1.XII.1656; TRz. 8419 p. 101. Potocki and Lanckoroński wished the army to enter winter quarters in Great Poland; Kersten, *Stefan Czarniecki* pp. 317–18.
[47] Vidoni, Wolbórz, 1.XII.1656; TRz. 8419 pp. 101–2.
[48] K. Pac to Brzostowski, 23.IX.1656; Czart. 386 no. 38, f. 159.

The widening conflict

they were unable to complete their journey and had to stay in Kalisz. John Casimir and Trzebicki argued with spirit and were able to prevent any binding resolution being adopted, nevertheless, it was questionable how much longer they could resist pressure for peace talks. John Casimir urged Louise Marie to come to Danzig as soon as possible. Meanwhile, however, he had to inform Vidoni of Charles X's expressions of goodwill and offers of peace preliminaries, and express his hopes for peace.[49]

The divisions between Poles and Lithuanians were worrying. The Lithuanians resented Polish opposition to a treaty with Muscovy and accused the Poles of attempting to sabotage the talks. In April, Galiński had already complained to Krzysztof Pac that the instructions he had been given by the senate council represented a grave obstacle to the achievement of an agreement, claiming that his hands had been tied by the senate council, which allowed him to agree nothing of import.[50] Pac was angered by the activities of Koryciński, who was in a unique position to hinder the talks: following the death of K.L. Sapieha, the Lithuanian vice-chancellor, and the illness of the grand chancellor, Albrycht Stanisław Radziwiłł, who was also shortly to die in his Prussian exile, Koryciński had temporary charge of the Lithuanian chancery, an opportunity which he used to frustrate the negotiations:

But several noble lords [from Poland], especially he who has temporary charge of the chanceries of Lithuania... are placing great obstacles in the path of a settlement; frequently, it is said, declarations intended for you have been changed; he almost succeeded in blocking that first proposal concerning the election, wishing rather to treat with the Swedes, although this certainly will not happen.[51]

A month later, Pac apologised for the complaints reaching the commissioners from the Court, claiming that they did not reflect John Casimir's view and complaining at interference of the Polish chancery in Lithuanian affairs.[52]

There was good reason to fear that a failure to reach agreement with Muscovy might provoke the Lithuanians into unilateral action and even bring about the collapse of the union: Lithuanians were talking of a separate treaty if the Poles refused to settle.[53] Reports indicated that this was no idle threat, as individuals took matters into their own hands: fearing prison, some had submitted to Alexis and sworn oaths of allegiance; others had accepted baptism into the Orthodox Church.[54] Krzysztof Pac's brother Mikołaj was among those who went over to the Muscovites. John Casimir found such reports worrying, fearing that talks with Sweden would bring the loss of all Lithuania 'for Lithuanians must look to their own fortunes'.

[49] Masini to Vidoni, Danzig, 21.XI.1656. TRz. 8419 p. 258.
[50] Galiński, 'Transactia ostatniego Rozgoworu' Czart. 2103 f. 138.
[51] K. Pac to Brzostowski, 23.IX.1656; Czart. 386 no. 38, f. 159.
[52] K. Pac to Brzostowski, 29.X.1656; Czart. 386 no. 40, f. 170.
[53] Vidoni, Lublin, 13.IX.1656; TRz. 8419 p. 72.
[54] Galiński, 'Transactia ostatniego Rozgoworu' Czart. 2103 ff. 140, 143.

Poland would also face the prospect of war with Muscovy 'which would reach the very gates of Warsaw'.[55]

Opponents of a Muscovite alliance failed to prevent the commissioners from reaching a settlement with Muscovy, signed at Niemież near Wilno on 3 November.[56] A last-minute attempt to secure the candidature of the tsar's infant son, rather than that of Alexis himself also failed: Trzebicki told the commissioners that agreement would be far easier to achieve in the Commonwealth for the tsarevich than for the tsar himself, and urged them to point out the difficulties that one man would face in ruling such a large state. In late November, before he knew the terms agreed at Wilno, John Casimir wrote that many senators saw only great problems with the tsar's candidature.[57] Nevertheless, the commissioners were grudgingly given permission to promise that a diet would be held as soon as possible to elect the tsar to the Polish throne. In return, Alexis promised his full commitment to the war against Sweden.

There have been some rather optimistic assessments of the significance of the treaty of Wilno. Lewitter suggested that an agreement was desirable for Poles and particularly for Lithuanians, since it promised security in the east. Gawlik regarded the treaty as the product of open and honest talks and a genuine desire for union. This assumption of the existence of substantial support leads Gawlik to explain the subsequent failure of the treaty in terms of foreign interference. This is a view accepted by Korzon and Wójcik, who saw Poland as being caught up in the 'whirlwind' of French and Austrian policy which sought in common, despite their opposition on most points, to block any union, especially since, he argues, both France and Austria were seeking to place their own candidates on the Polish throne.[58]

Historians working in the 1950s had perforce to present Polish–Russian relations in a favourable light. Wójcik's later assessment of Wilno, freed from some of these constraints, is more realistic, recognising that it was not based on firm foundations.[59] There was a large body of Polish opinion which not only opposed the tsar's succession but also further hostilities against Sweden, while Wilno did nothing to resolve the fundamental disputes dividing the two sides: the Muscovite occupation of Lithuania and the status of the Ukraine. Consideration of these issues, at the suggestion of the Muscovites, was postponed to the next diet along with the equally thorny problem of the succession, something which the Poles eagerly accepted,

---

[55] John Casimir to A. Leszczyński, Lublin, 12.IX.1656; Czart. 149 no. 110, p. 358; cf. A. Leszczyński to John Casimir, Częstochowa, 18.IX.1656; ibid. no. 117, ff. 377 8.
[56] Text: AGAD APPot. 45 ff. 118–22; AGAD ARadz. II, 21 pp. 281–2, 284, 289; Rudawski, *Historiarum* VII pp. 282–4.
[57] Trzebicki to commissioners, 9.IX.1656; Czart. 386 no. 45, f. 183; John Casimir to commissioners, 25.XI.1656; ibid. no. 57, f. 219.
[58] L. Lewitter, 'The Russo-Polish treaty of 1686 and its antecedents' *Slavonic and East European Review* 9 (1964) p. 9; Gawlik, 'Projekt unii' p. 108; Korzon, *Dola i niedola* I p. 159; Wójcik, 'Polska i Rosja wobec wspólnego niebezpieczeństwa szwedzkiego' p. 370.
[59] Wójcik, *Traktat Andruszowski* p. 26.

The widening conflict

since it offered endless possibilities of procrastination and they could be confident that the diet would never consent.

Nevertheless, the commitment made at Wilno to elect Alexis as John Casimir's successor was a serious obstacle to the realisation of Court plans to use the succession to improve its domestic position. Its original hope that it might persuade Alexis to allow the candidature of the tsarevich, who might fulfil the role previously assigned to Rákóczi's son, were soon dashed when Alexis insisted on his own candidature, despite the willingness he had expressed in April to consider the possibility of his son's election and even of his education as a Catholic.[60] Almost as soon as the treaty was signed, the Court began to seek ways to postpone the diet:

> The diet which is to be held in January, so they say, will be of great consequence and will be extremely turbulent... I fear it for the fatigue it is bound to cause me. All the pretenders to the succession will be intriguing; the Muscovites act openly, our Austrian and Transylvanian neighbours intrigue publicly and secretly.[61]

Those who had supported a settlement with Muscovy on tactical grounds, including Louise Marie, Lubomirski and Andrzej Leszczyński, agreed that it was essential to avoid holding a diet, which was bound to prove controversial, as long as possible.[62] It was hoped that the diet could be postponed until March, in order to await developments elsewhere. The queen was determined to stop the election of the tsar, and talked of persuading France, Denmark, Rákóczi and the sultan to campaign for the maintenance of the right of free election and against the tsar's succession.[63]

There were signs that such a policy might be popular in the long run, even among Lithuanians. For Wilno changed nothing essential in Polish–Muscovite relations: the two sides were united solely by common hostility to Sweden. The treaty, despite its pious phrases, brought no close military cooperation: both sides continued much as before; indeed, Alexis withdrew his forces from Riga, while the non-aggression pact he had signed with Brandenburg in September provoked doubts as to his commitment to fighting Poland's enemies. At least the promise of the succession meant that the Commonwealth had avoided territorial concessions in Lithuania or the Ukraine. Nevertheless, despite the optimism of the commisioners, who wrote to John Casimir of their hopes for an evacuation of Lithuania at least as far as the Berezina river before the diet, the Muscovites showed no signs of moving before they were sure of the succession.[64] Even Krzysztof Pac, long Koryciński's bitter opponent and a strong advocate of peace with Muscovy, approached de Lumbres, swearing that he was a supporter of France by inclination.[65]

[60] Vidoni, 27.IX.1656; TRz. 8419 p. 75; Louise Marie told Pac of her willingness to adopt the tsarevich as her own son to preserve the Catholic faith and the rights and liberties of the nobility, including the right of free election; Czart. 386, no. 35, ff. 148–9. In April, Alexis had been willing to consider such a scheme: Rykaczewski (ed.), *Relacje Nuncyuszów Apostolskich* II p. 297.
[61] Louise Marie to Mme de Choisy, 12.XI.1656; BNP FFr. 3859 f. 11.
[62] Vidoni, 18.XI.1656; TRz. 8519 pp. 95–6.
[63] Vidoni, Wolbórz, 13.XII.1656; TRz. 8519 pp. 106–7.
[64] Commissioners to Koryciński, 13.XI.1656; Czart. 2113 f. 102.
[65] De Lumbres to Mazarin, Danzig, 8.XII.1656; CPD I f. 258.

Pac's support for Wilno and a Muscovite alliance did not result from any great desire for a union but was motivated by tactical considerations just as much as the Court's. Lithuanians were well aware of the nature of Muscovite rule; Lithuanian dietines had already complained to John Casimir in August about Muscovite demands for total submission.[66] If the Muscovites were not prepared to evacuate Lithuania as Pac had hoped, then it might be necessary to explore the possibility of a swift peace with Sweden. Pac was receptive to de Lumbres's suggestion that Ferdinand III only desired a prolongation of the Polish–Swedish war in an attempt to prevent war breaking out in Germany.[67] Such an outcome was the last thing Pac wanted. De Lumbres was assured that the commissioners had exceeded their powers at several points and that the treaty would not take effect until ratified by the king and the senate council.[68] If the Muscovites could not be persuaded to evacuate Lithuania, it was essential to avoid a long war with Sweden. Without rejecting Wilno outright, Pac began to sound out de Lumbres on the possibility of a quick peace with Sweden.

The attraction of such a policy was increased by Jan Leszczyński's failure to win large-scale support from Austria. Austrian delays and prevarication caused Leszczyński to regret ever having come to Vienna.[69] When an agreement was eventually signed, its terms were desperately disappointing. In the treaty of Vienna of 1 December, Austria offered a mere 4,000 men, all of whom were to be paid by the Commonwealth.[70] The failure to persuade Ferdinand III to commit himself to the war on any significant scale was a great blow to those who saw Austria as the Commonwealth's saviour. Their policy had failed: neither Austria nor Muscovy had produced aid on the scale necessary to defeat the Swedes, while few had any desire to put Wilno into effect. Yet if they did not, the Commonwealth faced the hostility of Muscovy as well as Sweden and the renewed danger of partition.

Despite the failure of hopes in the Austrians and despite his opposition to the implementation of Wilno, John Casimir was reluctant to settle with Sweden, the attitude of the army notwithstanding. Nevertheless, he could not resist pressure for a new approach to Sweden through de Lumbres, although he did what he could to ensure that concessions were minor: he was unwilling to cede territory, although he was prepared to surrender the title of king of Sweden.[71] Vidoni accurately summarised John Casimir's predicament: 'The king is now shut up in Danzig like a prisoner and talks both of making peace on the enemy's terms and of fighting, which the army

[66] John Casimir to commissioners, Lublin, August 1656; Czart. 386 no. 6, f. 27.
[67] De Lumbres to Mazarin, Danzig, 15.XII.1656; CPD I f. 265.
[68] De Lumbres to d'Avaugour, Danzig, 18.XII.1656; CPD I f. 266.
[69] J. Leszczyński to B. Leszczyński, Vienna, 22.XI.1656; Czart. 385 f. 520.
[70] Wójcik, *Traktaty polsko-austriackie* document I pp. 31–5. It was too late to save Austria's reputation in Poland; many echoed Vidoni's opinion that if it had come a year earlier, the war would already have been over: Vidoni, 27.I.1657; TRz. 8420 p. 5.
[71] Pufendorf, *De rebus a Carolo Gustavo* IV p. 250. De Lumbres believed he could persuade John Casimir to change his mind on territorial concessions. De Lumbres to Mazarin, Danzig, 8.XII.1656; CPD I ff. 257–8.

The widening conflict

does not want, finally of the dangers of trying to escape'. While de Lumbres hoped to bring about a meeting of the two kings, John Casimir wrote secretly to Louise Marie that the Swedes were traitors worse than Turks or Tatars and urged her not to trust the French, who appeared too partial to the enemy.[72] Yet in the absence of effective aid from Austria or Muscovy, there was little else he could do.

Hopes for a quick settlement with Sweden were soon dashed, however. Charles X was in no mood to accept the Polish terms and was already seeking to break the deadlock by launching a new diplomatic initiative designed to attract foreign support through a new plan to partition the Commonwealth. The treaty of Labiau had been the first expression of this new policy; he now looked towards the Cossacks and Transylvanians, who had signed a treaty of eternal friendship in September.[73] Rákóczi, despite Lubomirski's efforts, had long been in contact with Sweden. Charles had at various times tempted him with promises of Polish territory, which Rákóczi was to rule as Sweden's vassal. In the autumn of 1656 rumours of renewed Polish offers of the succession to the Habsburgs persuaded him to turn a more favourable ear towards Sweden. On 6 December, Sweden and Transylvania signed the treaty of Radnot, which envisaged a partition of the Commonwealth: Rákóczi was to take much of Little Poland and Lithuania, with the title of king of Poland and grand duke of Lithuania; the Cossacks were to take the Ukraine; Brandenburg was to receive the parts of Great Poland it had already been granted in the treaty of Marienburg, while Sweden was to receive Royal Prussia.[74] If Frederick William still showed no sign of offering Charles his active support, the bait proved enough to tempt Rákóczi: on 22 January 1657, he entered Poland with an army of 41,000.

Rákóczi's invasion radically altered the military and diplomatic situation and provoked a fundamental reappraisal by the various factions in the Commonwealth. Once more, hopes of a diplomatic settlement had been dashed: if peace were to be achieved, a military solution was necessary. Furthermore, the rejection of hopes for a quick peace with Sweden brought renewed tension between Poles and Lithuanians, as the latter revived demands for a swift implementation of Wilno. Once more, the future was deeply uncertain; once more it was vital to attract more substantial and effective foreign aid than that granted in the treaties of Vienna and Wilno. At least the threat from Rákóczi spurred the army into activity; in February, it moved south to confront the new invader, abandoning Prussia for the moment to the Swedes. The Commonwealth was again fighting for its very existence, with no agreement as to the best means of salvation. In order to decide on the political and diplomatic line to be adopted, John Casimir called an extraordinary convocation of senators and representatives of the *szlachta* to assemble at Częstochowa. Here, he hoped, he would find sufficient support to reject the calls for an ignominious surrender to Sweden.

[72] Vidoni, Kalisz, 19.I.1657; TRz. 8420 p. 3. [73] Szilágyi *Transsylvania* II pp. 110–15.
[74] ibid. pp. 190–6.

5

Constructing a coalition: January–December 1657

The new Swedish coalition destroyed French hopes for a quick negotiated settlement. Koryciński complained to de Lumbres that he had been deceived, since Charles X had shown himself little inclined to peace: the more Poland conceded, the more hardline Sweden's position became. He dwelt on the efforts he had made to persuade the Poles to settle and stressed the reproaches he had suffered for delaying the Muscovite talks: 'This gives good sport to his enemies and to those who wish to criticise his conduct. He reproaches himself for the credulity which he has shown towards the Swedish proposals.' Despite de Lumbres's attempts to console him with news of *les civilités* which Mazarin was offering him, the chancellor continued to show much resentment.[1] French hopes of mediating peace in the short term were dead: Charles merely temporised, demanding that John Casimir call a diet to approve the powers of the Polish commissioners. John Casimir told de Lumbres that if no reply were forthcoming by the end of January, he would leave Danzig to put Wilno into effect.[2] When the reply finally came in March, after the meeting of Charles and Frederick William at Preussisch-Holland, it offered new talks, but although Charles hinted that he might be prepared to evacuate Poland for the right price, there was no indication of a major change of heart. Koryciński wrote angrily to Mazarin of his disappointment, claiming that the talks had failed because the Swedes did not treat honestly and lacked faith in a successful outcome.[3]

Foreign military aid was still essential. The government's most pressing task at Częstochowa was, therefore, to secure support for its preferred policy of a new approach to the Habsburgs, without exacerbating the existing divisions among senators. While Lithuanians reaffirmed their faith in Wilno and urged its swift implementation as the only hope of achieving a return to their estates, the Court, and those Poles who had supported Wilno on tactical grounds, had begun to reconsider. The treaty had failed to attract immediate large-scale Muscovite support, which it was now clear would only be forthcoming after the diet had ratified Wilno, a prospect which few relished. If the implementation of Wilno were to be avoided, however, it was vital to find an alternative source of support. It was to be hoped that the prospect of Alexis on the Polish throne and the threat posed to Austrian interests in Hungary by Rákóczi's alliance with Sweden might induce the Habsburgs to take a

[1] De Lumbres to Mazarin, Danzig, 12.I.1657; CPD I f. 286.
[2] De Lumbres to Mazarin, 19.I.1657; Harl. 4532 ff. 7–8.
[3] Koryciński to Mazarin, Danzig, 9.II.1657; CPP XI f. 189.

more positive line; the treaty of Vienna, inadequate though it was, and the movement of Austrian troops to the Silesian border indicated that Ferdinand might at last be concerned enough to act.

The first essential was to persuade Ferdinand to offer more support than he had agreed to provide in December. Although Lisola had been warmly welcomed by the king when he arrived in Danzig at the end of January, his reception generally was not so cordial. De Lumbres encouraged anti-Austrian feeling by spreading the story that the Poles had signed a treaty to elect archduke Leopold William to the Polish throne. Austrian policy was criticised even by those who were generally well disposed to Vienna: Lisola reported that John Casimir and senators of every faction believed that Austrian aid was far too little and far too burdensome to have any great value or general utility.[4] The government was wary of committing itself to the Habsburg alliance when the level of support it afforded was so small, especially since ratification might drive Muscovy into a league with Sweden. Given the Commonwealth's problems in paying its own army, few believed that it would be possible to support even the small number of troops the Austrians appeared willing to send. Led by Koryciński, the senators in Danzig refused to ratify the treaty, on the grounds that there were not enough present to do so. Lisola was constantly attacked over the terms and doubted whether he would secure ratification.[5] He was not told of the failure of the French peace initiative, while it was stressed that ratification was conditional on the Austrians agreeing better terms. The Poles demanded an immediate 12,000–15,000 men to face Rákóczi and requested that Vienna respond at once, otherwise peace would be made with Sweden.[6]

The king was anxious to head south and join forces with the queen and the Leszczyńskis, who were more favourably disposed towards Austria. He left Danzig on 10 February and arrived at Częstochowa on 2 March.[7] Many senators had gathered before the king's arrival, which gave them a chance to discuss the issues before the convocation formally opened on 3 March. The Leszczyńskis were angry at the refusal of the Danzig senators to ratify Vienna. Jan Leszczyński condemned Koryciński's campaign to block Wilno, criticising him for 'trumpeting the cause of war with Muscovy'.[8] He felt that the talks with Sweden breached the decisions of the senate council taken earlier in the year and had increased Austrian uncertainty.[9] The Leszczyńskis had, nevertheless, been unsure of the king's attitude, even if they wished no hint of this to reach Vienna. Andrzej Leszczyński told Vidoni that he was

---

[4] Lisola, Danzig, 3.II.1657; *Berichte* no. 51, p. 232. 'Summa eorum quae Consiliarius Aulicae Camerae Caesar. Franciscus de Lisola sermo. Poloniae Regi ac Excell. Dmi. Senatoribus ppsuit. die 3 Februar 1657' AGAD AKW Cesarskie k.25a 1 no. 6, p. 1.
[5] Lisola, Częstochowa, 5.III.1657; *Berichte* no. 53, p. 241; Vidoni, 27.I.1657; TRz. 8420 p. 5.
[6] Walewski, *Historia wyzwolenia* II pp. 27, 31; Kubala, *Wojna brandenburska* p. 111.
[7] Kersten, *Stefan Czarniecki* p. 328; there is no evidence to support Nani's assertion that he arrived on 24 February; Nani to Signori, *Zherela* p. 450. For his arrival on 2 March, see Chronicle of Zygmunt Koniecpolski, Częstochowa, 2.III.1657; BPANCr.1056 f. 58.
[8] J. Leszczyński to A. Leszczyński, Breslau, 8.I.1657; Czart. 388 no. 10, f. 19.
[9] J. Leszczyński to Lubomirski, Częstochowa, 14.II.1657; Czart. 388 no. 26, f. 40.

determined to combat Koryciński and all thoughts of peace with Sweden, complaining that the king and his advisors wished to destroy themselves and everybody else. He was worried that the king might make concessions to Sweden to obtain peace, including the possible cession of Danzig or Royal Prussia.[10]

The Leszczyńskis were prepared for a confrontation but were unsure of the attitude of Lubomirski and Piotr Gembicki, bishop of Cracow, who had opposed the offers made to Austria in 1655–6.[11] Leszczyński was worried that if Lubomirski supported peace with Sweden, ratification would fail. Lubomirski arrived in Częstochowa on 27 February.[12] The discussions which followed were heated but although there were many objections to ratification it was accepted in the end. Leszczyński was pleased with the outcome and assured Cieciszewski, the Polish resident in Vienna, that the ratification would be sent by the next post, after John Casimir's arrival, expected the following day.[13]

Evidently the betrayal of his trust by Rákóczi had persuaded Lubomirski that only the Habsburgs could now save the Commonwealth. Although Jan Leszczyński expected further opposition from Koryciński, Lubomirski's support reassured him that the chancellor would not succeed in blocking ratification, which he was confident John Casimir would accept.[14] He was proved right: despite the inadequacy of Austrian aid, the treaty was ratified on 7 March, although Bogusław Leszczyński was to go to Vienna with plenipotentiary powers to negotiate better terms.

The Court did not rely merely on the dramatic deterioration in the Commonwealth's military position to induce Vienna to send more aid: once again the throne was to be offered to the Habsburgs. Faced with the prospect of having to implement Wilno, the Court and Austrian supporters sought an alternative to the Muscovite election. Although Ferdinand had rejected the earlier offer, he was known to oppose the tsar's candidature, which might persuade him to send substantial reinforcements and to accept the new approach in order to preempt Alexis. From the Court's point of view, an Austrian candidature fitted better with its wider plans for reform: Ferdinand's second son Charles Joseph was young enough for plans of adoption by John Casimir and marriage to Louise Marie's niece to be feasible and, as a Catholic, would have the backing of the Church. Finally, there was good reason to hope that the prospect of a Muscovite succession might overcome traditional hostility to an Austrian candidature.

The offer was not, however, officially approved by the Częstochowa convocation. It was formally proposed by John Casimir and opposed by Koryciński, but no firm commitment was made, which angered the king, who complained bitterly about

---

[10] Vidoni, Częstochowa, 9.II.1657; TRz. 8420 pp. 6, 8.
[11] J. Leszczyński to Cieciszewski, Breslau, 12.I.1657; Czart. 388 no. 12, f. 22.
[12] Vidoni, Avvisi, Częstochowa, 3.III.1657; TRz. 8420 p. 199.
[13] J. Leszczyński to Cieciszewski, Częstochowa, 1.III.1657; Czart. 388 no. 43, ff. 59–60.
[14] J. Leszczyński to Cieciszewski, Częstochowa, 15.II.1657; Czart. 388 no. 27, f. 42; J. Leszczyński to Cieciszewski, Częstochowa, 1.III.1657; Czart. 388 no. 43, f. 60.

Koryciński's behaviour.[15] Nevertheless, there was concern that an Austrian candidature would alienate Lithuanians, who still saw the Muscovite succession as essential if they were to secure a return to their estates. Jerzy Zawisza, Krzysztof Pac and possibly Teodor Lacki were the only Lithuanians present, but Zawisza had been the leader of the Wilno commissioners and the Lithuanians could expect the support of Krasiński, who had been the Polish representative at the Wilno talks and was a strong supporter of the treaty.

There was much in Court policy in early 1657 to worry Lithuanians. Bąkowski had been dispatched to Moscow in January to apologise for the failure to hold a diet, offering Rákóczi's invasion and an outbreak of plague in excuse.[16] Meanwhile, John Casimir berated the Wilno commissioners for their indifference to the question of military cooperation, despite his frequent instructions that this was the *sine qua non* for an agreement.[17] Zawisza was worried that the convocation would reject Wilno and warned that Lithuanians would accept Alexis as their ruler if the Poles failed to agree to a joint peace. A group of Lithuanians, meeting in Brest under Paweł Sapieha, also expressed support for Wilno, urging John Casimir to reassure the tsar over the lack of progress towards its implementation.[18]

The Court had to take account of such sensibilities. To have pushed the Austrian succession too enthusiastically would have been to risk an open breach and an alliance between Lithuanians and anti-Austrian elements in Poland which might jeopardise the Court's election plans. As it was, Lithuanians still blamed Koryciński for the problems surrounding the Wilno negotiations and for attempting to block the implementation of the treaty. When the convocation discussed relations with Muscovy, there were serious differences of opinion, but it was decided to accept Wilno, which, John Casimir told Vidoni, was unavoidable.[19] The Wilno commissioners and supporters of the treaty had argued their case forcefully. In the face of such strength of feeling, supporters of an Austrian succession had to act circumspectly: there could be no question of adding to the Commonwealth's enemies by alienating Alexis through an offer of the crown to the Habsburgs while opinion remained so divided. Until such time as Ferdinand committed himself, it was necessary to keep any succession offer secret. Austria was still widely unpopular and the election plan could only succeed if the Habsburgs offered substantial and effective aid.

Such considerations induced the Court to confine knowledge of the plan to a few sympathetic senators. Louise Marie had outlined Court tactics to Vidoni a few days before the convocation opened. She said that both Alexis and Charles Joseph had their supporters; Vidoni replied that the latter would be better for the Catholic

---

[15] Vidoni, 26.III.1657; TRz. 8420 p. 17.
[16] Instructions to Bąkowski, Danzig 20.I.1657; AGAD LL.33 f. 98.
[17] John Casimir to commissioners, Danzig, January 1657; Czart. 150 f. 8.
[18] Vidoni, Częstochowa, 16.II.1657; TRz. 8420 p. 10; 'Puncta na Convocatiey Brzeskiey WXL Concludowane dnia 17.III.1657'; Czart. 1657 f. 240.
[19] Vidoni, Częstochowa, 16.II.1657 and 8.III.1657; TRz. 8420 pp. 10, 15.

religion but asked how Alexis could be prevented from joining Poland's enemies. The queen replied that the Poles would have to pretend to pursue negotiations with Muscovy but keep in contact with Austria and await the right moment to strike.[20] To prevent unilateral Lithuanian action, it was decided to send Pac to Muscovy to inform the tsar that a diet was to be held as soon as possible with the purpose of putting Wilno into effect, while urging him to send military aid immediately. Although this decision was officially to be kept secret from Vidoni, the king informed him that the diet was planned for 25 May, but that everything depended on the tsar's reply. The Court was playing for time; it was essential to stall the Muscovites long enough for Ferdinand to respond to the succession offer and to intervene in strength.[21] Talk of calling a diet in May was designed to put pressure on Ferdinand to accept the Polish offer and intervene immediately.

The document taken by Leszczyński was therefore not formally agreed in full council, as the 1655 offer had been; rather it was the work of a small group acting in collusion with the Court but without the knowledge of many senators. Leszczyński's plenipotentiary powers were drawn up in Koryciński's chancery, but Koryciński knew nothing of the succession offer.[22] The original of this document has disappeared. Walewski supposed that it was a binding promise of the throne by the senate.[23] In fact, as was made clear in the formal offer prepared in May, Leszczyński promised in the name of the king and of Andrzej and Jan Leszczyński, Trzebicki, Czarniecki and Lubomirski:

> by whatever resources, authority and powers they will possess ... to ensure that someone from the ... house of Austria should be elected king of Poland and grand duke of Lithuania by a free vote after the ... death of His Highness the present king, peacefully and without disturbing the Commonwealth; he above all who will be recommended by His Highness the king of Hungary.[24]

This document was not a new assurance of the succession for the Habsburgs but an offer made on behalf of a small group of senators, who were not in a position to make any kind of guarantee, given the opposition of so many, both Lithuanian and Polish. It gave notice of the establishment of a party in Poland dedicated to the promotion of the Habsburg election but the success of the plan depended on Vienna. As Louise Marie later wrote to Frederick William, there was a great difference

---

[20] ibid.
[21] Vidoni to Orsini, Częstochowa, 8.III.1657; TRz. 8420 pp. 109–11.
[22] Vidoni, Częstochowa, 26.III.1657; TRz. 8420 p. 17.
[23] The document was returned to John III Sobieski by Leopold I in 1683 but subsequently disappeared, along with the rest of the Sobieski family papers: Walewski, *Historia wyzwolenia* II p. 51, n. 6; M. Dogiel (ed.), *Codex Diplomaticus Regni Poloniae et Magni Ducato Lithuaniae* (Wilno, 1758–64) I p. 340.
[24] Obligatio super electionem regis ex domo Austriae, 27.V.1657; Copy, AGAD AKW Cesarskie, k. 25a, no. 10; Wójcik, *Traktaty polsko-austriackie* document 5, p. 51.

Constructing a coalition

between promising the throne and merely offering support in a future election.[25] Should Austria help to bring the war to a successful conclusion, it was hoped that Charles Joseph would be elected out of gratitude to the Habsburgs and because he would be a more popular candidate than Alexis. The Commonwealth's armies could then be turned against Muscovy in a war they were more suited to winning.

The offer to the Habsburgs was an attempt to create a political alternative to the Muscovite succession. The plan had some chance of success: fear of an interregnum had revived after Rákóczi's invasion, while a substantial body of opinion existed which was hostile to the tsar. The signatories of the document taken by Leszczyński to Vienna included some of the most important senators in Poland and the backing of the Catholic Church had been given by Vidoni, anxious to avoid a Muscovite election. While Lithuania remained a problem, Pac's attitude at the end of 1656 suggested that Lithuanian support for Wilno might evaporate if Austrian aid forced Sweden to settle quickly. Finally, the Court was aware that the presence of Austrian troops in the Commonwealth might prove necessary to overcome resistance to the election.[26] Much depended on the Austrian response to Leszczyński's mission. Although the Court had outmanœuvred its opponents very effectively at Częstochowa, Koryciński, who complained bitterly that the Court wished to reduce him to the status of a scribe, still believed that the *szlachta* supported him.[27]

Fate now struck a cruel blow. Although Ferdinand ratified the December treaty on 30 March, his death three days later, before Leszczyński even arrived in Vienna, deprived Poland of any hope of immediate aid and seriously hindered attempts to win greater support. Ferdinand's son Leopold I, not yet king of the Romans, was more circumscribed in his actions: his main concern was the imperial election, the first since the end of the Thirty Years War and the first in which Sweden would have any influence. The Poles could only expect further delays from Vienna.

These delays put a great strain on supporters of the Austrian succession. At the end of March, even before Ferdinand's death, Jan Leszczyński wrote to Cieciszewski bemoaning the long wait for reinforcements and saying that the Poles were at their wits' end. The delays made it difficult to justify the policy decided at Częstochowa: 'I am accused of raising false hopes and I do not know what to reply; let them at least declare that they are not withdrawing their support ... it is the ultimate cruelty not to reply to someone who wishes you well.'[28]

When Bogusław Leszczyński arrived in Vienna, he found that Leopold was extremely cautious, refusing to commit himself on the succession and requesting further guarantees from the Poles. Jan Leszczyński reacted angrily: 'I must confess that I am outraged that after so many declarations of our sincere affection, they dare

---

[25] Louise Marie to Frederick William, 2.I.1658; *Urkunden und Aktenstücke* VIII p. 275.
[26] Vidoni, 26.III.1657; TRz. 8420 pp. 17–18.
[27] Vidoni, Częstochowa, 1.IV.1657; TRz. 8420 p. 19.
[28] J. Leszczyński to Cieciszewski, Częstochowa, 31.III.1657; Czart. 388 no. 55, pp. 82–3.

After the Deluge

to treat in such an evasive way, renewing their scruples and doubts over those 4,000 men which they promised to send; in truth I despair of even that which has been agreed ever actually taking effect.'[29] The king was also desperate: even before he heard of Ferdinand's death, Vidoni found him greatly disturbed and complaining bitterly about Ferdinand, whom he did not expect to reach any decision.[30]

There was good reason for this anxiety. The military position was now so bad that if help did not arrive soon, John Casimir knew he might have to implement Wilno or settle with Sweden on whatever terms he could win. With a mutinous army and a desperate shortage of infantry, he could not think of mounting a new campaign, and he seriously considered capitulation.[31] The longer Vienna delayed, the more acute the crisis became. Lisola feared that the Poles would be driven to desperate measures and that 'the whole Polish people will regard us with implacable hatred'.[32]

As chances of Charles Joseph being elected by a grateful Commonwealth receded, Austrian supporters began to reconsider. Lubomirski's commitment to the plan had always been in doubt. His support had been a great coup for the Leszczyńskis, who had seen the chance to win him over when his hopes for Rákóczi's succession were finally dashed in January 1657, but he had long been anti-Austrian. In the light of his behaviour after Częstochowa, it is unlikely that his consent to the succession offer sprang from conviction. Rákóczi's treachery had forced him to reconsider his position; for the moment, it was to his advantage to cooperate with the Leszczyńskis and the Court: at Częstochowa John Casimir was to appoint a successor to Lanckoroński as Polish field hetman. Lubomirski's main rival was Stefan Czarniecki, castellan of Kiev and the king's favourite. The problem of the hetman's baton was one of the most difficult faced at Częstochowa; while the king wished to grant it to Czarniecki, he was faced with the determined opposition of a large section of the senate. Kersten suggests that Czarniecki's relatively humble origins explain this opposition, yet, as he admits, this explanation is weak; it will not do for the Leszczyńskis, who had allowed Czarniecki's daughter to marry into their family a year previously but who supported Lubomirski.[33]

It seems more likely that the Leszczyńskis saw an opportunity to win Lubomirski's support for the succession plan by a promise to back his candidature for the hetmanship instead of Czarniecki. Kersten agrees that such motives lay behind John Casimir's appointment of his old political enemy. There is no direct proof that such a deal took place, nevertheless it may be significant that Koryciński was excluded from the council meeting at which Lubomirski's promotion was approved.[34] Such a deal would explain why Lubomirski signed a document supporting a policy of which he had previously been the leading opponent. Once Lubomirski had been granted

---

[29] J. Leszczyński to B. Leszczyński, Kalisz, 26.IV.1657; Czart. 388 no. 72, f. 117.
[30] Vidoni, 1.IV.1657; TRz. 8420 p. 20.
[31] Vidoni, Częstochowa, 26.III.1657; TRz. 8420 p. 18; 1.IV.1657; TRz. 8420 p. 20.
[32] Lisola, Danków, 18.V.1657; *Berichte* no. 57, p. 271.
[33] Kersten, *Stefan Czarniecki* pp. 334–5.
[34] Vidoni, Częstochowa, 1.IV.1657; TRz. 8420 p. 19.

the baton, however, there was no guarantee that he would continue to support the Habsburg succession, since he could not be deprived of his office.

If Austrian delays gave Lubomirski an excuse to move away from support for Court policy, they also infuriated more convinced advocates of Charles Joseph and revived the position of de Lumbres, who rejoined the Court in early May. He had nothing new to offer; nevertheless, the doubts and divisions which he found at Court gave him an ideal opportunity to recover lost ground. There was widespread anger at the demands made in Vienna to Bogusław Leszczyński, especially the request for Austrian troops to garrison strongpoints on the Vistula and Warta rivers. Lubomirski stated that the army was desperate, believing that the Austrians were toying with the Commonwealth. He now urged peace with Sweden unless the Austrians sent immediate aid.[35] When de Lumbres confronted the queen over rumours that several leading senators, including the Leszczyńskis, supported an Austrian succession, she admitted the existence of the plan, though she denied her part in it, saying that: 'The ambassadors, against their orders and without the participation of the king and the Commonwealth, have promised their votes and those of their friends to allow the kingdom, or at least Great and Little Poland, to fall into the hands of the king of Hungary.'[36]

Despite the queen's protestations of innocence and de Lumbres's report that she still seemed little satisfied with the Habsburgs, such sentiments should not be seen as evidence that the queen wished to move closer to France, or supported peace with Sweden. She complained frequently at French attempts to prevent a rapprochement between Poland and Brandenburg, telling de Lumbres that the envoys to Vienna had been expressly forbidden to discuss the succession and attempting to persuade him that Sweden was scheming with Austria against France.[37] The strength of the queen's displeasure at Austrian delays is not to be doubted, but her cultivation of de Lumbres was motivated essentially by a desire to put pressure on Vienna by indicating that a settlement with Sweden was unavoidable if help did not come swiftly: Lisola was gravely worried in May by a new French suggestion that Louis XIV should offer to underwrite a deal in which Royal Prussia would be returned to Poland for a cash payment of 2,000,000 livres.[38] As yet, however, de Lumbres had no official backing for this offer and therefore was unable to channel anti-Austrian feeling. While Charles X campaigned actively with Rákóczi, the queen remained loyal to the policy of war and prospects for a settlement looked bleak.

It was essential to force a quick decision from Leopold, as Alexis stepped up the pressure by launching new diplomatic and military initiatives in the spring. A Muscovite envoy arrived in early May to press for the implementation of Wilno. He

---

[35] Walewski, *Historia wyzwolenia* II pp. 62, 67.
[36] De Lumbres to Mazarin, 23.V.1657; CPP XI f. 221.
[37] De Lumbres to Mazarin, 20.IV.1657; CPP XI f. 197.
[38] Lisola, Danków, 17.V.1657; *Berichte* no. 57, pp. 271–2.

left on 10 May with assurances that a diet would be held as soon as possible.[39] As the new campaigning season opened, the Muscovites moved into Livonia, seemingly willing once more to take the offensive. De Lumbres reported growing support not only for the Muscovite alliance but even for the election:

If peace with Sweden is not made soon, I see everyone here proceeding to make this nomination [of the tsar]; the Lithuanians eagerly, since the prince occupies all their country, and the Poles because he is offering them great advantages, promising to restore all the conquests he has made and to conquer Livonia to incorporate it in this kingdom. Those who previously opposed this seem presently to consent to it. Their reasoning is that the evil of which they wish to rid themselves is actual and that which they might fear is yet to come and uncertain, since it is possible that the king of Poland will outlive the grand duke. The rule of the latter will be less harsh and more supportable than might be supposed, since he is cultured enough and smacks little of the barbarian, treating the Lithuanians with all the consideration one would wish.[40]

It was essential, however, for Austrian supporters to give such an impression, for it was feared that the acceptance of Austrian aid and rumours of the succession offers might provoke the break-up of the Commonwealth. Nevertheless, Vidoni was confident that once the Austrian army had entered the Commonwealth, the election plan would succeed, claiming that many had declared that Leopold or Charles Joseph would be more welcome than Alexis. He was worried, however, that the acceptance of an Austrian king would prolong the occupation of Lithuania, which would prejudice the interests of the Catholic Church.[41] De Lumbres hinted at a possible split between the palatinates on the far side of the Vistula, together with Lithuania, and the rest of Poland, talking about a small Lithuanian cabal which was conducting its affairs in close secrecy but was spreading alarm and protesting that they would break the union if the Poles did not consent to the tsar's nomination.[42]

It is hard to determine the level of support for either a Muscovite or an Austrian candidature. The government's hints that it might proceed with the implementation of Wilno were partly designed to worry France and Austria in an attempt to persuade them to adopt a more energetic approach and partly to pacify Alexis. De Lumbres was certainly worried, reporting that the majority of the nobility supported the Muscovite election, while Vidoni also feared in early May that it might succeed, since even some that might be expected to share his opposition to the plan were wavering:

The matter is extremely delicate and I have made clear my opposition to those who support this move, who include some of the greatest figures in the kingdom. My protest may well provoke a great storm, which will be hard to contain and could cause irreparable damage. The bishop of Cujavia [Czartoryski], with whom I talked recently with all the zeal that I must

---

[39] De Lumbres to Mazarin, 15.V.1657; Harl. 4532, f. 69.
[40] De Lumbres to Mazarin, 20.IV.1657; CPP XI ff. 197–8.
[41] Vidoni, 15.V.1657; TRz. 8420 p. 32.
[42] De Lumbres to Mazarin, 23.V.1657; CPP XI f. 221.

devote to this matter, warned me not to speak to others in the same way, which should give Your Excellency good cause to reflect on the degree of circumspection with which I must proceed.[43]

Vidoni was worried enough to approach de Lumbres to urge him to use his influence to break any diet held to elect the tsar. De Lumbres replied that Charles X wanted the election of the tsar, or of an Austrian, hoping that this would provoke the Turk into moving against Poland.[44] Vidoni was determined to delay the calling of a diet, which de Lumbres felt was due to his desire to secure the succession for the Habsburgs. De Lumbres admitted the potential danger to Catholicism should Alexis be elected but added that there were signs that he was moderating his position, including a proposal for a conference between envoys of the Pope and the patriarch of Moscow to discuss a possible reunion of the Churches.[45]

The Court's position was eased considerably by the conclusion of the second treaty of Vienna (27 May), in which Austria finally promised further support, in the shape of 12,000 men and artillery. The cost, however, was still to be borne by Poland; Cracow and Poznań were to be held by the Austrians until the end of the war as surety, while Vienna was to receive half the proceeds from the lucrative Wieliczka and Bochnia saltmines.[46] Nevertheless, when news of the treaty arrived at the Polish Court on 6 June, it was received with joy and relief. Jan Leszczyński felt that it was of a 'miraculous excellence, since such significant reinforcements have been negotiated for such a small amount of money and such small rewards'.[47] John Casimir immediately issued a declaration rejecting talks with Sweden until Charles and his allies had left the Commonwealth and restored the status quo of 1655.[48]

The most useful result of the treaty, however, was not so much Austrian help, as the fact that it finally brought Denmark into the war. Frederick III had long been preparing an attack on Sweden but had not dared to move until the Habsburgs were committed. Once news of Austria's involvement reached Copenhagen, war was declared immediately, on 11 June. In July the Danes signed a formal alliance with the Commonwealth by which time they had already launched an attack on Swedish territory, aiming to win back the lands lost at Brömsebro in 1645.[49] It was this Danish threat to Swedish territory, rather than the entry of Austrian troops in June, which transformed the military situation. Charles had found Rákóczi a disappointing ally, and Sweden's military position had not changed significantly in the first half of 1657. On receiving news of the Danish incursion, Charles almost gratefully took the opportunity to leave the tangled political situation in Poland. He abandoned the

[43] Vidoni, 7.V.1657; TRz. 8420 p. 30.
[44] De Lumbres to Mazarin, 15.V.1657; Harl. 4532 f. 69; Vidoni, 15.V.1657; TRz. 8420 pp. 32–3.
[45] De Lumbres to Mazarin, 15.IV.1657; Harl. 4532, f. 69.
[46] Wójcik, *Traktaty polsko-austriackie* documents 2–4 pp. 38–49.
[47] J. Leszczyński to A. Leszczyński, 20.V.1657; Czart. 388 no. 87, f. 145; Lisola, Danków, 6.VI.1657; *Berichte* no. 61, p. 281.   [48] Copy, Harl. 4532, f. 83.
[49] Copia Confoederationis Dano-Polonicae contra Regem Sueciae, Copenhagen, 28.VII.1657; *Polonicae ex Archivo Regni Daniae* VI p. 92.

hapless Rákóczi to his fate, returning via Stettin to Sweden in early July. The Poles soon forced Rákóczi to surrender on 22 July; shortly afterwards the remnants of his army were crushed by the Tatars. Henceforth, the war changed fundamentally in nature. The Swedes no longer had a large army in Poland, although they still held a number of important cities, including Thorn, Cracow and Elbing, as bargaining-counters. The direct danger to Poland had lessened dramatically; nonetheless, final victory was still a distant prospect, as each Swedish garrison had to be reduced in turn.

The treaty of Vienna meant that negotiations with Sweden could finally be rejected. On 18 June, Trzebicki gave de Lumbres the Polish terms for a settlement, which called for the evacuation of all occupied territory by Sweden and its allies as a precondition for negotiations.[50] Nevertheless, despite this hardline attitude, Koryciński's forecast had proved accurate: the reaction of many to the terms of Vienna was negative. Stanisław Potocki was anxious to know more about the terms of the treaty and of the way in which agreement had been reached. He was particularly annoyed by the assignation of Cracow and Poznań after their capture to Austria as surety for the payment of the costs of the campaign, warning that this represented a danger to Polish liberty:

We must have certain reservations about something the dangers of which we have been warned by our forebears: namely the garrisoning of cities such as Cracow and Poznań by foreigners ... It behoves me to warn you that both soldiers and civilians are saying that thereby we will not have hereafter the monarchs we desire but those that we deserve.[51]

The Court could only hope that the long-awaited appearance of Austrian reinforcements would transform the situation. Initially, circumstances seemed promising. There were even hints that Koryciński might be willing to consider supporting an Austrian candidature: Louise Marie believed that he was displeased because he suspected that secret negotiations with Austria had taken place over the succession but that he was not opposed in principle and would like to be included.[52] In June, a joint Austrian and Polish army began the siege of Cracow, while in July, the defeat of Rákóczi and the recapture of Poznań from Brandenburg suggested that the tide had turned at last. Nevertheless, prospects for the successful accomplishment of the succession plan were poor, especially since the Austrians showed no sign of accepting the offer, or of agreeing to the marriage of Charles Joseph to Louise Marie's niece. Rumours of the offer abounded, however, and the queen feared that the presence of Austrian troops in the Commonwealth would lead Alexis to suspect that Leopold was seeking the throne.[53]

If such problems were to be overcome, it was essential to force Sweden to settle as soon as possible. It was to this end that the government sought to strengthen the

[50] De Lumbres to Brienne, Częstochowa, 19.VI.1657; CPP XI f. 239.
[51] Potocki to Trzebicki, 30.VIII.1657; Kubala, *Wojna brandenburska* dodatek XXI pp. 426–7.
[52] Vidoni, 13.VI.1657; TRz. 8420 pp. 41–2.   [53] Vidoni, 6.VI.1657; TRz. 8420 p. 40.

Constructing a coalition

anti-Swedish coalition by luring Frederick William away from his alliance with Charles. The treaty of Wehlau–Bromberg (19 September and 6 November 1657), which marked the successful realisation of this campaign, has long been criticised. Given the improvement in the military situation in the summer of 1657, Piwarski argues that the concessions made to entice the elector away from Sweden, especially the surrender of Polish sovereignty over Ducal Prussia, were unnecessary and gravely weakened the Commonwealth, since it cut it off from the Baltic along a wide strip of coast and represented a major threat to Poland's tenuous control of the mouth of the Vistula. Kamińska argues that it ended Polish influence on the Baltic and marked the decline of the Commonwealth's European position.[54]

It is suggested that it was Austrian pressure above all which forced the Poles to agree to talks and then to this disadvantageous settlement, directed more to securing Austrian interests: the detachment of Frederick William from his Swedish alliance in order that he might be won over to support Habsburg policy in the Empire.[55] The evidence for such a conclusion appears strong. Not only did John Casimir allow Lisola to act as a mediator, it was to Lisola that he assigned the secret instruction allowing the concession of sovereignty should Frederick William refuse to make peace on any other terms. Piwarski regards this as conclusive proof of Austrian dominance over Court policy and marvelled at the obedience of the Polish Court to imperial directives, which he explains in terms of the queen's dynastic plans and the pressure of a group of senators, especially the bishops, who acted in the spirit of orders from Vienna and Rome. He argues that the senate council accepted this arrangement and the concession of sovereignty because senators regarded the matter as unimportant, wanting a quick end to the war with Sweden in order to renew the war with Muscovy over the Ukraine and Belorussia; Frederick William therefore could set his own terms.[56]

Assessments of the treaty of Wehlau–Bromberg are frequently informed by a post-partition perspective which fails to take account of the complexity of the political and diplomatic situation. The importance of the granting of sovereignty in Ducal Prussia to Frederick William for the subsequent rise of Brandenburg-Prussia is undeniable; nevertheless, historians should not criticise John Casimir and his advisers if they were more concerned with the immediate problems they faced than with possible long-term consequences. Contemporary politicians were aware of the dangers of conceding sovereignty, which they accepted not because they were indifferent, stupid, or lacking in foresight, but because the alternatives seemed more damaging to the Commonwealth's interests: when the desire for a settlement with Frederick William first reemerged at the end of 1656, before Lisola arrived at the

---

[54] Piwarski, 'Rywalizacja francusko-austriacka' p. 399; A. Kamińska, *Brandenburg–Prussia and Poland 1669–1672* (Marburg-Lahn, 1983) p. 3.
[55] W. Odyniec, *Dzieje Prus Kólewskich 1454–1772* (Warsaw, 1972) p. 194; Piwarski, *Dzieje Prus Wschodnich* pp. 127–8.
[56] Piwarski, 'Rywalizacja francusko-austriacka' p. 398 and 'Stosunki szwedzko-brandenburskie' p. 449.

Polish Court and long before the second treaty of Vienna, the Commonwealth was faced with the prospect of immediate partition following Rákóczi's invasion. Later, despite the Austrian and Danish alliances, the government still faced enormous problems: it was essential to end the war with Sweden quickly to avoid the necessity of implementing Wilno without provoking a Lithuanian secession, while the terms of Vienna required the Commonwealth to bear the whole cost of Austrian intervention at a time when it could not pay its own troops.

The best way to achieve a quick end to the war was to construct as broad an anti-Swedish alliance as possible. Jan Leszczyński had already talked of a general alliance of the Commonwealth, Austria, Muscovy, Denmark, the United Provinces, Brandenburg and Courland.[57] He urged that the channels to the elector be kept open, feeling that a settlement was possible and keeping in touch with Hoverbeck through Nowiejski, canon of Warmia, sent to Poland ostensibly by Leszczyński's brother Wacław, bishop of Warmia, but carrying in fact peace feelers from the elector. Jan Leszczyński believed that once Frederick William declared his support for John Casimir, a general peace would soon follow.[58] His desire to tempt Frederick William away from Sweden did not mean, however, that he was prepared to settle at any price. He was angry with Gosiewski for agreeing to the Wierzbołów armistice, which he saw as unneccessary, arguing that John Casimir was entitled to ignore it, since Gosiewski had not been empowered to agree to it. He did not despair of Frederick William but felt that he could not wholly be trusted.[59]

If Jan Leszczyński supported talks with Frederick William, others were hostile. Many had wanted to deprive him of his duchy after the battle of Warsaw; this ill-feeling survived into 1657. A Brandenburg army had entered Great Poland at the end of August 1656 and had taken over many strongpoints from the Swedes. Most of the nobility of Great Poland had rejected the elector's call to accept his protection and had joined Jakub Weiher, palatine of Marienburg, in besieging Kalisz, looking for support from the royal army as it marched north to Danzig. Kalisz fell on 22 October 1656, and in November forces from Great Poland raided Brandenburg itself; mainly composed of cavalry, however, and lacking artillery, they could achieve little of significance. At talks in Zielenzig, the Great Poland delegates demanded the evacuation of all Brandenburg forces from Great Poland and asked for free passage for Polish troops to Swedish Pomerania. On 12 December a compromise was reached, in which Frederick William agreed to evacuate Zbąszyn

---

[57] 'Rationes ob quas perpetua ac firma Alliantia inter Imperatorem Domum Austriacum, Regem Daniae, Magnum Moschoviae Ducem, Electorem Brandenburgicum, Ordines Foederati Belgii, Ducum Curlandiae ab altera parte quam priorum contra Suecos concludenda sit.' Czart. 388 no. 56, f. 83.

[58] J. Leszczyński to Hoverbeck, Kalisz, 20.I.1657; Czart. 388 no. 15, f. 28; J. Leszczyński to Nowiejski, Kalisz, 24.I.1657; Czart. 388 no. 18, f. 32.

[59] J. Leszczyński to Trzebicki, Danków, 16.II.1657; Czart. 388 no. 28, f. 45; J. Leszczyński to Koryciński, Danków, 16.II.1657; Czart. 388 ff. 46–7.

Constructing a coalition

and Międzyrzecz and to consider the cases of Kalisz and Poznań. In return, a two-month armistice was signed, which was extended in March 1657.[60]

If Great Poland was ready to compromise with the elector owing to the lack of military support from the main royal army, others remained hostile. Opposition was led by supporters of peace with Sweden, with Koryciński once more prominent.[61] He wished to prevent the Poles settling with the elector, which would jeopardise prospects of peace with Sweden, claiming that Frederick William's recent enthusiasm for peace was dishonest and that he did not really wish to break with Sweden. Koryciński could not, however, prevent Lisola from persuading John Casimir and his fellow ministers to show him their terms for a settlement.[62] Despite this success for Lisola, Rákóczi's invasion and Frederick William's own decision to break contacts with Poland put an end to any immediate prospect of a settlement. At the Częstochowa convocation in early 1657, nothing was decided with regard to Brandenburg; hostility over its continued adherence to the Swedes prevented any closer contacts on the part of the Court.

If the government abandoned the idea of a settlement with Brandenburg in the immediate aftermath of Rákóczi's invasion, Gosiewski, still best placed to strike at Frederick William, continued to work for one. In February 1657, von Wreich approached him with instructions to negotiate a new armistice and closer relations. Wreich reported that Gosiewski was favourably disposed towards the conclusion of a general armistice but was apprehensive of the reception that his initiative would have at Court if he allowed himself to become too close to the elector. Wreich knew from Sapieha that Gosiewski was not trusted by the Court, despite Gosiewski's assurances that he had been given complete authority by the king and that any talk to the contrary was a French intrigue stirred up by his enemies.[63] Wreich's information was accurate: John Casimir was highly displeased that the elector had conceded nothing and felt that Gosiewski 'ought to have been more cautious in his handling of such a vital matter'.[64]

Many senators, far from being indifferent to the terms of an agreement, felt that Gosiewski was willing to concede too much to win over the elector and suspected his motives. For the Commonwealth was not in as strong a position with regard to Brandenburg in the summer of 1657 as Piwarski and others have argued. The policy of trying to force Frederick William to desert Sweden had failed: the royal army had

---

[60] Czapliński, 'Wyprawa Wielkopolan na Nową Marchię w r.1656 i układ w Sulęcinie' *Roczniki Historyczne* 23 (1957) pp. 262–72.
[61] J. Leszczyński to Lubomirski, 21.I.1657; Czart. 388 no. 16, ff. 29–30; printed in Kubala, *Wojna brandenburska* dodatek XV p. 419.
[62] Koryciński to Grzymułtowski, 25.II.1657; Czart. 400 no. 42, f. 221; copy in Czart. 150 f. 31. Lisola, Danzig, 3.II.1657; *Berichte* no. 51, p. 231. Koryciński also blocked an attempt to pardon Bogusław Radziwiłł, an important demand of Frederick William: Vidoni, 16.II.1657; TRz. 8420 pp. 10–11.
[63] Relation über geführte Verhandlungen mit Gonsiewski (Königsberg?) 13.XI.1656; *Urkunden und Aktenstücke* VIII pp. 201–2.
[64] Vidoni, Opole, 12.IV.1657; Levinson, *Die Nuntiaturberichte* no. 120, p. 84.

been unable to put any pressure on the elector after marching north to Danzig; this lack of support had forced the *szlachta* of Great Poland to suspend its attacks on Brandenburg, while Gosiewski was not strong enough to win a major victory unaided. Since neither Muscovy nor Austria was willing to turn their armies against Brandenburg, a military solution was impossible.

Furthermore, the elector could now negotiate on the basis of what he had won in the three treaties he had made with Sweden: recognition of sovereignty in Ducal Prussia, plus the palatinates of Poznań, Kalisz and Łęczyca and the county of Wieluń. While he had lost the cities of Łęczyca and Kalisz in October and Poznań in July 1657, he still held important strongpoints, including Piotrków Czarniecki and Kościan, which he had not yet surrendered despite the December armistice with Great Poland. These were important bargaining-counters which he could use in his campaign to win territory he really coveted: the bishopric of Warmia (Ermland), a wedge of territory which thrust deep into the heart of Ducal Prussia, or at least Braunsberg and the important prize of Elbing.

The demand for Warmia was subtle: the Church would oppose it, which meant that Frederick William was more likely to receive some other prize in compensation, such as Elbing, a base from which he could challenge Danzig's control of the Vistula trade. His ploy was successful. When Gosiewski suggested that peace could be made for the price of Warmia, the suggestion was poorly received, as it had been in January, when it had first been made by senators in Danzig.[65] Jan Leszczyński opposed the disposal of divine property, feeling there were other means by which Frederick William could be satisfied. Vidoni encouraged such sentiments, telling Leszczyński how dishonourable it would be for his brother Wacław, bishop of Warmia, and for the family if they agreed to something 'so damaging to the Commonwealth'.[66] The Polish instructions stressed the impossibility of ceding Warmia or allowing garrisons in towns subject to it but allowed the cession of Elbing if necessary, as a fief of the Polish Crown.[67]

It was a desire to avoid losing territory which led the Poles to consider the concession of sovereignty. Apart from Church objections, to cede Warmia to the elector would strengthen his strategic position to the Commonwealth's detriment.[68] When the senate council discussed the matter in July, the issue of sovereignty seems not to have provoked much discussion; far more time was spent on territorial concessions. The council rejected Frederick William's pretensions to Warmia and Allenstein, offering only the starosties of Lauenberg and Bütow, which had only reverted to the Commonwealth on the death of Bogislav XIV of Pomerania in

---

[65] Lisola, memorandum, 23.III.1657; *Berichte* no. 54, p. 250; Vidoni, 27.I.1657; TRz. 8420 p. 27.
[66] Vidoni, Kalisz, 27.I.1657; TRz. 8420 pp. 5–6.
[67] Instructio Regis Poloniae pro Episcopo Varmiensi et Domino Gąsiewski; Walewski, *Historia wyzwolenia* II dodatek XV p. xv.
[68] Vidoni, Kalisz, 27.I.1657; TRz. 8420 p. 6.

Constructing a coalition

1637.[69] Major opposition to the concession of sovereignty seems to have come only from Koryciński, who was not invited in case he caused trouble.[70] Jan Leszczyński's letters show no great concern with the matter: when he learnt of its concession, he merely expressed his opinion that the talks must be close to success, now that such a vital point had been settled.[71]

This lack of interest does not indicate that the senators thought the settlement with Brandenburg unimportant, merely that their priorities were different from those which historians believe they ought to have had. Senators, while appreciating the implications of surrendering sovereignty, were more concerned to protect actual territory than a theoretical sovereignty which meant little without the ability to back it with force. By 1657, the Poles had already made the elector at least three offers of sovereignty: before the treaty of Rinsk in 1655, and in March and June 1656 – offers which they could not expect him to forget.[72]

Jan Leszczyński, who was empowered to concede sovereignty in his talks with Hoverbeck, was worried that even this might be insufficient to tempt Frederick William to change sides. It was territorial concessions which concerned him, not the issue of sovereignty, which he felt was a sacrifice justified by the rewards it would bring.[73] It was inevitable that Frederick William would insist on sovereignty; the Poles therefore had to use this as a bargaining-counter to ensure that as little territory as possible was ceded. It was this concern, not Austrian pressure, which persuaded the government to concede this point.

There were internal political problems to consider as well. The Court was worried that Gosiewski was seeking an agreement with Brandenburg as a means of promoting his own desire for a Muscovite succession. Gosiewski's thinking is revealed in his instructions to Medeksza for the latter's mission to Alexis in 1657:

With regard to the elector... tell [the tsar] that although I had nearly persuaded him to desert Sweden and was on the point of reaching an agreement, I delayed the negotiations while I awaited His Imperial Majesty's reinforcements, whose arrival would demonstrate his good intentions towards the Commonwealth; this is important with regard to the election, even if the need for reinforcements is not pressing at present. I do not wish the king of Hungary alone to claim responsibility for persuading the elector to break with Sweden but for the tsar also to act as an intermediary.[74]

---

[69] This was under the terms of the 1526 treaty of Danzig, by which duke George of Pomerania was granted Lauenberg and Bütow as Polish fiefs. The Poles had promoted the dukes of Pomerania as a counterweight to the Teutonic knights in the fifteenth century.
[70] Vidoni, 6.VIII.1657; TRz. 8420 pp. 57–8.
[71] J. Leszczyński to W. Leszczyński, 18.VIII.1657; Czart. 388 no. 117, f. 210.
[72] The offer in October 1655 was made by bishop Jan Leszczyński; Vidoni to Orsini, 27.X.1655; TRz. 8418 p. 86; Piwarski, *Dzieje Prus Wschodnich* p. 120. The offers of 1656 were made by Podłodowski: Piwarski, *Dzieje polityczne Prus Wschodnich* p. 41
[73] J. Leszczyński to Trzebicki, Breslau, 24.VI.1657; Czart. 388 no. 93, ff. 159–60; J. Leszczyński to Cieciszewski, Breslau, 2.VII.1657; Czart. 388 no. 95, f. 166.
[74] Gosiewski, Instructions, 1.VIII.1657; Medeksza, *Księga pamiętnicza* p. 156.

After the Deluge

While Gosiewski sought an agreement with Frederick William to promote the Muscovite election, the Court was concerned that any diplomatic triumph would reflect well on Austria. It was essential to work closely with the Austrians to ensure that they, not Gosiewski and the Muscovites, derived the credit for any agreement and it was vital to move quickly, for Gosiewski, heartened by the tsar's move against Livonia and Ingria, demanded plenipotentiary powers to negotiate with the elector, after announcing his readiness to invade Ducal Prussia with 5,000 cavalry, 4,000 infantry and suitable artillery, claiming that he was in a good position to force Frederick William to reach a settlement.[75]

Circumstances had changed since late 1656, when the king had attacked Gosiewski for his reluctance to fight; this request provoked a hostile response from John Casimir and the senate, although Louise Marie was more favourably disposed. John Casimir suggested that Gosiewski's forces were insufficient to achieve the desired end and asked Lisola whether the Austrians were ready to use their army to force the elector to settle, to which he received an evasive reply.[76] If Gosiewski succeeded, the position of supporters of the tsar's election would be greatly strengthened.

Piwarski is therefore right to underline the importance of the Court's succession plans in motivating its support for an agreement with Brandenburg but wrong to suggest that it was merely acting under orders from Vienna and Rome. Austria's concern to lure Frederick William away from Charles was primarily motivated by a desire to be sure of his vote in the forthcoming imperial election, not by a desire to win the Polish succession: the latest Polish offer had already been rejected. It was the Polish Court which needed a quick settlement in order to preempt Gosiewski and keep control of the succession issue. There was still hope that the Habsburgs might accept the offer; even if they did not, however, it was essential to block Alexis. Louise Marie, who had not yet ruled out an Austrian succession, was one of the strongest supporters of a settlement with Brandenburg, helping to overcome John Casimir's doubts about the wisdom of agreeing the concession of sovereignty before even the treaty of Vienna. De Lumbres later wrote that Louise Marie sought to win over the elector whatever the price.[77] She was in direct contact with the electoral Court, emphasising her efforts on the elector's behalf in her letters to Frederick William's mother, Elizabeth Charlotte, and her role in persuading John Casimir and leading senators to forget the past and to allow Frederick William to keep his duchy, but hinting that if Frederick William did not settle quickly she would be forced to abandon him to the 'just vengeance' of the Poles.[78]

Thus there were important domestic reasons behind the government's wish to reach a speedy settlement. Similarly, there was good reason for the acceptance of Lisola's suggestion that he act as a negotiator on John Casimir's behalf, not just as

---

[75] Lisola, rel. ad imp., Danków, 16.V.1657; *Berichte* no. 56, p. 269.
[76] ibid.   [77] De Lumbres, *Relations* II p. 147.
[78] Louise Marie to Elizabeth Charlotte (June 1657); *Urkunden und Aktenstücke* VIII pp. 202, 204.

mediator. Historians have criticised the king for accepting this suggestion which, it is alleged, subordinated Polish to Habsburg interests and have usually depicted Lisola as the leading figure who first determined that the concession of sovereignty was necessary to achieve a settlement and then forced the weak-willed John Casimir to agree.[79]

The uncritical acceptance of Lisola's own account of the negotiations has led many to underestimate the subtlety of John Casimir's diplomacy. He was certainly convinced that a pro-Austrian policy represented the best means of finishing the war quickly and therefore of avoiding the need to implement Wilno. He also believed that it was vital to win over Frederick William, as a means of hastening the end of the war. Finally, it was essential to prevent Gosiewski from negotiating an agreement with the elector, partly to block plans to advance the Muscovite succession, partly because Gosiewski was suspected of being willing to concede too much. It was these considerations which persuaded John Casimir to listen to Lisola, who, observing with some justification that Gosiewski might constitute a threat to the success of the talks were he refused plenipotentiary powers, suggested that he should be forbidden to agree anything with the elector without the sanction of Lisola and Jan Leszczyński, at that point the proposed Polish envoy.[80] Lisola's suggestion neatly outflanked Gosiewski: taking him at his word with regard to his expressed desire for a settlement with Frederick William, it ensured that he would not be able to manipulate that settlement in favour of his political programme.

There was another reason for the acceptance of Lisola's suggestion. The official instructions to Gosiewski and Wacław Leszczyński, who had replaced his brother as the Polish envoy, maintained the position adopted in January, when the concession of sovereignty had been rejected. The secret instruction in which the king agreed to the concession of sovereignty if all else failed to persuade Frederick William to desert the Swedes was entrusted to Lisola alone, not to Leszczyński and Gosiewski. The instruction, however, contained an important proviso: 'Our Commissioners will promise ratification by the Estates at the next diet. They will further guard against being persuaded into agreeing any suspension of hostilities or neutrality [for the elector].'[81]

This explicit condition shows that the king was by no means abandoning all control to the Austrian ambassador. John Casimir knew better than most that he could not promise that a diet would ratify anything; furthermore, the fact that it was Lisola, not Leszczyński or Gosiewski, who was given the right to concede sovereignty meant that a future diet could refuse ratification on the grounds that the granting of plenipotentiary powers to a foreign envoy, who was in addition technically only the envoy of the king and not the Commonwealth, was illegal.

---

[79] Piwarski, 'Rywalizacja francusko-austriacka' p. 396; F. Schevill, *The Great Elector* (Chicago, 1947) pp. 179–80.   [80] Lisola, Danków, 16.V.1657; *Berichte* no. 56, p. 269.
[81] Instructio secreta pro tractata cum Electore Brandeburgica a Rege mihi soli ... commissa. Walewski, *Historia wyzwolenia* II dodatek XVIII pp. xviii–xix.

After the Deluge

Finally, the concession of sovereignty was dependent on Frederick William's active participation in the war. There was much room for future manœuvre: as with the Muscovite succession, there was hope that a necessary concession could later be redeemed.

Furthermore, after the capture of Poznań on 28 August, John Casimir wrote to Lisola specifically forbidding the concession of sovereignty.[82] Historians have suggested that this proves John Casimir's indecisiveness and have used Lisola's deliberate suppression of this inconvenient instruction as final proof that Polish interests were subordinated to those of Austria.[83] Yet, coupled with the qualifications given in the instructions, this letter could be used in the future to contest the sovereignty issue should it be felt this was necessary or desirable. Lisola was the king's ambassador, not the Commonwealth's; by writing his letter, John Casimir made it appear that Lisola had disobeyed his direct order. The Commonwealth, if it chose, could repudiate Lisola's action. Meanwhile, the king and queen could travel to Bromberg for the formal signing of the treaty on 6 November.

There was good reason for the Poles to be satisfied with the treaty: in the short term, they had achieved much for relatively little sacrifice. In contrast to the treaty of Vienna, the Commonwealth was not to bear the cost of Brandenburg's involvement in the war, while even if sovereignty was granted, major territorial concessions had been avoided: Poland kept Warmia and while it ceded the starosties of Lauenberg and Bütow, these were small territories that Poland had only ruled directly for twenty years and which remained fiefs of the Polish Crown. Elbing was ceded at Bromberg but Frederick William signed a document promising its return in exchange for a reduction of the aid he was required to send Poland in time of war and the payment of 40,000 thalers. Finally, Draheim was given to the elector for three years as security for the payment of 120,000 thalers in compensation for war damage.[84]

Piwarski, who considered that the treaty was forced on the Commonwealth, argued that its terms were seen by senators as conceding matters of secondary importance, which in any case might be challenged at a later date.[85] There is little evidence that the treaty was seen as unimportant but there was certainly sufficient opposition to indicate that a future diet might well repudiate it. Koryciński stated that he intended to protest against the treaty, pointing out that the elector had given no guarantees of good faith, asking if losses so large could be made good in the future and enquiring what would happen if Austria and Brandenburg should ever unite

---

[82] Lisola, Königsberg, 4.IX.1657; *Berichte* no. 75, p. 317.
[83] Piwarski, 'Rywalizacja francusko-austriacka' p. 396.
[84] The treaty was signed at Wehlau by Wacław Leszczyński and Lisola on behalf of the Commonwealth, and by Schwerin and Somnitz for Frederick William; Gosiewski signed at Wehlau on 19 September, with reservations, which were cleared up when the treaty was ratified at Bromberg on 6.XI.1657. The best account of the treaty is given by Kamińska, who criticises Moerner and others for inaccurately presenting its terms: Kamińska, *Brandenburg–Prussia and Poland* pp. 11–12.
[85] Piwarski, 'Rywalizacja francusko-austriacka' p. 399.

against Poland. He challenged the validity of the plenipotentiary powers granted to Lisola, which had been sealed by Trzebicki.[86] Lubomirski also expressed his opposition: 'His Excellency still takes umbrage at His Majesty's continued support for the Germans and even more so over the agreement with the elector, which he considers to be prejudicial to freedom and the product of the turbid minds of the Jesuits.'[87] While Vidoni assured Lubomirski that the king had acted out of his interest in peace and the well-being of the kingdom, the nuncio had his own doubts about the settlement: 'I advanced all the reasons I could think of, adding finally that all the elector's forebears had shown themselves to be enemies of the Crown and of the kingdom and that while he might seem inclined to peace at present, how much is this due to the necessity of the moment.'[88] The king listened, but stated that the matter was too far advanced to turn back and that the king of Hungary and the majority of senators supported a settlement. Vidoni's doubts, provoked by his concern for Catholic interests, show Piwarski's belief that Vienna and Rome were acting in concert on this issue to be misguided. The nuncio's concern was shared by some Polish bishops: Czartoryski was worried about the rights of the Church in Bütow; nevertheless, most seem to have followed Andrzej Leszczyński's lead in approving the treaty as a whole, which was ratified by nineteen senators.[89]

Piwarski was right in one respect, however: the Poles did see a chance that the terms might be contested in future years: John Casimir's conduct of the negotiations left much room for manœuvre. If in practice no concerted attempt was ever made to reassert Polish sovereignty, the Commonwealth did outmanœuvre Frederick William with some success over the territorial clauses. When the Swedes marched out of Elbing in 1660, the Poles moved in; despite never paying the required indemnity they successfully held on to the city until 1772. Braunsberg was returned to Poland by Frederick William in 1663, although an attempt by the Commonwealth to keep Draheim provoked the elector to seize it by force in 1668. For the loss of the two small starosties of Lauenberg and Bütow, the town of Draheim and a sovereignty that was more important in practical terms to the inhabitants of Ducal Prussia than to the Commonwealth, the Poles achieved substantial benefits: Frederick William's participation in the war was ultimately considerable. The fact that the Commonwealth's political problems after 1657 left it unable to reverse the tactical concession of sovereignty, which it had an opportunity to challenge in 1669 at the accession of Michael Korybut Wiśniowiecki when the treaty had to be reconfirmed by both sides, should not blind historians to the possibilities created by John Casimir's handling of the talks. If Poland ultimately lost out after 1668, it was more to do with its internal state than the treaty of Wehlau–Bromberg. That was something the statesmen could not foresee in 1657.

[86] Walewski, *Historia wyzwolenia* II p. 163; Vidoni, 1.VIII.1657; TRz. 8420 p. 55.
[87] Vidoni, Warsaw, 5.XI.1657; TRz. 8420 p. 71; Levinson, *Die Nuntiaturberichte* no. 163, p. 105.
[88] Vidoni to Orsini, Cracow, 22.IX.1657; TRz. 8420 p. 159.
[89] Soll to Vidoni, Bromberg, 6.XI.1657; Levinson, *Die Nuntiaturberichte* no. 164, p. 105.

6

The succession and the failure of the coalition: January–July 1658

By the end of 1657, after the withdrawal of the main Swedish army, Rákóczi's defeat and the construction of the anti-Swedish coalition, the immediate danger to the Commonwealth appeared to have passed. For the first time since 1656 it seemed that a quick end to the war was attainable and thought could be given once more to questions of the succession and political reform. Yet the optimism felt after the agreement with Brandenburg was soon dissipated. The Poles were anxious to take the offensive in the autumn of 1657 and fulfil their obligations to Denmark. Between September and November, Czarniecki mounted two expeditions into Swedish Pomerania with about 5,000 men. The Commonwealth's new allies, however, were more reluctant to commit themselves. Although Frederick William was keen enough to support Czarniecki, he was dissuaded by Austrian reluctance to fight outside the Commonwealth. With a delicate imperial election facing him in 1658, Leopold could not afford to risk breaking Westphalia by attacking Swedish possessions in the Empire: he had entered the war to prevent the partition of the Commonwealth, not to reopen the Thirty Years War.

This lack of support caused great problems for the Polish government and had serious implications for its election plans. The treaty of Vienna committed it to supporting the 12,000 Austrian troops now in the Commonwealth but it could ill afford the extra burden. Czarniecki's force, which consisted almost entirely of cavalry, could only mount a series of raids on Swedish garrisons, and did little to take the pressure off Denmark. Although a council of war at Poznań on 26 January 1658 agreed in principle that Denmark should be helped by her allies, no firm plans were drawn up; instead the Polish and Austrian armies were assigned to winter quarters. This marked the start of real anti-Austrian feeling: as troops entered their billets, local discontent grew apace, while the Austrians complained that the Poles were not meeting their obligations under the treaty of Vienna.

Most complaints came from Great Poland, where the bulk of the Austrians were billeted. Jan Leszczyński was already writing in October 1657 of the ill-feeling caused by 'these insolent Austrians'. Anger grew as it became clear that noble and Church land would not be spared.[1] The effects of such billets on Polish estates were

---

[1] J. Leszczyński to A. Leszczyński, 18.X.1657; Czart. 388 no. 139, f. 269; Vidoni to Orsini, Poznań, 16.XII.1657; TRz. 8420 p. 187.

The succession and the failure of the coalition

described by Piotr Opaliński, who asked for the burden to be spread by the enforcement of contributions from other palatinates:

> there is little that can be done when so many of our brothers have abandoned their devastated lands. Perhaps they will more swiftly fall prey to desperation ... for they already see themselves as lost and impoverished by contributions exacted with such violence from their estates. The number of such malcontents will rise so long as the country suffers such terrible oppression.[2]

The rapid growth of anti-Austrian feeling was a serious blow to Court plans. Since 1655 the Court and the senate council had persistently attempted to interest Vienna in the succession. Leopold's reluctance to prosecute the war with any urgency, however, and the rapidly escalating unpopularity of the Austrian troops destroyed hopes that a grateful Commonwealth would agree to the election of a Habsburg. The fear was already being expressed that Austria intended to seize the throne by force in order to destroy noble liberties.

It is usually argued that this development provided the perfect opportunity for de Lumbres to exploit the tension between Warsaw and Vienna to win over the queen and thereby achieve ever greater influence at the Polish Court. The queen, it is suggested, was only too willing to listen to these approaches: rejected by Leopold, who was not interested in the succession for Charles Joseph, or his marriage to her niece, and sensing a lack of support for a Habsburg candidate, especially in Great Poland, she began to consider a French candidature despite John Casimir's continued attachment to the Habsburgs.[3]

It is true that Louise Marie had been a reluctant supporter of a Habsburg succession, and there is no reason to doubt that she favoured a candidate from the land where she had grown up. Nevertheless, in the summer of 1657, she still shared the general mistrust of the French which de Lumbres reported was growing after the Treaties of Vienna and Copenhagen and the entry of Austrian troops into Poland.[4] He was unable to convince her that French diplomatic efforts in Istanbul, Königsberg, Moscow and Copenhagen were not directed against the Commonwealth:

> I could not entirely obliterate the impression which she has formed that these efforts are in Sweden's favour and that we are espousing Swedish interests against the king of Poland ... Her attitude to France has cooled and although she still has a great aversion to the house of Austria ... it is to be feared that she might change her mind and rejoin that side, unless France tries to win her back soon.[5]

---

[2] Piotr Opaliński to John Casimir, undated; Kubala, *Wojny duńskie* p. 422, n. 8.
[3] Wójcik, 'Stosunki polsko-austriackie w drugiej połowie XVII wieku' *Sobótka* 38 (1983) p. 493; Kubala, *Wojna brandenburska* p. 264; Bąkowa, *Szlachta województwa krakowskiego* p. 20; Piwarski, 'Rywalizacja francusko-austriacka' p. 210, based on Waliszewski, *Polsko-francuskie stosunki* p. 230.
[4] De Lumbres to Mazarin, Częstochowa, 3.VII.1657; CPP XI f. 253.
[5] De Lumbres to Mazarin, 4.VIII.1657; CPP XI f. 268.

After the Deluge

Despite this evidence of Louise Marie's displeasure with the French in the late summer of 1657, Kubala argues that it was precisely from this period that the French succession plan became the main motivating force for all her actions. He describes the exchange between de Lumbres and the queen but suggests that the anger stopped a few days later when de Lumbres confronted Louise Marie with a copy of a letter she had written to Bogusław Leszczyński stating her hostility to France for its championing of Sweden. According to Kubala, Louise Marie then stated that she desired the candidature of the duc d'Anjou or some other French prince, swearing that Leszczyński had not been empowered to offer the throne to Leopold for his brother or any other Habsburg prince.[6]

In the dispatch on which Kubala bases this assertion, the queen's attitude towards a French candidature seems much less categorical than he implies:

> She interrupted me, saying that she greatly regretted that I had not come earlier, and tried to persuade me that with the esteem and the trust which she said I had acquired with the king and all the senators and ministers, it would be easy for me to obtain everything I wish ... even a league against Austria, by making peace with Sweden, owing to the bad treatment the Poles were receiving from [the Habsburgs]. She then spoke of various proposals she had made to grant the crown of Poland to the duc d'Anjou or some other French prince.[7]

This is not a firm declaration of intent. It occurs in the midst of a heated discussion, in which the queen's main purpose is to deny that the Vienna treaty had included any firm offer of the throne. Far from expressing any commitment to a French succession, she was merely reminding de Lumbres of past offers, to stress that it was not just Austria which had been approached. At the most, it was a hint that if the French wished to take the matter further, offers had already been made which might be revived. The audience ended on an unfriendly note: the queen dismissed de Lumbres with more barbed comments, declaring that the alliance with Austria had only been made 'as a last resort', because Charles X had rejected the Polish terms, and complaining about the 1655 Anglo-French treaty, which she saw as pro-Swedish. As Kubala himself points out, the queen was deliberately misleading de Lumbres without telling a direct lie, since the throne had been offered to Ferdinand III, not Leopold.[8]

It was not until the end of September that Louise Marie went any further:

> The queen has hinted on several occasions and last night gave herself to be understood more clearly, that if France wished to aspire to the throne for one of its own she would demonstrate that she has not lost the affection which she owes to her native land, or her obligation to Their Majesties and to Your Eminence, and that she would do all she could to ensure the success of the plan.[9]

---

[6] Kubala, *Wojna brandenburska* pp. 262–3.
[7] De Lumbres to Mazarin, Cracow, 7.IX.1657; CPP XI f. 291. Kubala, *Wojna brandenburska* pp. 387–8, n. 6.
[8] Kubala, *Wojna brandenburska* p. 264; Mazarin replied by saying that he accepted the queen's assurances, but pointed out that rumours of the offer were circulating in Prague and all the German courts. Mazarin to de Lumbres, Paris, 16.XI.1657; *Lettres du Cardinal Mazarin* VIII p. 210.
[9] De Lumbres to Mazarin, Warsaw, 30.IX.1657; CPP XI f. 306.

The succession and the failure of the coalition

This approach was still only exploratory. She suggested that 200,000 écus would be necessary to ensure support. For the moment she was still principally concerned with the negotiations with Brandenburg, which the French wished to disrupt. Until Charles proved more reasonable, Louise Marie, far from serving French interests, supported building up the military pressure on Sweden. She had complained frequently about d'Avaugour's efforts to sabotage the Brandenburg talks. In October, she still maintained official government policy, stating that the Commonwealth refused to treat with Sweden without the participation of its allies.[10] More significantly, de Lumbres was deliberately kept away from Bromberg since it was felt that he would try and dissuade Frederick William from reaching an agreement.[11] The attempt by Blondel, the French resident in Berlin, to win the queen's support for peace talks with Sweden earned him a sharp rebuke.[12] Louise Marie was by no means convinced that the French were able or willing to deliver what they promised. For the rest of 1657 and in the first half of 1658, she kept in close contact with Frederick William, urging him to use his position as an elector to put pressure on Leopold in the period leading up to the imperial election in July, in order to persuade the Austrians to adopt a more active role in the war.

Nevertheless, Louise Marie was aware that even if Austrian military support was vital, prospects for an Austrian election were poor, despite the fact that Vienna, conscious of Austrian unpopularity, had at last decided to respond to the Polish offers: Auersberg presented a memorandum to the secret council on 6 December advocating a more active pursuit of the succession, while in a bid to placate Louise Marie, Leopold confirmed the grant made to her by John Casimir of the Silesian duchies of Oppeln and Ratibor.[13] When Lisola arrived to propose the Austrian succession, however, he was rebuffed by the queen, who told him that the king was in good health and that there were no plans at present to appoint a successor.[14]

The Austrian response came too late. Louise Marie had been prepared to support an Austrian candidature when there had seemed to be broad support for the idea

---

[10] Trzebicki to Vidoni, 29.X.1657; TRz. 8420 p. 87. It is true that at this point Louise Marie argued in favour of Brandenburg's neutrality in the war with Sweden, whereas John Casimir insisted on its participation; nevertheless, she later became an enthusiastic advocate of military action. Vidoni, Warsaw, 12.XI.1657; TRz. 8420 p. 72; Levinson, *Die Nuntiaturberichte* no. 165, p. 106.

[11] Des Noyers, Bromberg, 1.XI.1657; *Lettres* no. 128, p. 349; de Lumbres to Mazarin, Warsaw, 18.X.1657; Harl. 4532 pp. 124–5. Andrzej Leszczyński's plea that de Lumbres be banned from Court altogether was rejected; Louise Marie and Krzysztof Pac advised him to stay in Warsaw.

[12] [Blondel] 'ne réussit pas bien dans une audience qu'il eut avec la reine ... il la poussa indiscrètement et sans raison, en lui voulant persuader que, si elle voulait, on ferait la paix. Elle lui dit qu'elle le désirait plus que personne, et ensuite lui fit voir qu'elle n'était pas seule en Pologne, qu'il y avait des ministres et des sénateurs, et un conseil. Mais il rebâtit toutes les fois sa première instance avec une telle opiniatreté, qu'elle s'en impatienta, et dit, après qu'il fut sorti, mais tout bas, qu'il n'y avait pas moyen de traiter avec cet homme-là', Des Noyers, Poznań, 20.I.1658; *Lettres* no. 138, p. 377.

[13] Presentatum et lectum in Consilio Secret. die 6.XII.1657; Copy, CPA XVII f. 335; Confirmation of the duchies of Oppeln and Ratibor, Vienna, 28.I.1658; Copy, CPA XVII ff. 353, 366.

[14] De Lumbres to Mazarin, Poznań, 28.XII.1657; CPP XI f. 352; des Noyers reported the poor reception accorded the new offer: 'Je puis vous assurer qu'il y a tant d'aversion entre les deux nations que malaisément ils s'assujetiraient à cette maison.' Poznań, 1.XII.1657; *Lettres* no. 131, p. 359.

from the senate council. By the end of 1657, however, leading senators were expressing their hostility to the idea and their fears about the presence of Austrian troops in the Commonwealth. Lubomirski, who in October had attempted to stop the Austrians from garrisoning Cracow after it fell to the allied armies, told Vidoni

> of the jealousy with which he is regarded by the Court over the issue of the German garrison in Cracow. He justified himself by saying that he had only intended to return the capital city to liberty and that the German garrison should never have been allowed. What displeases him most is that, due to this affair, the nobility have come to loathe the house of Austria, feeling that it intends to win the throne by force, and that it is said that the crown might as well be given to the Swedes as to the Austrians.[15]

Concern over Austrian intentions did not mean that senators opposed an election in principle. Indeed, fear of an Austrian seizure of the throne increased support for the election of a candidate who might be brought up at Court under the watchful eye of the senate council. The Commonwealth's position was still weak enough for many to fear the consequences should John Casimir die before the war ended:

> I still consider it necessary to work towards the election of a successor to His Majesty, since, during the time that I have been with him, he has suffered from various indispositions, and although the times are unpropitious for dealing with such a matter, nevertheless, I feel it is worthwhile in every respect ... if there were an interregnum without a designated successor, I envisage the division of the kingdom between heretics and schismatics.[16]

De Lumbres had reported similar sentiments in September, and bore witness to the essential royal concern to maintain control of the future king:

> The majority of ... government ministers wish an election while the king is still alive, to avoid the divisions which, they believe, would inevitably occur if they waited until he should die. I understand that the king and queen support this move, even though it has been suggested to them that their power would thereby be significantly reduced ... if the successor is not dependent upon them ... For the sun is more appreciated when it is rising than when it sets.[17]

Louise Marie's interest in a French candidature grew as the extent of concern over Austrian intentions became apparent. It was further encouraged by Mazarin's positive response to the feelers she had put out in the autumn, when he told de Lumbres that the French would happily make available the sum suggested by Louise Marie 'to help ensure the succession for a French prince, or for someone who is a friend and ally of this Crown.'[18] He added that the French would be guided by the queen in this matter. This response was encouraging, for the queen had already told de Lumbres in September that she had serious doubts about the suitability of other candidates: Alexis offered little hope of conversion for himself or his son and although Charles Joseph had his supporters, including John Casimir, 'many would

[15] Vidoni, Warsaw, 5.XI.1657; TRz. 8420 p. 70.
[16] Vidoni, Poznań 11.I.1658; TRz. 8421 p. 7.
[17] De Lumbres to Mazarin, Warsaw, 30.IX.1657; CPP XI f. 305.
[18] Mazarin to de Lumbres, Paris, 16.XI.1657; *Lettres du Cardinal Mazarin* VIII p. 210.

The succession and the failure of the coalition

oppose him: those who have not forgotten the old enactment, accepted but not written down, forbidding the election of a prince from the house of Austria, so that liberty might not be destroyed, as happened in Bohemia and Hungary'.[19]

In November 1657 Louise Marie expressed a desire for peace to de Lumbres, who said she was 'returning to our side' because of the disgust she felt at Austrian behaviour and, to prevent a Habsburg coming to the throne, agreed to work for a French candidature.[20] The queen certainly realised that a French candidature might be viable, if only because of the unsuitability of those previously considered. Nevertheless, the extent to which she was committed has been exaggerated. Bąkowa accepts Kubala's assumption that she henceforth dedicated all her efforts to the achievement of a French election, arguing that she had already created a solid nucleus of support by early 1658, including Czarniecki, Lubomirski, Jan Leszczyński, Wielopolski, Wydżga, Morsztyn, Prażmowski and Gosiewski.[21]

Louise Marie was telling de Lumbres what he wanted to hear but her sincerity is open to question in the light of her other actions. Historians have been too keen to see these contacts as marking the definitive establishment of a 'French party'. Yet the attitude of leading senators was by no means clear. Kubala uses the evidence carelessly, conflating passages from de Lumbres's dispatches and interpreting them in the light of his assumptions that the queen's actions were all directed towards the achievement of a French election, and that she rapidly formed a powerful, coherent group working for a French election. In the same dispatch in which he revealed the queen's stated desire for a French candidature, de Lumbres reported that: 'Plusieurs ministres et senateurs m'ont aussi temoigné ne pas desirer un roi de cette maison [Habsburg] et protesté que par les traites de Vienne il n'y a aucune promesse ni obligation pour cela ...'[22] Kubala paraphrases this, not only mistranslating 'plusieurs' (several) as 'wielu' (many) but also inserting a phrase not present in the original: 'Many ministers and senators revealed their desire for a successor from the house of France and assured me that the Vienna treaty, a copy of which I was shown by the queen, contains no promises or undertaking with regard to the throne.'[23]

De Lumbres did discuss a French succession with several senators, but their reactions were cautious. It was one thing to oppose an Austrian succession, quite another to support a French candidate. Lubomirski told him 'that liberty is something which is cherished by the Poles, who would lay down their lives to preserve it, and that the example of the kingdoms of Hungary and Bohemia, which [Austria] has turned into hereditary monarchies from elective and free realms,

---

[19] De Lumbres to Mazarin, Warsaw, 30.IX.1657; CPP XII f. 305.
[20] De Lumbres to Mazarin, Warsaw, 10.XI.1657; CPP XI f. 327.
[21] Bąkowa, *Szlachta województwa krakowskiego* p. 21; Kersten states that Czarniecki was recruited in December 1657: *Stefan Czarniecki* p. 364.   [22] ibid.
[23] 'i wielu ministrów i senatorów objawiło życzenia sukcesji dla francuskiego Domu i zapewniali, że w traktacie wiedeńskim, którego kopię królowa mi pokazała, nie ma żadnej obietnicy ani obowiązania w sprawie sukcesji.' Kubala, *Wojna brandenburska* pp. 265, 389, n. 12.

causes Poles to fear the same fate'. De Lumbres suggested that to preserve liberty it might be expedient to elect a Pole or a foreign prince who was not a neighbour and therefore would be less able to threaten Polish liberties. Lubomirski passed over the first remark in silence but with regard to the second 'il demeurra d'accord'. Lubomirski's reaction, however, was non-commital: nowhere did he express actual support for a French candidature. De Lumbres went on to say that both Koryciński and Krzysztof Pac were 'well-intentioned' towards France but did not disclose their attitude towards a French candidature, although Kubala assumes they must have supported it.[24] By January, Bogusław Leszczyński, who had taken the succession offer to Vienna in the spring, had also changed his mind: 'He has promised his own vote in favour of a Habsburg prince and has even given the Austrians hope of those of his family, but having discovered the lack of sincerity of that house he has completely changed his mind.'[25] Nevertheless, Leszczyński did not openly state that he favoured a French candidature.

There is no doubt that, with the encouragement of de Lumbres and Louise Marie, the growth of anti-Austrian feeling caused some to consider a French candidature.[26] There is no evidence, however, that it was discussed as yet in anything but the most general of terms. The queen was perhaps encouraged by the initial response of a few, but this does not mean that she regarded the plan as anything more than one option among several, whose chances of success would depend on a number of circumstances. According to de Lumbres, as late as April Louise Marie had only confided fully in Lubomirski, Krzysztof Pac and Gosiewski 'and more openly to the last two, who are her creatures, than to the former'. Czarniecki had been told, but only in more general terms.[27]

If a French candidature was as yet merely a possibility, hopes for a quick settlement with Sweden rose after the withdrawal of the main Swedish army to Denmark. The September offer to return Prussia for a cash payment underwritten by the French was the first sign of a change in Swedish attitudes, though the refusal by de Lumbres to put the offer in writing provoked doubts as to Charles X's sincerity.[28] Nevertheless, as disillusion with Austria grew, so did interest in peace. Although Poland was committed to talking with Sweden only in concert with her allies and had rejected the French proposal of separate talks in November, the Austrian failure to fulfil its commitments under the treaty of Vienna could be used as a justification for Poland entering such talks. Kubala and others assume that for the queen and the 'French party', the succession was the main priority; in reality it was the prospect of peace with Sweden which was initially attractive. If this were achieved, thought could then be given to the succession; if it were not, a French candidate was unlikely to succeed. This suited Mazarin: although he responded

[24] De Lumbres to Mazarin, Warsaw, 10.XI.1657; CPP XI f. 327.
[25] De Lumbres to Mazarin, Poznań, 7.I.1658; CPP XII f. 7.
[26] De Lumbres to Mazarin, Poznań, 26.I.1658; CPP XII f. 24.
[27] Kubala, *Wojna brandenburska* p. 265; de Lumbres to Mazarin, Poznań, 20.IV.1658; CPP XII f. 73.
[28] De Lumbres to Mazarin, Poznań, 26.I.1658; CPP XII ff. 24–7.

favourably to approaches concerning the succession, he pointed out that for France the achievement of peace was of paramount importance.[29] If the French could persuade the Swedes to moderate their demands, then a more active pursuit of a French succession might be possible: 'We would not face as many problems ... as one might imagine, if we are able to restore peace to Poland, if the queen uses her influence as she promises and if we can engage the most important ministers and senators in our cause.'[30]

The government, however, was still committed to stepping up the military pressure on Sweden. Anti-Swedish feeling remained strong. Lubomirski suggested that now the Commonwealth had such powerful allies and Rákóczi had been repulsed, it might be able to wage war successfully on Sweden

> and, with the help of God, bring to his knees this public ravager of Christendom, for such I must call the Swede, who fights not out of the justice of his cause but solely because of his lust for war ... Truly one should have little faith in the Swedes ... the more they offer, the less they are to be trusted.[31]

Efforts continued to persuade Austria to pursue the war more actively. In January, talks were held in Berlin in which Frederick William, the Danish ambassador, and Jan Leszczyński tried to extract a firm commitment to a Pomeranian campaign.[32] Despite the queen's assurances to de Lumbres of her devotion to the French cause, she kept in close contact with Frederick William and urged the immediate commencement of the campaign: 'It is necessary either to ruin the king of Sweden or to treat with him. To achieve the former, it is necessary by whatever means to oblige the Austrians to join their armies to ours.'[33]

If it is assumed that the queen was wholly committed to the French at this stage, this letter is hard to explain. Kubala considers that her enthusiasm for the Brandenburg alliance stemmed from a desire for a French succession and that she expected to find in him 'a faithful friend, adviser and ally over matters close to her heart': peace with Sweden as a preliminary to a French election.[34] This interpretation is unconvincing. Whatever else Louise Marie expected from Frederick William, he was unlikely to support a French candidate for the Polish throne. The queen's correspondence makes no mention of the succession, beyond firm denials of any offer to the Habsburgs, and there is no indication that Frederick William was aware of the possibility of a French candidature until de Lumbres reported his lack of enthusiasm in February.[35] Louise Marie continued to encourage his desire for an offensive against Sweden, urging him to put pressure on Austria by refusing to vote

---

[29] Mazarin to de Lumbres, 14.XII.1657 CPP XI f. 349.
[30] De Lumbres to Mazarin, Poznań, 26.I.1658; CPP XII f. 24.
[31] Lubomirski to B. Radziwiłł, 13.XII.1657; WAP Wawel, ASang. 86 ff. 107–8.
[32] Copia literarum Sermi. Poloniae Regis ad Sermum. Electorem, Poznań, 30.XII.1657; Czart. 388 f. 287. The talks began on 3.I.1658; Opitz, *Österreich und Brandenburg* p. 49.
[33] Louise Marie to Frederick William, 26.XII.1657; *Urkunden und Aktenstücke* VIII p. 274.
[34] Kubala, *Wojna brandenburska* p. 262.
[35] Louise Marie to Frederick William, 2.I.1658; *Urkunden und Aktenstücke* VIII pp. 275–6; de Lumbres to Mazarin, Hamburg, 23.II.1658; CPP XII f. 44.

for Leopold in the imperial election unless he promised to assist in the conquest of Swedish Pomerania. Although the French also tried to persuade Frederick William to withhold his vote, they wished to prevent an invasion of Pomerania. Far from acting in the interests of France, Louise Marie was following official policy, investigating the possibility of separate talks with Sweden while keeping up the pressure on Austria and Brandenburg for a joint campaign. She took care to keep the elector informed of the progress of the peace plan, promising to tell him the terms on offer as soon as they arrived. She expressed her belief that negotiations should continue, which would not prevent the launching of a campaign, since the Austrians had now agreed to fight outside Poland.[36]

Louise Marie was a sensible and practical politician. If she was swift to appreciate that a French candidate might be suitable for the Court's wider plans with regard to the succession, she was aware that there were important obstacles in the attitude of John Casimir and the widespread suspicion, which she herself shared, that Mazarin favoured Sweden over the Commonwealth. Only if France succeeded in persuading Sweden to settle on terms acceptable to Poland would a French candidature be viable. If Louise Marie was naturally attracted to a French candidate and was prepared to sound out leading politicians as to their attitude, she would not commit herself as yet: the Commonwealth still needed military aid from Austria and Brandenburg to keep up the pressure on Sweden. Meanwhile, contacts with de Lumbres were a useful means of leaning on Austria. In an effort to worry Leopold, she resorted to threats, telling Vidoni of Polish fears that Austria would combine with Sweden and Brandenburg to partition Poland and stating that if Vienna was thinking in these terms, then the Commonwealth might unite with Sweden and invade Silesia.[37] She also put pressure on the French, however, demanding to know their attitude towards the succession:

time is short, partly since the ministers and senators, considering the lack of certainty about the king's health and the disorders which would ensue should he die during the war without a designated successor, are urging the king and queen to consider the matter, and partly since the Austrians are making strong moves in this direction, with attractive offers to the queen, who listens to them more than I would wish, despite the fact that those with regard for the liberty of their country wish the exclusion of the house of Austria from the succession.[38]

She told de Lumbres that she could not proceed without proof of French intentions, making it clear that if France failed to achieve peace with Sweden there could be no thought of any French succession and that 'in default of France, she can only look to a prince from the house of Austria'.

Such proof was at last forthcoming. In January 1658, Mazarin ordered 10,000 thalers each to be sent to Koryciński and Krzysztof Pac on condition that peace was

[36] Louise Marie to Frederick William, 26.XII.1657 and 19.I.1658; *Urkunden und Aktenstücke* VIII pp. 274, 277–8.
[37] Vidoni, Poznań, 4.I.1658; TRz. 8421 p. 5; Levinson, *Die Nuntiaturberichte* no. 174, p. 110.
[38] De Lumbres to Mazarin, Thorn, 13.I.1658; CPP XII f. 13.

The succession and the failure of the coalition

made and that they contributed to the succession: 'For it would not be right ... that we should sow and then harvest nothing.'[39] He also wrote personally to leading politicians, including Lubomirski, Koryciński and Pac, attacking Austrian behaviour and extolling the merits of peace with Sweden.[40] He told de Lumbres that more funds were available: 'There is something more efficacious than letters, and gifts are more eloquent than words.' He urged de Lumbres to tell him precisely what would be required for the queen, leading senators and the army, adding there was nothing France would not do to achieve peace. This was his main objective; as far as the succession was concerned, the princess palatine was writing directly to Louise Marie.[41] Encouraged, Louise Marie began to test opinion. Pac was persuaded by his wife to accept French money, while Louise Marie suggested to de Lumbres that more was needed for Prażmowski and especially for Morsztyn, who was well-regarded by several important magnates, including Lubomirski, over whom he had some influence.[42]

Yet Louise Marie was still aware that the success of such efforts was dependent on France's ability to persuade Sweden to settle. The Swedes were now offering to negotiate with all the allies together but the conditions were unclear enough to provoke doubt as to Swedish intentions and de Lumbres could not prevent Trzebicki and Bogusław Leszczyński demanding greater clarification.[43] Nevertheless, the senate council – unanimously according to de Lumbres – accepted the French proposal to mediate peace with Sweden and for negotiations on preliminaries to commence immediately. This decision was to be put to a convocation of senators and *szlachta* representatives which had been summoned to meet in Warsaw in March, the largest and most important political gathering since the Częstochowa convocation in early 1657. Louise Marie was active in this campaign:

One could not have asked for more from the queen, who took pains to talk to all senators and outline the reasons which I had told her and afterwards, aware of the opposition of vice-chancellor Trzebicki, she even spoke very sharply to him, threatening to tell the Warsaw convocation that he was the only obstacle to peace, which prompted Trzebicki to complain to the king; this provoked a row between Their Majesties.[44]

The debate was heated. Trzebicki and Andrzej Leszczyński strongly opposed French mediation, with Leszczyński stressing the help Austria had given Poland in

[39] Mazarin to de Lumbres, 11.I.1658; CPP XII f. 5.
[40] e .g. Mazarin to Lubomirski, 4.I.1658; CPP XII f. 2.
[41] Mazarin to de Lumbres, 4.I.1658; CPP XII f. 4.
[42] Pac only accepted after consulting the queen: de Lumbres to Mazarin, Poznań, 20.IV.1658; CPP XII p. 77. He had also accepted 5,000 thalers from Frederick William in September 1657 for his part in achieving the agreement at Wehlau: Frederick William to Hoverbeck, Wehlau, 21.IX.1657; *Urkunden und Aktenstücke* VIII p. 218. With almost all his estates under Muscovite occupation, Pac was in desperate need of money: de Lumbres to Mazarin, Cracow, 10.XI.1657; CPP XI f. 351. De Lumbres reported, with some degree of exaggeration, that Morsztyn governed Lubomirski absolutely: de Lumbres to Mazarin, Poznań, 20.IV.1658; CPP XII f. 77.
[43] Des Noyers, Poznań, 1.II.1658; *Lettres* no. 140, p. 381; de Lumbres to Brienne, Poznań, 26.I.1658; CPP XII f. 26; Copy to Mazarin, Harl. 4532 f. 160.   [44] ibid.

115

the past. Most of the lay senators present, however, supported the plan, as did the king.

It is important not to assume that support for French mediation implied support for a French succession. According to Kubala and Bąkowa, the queen had persuaded the king to support the French election by the end of 1657, and his acceptance of French mediation was the result of his conversion.[45] There is no evidence to support such a claim. Historians have too easily accepted Rudawski's pro-Austrian view that John Casimir had been browbeaten by his wife into accepting French mediation.[46] In reality, if John Casimir was prepared to bow to majority opinion in the senate, which urged the acceptance of French mediation, he refused further concessions. He resisted Louise Marie's suggestion that talks with Sweden should start immediately without the participation of Poland's allies and succeeded in preventing anything being put in writing with regard to peace preliminaries.[47] He won the argument. As the queen told Frederick William: 'His Majesty wishes to do nothing without your advice. He is sure that if we stay together nothing can shake us. If the Austrians send their troops, the combining of our forces will hasten peace. We cannot, however, count on them doing so.'[48]

The king was prepared to use the acceptance of French mediation as a means of putting pressure on Austria to agree to invade Pomerania but would go no further. If the succession plan were to progress, Mazarin would have to force Charles to make further concessions; the terms on offer were unacceptable and stimulated doubts about Charles's sincerity: 'Although the queen appears to remain firm in her resolve to promote the negotiations, she nevertheless is acting with more restraint, fearing that she will be criticised for her conduct if it transpires that the king of Sweden is not acting in good faith, of which she is ever fearful.'[49]

Such fears were vindicated when news arrived of a meeting between Schlippenbach and Schwerin in Berlin at which the Swedes offered to talk jointly with the Commonwealth and its allies, except Denmark, a few days after the arrival of the offer to talk separately.[50] De Lumbres reported that John Casimir was greatly disturbed by this; he was listening once more to the Austrians and had abandoned all thought of peace. Louise Marie unceremoniously ordered de Lumbres to go to Charles in order to clear up the matter; the ambassador's protests that this would mean he would miss the Warsaw convocation left her unmoved. If he could not resolve the matter, there was little hope for the French peace plan, let alone the succession.[51]

---

[45] Bąkowa, *Szlachta województwa krakowskiego* p. 21.   [46] Rudawski, *Historiarum* IX p. 398.
[47] Vidoni, Poznań, 26.I.1658; TRz. 8421 p. 9.
[48] Louise Marie to Frederick William, 26.I.1658; *Urkunden und Aktenstücke* VIII p. 278.
[49] De Lumbres to Brienne, 26.I.1658; CPP XII f. 26; Copy to Mazarin, Harl. 4532 f. 160.
[50] J. Leszczyński to Lubomirski, Berlin, 11.II.1658; Czart. 388 no. 175, f. 353. Schlippenbach was playing a double game: he also offered Frederick William a further share of Poland in a partition between Austria, Sweden and Brandenburg. De Lumbres to Mazarin, Berlin, 12.II.1658; *Urkunden und Aktenstücke* II p. 154.
[51] De Lumbres to Brienne, Poznań, 2.II.1658; CPP XII f. 36; des Noyers, Poznań, 1.II.1658; *Lettres* no. 140, p. 381.

The succession and the failure of the coalition

Rumours of the acceptance of French mediation caused a great stir in Berlin, as was intended. Lisola complained heatedly to Jan Leszczyński, who remarked: 'I confess that I do not grasp the reason why we should spurn this mediation and I am surprised that talk of peace should so upset Vienna, whose reinforcements are so much delayed, which is causing not just damage but destruction to our people.'[52] Leszczyński was exasperated by Austrian delays. In January he refused to leave Berlin until there was full agreement between Austria and Brandenburg:

> I cannot say how distressed I am by this delay in reaching a settlement, since it means the greatest danger for the Commonwealth; it immediately seemed to me that the Austrians were to blame, for they only offered 6,000 men, without cannon, which is the clearest signal that this merely represents a desire to quarter their troops for a long time in Poland, which is what they have hitherto been working for. They give this Court much cause for resentment.[53]

Nevertheless, Austria finally signed a defensive/offensive alliance with Brandenburg on 9 February. Leszczyński, still harbouring doubts as to Austrian sincerity, called for a council of war as soon as possible to discuss joint operations and the withdrawal of Austrian troops from Poland.[54]

The treaty of Berlin came too late to reestablish Austrian fortunes, since there was little time to exploit it before the Warsaw convocation. Trzebicki assured Vidoni that since John Casimir had told the ambassador that mediation had been accepted, Trzebicki had inserted some ambiguous phrases into the reply given to de Lumbres to avoid upsetting Leopold and to leave a loophole to facilitate retraction if necessary.[55] The king, however, was less encouraging and Vidoni reported increasing bitterness over Austrian behaviour. Despite the Berlin agreement, Austria was now quibbling over money and insisting that the invasion of Pomerania depended on the rejection of French mediation.[56] Such prevarication seemed all too familiar and did nothing to improve Austria's standing.

The Warsaw convocation opened on 20 February, with Trzebicki reading the royal proposals the next day. Since de Lumbres was absent and Lisola only arrived towards the end of proceedings, two of the most informative sources for the period reveal little about its course. The pro-Austrian Rudawski is unreliable; nevertheless, Walewski and Kubala follow him exactly, arguing that the king defied the wish of the majority over the acceptance of French mediation, declaring that the matter was for him to decide and refusing to allow debate.[57] Yet, apart from Rudawski's account, there is little evidence of opposition to the acceptance of French mediation. According to des Noyers, all senators strongly supported the king's wishes.[58]

---

[52] J. Leszczyński to Cieciszewski, Berlin, 8.II.1658; Czart. 388 no. 172, f. 345.
[53] J. Leszczyński to A. Leszczyński, Berlin, 11.II.1658; Czart. 388 no. 174, f. 347. For the threat not to leave Berlin, see Lisola, Berlin, 14.II.1658; *Berichte* no. 92, p. 368.
[54] Moerner, *Kurbrandenburgs Staatsverträge* no. 123, pp. 229–33; declaration by Jan Leszczyński, 9.II.1658; no.123c, p. 232.
[55] Vidoni, Warsaw, 16.II.1658; TRz. 8421 p. 11; Levinson, *Die Nuntiaturberichte* no. 178, p. 114.
[56] Vidoni, Warsaw, 16.II.1658; TRz. 8421 p. 11.
[57] Rudawski, *Historiarum* IX p. 398; Walewski, *Historia wyzwolenia* II p. 247; Kubala, *Wojny duńskie* pp. 40–1.   [58] Des Noyers, Warsaw, 21.II.1658; *Lettres* no. 142, p. 384.

French mediation had powerful supporters, including Lubomirski, Bogusław Leszczyński and Gosiewski. The higher clergy remained virtually isolated in opposition. Andrzej Leszczyński in vain reminded the convocation of the benefits Austria had brought Poland:

One can only marvel at the whole Commonwealth and at the king for forgetting the aid they had so recently received from Austria. The Polish king, born of an Austrian mother, rescued by Austrian arms and restored to his kingdom after his exile, should be ashamed to have forgotten so quickly. If this is what our neighbours are saying, what of more distant countries? They will say that Poles are the most ungrateful of nations and that they violate friendship instead of cultivating it.[59]

Vidoni stressed the queen's role in whipping up support for French mediation: 'She openly incites everyone against the Germans; it is therefore said that she must have received some great slight from them, or some great promises from France.'[60] Rudawski suggested that the queen was to blame for the lower clergy's refusal to support the bishops over mediation: 'The clergy ... long resisted the command of that woman until at last they agreed, compelled by pseudo-politicians, but chiefly in the last analysis, by the wish of the king himself.'[61]

There is no doubt that the queen worked tirelessly to win support for French mediation and that she used promises of money or favours to this end. When de Lumbres returned to Warsaw in March, Louise Marie assured him that she had won over several senators for the French cause, especially Czarniecki

who, as a result of the promise made to them of pensions, has spoken out forcefully on our behalf, talking favourably of our mediation, and in order more effectively to oppose the Austrian designs, has even effected a reconciliation with Lubomirski, with whom he did not have good relations due to rivalry between them over the command of the army.[62]

Nevertheless, the queen's efforts alone do not account for the complete failure of the bishops to block French mediation. They were unable even to ensure that the clergy as a whole followed their lead, due to widespread anger at the behaviour of Austrian troops, expressed in the protest of the clergy of the diocese of Poznań issued at the end of January, which later achieved notoriety when circulated at the imperial diet.[63] This document, signed by Tolibowski, bishop of Poznań, attacked the exactions of Austrian troops and the unwarranted demands they placed on the clergy. Rudawski pointed out that of all the episcopate of Great Poland, only Tolibowski had signed, concluding that here was proof that the protest was unrepresentative of clerical views and had been foisted upon the clergy by the

---

[59] Rudawski, *Historiarum* IX p. 399.
[60] Vidoni, Warsaw, 4.III.1658; TRz. 8421 p. 13; Levinson, *Die Nuntiaturberichte* no. 180, p. 115.
[61] Rudawski, *Historiarum* IX p. 398.
[62] De Lumbres to Mazarin, Poznań, 11.IV.1658; CPP XII f. 63.
[63] *Querelae Universi Cleri in Maiori Polonia et Diocesi Posnaniensi super Barbara Austriaci Militis Insolentia in Ordinem Ecclesiasticum et Christi Patrimonium Exercita ad Sacram Regiam Maiestatem Hungariae et Bohemiae etc.* (Poznań, 1658).

queen. Yet it was not the higher clergy on the whole who suffered the depredations of the Austrian troops but the parish clergy and monastic houses who had troops quartered on them, or who saw their income drop as local people were unable to meet tithe obligations. When Vidoni took this matter up with Andrzej Leszczyński, he was told that for the moment it was difficult to do anything about such problems.[64]

Tolibowski proved more sympathetic to the complaints of the lower clergy. In January he raised the problem of troops being billeted on religious houses; Vidoni appreciated the problem, mentioning it to Andrzej Leszczyński, who again put politics before the welfare of the clergy, declaring that the time was not right for the visitation of his archdiocese which the Pope and Vidoni were urging. While Vidoni acknowledged that the Commonwealth's needs were great, and argued that the clergy should give voluntarily and with papal approval, without prejudice to its tax-immunity, he was increasingly concerned about the aggravation caused by Austrian troops, 'which truly is insupportable'. If Tolibowski, in common with his episcopal colleagues, eventually opposed the acceptance of French mediation, the lower clergy were ready to support it.[65]

The general mood was hostile to Austria when Lisola arrived in Warsaw in early March, shortly before the convocation closed on 15 March. He was met with bitter complaints about Austrian delays.[66] Leopold was accused of bringing even more troops into Poland than the 12,000 allowed by the Vienna treaty. Lisola blamed Louise Marie for this hostility and immediately began a campaign to secure the rejection of French mediation. Kubala and Walewski, basing their opinions almost entirely on Lisola, conclude that the king was a reluctant supporter of the French mediation, forced to accept it by Louise Marie and by the attitude of those who, angered by the excesses of Austrian troops, suspected him of intriguing with Vienna.[67] Walewski stated that John Casimir's inability to stand up to Louise Marie put him in an ambiguous position:

The king commanded that Lisola be told that he was committed but he gave his royal word that he would delay talks in so far as it was possible, to ensure that they took place without French mediation, but he demanded that the Austrian army should move within two or three weeks, otherwise he would not feel bound by his word. The king refused to give this understanding in writing. Thus John Casimir adopted a false position: he had told France that he accepted their mediation and the Austrians that he would do his best to obstruct it.[68]

The impression given by Walewski, and by Kubala, who follows him almost verbatim, is that John Casimir was eager to reject French mediation but unable to do so. Yet Lisola's actual report, on which this account is based, gives a different

[64] Rudawski, *Historiarum* IX pp. 399, 406; Vidoni to Orsini, Poznań, 16.XII.1657; TRz. 8420 pp. 187–8.
[65] Vidoni to Orsini, Warsaw, 12.II.1658; TRz. 8421 p. 86; Vidoni to Orsini, Warsaw, 23.II.1658; TRz. 8421 p. 91; Rudawski, *Historiarum* IX p. 399; de Lumbres to Brienne, Poznań, 11.IV.1658; CPP XII f. 67.
[66] Lisola, Warsaw, 10.III.1658; *Berichte* no. 94, pp. 384–6.
[67] Kubala, *Wojny duńskie* p. 43. [68] Walewski, *Historia wyzwolenia* II p. 248.

After the Deluge

picture. John Casimir was prepared to abandon French mediation but only if the Austrians took the offensive:

His Majesty declared that he was not averse to promising this but under this condition, that Your Majesty's army, under the terms of the treaty of Berlin, should enter Pomerania or Holstein against the Swedes in two or three weeks; if not, then he intended in no way to bind himself to this end; and since he will not give up any means of avoiding ultimate defeat, whether by mediation or by arms, he will return completely to negotiation through mediators.[69]

This was a blunt statement of the position, not a categorical promise: if Leopold wished to restore Austrian fortunes in Poland, he must prosecute the war more vigorously. Far from supporting French mediation because his wife told him to, John Casimir did so in order to put pressure on the Austrians to give Poland genuine military aid. He was resolute in the face of threats from Lisola:

Having seen relations with the king of Hungary manifestly break down, I begged His Majesty to show his zeal for public order and reach agreement. In discussing these talks, he lost his temper, saying that Lisola had threatened that the German troops would not leave the kingdom until French mediation was abandoned and that this was not the sort of talk one expected from friends. He threatened to summon the Tatars and Cossacks to invade Silesia and to tell the tsar that the king of Hungary wished to take control of the kingdom... He says he will write to the king of Hungary to say he is willing to treat separately with Sweden.[70]

Vidoni attempted to soothe John Casimir, who asked him to make Lisola understand that it was impossible to withdraw French mediation. Meanwhile, Lisola talked to the queen, who gave him the same message. He then complained bitterly to Vidoni, who calmed Lisola sufficiently to win certain concessions, although the nuncio was worried that a complete breakdown in Polish–Austrian relations was imminent. Lisola's attitude seems merely to have strengthened John Casimir's resolve to stand by French mediation. On his return to the Polish Court, de Lumbres reported that John Casimir had applied himself 'with much vigour' over the issue and had given his positive assurance that French mediation had been accepted.[71]

The Court's deliberately ambiguous position certainly worried Lisola and de Lumbres, but their response was not always what the Court desired. Following the humiliating defeat for Austrian interests at Warsaw, Lisola began to work towards creating a strong Austrian party to counteract what he saw as the queen's pernicious influence. In March, he wrote of the foundation of a powerful faction.[72] Inevitably, this group had an episcopal nucleus, led by Andrzej Leszczyński and Trzebicki, who made great efforts to win support. They suggested that their stand would please

[69] Lisola, Warsaw, 18.III.1658; *Berichte* no. 94, p. 391.
[70] Vidoni, Warsaw, 11.III.1658; TRz. 8421 p. 15.
[71] De Lumbres to Brienne, Poznań, 11.IV.1658; CPP XII ff. 67–8; Copy to Mazarin, Harl. 4532 f. 197.
[72] Lisola, Warsaw, 10 and 28.III.1658; Walewski, *Historia wyzwolenia* II p. 246; Lisola to Portia, Warsaw, 26.III.1658; ibid. p. 249.

The succession and the failure of the coalition

John Casimir, who had accepted mediation against his better judgement to please the queen, but their support was insufficient to recover the Austrian position.[73] Although John Casimir was generally pro-Austrian, he was embarrassed by the rigid attitudes of Leszczyński and Trzebicki who were unwilling to compromise and accused them of failing to recognise the political problems caused by Austrian unpopularity. Even Jan Leszczyński, who distrusted the French, felt on occasion that Austrian supporters went too far in their support of Vienna:

> I am writing to [Trzebicki] but not about everything, for he is too partisan, trusting Lisola more than us. He does not see, or does not want to see, that the prolongation of the war is necessary for the Austrians, who want our laws and those of our allies to be consumed in this war. They therefore proceed by delays, for they trust neither the elector, nor the Danes, nor the Swedes, whom they wish to destroy. They promised to conclude an alliance with the king of Denmark nine months ago; to date nothing has happened ... I do not speak without foundation, since I have a letter from Cieciszewski, who writes that the Austrians have admitted that some people, wishing to subject us to their rule, advised that they should not take up arms on our behalf but should wait for our ultimate destruction, so that we, in complete penury and brutalised by Swedish rule, would turn in desperation to Austria and throw ourselves unconditionally on their mercy. He tries to justify the Austrians by writing that such advice was rejected; nevertheless, they do not hurry to save us.[74]

As vice-chancellor, Trzebicki was in a unique position to frustrate Court attempts to move away from a pro-Austrian policy, especially since the incapacity of the dying Koryciński meant that most government business in Poland had to be channelled through his hands. In early April, Vidoni reported John Casimir's anger at Trzebicki for not specifying in a letter to de Lumbres the acceptance of French mediation, as he had been ordered to.[75] Trzebicki's dogged oposition to the French peace plan was a continual embarrassment. He showed Lisola important documents and leaked vital information: when he was absent from Court for three weeks in April 1658, Lisola complained that he had been unable to see a copy of Rey's instructions for his mission to the imperial diet in Frankfurt.[76]

It was the inflexibility of Trzebicki and other Austrian supporters, rather than commitment to the French cause, which prompted the Court to remove as many as possible from sensitive government posts. Already in August 1657, Trzebicki had been nominated to succeed Piotr Gembicki as bishop of Cracow, despite a previous royal promise to bestow what was the richest diocese in Poland on Andrzej Leszczyński.[77] Since this position was incompatible with state office, when official

---

[73] De Lumbres to Brienne, Poznań, 11.IV.1658; CPP XII f. 67.
[74] J. Leszczyński to B. Leszczyński, Berlin, 24.I.1658; Czart. 388 no. 160, ff. 312–13.
[75] Vidoni, Warsaw, 1.IV.1658; TRz. 8421 p. 19.
[76] Lisola, Poznań, 10.IV.1658; *Berichte* no. 96, p. 397.
[77] Trzebicki had been nominated on 30.VIII.1657; *Repertorium Rerum Polonicarum ex Archivo Orsini in Archivo Capitolino* Elementa ad Fontium Editiones III ed. W. Wychowska-de Andreis (Rome, 1961) p. 29; this was confirmed by the Pope on 25.II.1658. For the promise to Leszczyński, see Vidoni, 26.VII.1657; TRz. 8420 pp. 49–50.

confirmation was received from Rome, Trzebicki would have to surrender the vice-chancellor's seals, despite Austrian attempts to prevent this.[78] When Lisola suggested that the Poles seek mediation from the imperial diet, John Casimir agreed, but the ambassador sent to Frankfurt was Władysław Rey, the queen's chancellor, much to Lisola's disgust. Louise Marie also worked for the recall of the blatantly pro-Austrian Cieciszewski from his post as resident in Vienna and his replacement by one of her clients, rather than the pro-Austrian Rudawski. Faced with such attitudes, Lisola threatened to leave Warsaw, only staying after a direct plea from Vidoni.[79] The unwillingness of Trzebicki and other Austrian supporters to compromise meant that, after Trzebicki's replacement by Prażmowski, a client of the queen 'the house of Austria will not have a single partisan in the Polish or Lithuanian chanceries'.[80]

Historians traditionally assume that this elimination of Austrian supporters from the government represented the final triumph of a French party, led by Louise Marie. It is true that the queen continued to sound out opinion, testing both the Polish response to a French succession and French willingness to back it. An important target was Jan Leszczyński 'who enjoys a high reputation in the Commonwealth'. The queen had suggested to de Lumbres that since Leszczyński's attitude was unclear, it might be appropriate to pay him a pension similar to the one accorded to Czarniecki.[81] Bąkowa suggests that Leszczyński had already been won for the French candidature by the end of 1657; in reality, although he supported an election, he was not committed to any specific candidate:

He has even stated that, with regard to the election of a successor, he will follow the opinions of [Lubomirski, Krzysztof Pac and Gosiewski]. This would be a great victory but it is necessary that he gives greater proof of his sincerity ... It is true that I have noticed a certain change in his manner but his behaviour in the past gives me good cause for suspicion in the present, although he is the queen's principal official and appears to depend upon her, and although he has told her that he recognises that it would be good for Polish liberty not to fall under Austrian domination.[82]

De Lumbres was right to doubt the extent to which Leszczyński was prepared to commit himself. While Leszczyński was deeply disillusioned with Austrian behaviour, he still hoped that an active anti-Swedish coalition based on the Polish–Brandenburg alliance was possible. He assured Hoverbeck that money would be forthcoming for the war-effort following the decisions taken on taxation at the Warsaw convocation.[83] If in March Leszczyński was concerned about Frederick William's commitment, worried that the slightest thing might upset him, in May he

---

[78] De Lumbres to Mazarin, Poznań, 27.IV.1658; CPP XII f. 79.
[79] Lisola, Warsaw, 18.III.1658; *Berichte* no. 95, p. 392; Vidoni, Warsaw, 11.III.1658; TRz. 8421 p. 14; Levinson, *Die Nuntiaturberichte* no. 182, p. 117.
[80] De Lumbres to Brienne, Poznań, 4.V.1658; CPP XII f. 90.
[81] De Lumbres to Mazarin, Poznań, 20.IV.1658; CPP XII f. 73; de Lumbres to Mazarin, Poznań, 11.IV.1658; CPP XII f. 68.   [82] De Lumbres to Mazarin, Poznań, 20.IV.1658, CPP XII f. 73.
[83] J. Leszczyński to Hoverbeck, 20.III.1658; Czart 388 no. 180, f. 377.

The succession and the failure of the coalition

was more optimistic, feeling that the elector's support was firm and stating that he had always believed that the best plan was to attack the Swedes in Pomerania.[84] His enthusiasm for military action stemmed from his pessimistic assessment of the chances for successful peace talks:

I confess that I have no great faith in these peace proposals; apparently they wish, under the pretext of seeking peace, to obstruct the joining of forces by Leopold and the elector. It is up to us, however, to persuade Austria and Brandenburg to attack the Swede; the Austrians, however, may still wish to wriggle out of their commitment, having already promised to move at the start of April. I do not trust them, being well acquainted with their offers. We should seek an alternative course of action.[85]

Gosiewski, frequently regarded as a supporter of the French election, was also ambivalent in his attitude. His support for Muscovy and the treaty of Wilno had been shaken by the reports he had received from Medeksza, whom he had sent to negotiate with Alexis. In January a drunk Muscovite told Medeksza that the tsar greatly regretted not continuing the war with Poland after taking Wilno and that he did not immediately turn on Sweden. He was once more preparing for war and massing troops on the Lithuanian border. Medeksza reported over 1,000 carts approaching the frontiers loaded with provisions. In the border areas, the countryside was deserted, with more than a third of the inhabitants gone. Reports of forced conversions to Orthodoxy continued, and Muscovite soldiers boasted that the tsar would occupy the whole Commonwealth.[86] When at last Medeksza succeeded in putting Lithuanian demands to Alexis on 8 February, he made little progress. All attempts to obtain a promise to evacuate occupied estates and to release Lithuanian prisoners were met with polite excuses. Lithuanians had supported Wilno to win their estates back, yet the tsar's treatment of the occupied territories provoked doubts as to whether the lands and titles would be returned after his election. Ominously, while Medeksza was kept waiting, the Swedish ambassador was received with courtesy, which bore out Frederick William's warning that Sweden wished to make peace with Muscovy whatever the cost.[87]

Nevertheless, although such reports prompted Gosiewski to respond to the queen's overtures concerning the French succession in April, he did not prove as easy to persuade as Louise Marie had hoped, despite her support for him in his rivalry with Paweł Sapieha, who had been appointed Lithuanian grand hetman over his head in 1656. Gosiewski reminded de Lumbres of the farcical short reign of Henry Valois, which was not a good precedent.[88] In May Gosiewski sent an agent to Poznań to confer with Louise Marie and de Lumbres, and then to France to discover

---

[84] J. Leszczyński to Lubomirski, 25.III.1658; Czart 388 no. 188, f. 383; J. Leszczyński to Turski, 26.V.1658; ibid. no. 191, ff. 393–4.
[85] J. Leszczyński to Lubomirski, 25.III.1658; Czart 388 no. 188, f. 383.
[86] Medeksza, *Księga pamiętnicza* pp. 110, 114, 147.
[87] ibid. pp. 123, 128, 164. Frederick William to Louise Marie, undated (December 1657), *Urkunden und Aktenstücke* VIII p. 275.
[88] De Lumbres to Mazarin, Poznań, 11.IV.1658; CPP XII ff. 63–4.

the intentions of Louis XIV. When Louise Marie suggested that the time was not ripe, Gosiewski took offence, seeing this as evidence of a loss of enthusiasm on her part. De Lumbres had to work hard to patch up this disagreement, but was forced to prevaricate when Gosiewski asked for money for the troops under his command. The ambassador suspected that Gosiewski was worried that if the succession plan succeeded solely through the queen's efforts France would feel that it only had an obligation to her and would be slow to recognise the contributions of others.[89]

It is significant that Gosiewski should accuse Louise Marie of losing enthusiasm for the French plan. Too often it is assumed that the queen worked in close cooperation with de Lumbres and that the latter's reports reveal her true feelings. Although Louise Marie had undoubtedly been encouraged by the positive French response to the proposed candidature, she was still far from committed. The succession had reemerged as an important issue, but a firm commitment was impossible because of the uncertain international situation. In March and April, a wide range of proposals was considered, including Leopold I (rejected as being too powerful), his brother Charles Joseph, Condé, Mattia de' Medici, the son of the duke of Courland, and Frederick William, whose candidature was unlikely owing to his continued refusal to consider conversion to Catholicism. Although the son of the duke of Longueville was Louise Marie's preferred candidate, she once more sounded out Vidoni as to the Pope's attitude to Mattia.[90] Yet the idea of Mattia as a compromise candidate was again rejected by Austrian supporters: Andrzej Leszczyński immediately repeated his opposition to any Italian or French candidate.[91] Such rigidity was dangerous for the Court's chances of achieving an election; when Leszczyński died in April, he was therefore replaced not by Czartoryski, as Austrian supporters had hoped, but by the less energetic and more tractable Wacław Leszczyński.[92]

Flexibility was vital because the international situation was still too fluid to permit any firm commitment to a particular policy. If Louise Marie had suggested a French candidature at the Warsaw convocation and if the majority of senators still favoured an election, no agreement was yet possible over the best candidate:

One is accustomed enough to hearing discussion of the succession among the Poles and I have talked of it with Their Majesties on many occasions but I perceive that everyone sees the matter in their own way ... May it please God that such a necessary goal be attained but its resolution must wait, for it is not possible at present to take any decision, since I foresee that some will argue against an election *vivente rege* for their own purposes, especially religious dissidents, since the division of the Commonwealth helps them to advance their pretensions.[93]

[89] De Lumbres to Mazarin, Poznań, 11.V.1658; CPP XII f. 96.
[90] Vidoni, Warsaw, 9.IV.1658; TRz. 8421 p. 20.
[91] Vidoni, 4.III.1658; TRz. 8421 p. 13.
[92] Vidoni, Warsaw, 22.IV.1658; TRz. 8421 p. 22; Levinson, *Die Nuntiaturberichte* no. 191, p. 122; Lisola, Poznań, 24.IV.1658; *Berichte* no. 98, p. 402.
[93] Vidoni, Warsaw, 9.IV.1658; TRz. 8421 p. 20.

The succession and the failure of the coalition

Furthermore, as was clear to Gosiewski, Louise Marie's enthusiasm for the French had substantially diminished since the Warsaw convocation.

This was due to a dramatic change in the international situation on both western and eastern fronts. Just as it seemed that the Austro-Polish alliance might collapse, Charles X led his army over the frozen Little Belt in a surprise attack on Copenhagen, which forced Frederick III to accept the humiliating treaty of Roskilde (26 February 1658). The defeat of Denmark was a great blow to the Commonwealth and put new strains on the alliance with Austria and Brandenburg. The most immediate worry concerned Charles's intentions: while the Poles feared he would return to finish off the work he had left incomplete in 1657, Leopold and Frederick William were afraid that he would use their alliance with Poland as an excuse to invade the Empire.

The most surprising result of Roskilde was that it at last galvanised Vienna into a more positive approach. Worried at growing French influence in Warsaw and afraid of a separate Polish settlement with Sweden, freeing Charles for an attack on Bohemia, Leopold at last decided that a preemptive strike at Pomerania might be necessary. He therefore ordered Montecuccoli to do everything in his power to promote joint action with Frederick William against Sweden. Yet Leopold's enthusiasm was almost immediately dampened by Frederick William. Long in favour of the Pomeranian campaign, the elector had changed his mind, fearing that now Charles's hands were free, he would turn on the ally who had betrayed him.[94] In April, when John Casimir called a council of war in Poznań to discuss the proposed campaign to Pomerania and Holstein, in direct contrast to the situation at the start of the year, it was Austria which favoured an active policy and Brandenburg which dragged its heels, as Lisola tried to win Polish support for an attack on Pomerania.[95]

Lisola still insisted, however, on the rejection of French mediation as the precondition for an attack on Pomerania, which caused the Poles to suspect that the new-found Austrian enthusiasm for offensive action was merely a political ploy; they had heard enough Austrian promises in the past to justify scepticism.[96] Nevertheless, the Austrians did make a concrete offer. Lisola gave assurances that Leopold was ready to send 5,000 men for the campaign in Prussia and 15,000 under Montecuccoli for the attack on Pomerania and Holstein, adding that Austria did not fear a French attack in Alsace and had sufficient forces to meet one in any case. He could not, however, convince Brandenburg of Leopold's sincerity. Frederick William, now fearing a Swedish attack, did not wish to risk waging war outside his own frontiers, especially since the Dutch and the Frankfurt diet strongly opposed

---

[94] Opitz, *Österreich und Brandenburg* pp. 85–97; A. Waddington, *Le Grand Electeur Frédéric Guillaume; sa politique extérieure* (Paris, 1905) I p. 403; Pribram, *Franz Paul Freiherr von Lisola und die Politik seiner Zeit* (Leipzig, 1894) p. 401; Vidoni, Poznań, 24.IV.1658; Levinson, *Die Nuntiaturberichte* no. 193, p. 124.
[95] Opitz, *Österreich und Brandenburg* pp. 86–7.
[96] Lisola, Poznań, 24.IV.1658; *Berichte* no. 98, pp. 398–402.

any campaign in the Empire. Until Charles's plans were known, he felt it was dangerous to divide his forces, or to leave Ducal Prussia unprotected.[97]

Instead, he now advocated peace with Sweden, pointing to the opposition of the imperial diet to any breach of Westphalia, to the support even of some Catholic princes for Sweden, to the loss of Denmark as an effective ally after Roskilde, to the bad feeling in Pomerania after the Polish attacks of 1657, which led the inhabitants to prefer Swedish rule, to the unreliability of Austria before the imperial election, and finally to the danger of alienating the tsar, the Cossacks, the Tatars and the Transylvanians. He then suggested that military operations against the Swedes be confined to Prussia, for which he was prepared to contribute troops, and that peace talks begin between Poland and Sweden, with the acceptance of French mediation if this could not be avoided.[98]

The change in Brandenburg's position was a severe shock for the Poles and particularly for the queen. Since Bromberg she had maintained close contacts with Frederick William. Her last letter before the Poznań conference was confident and friendly in tone: 'Although the queen has never doubted the resolve of M. the elector she was delighted to hear ... of his goodwill ... It is to be feared that the natural arrogance of the Swedes will cause them to stand aloof, but if they see Poland and Brandenburg united they will moderate their position.'[99] Louise Marie now joined John Casimir and the senate in condemning Frederick William for hindering the attack on Pomerania. Yet, even though Austria was now prepared to invade Pomerania, with the imperial election looming in July, Leopold was unwilling to risk breaking Westphalia without Frederick William's backing. A proposal to limit the campaign to Holstein was rejected, and all that could be agreed was a resumption of hostilities in Royal Prussia. The council ended on 19 May, and the Poles immediately sent Morsztyn to Berlin for separate talks with Frederick William, urging a more aggressive policy.[100]

Morsztyn's discussions in Berlin went slowly. He hoped to win a promise from the elector to help maintain the Austrian troops in Poland if he was reluctant to mount a campaign in Pomerania. More importantly, John Casimir wished to know whether Frederick William would support an attack on Pomerania after the election; if not, John Casimir demanded free passage for Polish troops through the electorate. Frederick William, who wished to avoid this, continued his doomed peace initiative: he refused to send a copy of his ratification of the February alliance with Austria to Leopold in an attempt to renegotiate its terms, while sending von der Goltz to Poland to urge a settlement, and Schwerin and Weimann to Charles, only to have his

---

[97] Opitz, *Österreich und Brandenburg* pp. 87–8.
[98] Masini reported that Frederick William might abandon his allies if he were threatened by Charles Gustav: Vidoni, Warsaw, 6.V.1658; Levinson, *Die Nuntiaturberichte* no. 195, p. 126.
[99] Louise Marie to Frederick William, 13.IV.1658; *Urkunden und Aktenstücke* II pp. 283–4.
[100] Opitz, *Österreich und Brandenburg* p. 89.

The succession and the failure of the coalition

offer of mediation rejected.[101] It was all too clearly an attempt to play for time until the imperial election was over and Sweden's intentions were better known. Von der Goltz found John Casimir and Louise Marie only too pleased to support the peace initiative but they refused to drop French mediation. Meanwhile, another council of war was called by John Casimir, which discussed the forthcoming campaign in Prussia and defensive measures to be taken by the allies against possible Swedish attacks.[102]

Despite such problems, Roskilde was an even greater blow to French hopes of building on the favourable outcome of the Warsaw convocation. French influence was dependent on persuading Sweden to settle on acceptable terms; after Roskilde however, Charles was in no mood for concessions. With Poland fearing a new attack, Louise Marie's attitude towards the French cooled noticeably: she berated de Lumbres for the French failure to persuade Sweden to alter in any way its attitude to peace, while the Poles remained deeply suspicious of Charles's latest offer to restore Prussia for money.[103] De Lumbres reported that the queen seemed annoyed at the French, behaving 'very coldly in this matter', stating that although she did not wish to see an Austrian prince wearing the Polish crown, it might come to this if the French did not produce better results. Reports from Frankfurt of French approaches to Brandenburg had aroused fears that they were attempting to persuade Frederick William to abandon the Commonwealth.[104]

Another factor had influenced this change in policy. Gosiewski's cautious interest in the queen's approaches in the spring had been an encouraging sign that Lithuanian opinion might be ready to shift away from support for Wilno. Hopes for a softening of Lithuanian attitudes, however, were destroyed by the tsar's renewed call for the implementation of Wilno, which, as Medeksza made clear, he was now ready to back with force. Lithuanians were still resentful about what they saw as Polish indifference to their plight. Zawisza had complained to Vidoni in October 1657

> with great feeling that he sees in His Majesty neither urgency nor concern for Lithuanian interests and therefore the Poles neither know nor care, although the grand duchy has aided Poland. He said that it seems as if the king's plan is to finish the war with Sweden first and then to turn on Muscovy with all his forces, which he considers is a difficult and time-consuming task involving great danger for the Catholic Church.[105]

---

[101] Instructions to Goltz, 5.II.1658; *Urkunden und Aktenstücke* VIII pp. 355–6; Pufendorf, *De Rebus Gestis Friderici Wilhelmi Magni, Electoris Brandenburgici* (Berlin, 1695) VII p. 431; Opitz, *Österreich und Brandenburg* pp. 91–92; Waddington, *Le Grand Electeur* p. 406. Libiszowska overlooks the radical change in Frederick William's policy, misinterpreting Morsztyn's mission as an attempt to distance the elector from Austria: 'Ludwika Maria w Berlinie (28.VI-3.VII.1658)' K. Matwijowski and Z. Wójcik (eds.), *Studia z dziejów Rzeczypospolitej szlacheckiej* (Wrocław, 1988) pp. 228–9.
[102] Opitz, *Österreich und Brandenburg* pp. 92–5.
[103] De Lumbres to Mazarin, Poznań, 11.V.1658; Harl. 4532 f. 212.
[104] De Lumbres to Mazarin, Rogoźno, 25.V.1658; CPP XII, f. 102.
[105] Vidoni, Warsaw, 20.X.1657; TRz. 8420 p. 69.

Lithuanian concern was heightened at the Warsaw convocation, where most Poles favoured war with Muscovy in the long run to avoid the implementation of Wilno. Nevertheless, war could not be considered yet; it was, therefore, decided to stall Alexis with promises of the throne, maintaining that under present circumstances it was impossible to hold the diet. Alexis, however, was determined to force the issue: he demanded strict implementation of the terms of Wilno and the appointment of plenipotentiaries to settle everything by the end of June at the latest; if not, war would be resumed. The Muscovite envoys arrived in Poznań in mid-April, offering peace and joint operations against the Swedes but with the 'harsh condition' of the succession.[106]

Since the situation on the western front was so uncertain, it was impossible to resist Muscovite pressure any longer: on 9 May a diet was called for mid-June. It was called solely due to Muscovite pressure; in every other respect, it came at an inconvenient time. The international situation was still deeply uncertain, with Charles's intentions remaining a mystery and with the imperial election not taking place until the end of July; only then would it become clear whether Austria's promises of more resolute action were reliable. Following the French failure to persuade Sweden to accept reasonable terms and reports that Charles was planning a new landing in Prussia, the Poles could not afford to break the Austrian alliance.[107] On the other hand, Frederick William's hesitancy and the unrealistic Austrian position with regard to Muscovy, in which Leopold desired peace to be maintained without Alexis succeeding, provoked doubts as to whether reliance on Austria would solve the Commonwealth's problems. There was a real possibility that Poland might once more have to fight on two fronts. Despite encouraging developments in the Ukraine, the government was once more dependent on the decisions of foreign powers; no firm policy could be decided until the international situation was clearer.

The prospect of the tsar's election, however, might prove sufficient to persuade France or Austria to break the deadlock. In early June, de Lumbres wrote to Mazarin that the peace talks were at their crisis and that they must succeed within six weeks, since the decision had been taken to treat with Muscovy. Louise Marie was already complaining at French indifference to the succession, and John Casimir doubted whether the Swedes would honour any treaty which was concluded.[108] According to de Lumbres:

The uneasy atmosphere at this Court is caused by the lack of belief in the possibility of making peace with Sweden and by the necessity of settling with the tsar. The failure of the former plan has so greatly embarrassed the queen that she is doing little to advance the designs of

[106] Lisola, Poznań, 3.V.1658; *Berichte* no. 98, p. 405; Vidoni, Warsaw, 1.IV.1658; TRz. 8421 p. 19.
[107] Opitz, *Österreich und Brandenburg* pp. 111–13.
[108] De Lumbres to Mazarin, 1.VI.1658; CPP XII f. 108; de Lumbres to Mazarin, 8.VI.1658; CPP XII f. 110.

The succession and the failure of the coalition

France with regard to the succession... Her excuse is that it is impossible to achieve without a settlement with Sweden, otherwise the Poles will believe that we have little concern for their repose and well-being and little power over the king of Sweden.[109]

Louise Marie told him that it had been decided to nominate Alexis so that at least Poland might recover what it had lost. A few days later, she said that following complaints about Rey's behaviour in Frankfurt, she had written to him asking him to act with more restraint, so as not to give too much offence.[110] Much had changed since March.

In a last bid to force a decision before the diet assembled, Louise Marie visited Berlin in person at the end of June. Historians have traditionally assumed that this visit was merely another indication of her dedication to France, an attempt to win Frederick William's support for peace with Sweden and to persuade him to put pressure on the Austrians by refusing to vote for Leopold in the imperial election. Such was Rudawski's view:

The queen, in order to please the French, hastened from Poznań to Berlin to consult with the elector of Brandenburg, whom she had already persuaded with difficulty to ally with His Majesty the king of Hungary and Bohemia. Accordingly, she persuaded the elector, first by secret arguments, then quite openly, to desert the Austrian side and to support the Poles. For if the elector wished to follow her advice, his son might become a Pole. The elector replied that he could by no means abandon Austria, since if he did so, he would bring the ultimate crisis upon his head. He never desired the kingdom of Poland for his son, nor would he even accept it, given its current miserable state... Unable to glean anything more from the elector, the queen returned to the king, three days after leaving Poznań.[111]

Kubala follows Rudawski's line, suggesting that Louise Marie's visit was motivated by a desire to set Frederick William at loggerheads with Austria. Libiszowska, who rightly draws attention to the propaganda impact of the meeting but who overestimates the queen's influence on Polish policy, rejects Rudawski as a biased source but still assumes that the visit was motivated by a desire to cut free from the Austrian alliance, while persuading Frederick William to accept French mediation.[112]

It was Frederick William, however, not Louise Marie, who was urging a quick settlement with Sweden in May and June, on terms which would bring no benefit to the Commonwealth or the Polish monarchy. Denmark's defeat and Charles's hardline attitude had destroyed the premise on which Louise Marie's position had been based in the autumn: that the acceptance of French mediation would bring peace on reasonable terms, thereby opening the way to a French candidature. Neither as committed to this policy nor as dominant at Court as she is often portrayed, Louise Marie had abandoned for the moment this line to return to the

---

[109] De Lumbres to Mazarin, Sieraków, 15.VI.1658; CPP XII f. 116.
[110] De Lumbres to Brienne, Sieraków, 22.VI.1658; CPP XII f. 125.
[111] Rudawski, *Historiarum* IX pp. 414–15.
[112] Kubala, *Wojny duńskie* p. 57; Libiszowska, 'Ludwika Maria w Berlinie' pp. 228–31.

only realistic alternative: to rely on military support from a newly willing Leopold to force Charles to be more tractable. In this respect, Frederick William, cultivated so assiduously for so long, had proved a disappointment.

Far from going to Berlin to persuade Frederick William to abandon Austria, Louise Marie brought a letter from Lisola urging an immediate joint attack on Pomerania and sought to win Frederick William's support.[113] Blondel reported that Louise Marie had come to confirm Frederick William in his determination to remain allied to Poland and to persuade him to execute the decision taken at Poznań in April to invade Pomerania, which the elector did not wish to implement. Although Louise Marie told Blondel, whom she disliked, that it was necessary to use Frederick William to achieve a settlement, she suggested he was too close to Sweden and complained bitterly about French and Swedish behaviour, stating her opposition to any peace conference.[114] The queen was well received but there is reason to doubt des Noyers's assertion that she obtained everything she desired.[115] According to Blondel, the meeting with the elector was not a happy one: 'Her apprehension and extreme annoyance, together with that which I have discerned in the eyes of Their Excellencies the elector and the electress, makes me believe that they are not at all satisfied with each other.'[116] Des Noyers remarked that Frederick William was such a feeble prince there was no profit to be made, which suggests that the queen was disappointed at the elector's refusal to stand by his promises to support the Pomeranian invasion.[117]

Much had changed since the cordial scenes at Bromberg in November. The queen failed to extract any pledge of support from the elector and returned disappointed to Warsaw, where she immediately persuaded a reluctant de Lumbres to go to Charles to try and obtain satisfactory terms for peace, arguing that this was the only way to prevent the diet throwing itself into the arms of the tsar. As de Lumbres pointed out this prevented him from attending the diet, since he could not hope to return in time, but he was unable to convince Louise Marie.[118] She could not expect de Lumbres to win any real concessions from Charles; the inference is that she wished him out of the way, as she had at Częstochowa in 1657 and at the Warsaw convocation in 1658, to leave her hands free to pursue policies of which the French ambassador might disapprove. He had failed once again; for the moment there could be no thought of any campaign for a French election.

---

[113] Pufendorf, *De Rebus Gestis Frederici Wilhelmi* VII p. 433; Lisola, Poznań, 29.VI.1658; *Berichte* no. 106, p. 434; Waddington, *Le Grand Electeur* I p. 406, n. 3. Opitz, *Österreich und Brandenburg* p. 102.
[114] Blondel to Mazarin, Berlin, 2.VII.1658; *Urkunden und Aktenstücke* II pp. 172, 174.
[115] Des Noyers, Sieraków, 7.VII.1658; *Lettres* no. 159, p. 418.
[116] Blondel to Mazarin, Berlin, 2.VII.1658; *Urkunden und Aktenstücke* II p. 174.
[117] BNP FFr. 13020 f. 56; the latter half of this phrase is omitted in the published edition: *Lettres* no. 159, p. 418.
[118] De Lumbres to Mazarin, Stettin, 16.VII.1658; Harl. 4532 f. 235.

7

Political reform

Despite the uncertainty of the international situation and its inability to find a suitable candidate, the Court remained committed to an election *vivente rege*. This has long been seen as a crucial and fateful error. By concentrating on the election, it is argued, the Court squandered a unique opportunity to restore the Commonwealth's political system to health through reforming diet procedure and, above all, through sweeping away the pernicious *liberum veto*. Louise Marie is usually seen as being chiefly to blame, as the driving-force behind the French election campaign which stimulated the formation of pro-French and pro-Austrian parties and diverted attention from reform of the diet, seen as the essential precondition for strengthening the state, thus squandering the favourable situation which had arisen since the Muscovite and Swedish invasions.[1]

From November 1655, there was certainly an encouraging atmosphere with regard to reform, and no shortage of proposals to limit or abolish the *liberum veto*. Vidoni wrote in January 1656 of the goodwill shown by senators, which provided an opportunity to improve the state of the Commonwealth now that the king had returned to Poland.[2] Des Noyers reported that: 'All our senators and all our nobles are agreed that they must change their method of government.'[3] Reform was first discussed at Oppeln in November, although no firm decisions were taken. The first concrete proposals, calling for the limitation or abolition of the veto, emerged over the next few months:

In this connection one can immediately state that after more senators have gathered here, the Commonwealth will be restored to its former order and reputation; i.e. liberty in all things will remain for everyone, but the licence which brings ruin will be destroyed, so that it will not be permitted that an individual, for any private reason whatsoever, should be able to break a diet, which we need in order to pay the army, thus provoking the ruination of the Commonwealth at the cost of us all.[4]

[1] W. Czermak, 'Próba naprawy Rzeczypospolitej za Jana Kazimierza' *Biblioteka Warszawska* 51 (1891) p. 524; Czapliński, 'Próby reform' pp. 303, 318 and 'Sejm polski w latach 1587–1696' in J. Michalski (ed.), *Historia Sejmu polskiego* I pp. 280, 296; Ochmann, 'Plans for parliamentary reform' pp. 163, 169; A. Przyboś, 'Plan elekcji za życia Króla, opracowany przez Kanclerza Koronnego Mikołaja Prażmowskiego 1 maja 1665r.' *Studia Historyczne* 25 (1982) p. 307.
[2] Vidoni to Orsini, Lwów, 20.II.1656; TRz. 8419 no. 16, p. 165.
[3] Des Noyers, Oberglogau, 26.I.1656; *Lettres* no. 22, p. 64; S. Wydżga, *Pamiętnik... spisany podczas wojny szwedzkiej w roku 1655 do 1660* ed. K. Wójcicki (Warsaw, 1852) p. 106.
[4] A. Leszczyński to John Casimir, undated (January 1656); Grabowski, *Ojczyste spominki* II p. 94.

Rákóczi's envoy Mikes, in his conferences with the group of exiles gathered round Lubomirski in Hungary, reported a general desire for reform of the veto: 'We do not desire licence but liberty, and we will abolish this ancient and pernicious law.'[5]

A more extensive proposal was drawn up at the end of 1656, when it was thought that a diet would soon be held to implement the treaty of Wilno. The 'Proposal for the successful convening, opening and concluding of the diet which, please God, will soon assemble' warned of the dangers of allowing the will of the majority to be thwarted but suggested that consideration of the principle of unanimity should be left to better times.[6] After Rákóczi's invasion, however, plans to hold a diet were swiftly abandoned and there was no further mention of reform until the autumn of 1657, when Montecuccoli reported a discussion at the siege of Cracow: '[Koryciński] and many others plan to change the form of the government of Poland, since a dissolute licence and a great state of servitude exist under the pretext of liberty, in that a simple gentleman can block all the proceedings and the very conclusion of a diet.'[7] This renewed interest stimulated the preparation of the most extensive plan yet for political reform: 'The decision of John Casimir that the traditional form of diet procedure should be preserved and that agreements reached should be faithfully kept', possibly drafted by Lukasz Opaliński, which again recommended the limitation of the right of veto, although not its complete abolition.[8]

This document was to be submitted to the Warsaw convocation in February 1658 in an attempt to give the diet a lead and to build support for the plan. Ochmann suggests that at the time it was drafted, the king and his senators took a fairly concerted view of the reform issue, with Opaliński arguing that the document should be published to stimulate open discussion and to ward off fears that the Court was planning to introduce absolute rule. The lack of information on the Warsaw convocation makes it difficult, according to Ochmann, to determine the fate of the proposals, but it was never published and the royal instructions for the 1658 diet made no mention of reform of the veto, despite calls for its limitation in the instructions issued by certain dietines to their envoys. Reform may not even have been discussed at the diet of July–August 1658, while the 1659 diet merely decided to refer the matter to a special commission.[9]

The failure of the Warsaw convocation to approve the proposal, despite apparently widespread support for reform of the veto and despite the fact that the

---

[5] Mikes, 'Relatio itineris ad Luboulam et resolutionis procerum Poloniae 14 18.XII.1655'; Szilágyi *Transsylvania* I p. 515.
[6] 'Szczęśliwego złożenia, zaczęcia i konkludowania sejmy da P. Bog blisko przyszłego sposób' BPANCr. 1062 pp. 150–1.
[7] Montecuccoli to unknown, 1.IX.1657; Walewski, *Historia wyzwolenia* II dodatek X p. viii.
[8] 'Decyzja Jana Kazimierza że sposób sejmowania starożytny zachowany będzie, że związki zawarte wiernie dochowane zostaną' Czart. 388 no. 141, pp. 272–5; printed in Kubala, *Wojny duńskie* dodatek XII pp. 534–6.
[9] Ochmann, 'Plans for parliamentary reform' pp. 174–6; Czapliński, 'Próby reform' pp. 318–20; cf. 'Instructions of the palatinate of Sieradz', 21.VI.1658, which criticise the damaging effects of the veto on the Commonwealth: Teki Pawińskiego 8342 p. 689.

Political reform

convocation seemed to go well as far as the Court was concerned, requires explanation. Either opposition appeared among senators and envoys to the convocation or the Court lost enthusiasm and failed to give the plan adequate support. The consensus among historians tends towards the former interpretation. Regarding the Court as providing the impetus behind plans to curb or abolish the veto, Czapliński suggests that opposition emerged owing to concern that the Court would use reform of the diet as a springboard for further constitutional change, which, he assumes, by early 1658 meant the French election. The Court's substantial patronage powers would enable it to realise all its plans, including a radical transformation of the constitution. He argues that neither Opaliński nor other senators supported too extensive a strengthening of royal power, owing to their fear that the fundamental rights of the noble Commonwealth would be violated: the right of free election, the duty to call the diet, the necessity for agreement on taxation from both chambers and religious toleration.[10] The assumption is that the Court still saw diet reform as essential but only as the necessary preliminary to an election *vivente rege*; as senators increasingly realised that this was the case, they abandoned support for reform of the diet. Thus the apparent pursuit of Court interests at the expense of the interests of the state, or at least of the magnate elite, provoked opposition to the diet reform which was essential for the Commonwealth's well-being.

For Czapliński and Kersten, such a split between Court and magnate elite is highly significant. For the support of many leading magnates for diet reform apparently runs counter to the theory of the magnate oligarchy which sees the magnates as being essentially responsible for the triumph of decentralist forces and the veto. Thus Czapliński expresses surprise that it appeared to be senators who spoke most frequently and sensibly, relatively speaking, about reform, asking whether it was the magnates who represented the voice of political commonsense but were 'drowned out by the benighted *szlachta* masses, as bourgeois historians once argued?' To resolve this apparent contradiction, he suggests that magnates saw that strengthening the state was necessary since: 'Under the circumstances of the time it could not fulfil its basic function, namely the defence of its territory, and was unable to guarantee magnate interests.'[11]

Kersten argues that magnate rule was not necessarily inconsistent with the limitation of the powers of dietines, or even of far-reaching diet reform, suggesting a conflict between the magnate desire for economic decentralisation and their interest in maintaining the internal and external power of the feudal Commonwealth, which had led them initially to support diet reform. Ultimately, however, magnates were responsible for the triumph of the veto. The waning of enthusiasm for reform was due to two factors: the political power of the *szlachta*, which was still considerable,

---

[10] Czapliński, 'Próby reform' p. 317.
[11] For example in the Ukraine, where the state was incapable of providing the infrastructure which would enable the magnates to extract maximum economic advantage from their estates, and which many had observed in western Europe. ibid. pp. 306–7.

and the attitude of the Court, whose plans were resisted by the 'magnate opposition in a very close alliance with the *szlachta* – i.e. with a whole class'.[12] Ochmann extends this argument, emphasising the difference in the nature of the reform proposals put forward by particular magnate groups, distinguishing between a maximum programme, which sought to deprive the chamber of envoys of all legislative initiative in important state matters in favour of the senate and a minimum programme, which sought to increase the efficiency of the diet by changes in procedure, essentially through the curtailment of the veto. Both programmes, she argues, were supported by the Court and by magnates, but each group had a different view of the main objectives of reform, seeking either the strengthening of the king's position with regard to the other two estates, or to make the senate the dominant estate, while pretending to strengthen royal power. The chances of reform succeeding were vitally hampered by disputes over these priorities, since the *szlachta*, ever-watchful of their rights and liberties, were innately suspicious of reform schemes.[13]

Ochmann divides the magnate elite into regalists, who linked their ambitions and interests with the Court and republicans, who sought support from the *szlachta*, blurring the ideological differences separating them from the mass of ordinary nobles and opposing the Court's alleged wish for *absolutum dominium*. Thus the regalists were confronted not only by the *szlachta* but also by the anti-royal opposition within their own class. The two groups within the magnate elite were only linked by a convergence of interests with regard to the role and prestige of the senate but their goals were essentially different: the regalists wished to strengthen the position of the monarch and the senate at the expense of the chamber of envoys, while the republicans sought new prerogatives for the senate at the expense of royal power and defended the preponderance of the chamber of envoys, whose actual weakness made its manipulation possible.[14]

The Court's mistake was to pursue the election at the expense of diet reform, which many republicans were ready to accept in some form and which would have benefited central authority. It received support from the regalists, largely new magnates or those seeking to establish their family fortunes who were prepared to support the Court's programme in order to gain access to Court patronage and French money and favour. Ultimately, however, such men could not be relied upon. They were prepared to see an increase in the power of the senate at the expense of the chamber of envoys but it was not in their class interests to allow too great an increase in royal power. Ochmann takes up Czapliński's suggestion that regalist views on the Court's reform programme were merely self-seeking, intended to win favour from the king, who controlled the distribution of offices and royal land, and that in most cases the promises were not matched by any real effort to implement them: 'Speeches on the floor of the senate cost magnates little but won them royal

---

[12] Kersten, 'Problem władzy w Rzeczypospolitej czasu Wazów' in Gierowski (ed.), *O naprawę Rzeczypospolitej* pp. 34–5.
[13] Ochmann, 'Plans for parliamentary reform' p. 163.   [14] ibid. p. 166.

favour.'[15] She argues that reform failed because, while regalists were insincere in their support for the royal programme, their opponents could count on widespread support among the *szlachta*, which was a much stronger political ally than the king. Support for royal aims was merely due to the desire of 'new' magnates to further their careers. While opposition magnates had to ensure continued support from the ordinary nobility, regalists could relatively easily free themselves of any dependence on the king. If regalist support for royal plans rested on shaky foundations, republican support for diet reform disappeared as the nature of royal intentions became clearer: senators were really only concerned with increasing senate power, not the power of the monarchy, and were unenthusiastic about diet reform. Thus the resolutions of the Warsaw convocation were not published, and the diets of 1658 and 1659 failed to introduce concrete reforms.[16]

Ochmann's underlying assumption is that the Court accepted the view that reform of the diet and the abolition of the veto was essential but that increasingly it regarded diet reform merely as the necessary first step towards the achievement of the French election. Yet at the time of the Warsaw convocation, when the plan appears to have foundered, the Court was not yet committed to a French election: Louise Marie had sounded out opinion, no more, and in any case her enthusiasm waned sharply after Roskilde, while John Casimir can by no means be regarded as committed to a French election at this stage. There is no evidence from early 1658 to suggest that senators feared that the destruction of the veto would open the door to a French election.

Vidoni's reports, which have not been used by any historian examining this question, suggest that after Opaliński presented his proposals for discussion at the end of 1657, support for reform of the veto evaporated among senators not because the Court promoted such an idea but because the Court itself lost interest. Although Vidoni frequently mentioned the plan to introduce majority voting in December and January, and although he subsequently discussed many of the issues actually raised at Warsaw, he made no further reference to the scheme, which appears to have foundered even before the convocation opened.[17]

In 1659, John Casimir remarked that the establishment of majority voting might not necessarily lead to the strengthening of his power, asserting that he did not mind the veto, for with the army on his side he could rule at will by breaking disobedient diets. Kubala and Ochmann suggest that he was seeking to confuse his opponents at a time when the campaign to elect a French prince was beginning in earnest; nevertheless, it is worth considering whether John Casimir was expressing his honest opinion.[18] It is true that the introduction of majority voting would have done much to expedite the progress of government business; nevertheless, even if the king

---

[15] Czapliński, 'Próby reform' pp. 306–7.
[16] Ochmann, 'Plans for parliamentary reform' pp. 166–7, 176.
[17] See Czapliński's demolition of the theory that Jan Leszczyński collected signatures after the end of the convocation on a document endorsing plans to reform the diet: 'Próby reform' p. 320; Bąkowa nevertheless still accepts the document as valid: *Szlachta województwa krakowskiego* p. 23.
[18] Kubala, *Wojny duńskie* pp. 348–9; Ochmann, 'Plans for parliamentary reform' p. 177.

had significant means at his disposal to influence the course of diet debates, it might also force him to accept policies which he opposed, including further restrictions on royal power. During discussions on majority voting in early 1658, Vidoni remarked: 'This would even be harmful to the kingdom, since it would be easy for the majority to combine against His Majesty, whereas [at present], when something does not please him, he can cause the breaking of the diet.'[19]

After 1652, John Casimir had been swift to appreciate the potential advantages which the veto afforded the monarchy. For years, the diet had been the main source of the increasing restrictions on royal power; it was therefore useful for the king to be able to paralyse proceedings if necessary, either to prevent further inroads on royal authority or to end criticism of royal actions, as John Casimir had done in 1654 when Białobłocki broke the diet with royal approval during the storm over the Lithuanian hetmanship. John Casimir saw the veto as a useful way of ensuring no damage was done to his remaining powers if the diet was proving impossible to control. His experience with diets since 1648 did not lead him to suppose that the introduction of majority voting would turn the chamber of envoys into an obedient and cooperative body overnight; on the contrary, it might render it more capable of attacking royal authority.

While the Court seems to have gone along with the various plans to curb the veto which emerged between 1655 and 1658, the extent of its enthusiasm is open to question. It was ready to support the introduction of majority voting with regard to the conduct of government business, as in the 1656 proposals.[20] The 1657 'Decision' also proposed procedural reform where the ordinary business of government was concerned: the royal agenda for the diet was to be kept secret until the diet opened, with envoys from dietines given plenipotentiary powers to decide on all matters in accordance with the general view, while normal diet business was to be decided by a majority vote, although a two-thirds majority would be required for a measure to pass. Nevertheless, the Court was opposed to any further restriction of the veto. A clause in the 'Decision' specifically urged its retention with regard to constitutional matters:

Should there be a proposal which is obviously contrary to the law and is in clear breach of the fundamental laws of the fatherland, or plainly against enactments by the Commonwealth, then anybody who is justified by the law will have a valid right of contradiction, under condition that this does not constitute a pretext for the advancement of his private interests.[21]

This clause has not received much attention, yet it calls into question first the assumption that magnates lost enthusiasm for reform of the veto due to fears about Court plans for an election *vivente rege*, since such a restriction would make it possible to block an election on constitutional grounds, and secondly the view that

---

[19] Vidoni, Poznań, 2.I.1658; TRz. 8421 p. 4.
[20] Ochmann suggests that the 1656 'Proposal' was possibly a draft of the king's instructions to regional dietines; if this was the case, it remained a draft and was never circulated. 'Plans for parliamentary reform' p. 171.   [21] 'Decyzja Jana Kazimierza' pp. 535–6.

Political reform

the monarchy was the most enthusiastic proponent of the curtailment of the veto. On the contrary, the introduction of this scheme would effectively block royal chances of introducing the fundamental constitutional reforms it saw as essential. In May 1658 Vidoni, after expressing his concern at the great complexity of matters for discussion at the forthcoming diet and at the possibility of strong opposition to royal plans since there was no lack of 'disaffected and disturbed minds', remarked that if the situation became impossible, the king could break the diet 'as he has done before'.[22] Why should the monarchy surrender such a valuable weapon for an uncertain advantage? In the light of his experiences after 1648 it is at least understandable if John Casimir was unable to see a working partnership with the diet as possible. In his eyes a stronger diet was the last thing the monarchy wanted.

It was senators, not the Court, who initiated schemes for reform of the veto after 1655. From the outset, the Court was considering a more radical approach aimed at reform of the executive, not the legislature, something it had sought to achieve since 1648. The first reform plan which can definitely be linked to the Court, mentioned by des Noyers in January and March 1656, did include a proposal to introduce majority voting but urged a radical curbing of the power of the diet:

> There would no longer have to be a diet, or diets would only be held to give more force to the law. The equestrian order would only represent, while the king would govern with the senate; he would still appoint whomsoever he wishes to the senate and his vote would be worth twelve. He would be absolute, as he was previously, in the distribution of patronage and only in matters of war and in matters of state would he be required to take a vote.[23]

The *liberum veto* was to be replaced by majority voting but, more significantly: 'Diets would only be held to represent the needs of the provinces and not to discuss [affairs of state]. The king and the senate alone would govern.'[24]

Kersten doubts the value of this evidence, since it is not confirmed by any other source; he justifies his scepticism on the curious grounds that it is hard to imagine that Louise Marie and her foreign entourage would suggest such a radical limitation of the king's power. Czapliński considers that the scheme was hatched by Louise Marie and her foreign advisers and had little chance of obtaining the support of senators since, even assuming their support for increasing senate powers, it is difficult to imagine that they would have agreed to such a major curbing of *szlachta* rights. Kersten insists on regarding the class interests of the magnate elite as necessarily antithetical to the interests of the monarchy and concludes that if such a plan existed, since it would greatly increase the influence, and serve the interests of, the Court group of magnates, 'which one ought not equate with the interests of the

---

[22] Vidoni, Warsaw, 19.V.1658; TRz. 8421 p. 24; cf. de Lumbres: '... cette Diète ne se tiendra que pour faire voire au Moscovite qu'il l'on se met en devoir de la contenter, afin que, pendant cette Diète qui se peut trainer ou rompre comme l'on voudra, il ne se porte à temuer aucune chose contre ce Royaume ...' De Lumbres to Brienne, Poznań, 4.V.1658; CPP XII p. 90.
[23] Des Noyers, Oberglogau, 26.I.1656; *Lettres* no. 22, pp. 64–5.
[24] Des Noyers, Oberglogau, 30.III.1656; *Lettres* no. 41, p. 126.

After the Deluge

king in any way', it serves as an example of the extreme reform wing which essentially sought the strengthening of the senate, something which Kersten regards as different from the strengthening of royal power.[25]

It is impossible, given the lack of other evidence, to come to any firm conclusions on the scheme, not least considering that des Noyers is not always accurate in his observations on constitutional matters. Nevertheless, he explicitly stated that the scheme was discussed by the senators in exile in Silesia, while his own assessment, which must have reflected that of Louise Marie, differs greatly from Kersten's view that the plan would have limited royal power in maintaining that, if successful, the plan would ensure that Poland became one of the most powerful states in Europe.[26] The king's twelve votes might not appear many given a senate membership of 150, but since only a fraction of that number ever attended council meetings and even the diet only attracted a minority, the king would have had a good chance of a majority on most matters, given the usual preponderance of Court supporters among those who did attend; nevertheless, the implicit recognition of the principle of majority voting at council meetings, albeit with the king commanding twelve votes, may have been designed to allay senate doubts about the plan: the king had never previously been required to follow the majority opinion.

The main cause of concern to John Casimir was the weakness of the executive, not the legislature. The major problem faced by the government was not so much the failure of the diet to vote adequate taxes but the widespread underfulfilment of the quotas agreed. It was not that the diet controlled supply; indeed quite the opposite was true. As Koryciński complained in 1656: 'The best way to ensure the swift payment of the army is not to wait for a diet, since every time the Commonwealth reaches a decison, still nothing is resolved, for its execution must be confirmed by yet another diet.'[27] Reforming diet procedure would do little good by itself: the problem lay in the relationship between the diet and the localities. This point was made strongly in the Oppeln proclamation of 20 November 1655, which called the nation to arms against the Swedes. It was not just the *liberum veto* which was blamed for the Commonwealth's plight:

This has occurred not through our neglect or oversight but due to the behaviour of those of you who have pursued your own private interests, either by breaking whole diets, or by delaying so long over defence, in order finally to satisfy your ambitions. With regard to taxes voted by the diet, some dietines have simply not paid; others, who have paid, have been most profligate. Thus the army remains unpaid and is mutinous, refusing to obey the hetmans.[28]

It was this problem which John Casimir saw as the major weakness of the Polish system, not the shortcomings of the diet. Wherever possible, he tried to avoid calling

---

[25] Kersten, 'Problem władzy' p. 34; Czapliński, 'Próby reform' p. 311; Ochmann, 'Plans for parliamentary reform' pp. 170–1.
[26] Des Noyers, 26.I.1656; *Lettres* no. 22, p. 65.
[27] Koryciński to unknown, 1656; Czart. 149 no. 185, p. 674.
[28] Royal proclamation, Oppeln, 20.XI.1655; Michałowski, *Księga pamiętnicza* no. 340, p. 777.

Political reform

the diet, preferring to work through the senate council or the *ad hoc* commissions established to implement diet decisions, such as the commission called in Wilno in May 1655 to consider payment of the Lithuanian army:

> Great problems have transpired with regard to pay for the army ... which threaten the grand duchy of Lithuania with collapse, if effective payment of the army is not made by 9 August, which cannot be without public consent. A diet could be called but it would have by law to be a six-week ordinary diet, which is not necessary for the Poles, who have agreed to sufficient taxes until 1 January next year.[29]

After 1655, when the war made it impossible to hold a diet until 1658, the willingness of senators to cooperate in the exercise of executive authority and to take decisions which should normally have been referred to the diet confirmed John Casimir's view that he should base his attempt to strengthen central power on the senate council rather than the diet. Between 1648 and 1655, divisions among senators, rivalry between magnate factions, disagreements between Poles and Lithuanians and the determined opposition of malcontent magnates had meant that the government was unable to impose its authority. Following the events of 1655 John Casimir found himself in a much stronger position. With the death in disgrace of Radziwiłł and Opaliński and the disappointment of hopes that Charles X or anyone else was prepared to act as protector of the Commonwealth's rights and freedoms, John Casimir found his senators much more cooperative and aware of the Commonwealth's weaknesses.

The Court's reliance on senators and magnates has been criticised by historians, who argue that it should have exploited anti-magnate feeling among the *szlachta* to break the grip of the magnates upon the political structure. There is indeed some evidence of anti-magnate feeling after the Swedish invasion. An anonymous 'Advice for the Reformation of the Commonwealth' (1657) suggested a different and more radical solution: 'The greatest reason [for the weakness of the Commonwealth] is the poverty of the state. This poverty stems from the fact that private individuals have seized control of the state's private patrimony ... which they parcel out through extravagance, thereby impoverishing the country.' The result of this monopoly of the proceeds from the royal domain by private individuals was that 'the Commonwealth, deprived of its rightful income, must beg the nobility for subsidies in time of need; the nobility, exhausted by extravagance, cannot adequately respond.' The anonymous author then recommended that the proceeds from all starosties and royal leases be removed from private hands and returned to the state treasury, 'which would meet the state's requirements, both military and non-military'.[30]

The anti-magnate tone of this document is strong, demonstrating that the sentiments which had produced the execution movement a century earlier were still

---

[29] Royal proclamation to the inhabitants of the Pinsk district, 23.II.1655; *Akty otnoshiashchesia ko vremeni voiny za Malorossiiu* Akty izdavaemye Vilenskoi Kommisiei dlia Razbora Drevnikh Aktov XXXIV (Wilno, 1909) no. 32, p. 34.

[30] 'Rada do Poprawy Rzeczypospolitej, 1657'; Czart. 150 no. 94, pp. 401–2.

alive. It was the magnates and richest *szlachta* who monopolised these lucrative sources of income, which did much to ensure their continued social and political dominance.[31] The author blamed the disagreements which so disrupted the political life of the Commonwealth on competition for starosties:

The Commonwealth would be more harmonious, for this is the greatest cause of disputes and factions ... Hence diets and dietines are always stormy, since all aspire to one aim, namely to acquire some of these lands of the Commonwealth ... And His Majesty, unable to satisfy everyone amidst such great competition, brings down the hatred of the public upon himself, since by satisfying one, he must disappoint another.[32]

The transformation to absolutism in Denmark in 1660 and in Sweden in 1680 was achieved in part by a similar move, in which the power of the high nobility was broken by the *reduktion* of royal land in magnate hands, for which Frederick III and Charles XI received the support of anti-magnate elements among burghers and the lesser nobility. Ochmann suggests that there were many 'soundly thinking' individuals among the middle *szlachta* who were concerned at the disasters experienced since 1655 and that these included both strong critics of the magnates and the occasional royalist. She criticises John Casimir for ignoring such positive elements and for failing to seek an alliance with the *szlachta*, which he treated as a passive tool of the magnates, while the *szlachta*, seeing no prospect of an alliance with the king over the heads of the magnates, continued to dislike the Court and were willing to cooperate with the anti-royal opposition.[33]

It is difficult to see how John Casimir could have done otherwise, even if one scheme similar to the 'Advice' suggests that some at least in Court circles were considering such a move: 'If it were ever possible, it would be better not to distribute those accursed vacancies, which confound and impoverish the Commonwealth but to administer them directly and to meet public needs out of the income.'[34] There is no sign, however, of any wider interest in this scheme on the part of the Court. If regalist currents existed among the ordinary nobility, then John Casimir can be forgiven for not noticing them, or at least for not considering seriously an anti-magnate alliance with the *szlachta*. Conditions had changed since the great days of the execution movement, and the gap between magnates and *szlachta* had widened. Ochmann criticises John Casimir for only dealing with the ordinary nobility through the magnates but does not suggest how it could have been otherwise in a vast state with a tiny central bureaucracy, where the majority of nobles stayed on their estates most of the time and constituted some 6–8 per cent of the population.

[31] Ochmann, 'Anonimowy projekt reformy skarbowej z 1657 roku' *Sobótka* 30 (1975) p. 304.
[32] 'Rada do Poprawy Rzeczypospolitej' Czart. 150 pp. 408–9.
[33] Ochmann, 'Anonimowy projekt reformy skarbowej z 1657 roku' p. 307. For the anti-magnate feelings of certain dietines, see Leszczyński, 'Siedemnastowieczne sejmiki a kultura polityczna szlachty' in Gierowski (ed.), *Dzieje kultury politycznej w Polsce* (Warsaw, 1977) p. 59.
[34] 'Considerationes Salvandae Reip.'; Czart. 2576 p. 399; Targosz, *Hieronim Pinocci* p. 30, n. 1.

Political reform

The king had no opportunities for close contact with anything but a tiny minority and that was possible primarily at diets, which only met for six weeks or so every two years. He was utterly dependent on magnates and senators to support his policies at dietines, where so much that was important was ultimately decided: royal secretaries wrote countless letters to local magnates urging them to use their influence to secure support for royal proposals. The infrequency of diet sessions, the lack of a developed central bureaucracy, the slow circulation of information in such a large state and the importance of dietines within the political system precluded the formation of any permanent or coherent regalist party among the *szlachta* as a whole, except by the extension of royal patronage channelled through the magnate clienteles.[35]

From the king's point of view, the existence of positive currents of thought among the ordinary nobility was hard to detect. At diets, he had to endure endless private or local petitions and frequent criticism of his actions, while the only positive initiatives taken by the chamber of envoys tended towards the limitation of royal power. Even the idea for a *reduktion* put forward in the 'Advice' stemmed as much from a desire to avoid paying taxes as from a wish to strengthen the executive: 'Respect for the majesty of the king and the authority of the senate would be greater if revenues existed sufficient to satisfy the needs of the Commonwealth without having to depend so heavily on the *szlachta* when collecting taxes.' The result, in the opinion of the author, would be increased freedom for all: 'The *szlachta* is not free either, for they are disturbed by having to make contributions and by the obligation to support the *levée-en-masse* ... but we are all in the greatest servitude and must, as things stand, be at the mercy of our own soldiers.'[36]

Such sentiments merely confirmed Court prejudices in favour of the magnates. It was among the magnates that the king could use his still extensive powers of patronage to extend his influence and to build up a regalist party; it was precisely these powers which the 'Advice' sought to curb. Supporters of the Court might on occasion be self-seeking and insincere but the extent to which magnates could distance themselves from the Court should not be exaggerated. The proposal to end the granting of starosties would deprive the monarchy of its major political weapon and would leave it with the problem of administering the vast lands it would then control.

There was another problem. The Commonwealth's inefficient financial system meant that it, like other early modern states, depended on credit, particularly in moments of crisis. This was especially so between 1655 and 1660, when tax-collection was seriously disrupted by the war. To an extent, the government could raise loans in Danzig and the other merchant cities of Royal Prussia, but its main

---

[35] Even in the mid-seventeenth century, the circulation of printed books and pamphlets was limited and slow. Much material circulated in manuscript form, and speeches or reports were often copied into a scrapbook, the so-called *Silva Rerum*.

[36] 'Rada do Poprawy Rzeczypospolitej' pp. 410–11.

creditors were richer nobles and magnates. Since the diet met for such short periods and did not vote a proper budget, it was inevitable that the senate council in practice should take decisions on its own authority in unforeseen circumstances. If it were necessary to pay for a military expedition or a diplomatic mission, a security could be issued on council authority to the treasurer or another official, as a guarantee for the repayment of any expenditure at the next diet.[37] These sums were frequently considerable: the diet of 1658 agreed to meet a senate promise and repay 593,809 złoties to Paweł Sapieha; considering that 25.5 instalments of the land tax voted in 1658 brought in a total of 4,262,377 złoties, this was a substantial sum.[38]

The problem was that although the monarchy controlled the authorisation of such loans through the senate council, authorisation of repayment was in the hands of the diet. The difficulties of managing diets, their tendency to end without achieving anything and their inability to ensure that their financial demands were met by dietines, led to the dangerous situation in which the monarchy could not guarantee repayment and creditors had to look more to the diet or dietines than the Crown for satisfaction. Given the level of indebtedness, it was impossible to contemplate the sort of solution recommended in the 'Advice'. The idea of clawing back the three-fifths of the income from royal lands to which the monarchy was entitled might be attractive but it was impractical, given the extent to which the monarchy had become dependent upon political and economic cooperation with the magnates and the richer *szlachta* since the Union of Lublin. The executionist idea that the Commonwealth could survive as a domain state was a political anachronism, not a viable programme. If central authority were to be made more effective, then different means would have to be found.

If the monarchy could win control of its debts by asserting its financial independence through the senate council, then it might be possible to create a more stable system of private credit. The attitude of senators after 1655 indicated that this might be possible: in the extraordinary circumstances of the war, senators were quite willing to take responsibility themselves for decisions which ought to have required a diet. Senators, while they might resist attempts by the king to govern alone, were convinced of their own rights in this respect. Already in March 1655, John Casimir had sought advice as to whether the raising of troops without calling a diet was permissable. Jan Wielopolski, by no means a regalist, replied that while it was technically illegal 'sine communi consensu', nevertheless: 'Senators are not present at Your Majesty's side merely to be the guardians of the law but to be its interpretors; to them, as to every citizen, the supreme law should be the safety of the fatherland.'[39] Following the treaty of Wilno in 1656, John Casimir asked the senate

---

[37] Rybarski, *Skarb i pieniądz* pp. 16, 27.
[38] *Volumina Legum* IV pp. 521–2; Rybarski, *Skarb i pieniądz* p. 102. Sapieha claimed he was owed twice the amount; A. Rachuba, *Konfederacja kmicicowska i Związek Braterski wojska litewskiego w latach 1660–1663* (Warsaw, 1989) pp. 14–15.
[39] Wielopolski to John Casimir, 4.III.1655; AGAD APPot. 45 I p. 16.

Political reform

council whether a diet should be held in January, as called for in the terms of the treaty.[40] Even Jan Leszczyński, that good republican, was convinced that calling a diet was inadvisable, arguing that the senate had the necessary powers to act. He recognised that holding a diet might pose more problems for the government than it would solve:

> This diet has been rather hastily called and will bring no benefit to the Commonwealth ... if the senate cannot restore liberty, it certainly will not increase confusion ... I prefer liberty and that is why I wish to preserve it, but by confusion nothing will be preserved. We cannot postpone calling a diet, which is absolutely necessary, since without a diet it is impossible to preserve liberty, but we must suggest the business with which we start and end the diet, since if we allow private matters to be discussed, we will face new disorder.[41]

Leszczyński, despite his evident scruples, stated that should taxes be necessary, then the king should call a convocation of senators instead of a diet, which would avoid the problem of political confusion.

Koryciński's advice was similar. While his hostility to Wilno partly explains his opposition to calling a diet in 1656–7, he was also convinced that the major problem facing the Commonwealth was the payment of the army, which the calling of a diet in January would not help: the taxes for the second two quarters of 1655 voted by the 1655 diet had been due in December, but since the Swedes had invaded in July, these taxes had not reached the treasury. Holding a diet would not solve the problem, since the army would probably mutiny if, as was usual, the diet proved reluctant to meet the government's fiscal demands, while the government might be forced to make 'terrible promises ... which we would not be able to meet. While there is no diet, hope of one will persuade the troops to serve longer.' Since the army was only bound to serve until the expiry of the last quarter-year for which taxes had been voted at the start of April, he argued that the best time to hold a diet would be early April, which would keep the army in service under oath until 1 July, whereas a diet in January would only keep the troops in service until 1 March. He suggested that palatinates should bring their unpaid taxes with them so that the army could be paid immediately. This would not be illegal since the dietines would conclude nothing new, but merely implement decisions already taken, in the manner of normal post-diet meetings.[42] Rákóczi's invasion, in the event, gave the government an excellent excuse for postponing the diet. Nevertheless, the problem of paying the army remained: if a diet could not be held, money would have to be raised on the authority of the senate council to prevent the army disbanding.

The cooperation which he received from his senators after 1655 convinced John Casimir that the road to more effective government lay through the senate council.

---

[40] John Casimir to Grzymułtowski, 24.X.1656; Czart. 3487 p. 93. John Casimir to J. Weiher, Chojnice, 24.X.1656; Czart. 149 no. 143, p. 475.
[41] J. Leszczyński to A. Leszczyński, Vienna, 18.XI.1656; Czart. 384 no. 257, p. 507.
[42] Koryciński to unknown, 1656; Czart. 149 no. 185, p. 673.

At least council debates were not marked by the confusion and disorder seen at the diet. As Louise Marie pointed out:

Nothing can happen [at a council meeting] without the king's willing and commanding it. Matters resolved in the senate outside the meetings of the diet are decided by the king and he is not obliged to follow the majority opinion; it is sufficient for him to have the support of one senator for something to pass.[43]

During the war, John Casimir developed his policy of calling extraordinary convocations, such as those at Częstochowa in 1657 and Warsaw in 1658. These meetings included *szlachta* representatives as well as senators and were designed to give greater authority and legitimacy to royal policy, while allowing the government far greater control over their composition and course than would have been possible at a diet. It was important that they were given added authority by being seen to be more than the normal meeting of senators present at Court. This point was emphasised by Bogusław Leszczyński in defending the controversial clause of the treaty of Vienna which gave Austria the right to garrison Cracow after its capture: 'When the situation was already desperate, God assembled at His holy shrine at Częstochowa not a normal council . . . but more than twenty leading senators . . . and although the whole senate did not gather, which never happens in truth, the most eminent were present.' He considered that the failure of the Częstochowa convocation to sanction the surrender of Cracow to the Austrians was unimportant, since it had agreed that the Commonwealth could not save itself by its own efforts; following the Austrian demand for Cracow, he had been sent a declaration signed by John Casimir, Trzebicki and the senate council, giving him:

ministerial and royal authorisation and if it was permissible for the senate council to empower me, which nobody denies, the senate council had the authority to deal with this problem . . . since it was necessary for the good of the Commonwealth and since there was no chance to consult more widely by convoking a meeting of the equestrian order.[44]

It was not just with regard to foreign policy that John Casimir took important decisions on the authority of the senate council. In this period, a determined attempt was made to tackle the financial problem which lay at the heart of the Commonwealth's plight by circumventing the powers of the diet. The practice of running up debts in the name of the treasury and ordering payments for extraordinary purposes encroached on the fiscal powers of the diet. The senate council went further than this, however, in its attempt to meet the financial demands imposed by the war. In 1656, on the basis of a council decree, an excise was introduced in several towns, especially in the palatinate of Ruthenia, as a sales tax on all items worth more than five groszy. After the Częstochowa convocation, a decree was issued, proclaiming that to meet the needs of war

[43] Louise Marie to Mme de Choisy, 12.XI.1656; BNP FFr. 3859 f. 11.
[44] B. Leszczyński to Stanisław Potocki, Cracow, 16.IX.1657; Czart. 1656 p. 394, 397.

Political reform

with our lords senators and faithful advisors, gathered at our side, on the authority of the senate council, [we decree] a new tax for all common people in all towns and villages, both royal and, by special permission, ecclesiastical. This tax is uniform, equal and does not weigh more heavily on one man than on another.[45]

It was one thing to proclaim the new tax, another to collect it. To avoid criticism from dietines, the council made it clear that the new excise was subject to the approval of the next diet; nevertheless, it technically had no power to authorise this advance. There was more to this initiative, however, than an attempt to introduce a new tax without diet approval. The administration of the new tax, along with the *czopowe*, a tax on beer and spirits, was to be taken out of the hands of the dietines and given to the central treasury.[46] This was a bold attempt, carried out with the full backing of the senate council, to reverse the long trend of fiscal decentralisation, which had accelerated after 1641.

The cooperation of the senate council in this and similar matters convinced John Casimir that the key to strengthening central authority was to increase the power and prestige of the senate council. Historians examining the 1657 'Decision' have usually concentrated their attention on the proposal to limit the veto; more important perhaps was the proposal that, in addition to the senators-resident usually appointed by the diet, *szlachta* representatives should be nominated by the diet to attend Court and participate in meetings of the senate council alongside senators and government ministers.[47] It was emphasised that the diet would retain its powers to ratify council decisions but the intention was clear: the authority of the senate council was to be increased by making it appear a more representative body. Should the veto be retained and the senate council continue to cooperate, the theoretical right of the diet to ratify council decisions might not be fatal: if the diet constantly ended in anarchy or was broken, then its approval might become irrelevant; indeed, the continuation of the veto might be essential to increase the power of the extended council by default.

By early 1658, enthusiasm in Court circles for diet reform was waning. The proposals for the limitation of the veto contained in the 'Decision' were not submitted to the Warsaw convocation for discussion, despite Opaliński's wish to do so. Partly this was due to the fact that this assembly was not seen essentially as a preparatory meeting designed to agree on a reform programme to be submitted as soon as possible to the diet, as many historians have assumed: it was called primarily to deal with problems of foreign and financial policy, not diet reform. At that point it was not planned to hold a diet; the 1658 diet was only called subsequently in order to stall Muscovy with regard to the succession.

Another reason for the failure to discuss diet reform, however, was that Court

---

[45] ibid. pp. 314–15; Rybarski, 'Podatek akcyzy z czasów Jana Kazimierza i Michała Korybuta' *Studia Historyczne ku czci Stanisława Kutrzeby* I pp. 403–4.
[46] Rybarski, *Skarb i pieniądz* pp. 315, 317.   [47] 'Decyzja Jana Kazimierza' p. 536.

doubts about the wisdom of too drastic a limitation of the veto were increasingly echoed by important interest-groups within the Commonwealth who saw the veto as a vital safeguard of their rights and liberties. The Catholic Church was the first to express its concern: 'Among the matters to be discussed ... will be a reform of the laws and government of the Commonwealth; it is proposed to return to majority voting ... which I feel could be prejudicial to the clergy, since the votes of bishops are few and the laity would be dominant.'[48] Given the Church's privileged position with regard to taxation and the bitterness it had aroused during the war, this was an important point: in 1655, the Church had resisted with difficulty calls that its tax-exemption should be waived and that it should contribute to the *łanowa* infantry; if majority voting were introduced, it might prove impossible to protect Church privileges.[49] Furthermore, the Warsaw convocation also discussed the proposed terms for an agreement with the Cossacks, which included the creation of a duchy of Ruthenia on the lines of the grand duchy of Lithuania, with seats in the senate for representatives of the Orthodox Church; the implications of this plan had to be considered regarding the position of the Catholic and Uniate Churches in Lithuania and the Ukraine. Finally, there was the possibility of the tsar's succession under the terms of the treaty of Wilno: if majority voting were introduced and Alexis were elected the Church might face further pressure in the diet from Orthodox interests. Faced with these potential threats to its position, the Church saw the retention of the veto as important for the defence of its interests. The doubts of ecclesiastical senators, traditionally the strongest supporters of attempts to strengthen royal power, only reinforced those of the Court.

The proposal to abolish the veto also had important implications for Lithuanians, who feared the introduction of majority voting since the Lithuanian minority at the diet would be swamped: 'A Lithuanian participant talked at length with me on this matter, telling me that [this reform] will never happen, otherwise the Lithuanians would separate from Poland, since in that case, their votes would be inferior to those of the Poles, to whom they would be subordinated, rather than united.'[50] Lithuanians already resented the way in which their interests had tended to be subordinated to those of Poland, especially since 1654. At least the principle of unanimity and the threat of the veto afforded Lithuanians some protection and made it possible to force the Poles to reconsider controversial legislation. Majority voting would deprive them even of that.

Such doubts reinforced the Court's view that increasing the authority of the senate council, not the diet, should be the main priority. The maintenance of the

---

[48] Vidoni, Poznań, 27.XII.1657; TRz. 8420 p. 82.
[49] Vidoni to Orsini, Warsaw, 20.VI.1655; TRz. 8418 no. 19, p. 35; Hoverbeck to Frederick William, Warsaw, 20.VI.1655; *Urkunden und Aktenstücke* VI p. 700. In fact the Church contributed to state taxation, and on the same footing as the laity with regard to extraordinary taxation: H. Karbownik, *Ciężary stanu duchownego w Polsce na rzecz państwa od roku 1381 do połowy XVII wieku* (Lublin, 1980) pp. 161–2. Nevertheless, it was widely perceived as uniquely privileged and faced serious pressure to increase its contributions.   [50] Vidoni, Poznań, 2.I.1658; TRz. 8421 p. 4.

Political reform

principle of unanimity and increasing anarchy at the diet might indeed reduce it in practice merely to the forum for the expression of *szlachta* grievances and the presentation of petitions envisaged in the scheme reported by des Noyers in 1656. The tendency of historians to regard diet reform as essential has caused them to overlook the fact that while there is no evidence that the Warsaw convocation even discussed diet reform and certainly did not approve Opaliński's scheme for the introduction of majority voting, it both considered and approved the proposals for financial reform contained in the 'Decision', which criticised the fiscal structure of the Commonwealth and sought approval for the actions of the senate council since 1656:

> It is and has been a source of great difficulty with regard to the needs of the state that the ordinary expenditure of the fatherland is not covered by ordinary and proportional revenues, whence military service is burdensome for the army and it is difficult to bargain for taxes ... For which reason, so that such a situation will not occur again, we pledge that the *czopowe* and the excise in the towns will be assigned to meet the normal and constant expenditure of the Commonwealth ... which will be confirmed at the next diet.[51]

Czapliński makes only a bare mention of this clause, concentrating even then on its supposed class nature, claiming that the idea was 'dictated by the class interests of the richer *szlachta* and the magnate elite, since the excise, a tax fashionable in contemporary western Europe and in neighbouring Prussia, affected mainly the poorer elements of society'.[52] He misses the point by ignoring the fact that the decree introducing the excise specifically exempted all goods worth less than five groszy to ensure that the poorest people did not pay and that such taxes in western Europe were fashionable precisely because they enabled governments to circumvent noble tax privileges. The restriction of the tax to royal and ecclesiastical towns was undoubtedly to reduce opposition to its introduction from dietines; the important point was that this tax was to be a permanent part of the ordinary revenue of the state.[53] If reform of the legislature was not now seen as a priority, reform of the executive was seen as essential by the majority of the senate council; there is no evidence of any opposition to this proposal, which was later put to the diet.

The government hoped that, with such backing, the new tax would have become familiar enough to be accepted by the time the next diet met. On its introduction after the Częstochowa convocation it had met a mixed reception from dietines. Some did object to the way in which the new tax was introduced without the knowledge of the equestrian order and had already been operating for eight weeks 'to the great inconvenience of all, although nobody is participating and the Polish infantry has not received a single shilling from it'.[54] Nevertheless, others welcomed

---

[51] 'Decyzja Jana Kazimierza' p. 536.
[52] Czapliński, 'Próby reform' p. 318; Bąkowa sees the significance of the measure, but does not pursue the matter any further: *Szlachta województwa krakowskiego* p. 23.
[53] Rybarski, *Skarb i pieniądz* pp. 74, 324.
[54] Instrukcja od Koła Rycerskiego z Województwa Podolskiego za uniwersałem JKMści, Kamianets, 9.XI.1657; Czart. 402 p. 221.

this form of taxation over more traditional taxes which fell directly on noble estates. Two days after the original proclamation, the Środa dietine decided to introduce an excise of its own in royal, ecclesiastical and lay towns, which was seen as a way to avoid the constant government demands for new taxes: this decision, while it implied acceptance in principle of the government's right to introduce these taxes, was probably designed to preempt the government and keep control of the new tax at local level.[55]

It was to be hoped that such support might overcome objections to the crucial proposal concerning the way in which the new taxes were to be collected. In the summer of 1657, treasury secretaries were sent out to dietines to start collecting the new tax. This provoked an immediate response: the Środa dietine asked the king to suspend the excise until it received guarantees that it would continue to be administered by the palatinates. This plea, however, was rejected by John Casimir, who ordered that the excise and *czopowe* be surrendered to the administration of the treasury.[56]

The government attempted to override such objections by submitting the proposal to the Warsaw convocation. Government propaganda stressed that the convocation should be regarded as having the force of a diet. In his decree of January 1658 justifying the introduction of the excise, John Casimir emphasised the way in which the decision had been reached:

At the recent Częstochowa convocation ... in the presence of senators of rank, members of our council, both ecclesiastical and lay, and of a considerable number of representatives of the equestrian order, being unable in any way, due to constant wars and other important reasons, to hold a diet at that time, this measure was enacted by the senate council with unanimous consent ... It seemed to us, together with our counsellors, that the *czopowe* and excise, whose administration and disposal was at that time in the hands of the palatinates ... should be assigned to the care of His Excellency the Crown treasurer, unhindered by any decisions of particular dietines, which were abrogated by that council in the public interest.[57]

The government was backed by the senate council. Jan Leszczyński, always so concerned to protect and preserve the Commonwealth's liberties, wrote enthusiastically to Hoverbeck that he was sure that money would be forthcoming after the agreement of the general excise and *czopowe* in noble as well as royal and ecclesiastical towns.[58] The lack of senate opposition may be explained by the fact that the new tax was to be collected by the state, not the royal treasury, under the control of the treasurer, who was bound to submit his accounts to the diet. The plan certainly enhanced the prestige of the senate council: if it had been successfully implemented, it would have created an important precedent by greatly increasing its fiscal powers.

[55] Rybarski, *Skarb i pieniądz* pp. 315–6; 'Podatek akcyzy' pp. 405–6.
[56] Rybarski, *Skarb i pieniądz* p. 320.
[57] Royal proclamation, Poznań, 9.I.1658, printed in Rybarski, *Skarb i pieniądz* pp. 316–17.
[58] J. Leszczyński to Hoverbeck, Warsaw, 20.III.1658; Czart. 388 no. 186, p. 377.

Political reform

The approval of the excise and *czopowe* by the Warsaw convocation was an important victory for the government. Nevertheless, the main battle over control of the new taxes had not yet been won. It was vital that the treasury officials trying to collect the taxes had time in order for the system to become accepted, so that when a diet was called, it could be presented with a *fait accompli*. It is probable that John Casimir, far from seeing the convocation as merely preparatory to the meeting of a diet, intended to continue ruling as he had done since 1655, not calling a diet but relying on the senate council and periodic assemblies of notables. Unfortunately, the renewed Muscovite demands meant that the diet could no longer be postponed. It was therefore inevitable that the new taxes would meet the scrutiny of the diet before they were fully established.

John Casimir made great efforts to persuade the diet to accept the new taxes and especially their centralised collection:

Although His Majesty is certain of achieving eternal peace with His Majesty the tsar at the forthcoming diet, nevertheless, since he has urgent problems to deal with on other fronts, particularly the unfinished war with Sweden, the [Lithuanian] army ... cannot be disbanded and since it is impossible to keep it in service without supplies ... and although His Majesty and the senate council ought not to have introduced such taxes without the consent of the equestrian order, it was difficult to see any alternative.[59]

The response was mixed. Some dietines voiced their suspicion of the principle, at least with regard to the collection of the excise in noble towns: 'The levying of the excise and the *czopowe* on noble property represents a great burden on this estate and a threat to its freedom; let us hope, however, that these taxes will bring advantage to the fatherland ... but we fear that ... mountains of gold have been promised which will turn out to be illusions.' Despite these doubts, however, the Wizna dietine agreed to follow the view of other envoys: if they were in favour of the excise it should be accepted, although its envoys were instructed to block it if anyone protested at the diet.[60]

In general, dietines did not attack the tax itself and some even preferred it to more traditional forms of taxation, which, it was claimed, the nobility were unable to pay.[61] There was a favourable response to the idea from some Lithuanian dietines, which welcomed any plan to pay the grand duchy's armies: 'We well know that the army has received neither satisfaction for its services nor just reward for its labours and its courage, of the kind ... which it is customary to provide ... It behoves our envoys to do all they can to ensure that the means to satisfy the army, namely the excise, are put into effect.' At least the principle was accepted, even if noble exemption was requested:

---

[59] Royal instructions to the Pinsk dietine, 26.III.1658. *Akty otnoshiashchesia* no. 107, p. 122.
[60] Laudum Conventus Particularis Viznensis, 21.VI.1658; Teki Pawińskiego 8350, pp. 211–12.
[61] Rybarski, *Skarb i pieniądz* p. 321.

After the Deluge

We nevertheless recommend to our envoys that, in order that the noble estate should continue to enjoy the security and liberty which it currently possesses, they may not be subject to any excise and that such a tax be not collected in noble villages, although we permit its gathering in royal and ecclesiastical towns and villages.[62]

Nevertheless, if the majority was ready to accept the excise and *czopowe* as necessary evils, there was opposition over the key question of control. Most dietines rejected the proposal that the new taxes should become part of the ordinary revenue of the state and there was particular opposition to the levying of the tax without diet permission. Some expressed opposition to the whole plan:

The excise is a terrible yoke dreamed up for the poor nobility and the miserable peasants in the style of the [German] Empire; a tax payable on all things sold: cattle, grain, cloth, hides and barrels of beer brought to the inn ... Soon there will be an absolute regime, as exists in Germany, since the nobility will not send their beer to the inn but burghers will bring ale from the towns to noble villages; the next thing will be that fathers will have to pay a poll tax on stoves, on windows and on their own poor children. Thus it is in Turkey, where first only a little is requested, but as time goes on, ever more is demanded, as much as it pleases the government to ask.[63]

The government was defeated on this vital issue. The chamber of envoys was prepared to accept the taxes but with important reservations: they were to be regarded as extraordinary revenue and were only to run until the next diet. Furthermore, it was emphasised that the taxes were to be collected and administered by the palatinates, not the central treasury, and the proceeds were to be assigned exclusively to military expenditure.[64] Although the excise was renewed and extended at the 1659 diet this represented a real defeat for royal hopes of reform: while the tax could be collected, the government had failed to wrest the initiative in taxation away from the diet, despite strong senate support. Collection was to remain in the hands of the dietines. An important battle had been lost: after the final establishment in the 1650s of the fiscal powers of dietines, there were no substantial changes until 1717.[65] The response to the government's plans for even this small measure of financial reform underlined again that the diet was unwilling to address the fundamental problems revealed since 1655. John Casimir had been supported by the senate council, which had struggled to cope with the problems of fighting a war with such a decentralised political system, only to see his plans rejected by the diet.

Too often, historians have seen the abolition of the veto and reform of diet procedure as panaceas for all the Commonwealth's ills and assumed that supporters of reform all saw matters in this light. It is true that some would have agreed with

---

[62] Instructions of Kowno dietine for deputies to the diet, 21.VI.1658; Medeksza, *Księga pamiętnicza* p. 171.
[63] '*Speculum ... Prawdziwe Synom ... Koronnym*' Czart. 151 no. 159, p. 726.
[64] *Volumina Legum* IV pp. 524–5.
[65] A. Lityński, *Szlachecki samorząd gospodarczy w Małopolsce (1606–1717)* (Katowice, 1974) pp. 45, 69.

Political reform

this view, yet the problems of the Commonwealth ran deeper than the procedural difficulties of the diet; in the light of *szlachta* attitudes as displayed in 1658, which seemed all too familiar, John Casimir's doubts concerning the proposition that a reformed diet would lead to the strengthening of central authority are understandable. If the government could not win acceptance for such a reform, when the senate council was united in supporting it and a mere three years after the collapse of the Commonwealth in the face of its enemies had convincingly demonstrated the need for reform, then it was to be doubted if it ever could win acceptance for more radical measures even if majority voting were introduced. Although the 1658 diet was not as harmonious as some observers reported, the government on the whole succeeded in pushing through its programme, which included such controversial measures as the acceptance of French mediation and the ratification of Wilno. Yet with regard to internal reform, it seemed that the diet was, as it had been throughout John Casimir's reign, more interested in frustrating and restricting the actions of the government than cooperating in the exercise of power. The attitude of envoys in 1658 merely confirmed John Casimir's prejudices against the diet and threw him back on the senate council, which at least seemed willing to tackle the problems of the executive. The surrender of the *liberum veto* under such circumstances would deprive the monarchy of an important weapon which enabled it to block further restrictions on its power, without any guarantee that effective reform would follow.

8

Towards a French candidature: 1658–60

If the monarchy's reform plans, based on an increase in the power of the senate council, were to succeed, it would have to confront the problem of independent magnate power which had frustrated all its efforts between 1648 and 1655. Given the king's political and financial dependence upon the magnates, it was difficult to see how this could be achieved unless the monarchy were able to raise itself sufficiently above the magnate factions to dominate them and make it as dangerous for a Radziwiłł or a Lubomirski to oppose royal power as it had proved for Radziejowski. Moreover, it was not just the diet which was capable of placing restrictions upon royal power. The principle of free election of the king after the death of his predecessor meant that at regular intervals the Crown lost control of the political situation. From the death of one king to the coronation of the next, the royal patronage machine was suspended and the monarchy was unable to exert any influence upon the political struggle. It was royal elections above all which ensured the continuing and increasing weakness of the monarchy. If the diet was ever likely to place greater restrictions upon royal power, it was capable of manipulation and a degree of control impossible during a royal election: it was in the drawing up of the *Pacta Conventa* by the coronation diet that the most damaging limitations upon royal power were introduced. Agreeing to such conditions was necessary to achieve election, especially if it were contested. Thus, any reform which might be achieved by John Casimir could easily be undone upon his death.

The plan for an election *vivente rege* was designed to confront both these problems. First, the Court would be able to mobilise its extensive influence at the election diet to block as far as possible the inclusion of further restrictions on royal power, something which a king elected in the usual way was unable to do, since he could only activate his extensive patronage powers after his coronation. Secondly, the election of a foreign prince would give the monarchy a power-base outside the Commonwealth for the first time since 1600, which might reduce royal dependence upon the diet in matters of finance. Its increased wealth, allied to potential foreign backing at critical moments, would enable the monarchy once more to raise itself above the great magnate factions and restore its position of dominance, by increasing its already considerable power to manage and manipulate the political system.

Thus, an election *vivente rege* as far as the Court was concerned was no mere

Towards a French candidature

exercise in irresponsible dynasticism but the very centrepiece of its campaign for political reform. Frustratingly, however, despite the willingness of so many senators to accept the principle of an election after the disasters of 1655, the Court was no nearer realising its dream in 1658. Indeed, the 1658 diet came at an extremely awkward moment. On the one hand, hopes that military support from Austria and Brandenburg would bring a swift victory over Sweden had been disappointed by the reluctance of both these powers to take the offensive; on the other hand, the acceptance of French mediation had not opened the way to a quick negotiated settlement. Opinion among senators remained divided as to the best course of action:

Everyone without exception yearns for peace; some, however, argue that this should begin with a rapprochement with Muscovy, others that peace should be made quickly with Sweden in order to strike at Muscovite oppression; the greatest number, however, wish to subdue the Swedes but since they see that achieving this will be a difficult, lengthy and dangerous task, they argue that it is better to try to persuade the Muscovites to accept tolerable conditions; they wish in the meantime to keep alive Muscovite hopes of peace and the succession, and to persuade them to attack the Swedes, so that the king of Sweden, alarmed at this new enemy, will of necessity be forced to make peace with Poland.[1]

The imperial election was not until the end of July; only then would it become clear whether Austrian promises of more resolute action were sincere. Since it was reported that Charles X was planning a new landing in Prussia, the Poles could not afford to break with Austria, yet the behaviour of Austrian troops ensured that the Austrian alliance would remain unpopular. The diet was called primarily to stall Alexis and in the hope that the prospect of his election would persuade either Austria and Brandenburg or France to act with greater resolution. Once again, largely powerless to influence the course of events decisively, the Polish government could only play for time. For the moment there could be no thought of an election; apart from the discussions over Wilno, the problem of the succession was not broached during the diet.

The government approached the diet without a clear programme. The royal instructions, issued on 27 May, merely called for the ratification of the treaties with Austria, Brandenburg and Denmark, for consideration of the Muscovite demands for the succession and for measures to ensure the payment of the army. John Casimir's letters to senators before the meeting of the dietines adopted no firm line and did not call for political reform.[2] It was officially maintained, *pour encourager les autres* and to conciliate Lithuanian opinion, that its purpose was to settle the Muscovite succession:

Since this diet is only being held to satisfy the grand duke of Muscovy ... in order to implement the treaty signed at Wilno and since this prince is also approaching with a

[1] Lisola, Poznań, 16.V.1658; *Berichte* no. 100, pp. 412–13.
[2] e.g. John Casimir to Krzysztof Gembicki, 20.V.1658; BPAN Kórnik 1618 p. 57.

powerful army, it has been decided to enter negotiations with him, if it is impossible to do so first with Sweden. It is not that the Poles do not fear his rule ... but they believe that there is no other way to prevent the ruin of their country.[3]

When Vidoni tried to persuade Louise Marie that talks with Alexis must be ended, she stressed that the Poles had little choice, telling him

of the necessity of satisfying the tsar, since with three armies surrounding the Commonwealth, not including that of Brandenburg, the Poles regard the tsar as the least dangerous of their friends and enemies. He is the most likely to commit himself, while the king of Sweden offers no such hope; neither do the Poles expect any commitment from the king of Hungary, who has attracted much resentment due to the behaviour of his troops. Furthermore, the attitude of Lithuania gives great cause for concern: it is capable of settling with Muscovy on its own and its lead might be followed by the Cossacks and all the territories on the far side of the Vistula.[4]

The Court might not wish to settle with Alexis, but it was certainly prepared to use that threat to put pressure on both France and Austria. While de Lumbres asserted that the Austrians preferred talks with Muscovy to talks with Sweden, Leopold was sufficiently worried by the prospect of the tsar's election and the acceptance of French mediation to appoint his own commissioners to negotiate with Sweden; John Casimir stressed that if Leopold could secure Swedish aid in a war against Muscovy, he would be prepared to abandon French mediation.[5]

Much depended on the attitude of the diet. Despite the usual reports of a low attendance, when Krzysztof Pac, as Lithuanian grand chancellor-elect, read the royal proposals on 15 July following Koryciński's death the previous day, there were twenty-three senators present, a relatively high number for the start of a diet. Others soon began to arrive: forty-two senators appeared by the end of the diet, which made it one of the best-attended for some time. There was a particularly large number of ecclesiastical senators, probably due to the inclusion in the agenda of the Muscovite succession and the Cossack request for abolition of the Uniate Church.[6]

The Court did not pursue a strongly pro-French line. Louise Marie only returned from her unsuccessful Berlin mission on 15 July, having been absent

[3] De Lumbres to Brienne, 25.V.1658; CPP XII p. 99.
[4] Vidoni, Sieraków, 11.VI.1658; TRz. 8420 pp. 26–7.
[5] De Lumbres to Brienne, 25.V.1658; CPP XII p. 106; Instructions, Frankfurt 3.V.1658. Walewski, *Historia wyzwolenia* II document LIV p. lxv. For a full account of Austrian attitudes to Muscovy in early 1658, see Pribram, *Österreichische Vermittlungspolitik im polnisch-russischen Kriege 1655–1660* Archiv für österreichische Geschichte 75 (1889) pp. 452–75.
[6] For reports of low attendance, see: B. Radziwiłł to Gosiewski, Königsberg, 20.VII.1658, BPANCr. 342 p. 783; Krzysztof Racki to unknown, BJag. 5 p. 795. The figure of forty-two is based on the names given in *Theatrum Europeum* VIII, 2 pp. 653–4, Vidoni, Avvisi; TRz. 8421 p. 238, Chrapowicki, *Diariusz* p. 170, and the signatories of the plenipotentiary powers for the commissioners for the talks with Muscovy, drawn up in Warsaw on 25 July; Czart. 387 no. 4, pp. 19–20. The attendance of fourteen bishops was considerably higher than the best figure for the reign of Władysław IV, which was nine: Czapliński and Filipczak-Koczur, 'Udział senatorów' p. 676. Indeed, the figure of forty-two senators was not matched by any of Władysław IV's diets and was only surpassed in the early seventeenth century by those of 1627 and 1631.

Towards a French candidature

during the vital pre-diet period. John Casimir still favoured the Austrian alliance and he did what he could to curb anti-Austrian feeling. He cancelled a Corpus Christi procession at the request of the Austrians following a precedence dispute with the French, and when a delegation from Great Poland demanded the withdrawal of the Austrian army, he pointedly remarked that if they had not opened the gates of the kingdom to Sweden in the first place, they would not have had to endure the presence of foreign troops.[7] While he was not prepared to abandon French mediation, on hearing rumours of Charles's intention to attack Prussia, he urged the allies not to wait until Swedish troops were in Pomerania or Prussia but to mount a preemptive strike; he wished for more from Austria than the leisurely conduct of the siege of Thorn, which Souches had begun a fortnight earlier.[8]

Most senators favoured the Habsburg alliance. Jan Leszczyński, so disillusioned with Austria earlier in the year, now abandoned his flirtation with the idea of peace with Sweden, stating he had always believed that the best plan was to attack the Swedes in Pomerania.[9] During the diet, he was quick to reassure the pro-Austrian Cieciszewski that the interests of France were well known and that the French were not trusted as much as Cieciszewski imagined.[10] Hostility to Austria came principally from the chamber of envoys. If many dietines were prepared to accept the treaty of Vienna, there were vociferous complaints about the behaviour of Austrian troops and the government had great trouble in securing ratification. The general dietine of the Cracow palatinate asked for the withdrawal of the Austrian garrison from the royal castle of Wawel, while the most common demand was that the Austrians should not again be permitted to take up winter quarters in Poland. The Sieradz palatinate demanded compensation for the destruction wrought by the Austrians on their march to Great Poland from the siege of Cracow. Envoys from Łęczyca were instructed to beg the king not to deliver the palatinate up to ultimate ruin by granting winter quarters to the Austrians: 'Since we prefer to suffer any extremes rather than experience the kind of oppression that our brothers ... have endured.'[11] The main complaints were that the troops did nothing while sucking the land dry and that the Austrians were introducing more than the 12,000 allowed by the treaty.[12]

Nevertheless, the Court succeeded in persuading the chamber of envoys to ratify the Vienna treaty unaltered, through first obtaining senate agreement. It was to be

---

[7] Walewski, *Historia wyzwolenia* II pp. 287–8; Vidoni, Poznań, 24.VI.1658; TRz. 8421 p. 30.
[8] John Casimir to Montecuccoli, Warsaw, 24 and 30.VII.1658; Opitz, *Österreich und Brandenburg* pp. 111, 113.
[9] J. Leszczyński to Turski, Goslina, 26.V.1658; Czart 388 no. 191, p. 394.
[10] J. Leszczyński to Cieciszewski, Warsaw, 28.VII.1658; Czart. 388 no. 209, p. 461.
[11] Instructions for envoys from the Cracow palatinate, 21.VI.1658; *Akta sejmikowe województwa krakowskiego* II p. 638; instructions of the Zator dietine, 17.VI.1658; ibid. p. 619; instructions for envoys from the Sieradz palatinate, 21.VI.1658; Teki Pawińskiego, 8342 pp. 692–3; instructions of the Kowno dietine, 21.VI.1658; Medeksza, *Księga pamietnicza* p. 170; instructions for envoys from the Leczyca palatinate, 21.VI.1658; Teki Pawińskiego 8327 pp. 691–2.
[12] Vidoni, Warsaw, 13.VIII.1658; Levinson, *Die Nuntiaturberichte* no. 208, p. 131.

After the Deluge

hoped that once the Pomeranian campaign began, most Austrian troops would leave and that the storm of protest would die down. The *szlachta* opposed the presence of Austrian troops in the Commonwealth, not the anti-Swedish alliance, and general opinion was favourable to Frederick William, despite his reluctance to participate in the Pomeranian offensive which so infuriated the Court. While the Court vented its anger in an attack on the elector in Karwat's opening sermon, the reaction of dietines to the treaty of Wehlau–Bromberg was almost entirely favourable.[13] Opposition came only from followers of Paweł Sapieha, who opposed the return to Bogusław Radziwiłł of the Radziwiłł estates, promised to the Lithuanian army by John Casimir in 1656.[14] Nevertheless, Krzysztof Pac wrote to Radziwiłł of widespread support for the treaty in Lithuania, while the dietine of Halicz welcomed the proposal to confer Polish nobility on three Brandenburg politicians and diplomats, including Hoverbeck. If the payment of the Lithuanian army remained a problem, the treaty was duly ratified.[15]

Envoys welcomed the government's policy of using all possible means to obtain a quick and favourable settlement with Sweden. French mediation was accepted, as was the treaty of Vienna, despite the behaviour of Austrian troops. There was, however, opposition to the Muscovite succession. Lubomirski argued in the Cracow dietine that while he recognised the advantages of an agreement with Muscovy, he felt it was an inopportune moment to discuss the succession: such an election would immediately lead to war against Turkey and the Tatars, and he was generally opposed to the idea of holding a diet at all. His reservations were reflected in the instructions of the Cracow dietine, where his influence was extensive. He deliberately arrived late at the diet, to avoid discussion of the Wilno treaty.[16] Many dietines echoed his concern:

Our laws forbid the election of a new king during the lifetime of our Serene Highness ... our envoys ... after consulting with envoys from other palatinates, will make clear to His Majesty the tsar that his election will not be in accordance with our laws. With regard to this nomination: if it comes to the worst we command our envoys that, having consulted with envoys from other palatinates and having informed our palatine, they will call us out in the noble levy.[17]

Despite this opposition, the government succeeded in winning support for new

---

[13] Frederick William complained at the attack to Louise Marie in a letter dated 29 July: *Urkunden und Aktenstücke* VIII p. 285. The queen had promised to offer protection to Protestants at the Berlin meeting.
[14] J. Leszczyński to Hoverbeck, Warsaw, 16.III.1658; Czart. 388 no. 182, p. 370.
[15] Krzysztof Pac to Bogusław Radziwiłł, Wilkowiszki, 20.VI.1658; AGAD ARadz. dz.V teka 251, II, 208 pp. 77–8; instruction for envoys from the Halicz dietine, 17.VI.1658; *Akta grodzkie i ziemskie* XXIV p. 143; cf. instruction of the dietine of the duchy of Oświęcim and Zator; *Akta sejmikowe województwa krakowskiego* II p. 622.
[16] Vidoni, Warsaw, 8.VII.1658; TRz. 8421 p. 31; instructions for envoys from the Cracow palatinate, 21.VI.1658; *Akta sejmikowe województwa krakowskiego* II p. 636; Vidoni, Warsaw, 6.VIII.1658; TRz. 8421 p. 38.
[17] Instructions for envoys from the Sieradz palatinate, 21.VI.1658; Teki Pawińskiego 8342 pp. 686–7.

Towards a French candidature

talks with Alexis over the conditions to be attached to his succession. It was no more attracted than Lubomirski by the idea of a Muscovite election and was determined to renegotiate the terms of Wilno: it had already appointed commissioners in May, ostensibly to discuss the treaty's implementation, in reality to renegotiate its terms. The diet was quite prepared to accept this policy: it was not being asked to ratify the treaty as it stood, while the treaty itself had postponed consideration of vital questions, including the occupation of Lithuanian territory and the position of the Cossacks, which had to be settled before it could be implemented.

Changes in the Ukraine since Khmelnytskyi's death in August 1657 had worked to the Commonwealth's advantage. With Khmelnytskyi out of the way, Alexis had increased the pressure on the Cossacks to comply with the Muscovite interpretation of the treaty of Pereiaslav. Moscow's new assertiveness widened divisions already apparent within Cossack ranks. Vyhovskyi, elected temporary hetman until the majority of Khmelnytskyi's son Iurii, began to move away from Muscovy, supported by a significant part of the Cossack leadership. Although Vyhovskyi first signed a new agreement with Sweden at Korsun, Charles X was in no position to offer effective protection. If support were to be found against Muscovy, some kind of agreement with the Commonwealth was the only practical solution.

The Commonwealth sought to exploit these feelings by launching a new peace initiative shortly after Khmelnytskyi's death with the backing not only of the king but also of Lubomirski and Koniecpolski, both landowners whose large Ukrainian estates were occupied by the rebels.[18] In talks held during March and April, a radical new solution to the Cossack problem was devised which envisaged the creation of a duchy of Ruthenia from the palatinates of Kiev, Chernigov and Bratslav. The Commonwealth would thereby be turned into a tripartite state, in which the Cossack elite would receive the recognition it had hitherto been denied. The favourable reaction of Vyhovskyi and his supporters was encouraging and led to the signing of the treaty of Hadiach in September, which, it was hoped, established a definitive solution for the Cossack problem. For the first time, the Commonwealth could consider breaking the treaty of Wilno without risking a renewal of the Cossack–Muscovite alliance of 1654–5: 'It is said that the Muscovite is weak, and it is believed that he can achieve little this year. The Poles are rejecting hopes for renewed talks ... since they see that the king of Sweden is now tied down in Denmark, which frees the Polish armies to be thrown against the Muscovites in great force.'[19]

The government had to proceed with care, however; it had to avoid precipitating war with Muscovy before peace was achieved with Sweden, since this might yet provoke a split with Lithuania, where many still favoured a settlement with Muscovy: 'Our envoys will ask His Majesty to confirm and keep inviolate the peace settlement reached with the tsar ... so that it might restore us in our weakened

[18] Pernal, 'The Polish Commonwealth and the Ukraine' pp. 300–5.
[19] Lisola, report, 3.IX.1658; *Berichte* no. 111, p. 446.

circumstances to our former glory and security.'[20] The prospect of a settlement with the Cossacks did nothing to help Lithuania; on the contrary, it promised to prolong war with Muscovy. The government therefore kept up the appearance of being willing to implement Wilno. The diet accordingly drew up the terms under which Alexis was to be offered the throne, asserting the fundamental nature of Polish and Lithuanian liberties, with the basic right of free election of the monarch as the most important. Alexis was to succeed John Casimir after the latter's death but only if he did not interfere in the government of the Commonwealth until then. It was stressed that such an election, which took place against all the laws and customs of the state, was accepted for purely pragmatic reasons and was not to be repeated: in future, the right of free election was to be maintained and the tsar was not to attempt to influence the choice of his successor. On John Casimir's death, the primate would call a convocation diet as usual and Alexis would not begin to rule until after his coronation, at which he would have to swear to uphold the *Pacta Conventa*. As a mark of good faith, he was to withdraw from all occupied territory in Lithuania and begin military action against Sweden.[21] These terms might well prove unacceptable but it was to be hoped that the negotiations would at least delay a Muscovite attack until settlements had been reached with Sweden and the Cossacks.

This policy was strongly opposed by Vidoni, who was anxious to preserve the position of the Uniate Church, hated by Muscovite and Cossack alike. He received little support and was told bluntly by John Casimir

> that he did not wish to sacrifice himself and the whole kingdom on account of the Uniate Church; that if the Uniates had nothing to live on, then they must die of hunger; that if his father had lived, he would have done the same thing. He pointed out that in Germany the peace of Westphalia had abolished archbishoprics and bishoprics.[22]

This was also the attitude of the majority of envoys to the diet, although Vidoni's influence was sufficient to persuade the bishops to issue a formal protest against Alexis's proposed election. The Polish Catholic hierarchy, however, was by no means as committed as the papacy to supporting the Uniate Church, and some bishops were positively hostile. While Vidoni was pleased at the attitude of the most zealous, including Trzebicki, Czartoryski, Tolibowski and Ujejski, the bishop of Kiev, he was scandalised that others would only sign the protest if they could make clear their reservations. Vidoni hoped to secure the signatures of Tarnowski, archbishop of Lwów, and the bishops of Lutsk and Kamianiets, who were not present, but the division of the episcopate was a blow to his hopes of preventing the acceptance of the tsar's candidature. He was opposed most strongly by Zawisza, who, as bishop of Wilno and a commissioner for the talks with Muscovy, protested vehemently about attempts to block the treaty.[23]

[20] Instructions for envoys from Kowno district, 21.VI.1658; Medeksza, *Księga pamiętnicza* p. 170.
[21] Instructions for commissioners to treat with Muscovy, Warsaw, 25.VII.1658; Czart. 387 no. 7, p. 31.
[22] Vidoni, Warsaw, 23.VII.1658; TRz. 8421 p. 32.
[23] Vidoni, Warsaw, 30.VII.1658; TRz. 8421 pp. 34–5.

Towards a French candidature

Given that the government had not wished to call the diet, it had some cause for satisfaction at the outcome. While its tax reform proposals had been rejected, its foreign policy had been endorsed and it could continue along the lines established by the Warsaw convocation. There was, it is true, some criticism of the way in which the senate council had taken such important decisions and entered into agreements with foreign powers on its own authority without consulting the equestrian order.[24] This attack was not taken up in any major way, however, and the government's handling of the war since 1655 was largely approved. Nevertheless, despite the relative harmony of the 1658 debates and the approval of new taxes to pay the army, it could not be disguised that the Commonwealth was as dependent as ever on forces beyond its control.

At last, however, events were moving in its favour. Even as the diet hastily concluded its deliberations at the end of August when plague arrived in Warsaw, developments were taking place outside the Commonwealth which were ultimately to bring the end of the war with Sweden and open the way for the Court to launch an election campaign. On 18 July, Leopold I was finally elected Holy Roman Emperor in Frankfurt, which stimulated Polish hopes for more active Austrian involvement in the war. Shortly afterwards, Charles X ended months of speculation when he landed his army at Korsør in Zealand and marched on Copenhagen. Rejecting a return to the Commonwealth, or an attack on Brandenburg or Austria, he had decided to strike once more against Denmark, an enemy whom he thought he could defeat swiftly, in the hope of winning even greater dominance in Scandinavia and final control of the Sound.

Both these events were of fundamental importance for the Commonwealth. It could now be hoped that Austria would fulfil its commitments under the Treaties of Vienna and Berlin, while the Swedish attack on Denmark ensured that the Commonwealth would not face the prospect of another invasion which had threatened it ever since Roskilde and gave it hope of further foreign aid: the maritime powers were concerned to keep control of the Sound divided between Sweden and Denmark. Under their treaty of 1649, the Dutch were obliged to aid Denmark, as they had not been in 1657 when Denmark had been the aggressor. It was hoped that once the Pomeranian offensive was launched, a settlement would soon follow.

These changes in the international situation made the adoption of a pro-French policy more unlikely. Despite her coolness towards France before the diet, the queen's natural preference for a French candidature was encouraged by the strong anti-Austrian feelings displayed at the diet. She actively fostered such sentiments, lending her support to the widespread and ultimately successful opposition to the granting of Polish nobility to Lisola. When Trzebicki attempted to persuade Tolibowski to intervene on Lisola's behalf, he was told that Louise Marie had

---

[24] Instructions for envoys from the Sochaczew dietine, 21.VI.1658; Teki Pawińskiego 8346 p. 2.

After the Deluge

opposed such action and that Pac had told Lisola he must lobby on his own behalf, which Lisola refused to do; understandably he was said to be mortified.[25]

While Louise Marie still expressed doubt as to French sincerity over the succession plan when de Lumbres returned from his mission to Charles X, she agreed to continue her work for the French cause, telling de Lumbres that the Poles did not desire the tsar's succession, through fear of domination, or of any German or Italian prince and hinted that if the duc d'Anjou was impossible, then there were several who favoured the son of the duc de Longueville.[26] De Lumbres reported that the queen had 'worked marvellously' during the diet, and that she continued to display great affection for France, expressing her desire for a French succession.[27] This renewed enthusiasm was encouraged by a resurgence of interest among senators, including the new primate, Wacław Leszczyński, who would act as interrex after John Casimir's death. Many of the major offices of state were now filled by men potentially favourable to a French candidature, including Crown vice-chancellor Bogusław Leszczyński, Crown grand chancellor Prażmowski, Crown treasurer Jan Kazimierz Krasiński and Crown referendary Jan Andrzej Morsztyn; according to des Noyers, all these men were 'creatures of the queen'.[28]

Nevertheless, neither the international situation nor John Casimir's attitude permitted an active pro-French campaign. Charles's new offer, which demanded Livonia and the payment of 5 million thalers for the return of Prussia, was rejected.[29] If the diet was willing to accept the cession of Livonia, the Court, hoping for an early offensive in Pomerania, felt that the Commonwealth might do better.[30] At two inconclusive meetings between Lisola and Polish representatives (17 and 20 August), the Poles argued that an offensive campaign against Sweden must be launched immediately and that those Austrian troops not involved should withdraw to Silesia.[31] Eventually, Polish persistence was rewarded. The long-awaited Pomeranian campaign began in August, once Frederick William, relieved that Charles did not intend to attack Ducal Prussia, regained his enthusiasm. Louise Marie once more urged him to take the offensive:

Your expedition into Prussia was approved by everyone while an enemy attack was feared, but now the queen cannot refrain from mentioning that she believes that it would be much

---

[25] Vidoni, Warsaw 3.IX.1658; TRz. 8421 pp. 43 4.
[26] De Lumbres to Mazarin, Warsaw, 29.VIII.1658; CPP XII p. 134.
[27] De Lumbres to Mazarin, Warsaw, 7.IX.1658; CPP XII p. 138.
[28] Des Noyers, Warsaw, 11.VIII.1658; *Lettres* no. 164, pp. 429–30.
[29] Des Noyers, Warsaw, 18.VIII.1658; *Lettres* no. 165, p. 431; de Lumbres to Brienne, Warsaw, 29.VIII.1658; CPP XII p. 136.
[30] Chrapowicki, 13.VIII.1658; *Diariusz* p. 169. Louise Marie was angered by the Swedish attitude: 'La Reyne attend l'ambassadeur de Lumbres pour luy faire des reproches d'avoir escouté et resçut des propositions aussi désraisonables que celles qui luy ont esté faites a Wismar. Dieu nous ayant délivrez de tous nos autres ennemis et nous restant 70,000 hommes, qui n'auront plus affaire que contre les Suedois, il y a apparence, qu'ils n'en seront pas quittes pour nous [rendre] ce qu'ils nous ont usurpez.' Louise Marie to Frederick William, 23.VIII.1658; *Urkunden und Aktenstücke* VIII pp. 288–9.
[31] Lisola, Ujazdowa, 25.VIII.1658; *Berichte* no. 110, pp. 440–2.

more honourable and advantageous to enter Jutland with support for the king of Denmark... since the forces of [Lubomirski] and Souches are sufficient for reducing the Swedish garrisons [in Prussia].[32]

The government was following the course laid down since the end of 1657: attempting to force Sweden to negotiate by attacking Pomerania in conjunction with Austria and Brandenburg, while keeping up more informal contacts through the French. Until this policy bore fruit, there could be no thought of an election campaign.

Three basic obstacles still remained: Lithuanian support for the treaty of Wilno, which meant that the union might be threatened if the Court officially pursued an alternative candidate to Alexis; the dependence upon both Austrian military support and French mediation; and the lack of agreement both at Court and within the senate council over the most suitable candidate. The extent of anti-Austrian feeling at the 1658 diet and the interest expressed by several leading senators in a French candidature did much to persuade Louise Marie that such an option was feasible; nevertheless, John Casimir still favoured Austria, especially once the Pomeranian campaign was launched.

It was only in 1660 that these obstacles were finally cleared away. The first to be removed was the problem of Lithuania, where the situation changed dramatically and suddenly. The conflicting interests of Poland and Lithuania with regard to foreign policy had been a major destabilising factor between 1654 and 1658, when there was an ever-present danger of a collapse of the union. Disputes had continued throughout the spring and summer of 1658. Gosiewski, despite his flirtation with the idea of peace with Sweden in the spring, soon reverted to his former support for a settlement with Muscovy, once more expressing his fear that the interests of Lithuania were to be sacrificed and reviving the spectre of a Lithuanian split should peace be made with Sweden rather than Muscovy. There were reports of Lithuanian displeasure with the lack of Polish aid and rumours that Gosiewski was trying to win support for a settlement with Muscovy.[33]

Gosiewski's attitude was worrying, as he warned that beginning peace talks with Sweden before the achievement of a settlement with Muscovy might provoke a Lithuanian secession.[34] Gosiewski was just as ready to lead Lithuania out of the union if necessary as Radziwiłł had been in 1655, even if he preferred to see Alexis rather than Charles X in the role of Lithuania's saviour:

[Gosiewski] always took the side of the tsar and has taken control in Lithuania, which he will not leave with his troops. He is waiting to see where victory will come; let Poland do what it likes, [he] will gather the *szlachta* around him and, expressing his good wishes to the tsar, will

[32] Louise Marie to Frederick William, 1.IX.1658; *Urkunden und Aktenstücke* VIII p. 291. On 13.VIII.1658, the elector had written to Louise Marie, still talking of peace with Sweden and urging the Poles not to treat separately: ibid. pp. 286–7.
[33] Vidoni, Sieraków, 11.VI.1658; TRz. 8421 p. 26.
[34] Lisola, Poznań, 19.VI.1658; *Berichte* no. 105, p. 433.

not obey His Majesty's orders if commanded to attack but will act as a wise head seeking to find a way of mediating.[35]

It was even suggested that if Poland attacked Muscovy Gosiewski would be willing to resist, something that Janusz Radziwiłł had rejected in his dealings with Sweden. Gosiewski was optimistic that he would be followed by Sapieha's army, alleging that Sapieha was more concerned with Polish than with Lithuanian interests. His position in the weeks before the diet was worrying, since Alexis was making a determined effort to attract support for his campaign to achieve the succession, promising resolute action should he be elected; such talk merely increased Polish opposition to the plan.[36]

It was vital, therefore, that if the war with Muscovy were to resume, the Poles should not be seen as the aggressors, for that might alienate Lithuania finally and irrevocably. Despite his earlier expressions of support for peace with Sweden and the French succession, and his close identification with Louise Marie and the Court, Krzysztof Pac had not abandoned hope of a settlement with Muscovy, which he still regarded as the best solution for Lithuania, and he took a close interest in 1657–8 in Gosiewski's negotiations with Alexis. During the diet, he wrote to Brzostowski of Lithuanian attempts to ensure that a commission was appointed to ratify any agreement made at Wilno without the need to call another diet.[37] He warned Brzostowski to ignore any orders from Warsaw which did not emanate from the Lithuanian chancery:

We are aware that certain private ordinances are reaching you which do not proceed from the Lithuanian chancery and which urge you to delay the talks ... You must be careful to pay no heed to such documents; on the contrary, you must settle as swiftly as possible, for such is the wish of Their Majesties. If any more such letters arrive, I ask you to note from which chancery they derive and to send me copies.[38]

Signs, however, that Gosiewski's hopes of a settlement with the tsar were unreasonable had been evident as early as March. Alexis showed little interest in the prospects of a settlement splitting Poland and Lithuania, insisting upon the full implementation of Wilno. He had begun military preparations long before the diet but postponed a decision until the new talks opened, preferring to look for an agreement with Sweden.[39] Medeksza's reports of the tsar's treatment of the occupied areas and of the warnings of Commonwealth prisoners also indicated that prospects of a reasonable settlement were receding. He warned that Muscovy was not to be trusted and reported that he had heard threats from Muscovite soldiers that all of Poland and Lithuania would be occupied.[40]

When the diet failed to accept the full implementation of Wilno, Alexis finally lost

---

[35] Medeksza, *Księga pamiętnicza* pp. 158–9.   [36] Vidoni, 30.V.1658; TRz. 8421 p. 25.
[37] Pac to Brzostowski, Warsaw, 9.VIII.1658; Czart. 387 no. 32, p. 176.
[38] Pac to Brzostowski, 20.VIII.1658; Czart. 387 no. 35, p. 188.
[39] Medeksza, *Księga pamiętnicza* p. 146.   [40] Medeksza to Gosiewski, 12.III.1658; ibid. p. 147.

Towards a French candidature

patience. On 27 August, news arrived in Warsaw that the Muscovite commissioners had left Wilno without waiting for the arrival of the Commonwealth's ambassadors.[41] The Muscovites refused to talk to Gosiewski, and John Casimir wrote to Frederick William blaming Muscovy for the breach.[42] Shortly after the end of the diet, Muscovy began military action against Lithuanian forces. Gosiewski had to abandon his intention of relieving Wolmar in Livonia, which was under attack from Sweden, to turn against Muscovite troops in Samogitia.[43] His pro-Muscovite policy in ruins, Gosiewski was defeated and captured after a surprise Muscovite attack on 21 October.

The option of peace with Muscovy now seemed less attractive to Lithuanians. Their support for Wilno had always been tactical: they were just as wary as the Poles of Muscovite despotism, of which many had direct experience, hoping that with Polish support Alexis would be forced to accept constitutional restraints on his power and they would be allowed to return to their estates. For two years, suspicions that Polish lack of enthusiasm for Wilno might lead to the permanent occupation of Lithuania by Muscovy had seriously undermined Lithuanian faith in the union. Now, however, Polish military support was vital if the Muscovites were to be driven out. An early settlement with Sweden was therefore necessary to release Polish forces for the war in the east. Pac and other Lithuanians were now ready to listen to French arguments that the Austrians were only interested in prolonging the war in order to prevent any Swedish intervention in the Empire. Pac, although hopeful that a settlement with Muscovy was still possible, and despite his feeling that the Poles bore a great deal of the responsibility for preventing one, expressed support for the French peace plan: 'Your Grace can see what sort of state Poland is currently in ... and that we must fall under the domination of one of these two powers, either of Austria or of Muscovy ... Peace with Sweden will be the source of happiness for our ravaged Fatherland and for our neighbours.'[44] By the end of August, Lisola reported that Pac had been completely won for the French cause.[45] If the government had failed in its attempts to delay the start of war with Muscovy, at least it was Alexis, not the Poles, who appeared to be responsible for breaking off negotiations. For the first time since 1656, Poles and Lithuanians seemed to have a common interest in ending the war with Sweden as soon as possible, in order to turn on Muscovy.

Not all Lithuanians supported this line; as administrator of the Lithuanian treasury after Gosiewski's capture, Pac was deeply unpopular with the army and Sapieha's continuing desire for a Muscovite peace was ominous, presaging a new struggle for dominance between the great Lithuanian magnate families.[46]

[41] Chrapowicki, *Diariusz* I p. 170.
[42] J. Leszczyński to Bieniewski, Warsaw, 7.VIII.1658; Czart. 388 no. 211, p. 467.
[43] John Casimir to Frederick William, 29.VIII.1658; *Urkunden und Aktenstücke* VI, p. 68.
[44] K. Pac to B. Radziwiłł, Szamotuły, 12.V.1658; AGAD ARadz. dz.V, teka 251, 11208 p. 61.
[45] Lisola, Ujazdowa, 11.IX.1658; *Berichte* no. 112, p. 449.
[46] Rachuba, *Konfederacja kmicicowska* pp. 67, 80.

Nevertheless, the Court could now promote an election *vivente rege* without risking the collapse of the union: indeed, henceforth Lithuanians were to be amongst the most dedicated supporters of the idea. Furthermore, the fear that Alexis might seize the throne now that war had once more broken out meant that many were prepared to support an election to ensure the preservation of Polish liberties. Nevertheless, the international position still prevented the Court from launching a campaign; this position did not change for as long as the war with Sweden lasted.

It took nearly two years to end. From the second half of 1658, the allies conducted a war of attrition in the Commonwealth, picking off the remaining Swedish garrisons, while taking the offensive in Pomerania and Denmark. This campaign and the attitude of England, the United Provinces and France, who signed the first concert of the Hague in May 1659, calling for peace between Sweden and Denmark on the basis of Roskilde, ensured that Charles X's second Danish war was far less successful than the first. The Pomeranian campaign went relatively well, while the English and the Dutch defeated the Swedes at sea and kept trade flowing. Although Charles was still planning new campaigns in early 1660, his premature death in February and the accession of the infant Charles XI at last opened the way to a settlement. Sweden quickly concluded peace with the Commonwealth, Austria and Brandenburg at Oliva (3 May 1660) and with Denmark at Copenhagen (6 June). The result was reasonably favourable for the Commonwealth: John Casimir surrendered his claim to the Swedish throne and the Commonwealth recognised *de iure* Swedish rule of most of Livonia, which Sweden had already controlled *de facto* in 1655. After five years of fighting, Sweden had obtained virtually nothing from the Commonwealth. It was a vindication of the policy which the government had pursued consistently since early 1658, a policy which sought to use both the Austrian alliance and French mediation to achieve a reasonable settlement.

The government had played a weak hand with some skill. Unable to end the war unaided and finding it difficult to attract effective support, it had successfully played off one side against the other, using the threat of reaching a settlement with Sweden mediated by France to persuade Austria to pursue the war more actively, without giving in to French pressure to accept unsatisfactory peace terms. While charting such a tricky course, it was impossible for the Court to commit itself with regard to the succession once its original offers had been rejected by Vienna and the behaviour of Austrian troops had destroyed hopes that a Habsburg would be accepted easily by a grateful Commonwealth. Nevertheless, the Court's interest in an election had not abated; indeed it had intensified in 1658, when its plans for financial reform had been rejected by the chamber of envoys. It was now essential to prepare the way and decide upon a suitable candidate.

It is usually assumed that the Court was by now strongly backing a French candidature. Yet, although the queen had certainly explored the possibility with increasing interest and although she had suggested a French candidature in several discussions of the election, neither she nor John Casimir was as yet committed. The

Towards a French candidature

Commonwealth still needed Austrian military support and the presence of Austrian troops in the kingdom might create problems if, as was by now certain, an Austrian candidate were not backed by the Court. It was the achievement of the election which was vital; the identity of the candidate was important, but secondary. The Court could not risk backing someone who did not enjoy the widest possible support among senators. It was aware that attachment to the principle of free election was strong; if this were to be overcome, the election campaign would have to be managed with great care. It was vital not to risk squandering the almost universal support among senators for the principle of the election by pushing a particular candidate too strongly. Any attempt to nominate a successor would be met with instant opposition; it was important that the Court allow a proper election to take place, in which it at least appeared to be neutral.[47] Yet, as the 1656 dispute with Lubomirski over Rákóczi had shown, it was essential that the Court should control the election and ensure that its preferred candidate should emerge victorious.

The Court therefore concentrated after 1658 on nurturing senate support for the principle of an election, while seeking to promote as wide a measure of agreement as possible over suitable candidates, without openly committing itself. Support for an election remained strong and, following pessimistic reports about John Casimir's health from the royal doctor, there was extensive discussion of suitable candidates. In December 1658, a meeting called by Lubomirski considered several possibilities. The express desire to exclude neighbouring princes as a potential danger to liberty effectively ruled out an Austrian candidature. Among those discussed were the brother of the elector of Bavaria, Mattia de' Medici, and James, duke of York. Two French candidates were mentioned: the son of the duc de Longueville and the duc d'Enghien, although doubts were expressed about the latter, whose father was still in rebellion against the French Crown. Although no firm decision was taken, it was decided explicitly to exclude the Habsburgs from consideration.[48]

Yet de Lumbres was still doubtful about the queen's intentions. He noted in describing this meeting that Louise Marie had not spoken a word to him about it and expressed his concern that the queen was once more listening to the Austrian proposals. The queen's reticence may have been motivated by a desire to pressurise Mazarin into giving official backing to a French candidate but other evidence suggests that the Court was still considering the possibility of a compromise candidate who might be less politically sensitive than an Austrian or Frenchman. When Vidoni discussed the matter with Louise Marie for over an hour in March 1659, urging her not to miss this golden opportunity, she replied that French and Austrian candidates would encounter great difficulties, as would other German princes, and suggested that the Pope might like to propose a better candidate.[49]

---

[47] Such was the view put forward by Pinocci in 1658: 'Progetto circa il successore'; WAPCr. AP. 358 pp. 163–70; Targosz, *Hieronim Pinocci* pp. 45–6.
[48] De Lumbres to Mazarin, Danzig, 7.XII.1658; printed in Waliszewski, *Polsko-francuskie stosunki* document XCVI p. 235.   [49] Vidoni, Warsaw, 18.III.1659; TRz. 8422 p. 18.

After the Deluge

The queen's proposal may not have been entirely serious, and it is possible that her statements to Vidoni were designed to camouflage her support for a French candidature to which Rome might object. At no point, however, had Vidoni expressed hostility to a French candidature, though he knew that it had been discussed. Nevertheless, in April 1659, Louise Marie asked for further information concerning Mattia's suitability, since John Casimir continued to favour him, which suggests that the king still had his doubts about a French candidature. In July, talks were still proceeding with Mattia with regard to a possible candidature. There was some concern, however, that Mattia was too old, especially from the point of view of the plan to marry the candidate to the queen's niece, who was still only thirteen.[50]

Mazarin was unenthusiastic about the queen's preference for Longueville or d'Enghien. His preferred candidate was the duke of Neuburg, whose son could marry the queen's niece. He also suggested prince Almerico d'Este of Modena, whose nephew was married to Mazarin's niece, Laura Martinozzi.[51] Both candidates, along with the duke of York, were still under consideration in the summer of 1659, when Vidoni again discussed the succession with Bogusław Leszczyński. The nuncio was quite prepared to support any of the candidates suggested by Mazarin. He was attracted by Almerico d'Este, but John Casimir was worried that he was too young and inexperienced to succeed: if the Court was going to argue that one of the most pressing reasons for suspending the normal electoral process was to avoid the danger of an interregum in time of war, it would be tactically unsound to propose an infant. Vidoni also praised the virtues of Neuburg but, apart from being too old, he was also married while his son was too young. It was felt that the elector of Bavaria's brother would not be interested, but a case was made by Prażmowski for the duke of York, whose candidature, he felt, would not be welcome to Sweden.[52]

The Court, far from seeking the election of a French candidate at all costs, was searching for someone with the widest possible support among senators, who would yet be capable of being tied to the Court through a marriage to Anne Henriette, thus preventing the formation of a reversionary interest. In August 1659, it seemed as if its efforts were bearing fruit when a secret document was signed by leading senators in which the need for an election was stressed. John Casimir agreed to abide by the decision of the senate and the *szlachta*, and promised that he would not treat unilaterally with any pretender to the throne. The senators agreed in return to three conditions put forward by John Casimir: that the candidate should be a Catholic, that he should be younger than the king and that he should marry the queen's niece.[53]

If the Court were to gain the political advantage it hoped for from an election it

[50] Vidoni, Warsaw, 26.IV.1659; TRz. 8422 p. 39; Warsaw, 5.VII.1659; TRz. 8422 p. 67.
[51] Mazarin to Louise Marie, Aix, 26.II.1659; Waliszewski, *Polsko-francuskie stosunki* document XCVII, p. 236.
[52] Vidoni, Warsaw, 18.III.1659; TRz. 8422 pp. 18–20; Warsaw, 28.VI.1659; TRz. 8422 p. 66.
[53] Ochmann, *Sejmy lat 1661–2. Przegrana batalia o reformę ustroju Rzeczypospolitej* (Wrocław, 1977) p. 15.

Towards a French candidature

was essential to ensure that the right candidate won. By 1660, a final decision was necessary and the Court opted for d'Enghien. He was young enough to be a viable candidate for the hand of the queen's niece, while being old enough to fulfil the role of king-elect. Oliva removed the need for Austrian military support, while Austrian behaviour in 1659 had persuaded John Casimir that an Austrian candidature was impossible. Furthermore, despite Lisola's urgings, Leopold I was reluctant to allow the betrothal of Charles Joseph to Louise Marie's niece, who was in any case in France under Mazarin's control, which rendered the prospect of an Austrian marriage unlikely.[54] The peace of the Pyrenees, in which Condé was rehabilitated, removed one further obstacle.

D'Enghien's virtues contrasted with the drawbacks of his main rivals: France was willing to provide financial backing which would be vital if the election campaign were to succeed and if the Court were to realise its wider political plans. Many senators were prepared to accept a French candidature, feeling that since France was not the Commonwealth's neighbour, it was less likely to threaten noble liberties than Austria or Muscovy. Although less contentious alternatives, such as Mattia de' Medici, proved attractive, none of them commanded the sort of resources which would enable them to avoid the risk of falling into the same state of financial dependency upon the diet which had so afflicted the Vasas after 1600. Since it was clear by 1660 that an Austrian candidature was out of the question, the only realistic alternative was to look to France. Louise Marie wrote to her sister in February arguing that a German or Italian prince would not be powerful enough to persuade Poles to take a stand against Austria, while doubts about taints of illegitimacy in the ancestry of d'Enghein's leading French rival, the son of the duc de Longueville, provoked concern that he would not be well-regarded in Poland. Moreover, the queen's sister let it be known that she considered d'Enghien to be the most suitable candidate for her daughter's hand. Faced with such pressure, Mazarin finally relented. News of his consent reached Poland in October 1660, while an official sanction was issued on 30 November. De Lumbres was issued with plenipotentiary powers to negotiate the succession; his instructions, drawn up on 20 December, reached Poland in early February 1661.[55] At long last, the Court could launch its election campaign.

---

[54] Vidoni, 5.I.1659; TRz. 8422 p. 3; Warsaw, 8.II.1659; ibid. p. 7; Warsaw, 1.III.1659; ibid. p. 14; Warsaw, 8.III.1659; ibid. p. 17.

[55] Waliszewski, *Polsko-francuskie stosunki* pp. 79–82. Brevet pour M-r. le Prince et M-r. le Duc d'Anguien... au sujet de la succession à la couronne de Pologne... 30.XI.1660; ibid. document XIII, p. 239; Mémoire pour servir d'instruction secrete au sieur de Lumbres ... 20.XII.1660; ibid. document CVI p. 240.

9

Conclusion: the succession and the failure of reform

The moment seemed propitious. The principle of an election *vivente rege* appeared to have the support of most influential senators and it was hoped that d'Enghien would benefit from a wave of gratitude towards France for its role in mediating peace with Sweden. Furthermore, the Commonwealth was still at war with Muscovy: the prospect of a seizure of the throne by Alexis and the need to avoid an interregnum were still powerful arguments in favour of an election; after Oliva, Sapieha dropped his demands for peace with Muscovy and supported the war-effort. The successful liquidation of one of the Lithuanian army confederations, formed in 1659 in anger at the massive arrears in pay which had built up since 1655, and the settlement of Sapieha's financial dispute with the Commonwealth, stimulated hopes that the Lithuanian army might be won over.[1]

Confident of senate backing for the principle of an election, the Court now sought to win wider support. Whatever the Court's long-term aims, it was important in the short term to appear to act constitutionally: it was therefore necessary to secure diet approval for an election. It was this consideration which led the Court to conquer its doubts and risk suggesting the introduction of majority voting. This move was tactical: aware that the plan was bound to stir up opposition and confident of its ability to influence the diet, especially with the large sums of money promised by France, the Court sought to ensure that its campaign was not derailed at the outset by the veto. In June 1660, a new commission met to consider reform proposals, including two drawn up in 1659 which called for the curtailment or abolition of the veto, and diet reform was at last included, alongside the call for an election, in the royal instructions for consideration by the diet which was called for May 1661.[2]

The Court endeavoured to keep its plans a secret known only to its most trusted confidants, whose signatures it began to collect on a document pledging support for d'Enghien towards the end of 1661. In public it concentrated on propaganda proclaiming the need for an election and establishing the Commonwealth's first newspaper, the *Merkuriusz Polski*, run by royal secretary Hieronim Pinocci, to campaign in its favour.[3] Louise Marie and John Casimir embarked on a tour of the

[1] Rachuba, *Konfederacja kmicicowska* pp. 78–80.
[2] Ochmann, 'Plans for parliamentary reform' pp. 177–8.
[3] A. Przyboś, *Merkuriusz Polski* (Cracow, 1960); Libiszowska, 'Pierwsza gazeta polska Merkuriusz Polski i jej rola w walce o reformę ustroju w połowie XVIIw.' *Prace Polonistyczne* 12 (1955) pp. 187–205.

Conclusion

Commonwealth, visiting local dietines to try and drum up support for an election. John Casimir reminded the *szlachta* that only the election of Władysław IV in 1632 had been entirely peaceful and that was only because the candidate had been the previous king's son: precedent suggested that civil war was likely if there were to be a contested election between rival foreign candidates. Such a conflict in time of war might threaten the Commonwealth's very existence. In a speech to the diet on 4 July 1661, he warned that if the election failed the Commonwealth faced the prospect of partition between rival powers fighting for dominance, a danger which had been only too evident since 1655.[4]

The Court faced a dilemma. Much of the support for an election had come from senators who were convinced not only that it was necessary to win foreign support in the war against Sweden, but also that it was the only way in the extraordinary circumstances of the war to preserve Polish liberties, including the right to free election. Thus, they were willing to support an election *vivente rege* in principle but not for the same reasons as the Court, which hoped to use it to effect a permanent transformation in the position of the monarchy. The Court was aware of this problem and maintained in public that it would remain neutral in any election, preserving the principle of the right of free choice. Yet the debates over the succession after 1655 had demonstrated that it was essential for the Court to ensure the election of its own candidate if it were to realise its wider plans and not merely establish the dangerous focus for malcontent magnates which the 1656 Rákóczi candidature had threatened to become. It had decided by 1660 to back d'Enghien; this, however, ran the risk of alienating senators who were, for whatever reason, willing to accept the principle of an election, but who objected to the Court candidate, including the ecclesiastical senators, who had been enthusiastic advocates in 1655 of offering the throne to the Habsburgs on a hereditary basis, and who remained loyal supporters of Austria.

It proved impossible to keep d'Enghien's candidature a secret. Already in 1660, some leading senators were expressing doubts about Court policy. Jan Leszczyński wrote to Lubomirski in May of his opposition to reform and to the election of anybody, be it a French or an Austrian candidate. Leszczyński, Lubomirski, Trzebicki, Łukasz Opaliński, Wieloposki and Krzysztof Gembicki began to organise opposition among the *szlachta*.[5] At the diet Trzebicki strongly opposed the abolition of the veto and although only three other senators (Krzysztof Pac, Ujejski and Lubowiecki) mentioned it at all, Trzebicki, Leszczyński, Sielski, Wielopolski and Opaliński conducted a powerful campaign behind the scenes. Their efforts were rewarded: by referring the matter to yet another commission, the diet effectively declared its lack of interest.[6]

---

[4] Ochmann, *Sejmy lat 1661–1662* pp. 36, 108–10.

[5] J. Leszczyński to Lubomirski, 1.V. and 16.V.1660; BPANCr. 1065 ff. 311–12, f. 88; Czapliński, 'Próby reform państwa' p. 327; Bąkowa, *Szlachta województwa krakowskiego* p. 30.

[6] Ochmann, *Sejmy lat 1661–1662* pp. 17–18, 20, 74; Przyboś and Rożek, *Biskup krakowski Andrzej Trzebicki* p. 42.

After the Deluge

Despite this setback, the Court was determined to pursue the election. Although the 1661 diet did not reject the idea outright, growing opposition led to a ban on its further consideration by the 1662 diet. Undeterred by this rebuff, the Court pinned its hopes on the use of more dubious tactics, including a possible recourse to military means, something which it had considered since at least 1658. Its plans received a setback when confederations of the Lithuanian and Polish armies expressed their opposition to the election. When the Court approached France in the hope of securing sufficient money to buy off the confederates, the sums it required were far greater than the French were prepared to grant. Nevertheless, in 1663 the marriage of d'Enghien and Anne Henriette took place, while the Court succeeded in winding up the military confederations with the help of the taxes voted by the 1662 diet.[7]

The Court proved unable, however, to achieve its aims. In 1664 it struck against Lubomirski, by now one of the leading opponents of the election and eminently capable of using his political influence to frustrate the Court. Lubomirski's successful impeachment at the diet of 1664–5 merely deepened the political crisis, however, as the Court's tactics provoked outrage, seeming to confirm opposition claims that it sought *absolutum dominium*. The diets of 1664–5 and 1665 were broken by vetoes exercised by Lubomirski's supporters, while Lubomirski fled to Silesia where he sought the protection of the Habsburgs, who were determined to block the French election. In 1665 he raised the standard of rebellion. Although he won a bloody victory over royalist forces at the battle of Mątwy in 1666, he failed to secure his full rehabilitation, withdrawing once more to Silesia, where he died in January 1667.

Lubomirski's *rokosz* effectively ended Court hopes of achieving the election and plunged the Commonwealth into anarchy. Both the diets held in 1666 were broken, as was the first diet in 1668. The treaty of Hadiach had not been ratified by the 1659 diet, and the Cossacks, whom the Court had seen as a possible source of military support, had split between Muscovite and Polish supporters. Despite the great successes of the 1660–1 campaigns against Muscovy, the war-effort suffered from the growing political chaos, in which the breaking of successive diets meant that taxes to pay the army were neither voted nor collected. In consequence, the Commonwealth proved unable to follow up its victories in 1660–1 and had to make an unsatisfactory peace at Andrusovo in 1667, surrendering Smolensk, the palatinate of Chernigov, Kiev and the left-bank Ukraine. On the queen's death in 1667, John Casimir, weary of the long struggle, decided to play his last card and implement a plan which had been under consideration since 1662. In 1668 he declared his intention to abdicate, after securing the promise of a pension from Louis XIV, and he withdrew to France, where he died in 1672, ending his days as abbot of St Germain-des-Prés in Paris. His hope that a French-backed candidate

---

[7] Codello, 'Konfederacja wojskowa na Litwie w latach 1659–1663' *SMHW* 6 (1960) p. 34; Rachuba, *Konfederacja kmicicowska* esp. pp. 135–220; W. Klaczewski, *W przededniu wojny domowej w Polsce. Walka sejmowa lat 1664–1665* (Lublin, 1984) p. 21.

Conclusion

would be elected was nevertheless to be disappointed. Despite a great effort by French supporters, the 1669 election saw the rejection of all foreign candidates in favour of a native nonentity: Michael Korybut Wiśniowiecki, son of Jarema, the great popular hero of the early years of the struggle against the Cossacks. The breaking of Wiśniowiecki's coronation diet before it had even run its six-week course – the first time this had occurred – was an ominous portent of what was to follow. It was an appropriate death-knell for the last plan to reform the Commonwealth's political system which might have rescued its international position before it was too late.

The main aim of this study has been to examine attitudes to political reform in the Commonwealth in the aftermath of the disastrous collapse of 1654–5, and the reasons for the adoption of the campaign to elect the duc d'Enghien as successor to John Casimir *vivente rege*. A detailed examination of the failure of this campaign in the 1660s would require another book. Nevertheless, it is clear that traditional explanations of that failure need to be reexamined, especially the assumption that the Court, for private reasons, or because of blind obedience to foreign interests, ignored the need for political reform to embark on an irresponsible dynastic adventure. Too often, the failure of the election campaign in the 1660s is taken to be proof that it was ill-conceived.

It is incontestably true that the election campaign aroused substantial and growing opposition after 1660, which the Court was unable to overcome. Studies of the 1660s have largely concentrated on the growth of this opposition; overwhelmingly they suggest that its triumph was inevitable because the Court chose the wrong option: instead of concentrating on diet reform, which was both desirable and attainable, it tried to force through an election which went against the grain of the Commonwealth's political tradition, thereby destroying all chance of achieving the abolition of the veto. It failed to exploit *szlachta* resentment against the magnates, and its crude methods, including 'blatant bribery on a scale never before known', alienated *szlachta* opinion. Its willingness to contemplate the use of force after 1662 was the ultimate and fatal error, which enabled the magnate opposition to exploit the situation in its favour.[8] Klaczewski argues that John Casimir's defeat at the diets of 1664–5 marked the end of hopes for an alliance between the monarchy and the *szlachta*, concluding that 'power in the state passed all the more into the hands of the magnate oligarchy'. He assumes that there were three political forces in the Commonwealth: the king, the *szlachta* and the magnates, suggesting that the magnates 'as a whole' realised the necessity for the existence of a strong state structure. Yet, his own account of the diets of 1664–5 demonstrates that both the *szlachta* and the magnates were divided amongst themselves and that the king received substantial support from both magnates and ordinary nobles. Indeed Mazovia, where the petty nobility was dominant and magnate influence was at its

[8] Ochmann, *Sejmy lat 1661–1662* p. 244.

weakest, was consistently royalist, although not necessarily in favour of a French election.[9]

Neither the *szlachta* nor the magnates acted as collective political entities, and the *szlachta* was not naturally and inevitably opposed *en masse* to royal aims. Even before 1655, there was no coherent or organised magnate opposition to John Casimir's controversial policies. To represent the political alternatives after 1655 in terms of a struggle between *szlachta* democratic republicanism exploited by self-seeking and unscrupulous magnates and absolutism promoted by an isolated Court is to oversimplify. The Court's ultimate failure should not obscure the fact that its support was sufficient to achieve the impeachment of Lubomirski, whose position was far more powerful than that of Radziejowski in 1652. It was the monarchy's apparent strength, not its weakness, which provoked fears of absolutism and which ensured the triumph of Fredro's view of the veto as essential to the preservation of liberty.[10] In fact, a vital reason for the adoption of the election campaign was that it seemed to have a better chance of success than reform of the diet. At the 1661 diet, in contrast to the reservations expressed about diet reform, only one senator – Andrzej Olszowski – spoke out against the election plan. One other, Łukasz Opaliński, did not refer to it directly; all other senators who expressed their opinion in open session either supported it strongly, like Krzysztof Pac and Lubowiecki, or accepted it in principle. When the king discussed the election with the senate only Olszowski, Czartoryski and Fredro opposed it, with the first two merely arguing for its postponement to more settled times and only Fredro opposing it outright. By 8 June fifty senators had expressed their agreement.[11]

The Court's belated conversion to support for majority voting was based on the calculation that it could secure a majority in the diet for its election plans. This confidence appears to have been justified: it was not just in the senate that it received support. Although no detailed instructions have survived from Lithuanian dietines, opinion in the grand duchy, still occupied by Muscovite troops, seemed overwhelmingly in favour of an election: it was reported that only one dietine opposed it. Krzysztof Pac succeeded in winning the support of eighteen dietines, while the vice-chancellor Naruszewicz influenced a further five. At the diet, M.K. Pac and Jewłaszewski warned that Lithuania could only be saved if the election were agreed. When opinion among Polish envoys seemed to be drifting away from support for the election Krzysztof Pac declared that Lithuanians were ready to take up arms in support of the election, and, as he repeatedly stressed, were even prepared to break the union if the Poles rejected the idea. These threats were repeated in a published manifesto signed by forty Lithuanian senators and envoys. Of the leading Lithuanian magnates, only Paweł Sapieha did not sign.[12]

In Poland, the situation was rather less promising; nevertheless, if the majority of Polish dietines were opposed to diet reform in 1661, with only the Kiev dietine

[9] Klaczewski, *W przededniu wojny domowej* pp. 5–6, 47–8, 106. [10] See above, p. 14.
[11] Ochmann, *Sejmy lat 1661–1662* p. 91. [12] ibid. pp. 111, 114, 125.

Conclusion

regarding it as necessary, attitudes to the election were less categorical. Although the important dietine at Środa, along with those of Halicz, Wizna, Czersk and Zakroczym rejected the idea outright, others were prepared to accept it, albeit with reservations. There was a general concern that the principle of free choice be meticulously observed and if most dietines ignored the king's request for envoys to be granted plenipotentiary powers to agree to the election, this was by no means unusual, and most instructed their envoys to decide on the basis of their discussions with representatives of other palatinates. If only the dietines of Sieradz, Wieluń, Żytomierz and Royal Prussia expressed their support, this should be considered together with the widespread support from Lithuania. If the *szlachta* was far from expressing complete approval, which was hardly to be expected, neither did it reject the election outright.[13]

Attention usually focusses on the way in which this cautious attitude on the part of the *szlachta* and leading senators turned increasingly to opposition. Yet, if the opposition grew in strength and became increasingly vocal, the Court maintained a level of support which cannot be explained away in terms of simple bribery. The magnate elite did not consist of a closed group of families inevitably opposed to Court interests and seeking to seize control of the 'helm of state'. It is quite clear that the Commonwealth was a class state in the sense that it was dominated by a class-conscious nobility which excluded all non-nobles from a share in the exercise of political power. This does not, however, imply that the ruling class was united in its political outlook, or acted as a collective political entity. Factional rivalry was intense, and the monarchy could in practice exploit this situation to win support from even the most powerful and economically independent magnates. Between 1655 and 1668, both *szlachta* and magnates were deeply and fundamentally divided, not over the basic ideals of the Commonwealth's political system, which all accepted, but over the best means to preserve them. While the Court was accused by its enemies of seeking to destroy those liberties and of wanting to introduce absolute rule, there were many who, conscious of other dangers to the Commonwealth and its liberties, were prepared to support it. In this context, the Court's suggestion that the candidate should be a young adult who would be brought up under its supervision was clever: while it appealed to senators as a means of ensuring that the future king would be instructed in Polish ways, so that when he succeeded, the constitution would be preserved, it would also ensure that the king-elect would remain under Court influence, especially if he married Louise Marie's niece.

Behind the rhetoric about republican virtue and noble liberties the battle was essentially one for control, as it had been since the disagreements between the Court and Lubomirski in 1656 over a Transylvanian candidature. The inability of any faction, including the Court, to dominate this political battle led to the stalemate which so paralysed the Commonwealth. The shock of the Swedish deluge had provided John Casimir with the best opportunity since 1569 to transform the

[13] ibid. pp. 38–49.

After the Deluge

position of the monarchy: the disgrace of Radziwiłł and Opaliński had demonstrated that malcontent magnates could not take their opposition too far, while the monarchy could act as a patriotic rallying-point for the opposition to Sweden.

For the Court it was not diet reform but the election which was essential if this political stalemate were to be broken. Too often this choice of priorities has been condemned by historians who either, like Lelewel in the nineteenth century, regard democratic republicanism as the embodiment of a romantic 'national idea', or who believe that, with a few procedural adjustments, the diet would have developed into an effective, modern parliamentary body. Such criticisms of the monarchy depend upon a set of anachronistic and whiggish assumptions derived from knowledge of modern systems of parliamentary democracy. Yet the diet was not essentially regarded by the *szlachta* as a partner in government but as a check upon it: a forum for the expression of private and local grievances, in which government proposals could be scrutinised to ensure they did not contravene local rights and privileges and the limits of royal power could be further defined. It was the king's task to initiate policy, the diet's to approve it or reject it. From the monarchy's point of view, therefore, the diet appeared to be the principal source of the ever-increasing restrictions on its freedom of action.

For the monarchy, the main problem after 1569 was how to manage the diet in practice to prevent the increase of restrictions on executive power and to ensure that taxes were raised and government business was carried out. Just as important was the need to manage the local and provincial dietines which played such a vital role in the execution of diet enactments. Historians have tended to assume that the introduction of majority voting would have solved this problem. In the 1650s and 1660s, however, John Casimir saw the veto as a useful weapon in his perennial battle to manage both diet and dietines. In the 1660s, the destructive effects of the veto became only too apparent, yet before 1660 it appeared to have certain advantages from the king's point of view. The ability to break diets and dietines enabled him to avoid or block further restrictions on his power and to put an effective end to criticism when it got out of hand. John Casimir sanctioned Białobłocki's veto of 1654 and seriously considered breaking the 1662 diet to prevent it banning further consideration of the election, only desisting because he needed the taxes which the diet proved willing to vote in order to pay the army.[14] In the struggle over the impeachment of Lubomirski in 1664–5 John Casimir found the veto extremely useful: by breaking the general dietines at Środa and Proszowice, Court supporters prevented the appearance at the diet of envoys from two of Lubomirski's most important power-bases, which did much to ensure that the impeachment was successful. Despite attempts by Lubomirski's supporters to break the diet and thereby prevent a verdict, Court supporters, who were in the majority, successfully

[14] Ochmann, *Sejmy lat 1661–1662* p. 202.

Conclusion

blocked attempted vetoes until Lubomirski had been sentenced. Once that was achieved, the Court was happy to allow Telefus to lodge a successful veto.[15]

The decline of the diet and its growing paralysis through increasing use of the veto potentially gave the political initiative to the king and the senate council. Between 1655 and 1660, with the backing of his senators, John Casimir governed effectively, considering the circumstances, and developed the technique of securing support for important political initiatives by summoning large-scale convocations of senators and representatives of the *szlachta*, which were not subject to the procedural handicaps of the diet, and where majority decisions were sufficient to decide policy. With the diet effectively deprived of its capacity to place further restrictions on royal power through the king's ability to engineer its premature end if necessary, the onus of government would in practice increasingly be thrown back upon the senate council, as it had been between 1655 and 1658; the diet would remain as a forum for the expression of grievances, as envisaged in the plan mentioned by des Noyers in 1656.

It was not just the Court which feared the implications of abolishing the veto. The diet was not a modern representative parliament; it was an assembly of delegates from provincial dietines. The veto was essential if provincial interests were to be respected: the principle of unanimity before 1652 had frequently served the positive function of enabling provincial delegates to invite the diet to think again and work out a compromise which took account of their local interests. Given the doubts of substantial interest-groups about the implications of majority voting and the apparent usefulness of the veto as a weapon of the last resort for the monarchy in its battle to manage diet and dietines, it should not be regarded as surprising that diet reform failed after 1655: the election campaign was by no means the only factor involved. More mature parliamentary bodies than the seventeenth-century Polish–Lithuanian diet have failed to solve the problem of convincing ethnic and religious minorities that their interests can be safeguarded within the framework of majority rule. The abolition of the veto might well have saved the diet as an effective parliamentary body; it might just have easily have led to the break-up of the Commonwealth.

The Court had shown little interest in diet reform before 1655 and remained sceptical of its value. John Casimir's attempts at political reform between 1648 and 1655 had concentrated on improving the monarchy's position through increasing its control over its servants. His demands for compensation in March 1655 for surrendering his claim to Sweden demonstrate that, like his father and brother before him, John Casimir saw the issue of the succession as the key to increasing royal authority. Before the Swedish Deluge, such plans met with fierce opposition from senators; the war transformed this situation. By 1660, if senators had

[15] Klaczewski, *W przededniu wojny domowej* pp. 40–2, 68; Czermak, 'Sprawa Lubomirskiego w roku 1664' in Czermak, *Ostatnie lata Jana Kazimierza* ed. A. Kersten (Warsaw, 1972) p. 221.

After the Deluge

increasing doubts about diet reform, they appeared to be much more in favour of the principle of an election, if not a French candidature. Even once opposition to the idea began to grow, there were signs that a compromise might be possible: Andrzej Trzebicki did not actually speak out against the election in principle and in 1662, although he favoured the candidature of the duke of Lorraine, he was prepared to accept d'Enghien, so long as he married a sister of Leopold I rather than Lousie Marie's niece, which suggests that his opposition to majority voting in 1661 stemmed more from his fears for the implications for the Church and royal power than any desire to block the election.[16]

It was the failure to agree on a candidate before 1660, however, when fear for the Commonwealth's future was at its height, which ultimately doomed the election campaign. Once the war with Sweden was over, domestic political rivalries re-emerged. The most damaging conflict was between the Court and Lubomirski. Between 1657 and 1660, the Court had tried to win Lubomirski over, apparently with some success. He signed the offer to the Habsburgs in the spring of 1657 and later was a prominent supporter of the queen's campaign to find an alternative candidate to a Habsburg. In December 1658 it was Lubomirski who called the convocation of senators in Thorn which discussed possible candidates for the throne and which issued a declaration implicitly excluding an Austrian candidate, while explicitly suggesting that a French candidature might be compatible with the preservation of the Commonwealth's liberties.

Lubomirski's interest, however, was occasioned more by a fear of the alternative than genuine support for the Court. Although he had signed the 1657 offer to the Habsburgs he was horrified by the terms of the second treaty of Vienna, which not only awarded the Austrians the rich proceeds from the salt mines at Bochnia and Wieliczka but also allowed them to garrison Cracow, which struck a blow at his most important power-base in Little Poland, where he was highly popular among the local nobility. Given John Casimir's clear support for an Austrian candidature, which remained strong until 1658, Lubomirski had a great deal to gain by supporting Louise Marie.

Once the danger from Austria had passed following the withdrawal of Austrian troops from the Commonwealth, all Lubomirski's old inclinations reemerged. Although he later justified his opposition on the grounds that it was a threat to noble liberties, it was not the principle of the election to which he was opposed but its domination by the Court.[17] He had long had his own ambitions with regard to the election, of which his support for Rákóczi in 1655–6 was but one manifestation. From 1655 Lubomirski regarded himself as a potential candidate for the throne. A Piast candidature might be regarded with great suspicion by magnates, since the

[16] Przyboś and Rożek, *Biskup krakowski Andrzej Trzebicki* p. 44.
[17] Lubomirski published an extensive defence of his actions after his impeachment, full of appeals to republican liberty: *Jawnej niewinności manifest. Boga, światu oyczyźnie ... podany z przydaniem perspektiwy na proces, responsa na informatia, discursu ziemianina y inszych rzeczy wiadomości godnych* (1666).

Conclusion

monarchy's great patronage powers would give a native candidate a golden opportunity to favour his own family and clients over their rivals; nevertheless, Lubomirski knew that it was traditionally popular among the ordinary nobility. He had good reason to believe that his candidature would be welcome: despite his dealings with the Swedes in 1655 he had not gone over to Charles X, and his reputation did not suffer like those of Radziwiłł or Opaliński. His military feats after 1655 won him great popularity, while he possessed a firm power-base in his domination of the politics of Little Poland in general and the Cracow palatinate in particular.

Suspicions about Lubomirski's ambitions were an important source of tension which continued throughout the war. In 1656, he strongly opposed the marriage of his relation Jan Zamoyski to Maria Casimira d'Arquien, one of the queen's French entourage, fearing that this would lure Zamoyski into the Court circle.[18] Meanwhile, John Casimir proved extremely reluctant to trust Lubomirski in military matters, although he was finally forced to appoint him Crown field hetman at Częstochowa in March 1657. Jan Leszczyński told Vidoni during the Częstochowa convocation that Lubomirski was capable of competing for the crown and that he would face no great obstacles apart from John Casimir's hostility.[19]

Lubomirski was prepared to support the general principle of an election so long as there was a danger of the seizure of the throne by Austria or Muscovy. Once the Austrian army had withdrawn and the Court began to enlist the support of an impressive array of senators for the candidature of d'Enghien, Lubomirski feared for his own position and moved into open opposition. He took this step not because he was opposed to strong royal government, despite the pious platitudes of his *Manifesto*, but to strong royal government over which he had no influence and from which he could expect no benefit. In this, his attitude was typical of his fellow magnates.

Yet if Lubomirski was successful in blocking Court plans, the Court was equally successful in frustrating his ambitions, and he died in exile two years before a native candidate, Michael Korybut Wiśniowiecki, was indeed elected in 1669. It is unlikely, however, that Lubomirski himself would have been successful had he lived: he had too many important magnate rivals. Although Wiśniowiecki was the scion of a great and famous house and the son of Jarema Wiśniowiecki, who had been the sort of popular hero in the early years of the Cossack revolt that Lubomirski had become after 1655, he was too young and inexperienced to cause his peers any great concern. The leading magnates who had supported the French election campaign and had tried to secure d'Enghien's election in 1669 immediately passed into opposition; such prominent figures as Krzysztof Pac and John Sobieski set about frustrating royal policy just as Lubomirski had frustrated them in the 1660s.[20] This

---

[18] Cefali to Vidoni, Lublin, 26.VIII.1656; T.Rz. 8419 p. 256.
[19] Vidoni, Częstochowa, 16.II.1657; T.Rz. 8420 p. 9.
[20] In 1677, Pac attacked Sobieski, by now himself king, for attempting to strengthen the power of the senate, something which Pac had supported in the 1650s and 1660s. Wójcik, *Jan Sobieski 1629–1696* p. 267.

was not because they had reverted to a 'natural' tendency on the part of the magnate stratum to resist central authority but because they had suffered a setback in the battle between magnate factions for central control which raged behind the rhetoric about noble freedom.

It was the Court's failure to maintain the cooperative relationship it had enjoyed, on the whole, with the senate council between 1655 and 1660 which was the true cause of the deepening political chaos. While the threat of partition remained, the majority of senators were ready to back Court policy as the best means in such a difficult situation of preserving the constitution and of strengthening the state, confident in the senate council's ability to act as 'guardians of the king and the law'. After Oliva and the successful campaign of 1660–1 which drove the Muscovites out of much of Lithuania, however, chances of success were significantly reduced: ignoring the extent to which success against Sweden at least had been dependent on foreign support, many came to believe that the Commonwealth's traditional system had been vindicated and that the need for reform was not as pressing as it had seemed in 1655. The choice of a French candidate, for eminently sensible reasons, alienated many who were prepared to support an election *vivente rege*, especially the episcopate, traditional supporters of strong royal power. Once again it was the monarchy, with its radical reform plans, which appeared to be the greatest threat to republican liberty.

The monarchy, by failing adequately to appreciate that much support for the election derived largely from a desire to protect the essence of the Commonwealth's political system, lost the vital propaganda battle: the *Merkuriusz Polski* dwelt too much on the virtues of strong royal government and the restoration of hereditary monarchy in Denmark and Britain in 1660, while the Court's refusal to accept the 1662 ban on the further pursuit of the election and its willingness to countenance the use of force provoked genuine concern as to its intentions. In the face of possible partition, or of the seizure of the throne by Austria or Muscovy, an election *vivente rege* seemed the only means of ensuring that the death of John Casimir would not be followed by the destruction of noble liberties by a foreign ruler. If the Court saw the election essentially as a means of increasing its political power and influence by bringing up a successor under its influence, senators saw the scheme as a means of ensuring that the king-elect was brought up to respect the fundamental principles of the 'Golden Freedom'. The Court's vague and ambiguous position merely provoked fears that it saw the election as the first step on the road to *absolutum dominium*, something which it did little to deny and which its pursuit of the election after it had been banned by the 1662 diet seemed merely to confirm.

In the last analysis the Court proved unable to manage the rival and competing forces within the Commonwealth's ruling class to produce an alliance strong enough to force through its programme. The monarchy faced neither a challenge from a united magnate oligarchy over control of the 'helm of state' nor a simple ideological battle between absolutism and democratic republicanism in which the latter was

Conclusion

always bound to win, but a complex and shifting situation in which the issue among leading magnates was not so much whether central power should be strengthened but which factions or factional alliances were to dominate politics at the centre once reform was achieved. Many leading magnates were quite content to back royal plans because they expected, in the event of a successful realisation of Court plans, to benefit in the long term from the strengthening of royal power. Given the bitter factional rivalry within the magnate elite it was impossible for the Court to avoid provoking the opposition of magnates who feared that their rivals would benefit in this way.

It has been the aim of this study to explain royal policy not to justify it. It would have taken someone of wider political vision than John Casimir to turn the multinational, religiously plural Commonwealth into an effective parliamentary monarchy, examples of which were singularly lacking in mid-seventeenth century Europe. Nevertheless, the campaign to elect d'Enghien *vivente rege* was not an irresponsible irrelevancy which fatally diverted attention away from the more important task of diet reform but the centrepiece of an attempt to end the crisis of government in the Commonwealth by strengthening the executive through improving the position of the monarchy. Central to this concept was a partnership between Crown and senate council which had seemed to emerge after the shock of 1655 but which gradually broke down after 1660. The tragedy was that if the Court could still win enough support for its plans to appear dangerous it could never quite win enough to triumph.

Nevertheless, the campaign for an election *vivente rege* under John Casimir came closer than any attempt before the late eighteenth century to breaking the political stalemate which was the true source of the Commonwealth's weakness. After 1668, the Commonwealth was left behind as its neighbours transformed themselves into military powers with which it could no longer compete. A state system emerged in east-central Europe predicated upon the Commonwealth's internal weakness; its neighbours cooperated in ensuring that weakness continued. A hundred and thirty-three years after John Casimir's abdication, when his prophecy to the 1661 diet about the dangers of ignoring reform had proved only too prescient, King Stanisław Augustus Poniatowski successfully presided over the establishment of the Constitution of 3 May 1791 which abolished the *liberum veto*, strengthened the royal government by streamlining the royal council and introduced a hereditary monarchy. It was too late to save the Commonwealth but the Constitution of 3 May, stripped of its Enlightenment rhetoric, achieved essentially what John Casimir had sought. In the mid-seventeenth century, it had been impossible to convince the mass of the nobility that liberty could be preserved by increasing royal power. The failure of the election campaign, however, was by no means inevitable: John Casimir may have been unsuccessful; he was not wilfully irresponsible.

Bibliography

MANUSCRIPT SOURCES

Archiwum Główne Akt Dawnych, Warsaw

Libri Legationum
33   1649–66

Archiwum Koronne Warszawskie
Karton 11b   Szwedzkie
Karton 25a   Cesarskie

Archiwum Radziwiłłowskie
Dział II, ks. 21   Acta publica variaque miscellanea 1655–6
Dział V: Wybrana korespondencja

Archiwum Publiczne Potockich
45   Silva rerum Jana Wielopolskiego starosty bieckiego

Zbiór Anny z Potockich Branickiej V

Biblioteka Narodowa, Warsaw

Zbiory Baworowskich
261

Biblioteka Ordynacji Zamoyskiej
934   Varia historico-politica et poetica 1583–1661

Biblioteka Uniwersytetu Warszawskiego

66

Bibilioteka Jagiellónska, Cracow

5   Akta publica et epistolae 1606–74
6357   Miscellanea

Bibliography

Biblioteka Muzeum im. Ks. Czartoryskich, Cracow

Teki Naruszewicza
148 (1655), 149 (1656), 150 (1657), 151 (1658), 152 (1659), 160 (1660)

General Collection
- 384 Korespondencja Jana Leszczyńskiego z lat 1653–6
- 385 Akta za Jana Kazimierza 1655–6
- 386 Akta i listy dotyczące rokowań z Moskwą i wojny ze Szwecją 1656
- 387 Transakcje z Moskwą 1658
- 388 Korespondencja Jana Leszczyńskiego z lat 1656–60
- 393 Akta za Jana Kazimierza od 1650 do 1655
- 394 Akta za Jana Kazimierza 1648–65
- 399 Akta za Jana Kazimierza 1655–68
- 400 Akta za panowania Jana Kazimierza od 1648–68
- 401 Senatus Consulta 1658–68
- 402 Originały za Jana Kazimierza 1648–70
- 425 Akta za Jana Kazimierza, Michała i Jana III, 1655–92
- 917 Kopje historyczne 1553–83 (fragmenty Tek Naruszewicza)
- 977 Lauda et acta terrarum Prussiae 1650–66
- 1656 Silva rerum 1655–67
- 1657 Silva rerum 1583–1673
- 1774 Akta sejmikowe województw poznańskiego i kaliskiego 1601–1703
- 2103 Akta dotyczące stosunków z Moskwą, 1657–64
- 2113 Akta dotyczące rokowań z Moskwą, 1656
- 2576 Akta z czasów Władysława IV i Jana Kazimierza
- 3487 Manuskrypta za królów 1645–93

Biblioteka Polskiej Akademii Nauk, Cracow

- 342 Korespondencja
- 354 Suplement do listów Sapieżyńskich
- 363 Listy oryginalne królow
- 426 Zbiór różnych dokumentów z lat 1532–1812
- 1056 Listy 1621–1864
- 1062 Summarius consiliorum, rerum gestarum, literarum et legationum ac responsum variorum
- 2253 Księga pamiętnicza Jakuba Michałowskiego
- 2254 Księga pamiętnicza Jakuba Michałowskiego
- 2255 Księga pamiętnicza Jakuba Michałowskiego

Teki Pawińskiego
- 8319 Akta sejmikowe ziemi czerskiej
- 8327 Akta sejmikowe województwa łęczyckiego 1573–1678
- 8331 Akta sejmikowe ziemi lomżyńskiej I 1574–1673
- 8336 Akta sejmikowe województwa płockiego 1572–1692

Bibliography

8338 Akta sejmikowe województwa sandomierskiego
8342 Akta sejmikowe województwa sieradzkiego I 1574–1668
8346 Akta sejmikowe województwa rawskiego 1583, 1657–1790; ziemi gostyńskiej 1668–1790; ziemi sochaczewskiej I 1658–99
8348 Akta sejmikowe ziemi warszawskiej 1621–99
8350 Akta sejmikowe ziemi wiskiej I 1576–1699
8353 Akta sejmikowe ziemi zakroczymskiej I 1573–1704
8355 Akta sejmikowe różnych województw

Teki Rzymskie
Letters and dispatches of Pietro Vidoni, 1652–60 (copies)
8418 (1655), 8419 (1656), 8420 (1657), 8421 (1658), 8422 (1659–60)

Wojewódzkie Archiwum Państwowe, Cracow

Oddział III   Archiwum Pinoccich: 358

Wojewódzkie Archiwum Państwowe, Cracow: Oddział na Wawelu

Archiwum Sanguszków
67 Zbiór materiałów historycznych 1605–1729
86 Korespondencja XX. Sanguszków ... z Sapiehami 1622–1739

Biblioteka Zakładu Narodowego im. Ossolińskich, Wrocław

Teki Lukasa   2976/II, 2978/II, 2979/II, 3008/II, 3010/II
3564/II   Listy i diariuszy, 1648–74

Biblioteka Polskiej Akademii Nauk, Kórnik

1618   Listy oryginalne królów

British Library

Harley 4532   Lettres de M. de Lumbres touchant la Pologne 1657–61

Archives de la Ministère des Affaires Etrangères, Paris

Correspondance Politique: Pologne XI 1650–7
Correspondance Politique: Pologne XII 1658–60
Correspondance Politique: Danzig I (to 1661)
Correspondance Politique: Autriche. Vienna XVII 1648–59
Correspondance Politique: Suède XXI

Bibliography

Bibliothèque Nationale, Paris

FFr. 3859   Lettres de Louise Marie de Gonzague à Mme de Choisy
FFr. 13019 Correspondance d'Ismaël Bouillaud I
FFr. 13020 Correspondance d'Ismaël Bouillaud II
FFr. 13040 Correspondance d'Ismaël Bouillaud XXII

PRINTED SOURCES

Actorum et gestorum Sueco-Polonicorum semestrale. Das ist Halb-jährige Erzehl- und Darstellung aller in Jüngsten von Ih. Königl. Majestät zu Schweden &c. in das Königreich Polen fürgenommenen Feldzug, vom Herbst, dess 1655, biss Ostern 1656 fürgenommener und verrichteter Handlungen, gewechselter Schrifften, und anderer Begebenheiten ... (Semestrale secundum) (Frankfurt-am-Main, 1657)

Akta grodzkie i ziemskie z czasów Rzeczypospolitej polskiej z archiwum tak zwanego Bernardyńskiego (Archiwum Ziemskiego) we Lwowie XXI, ed. Prochaska, A. (Lwów, 1888)

Akta sejmikowe województwa krakowskiego II, ed. Przyboś, A. (Cracow, 1955)

Akty otnoshiashchiesia ko vremeni vojny za Malorossiiu (1654–1667) Akty uzdavaemye Vilenskoi Kommisiei dlia Razbora Drevnikh Aktov XXXIV (Wilno, 1909)

Baliński, M. (ed.) *Pamiętniki historyczne do wyjaśnienia spraw publicznych w Polsce XVII wieku* (Wilno, 1859)

Carta de un Cortesano de Roma para un correspondiente suyo, en que le dà cuenta del fin de los successos de Prencipe Casimiro, hermano del Rey de Polonia, primo de nostro Rey Phelipe III, que viniendo à la guerra de Portugal fue preso en Francia, y de su entrada en la Compaña de Iesus (1643)

Chéruel, M.A. and d'Avenel, G. (eds.) *Lettres du Cardinal Mazarin pendant son ministère* Collection des Documents Inédites sur l'Histoire de France (Paris, 1872–1906)

Chrapowicki, J.A. *Diariusz* I (1656–64) ed. Wasilewski, T. (Warsaw, 1978)

Collectanea e rebus Polonicis Archivi Orsini in Archivo Capitolino Romae I Elementa ad Fontium Editiones XIV ed. Wychowska-de Andreis, W. (Rome, 1965)

Coxe, W. *Travels into Poland, Russia, Sweden and Denmark. Interspersed with Historical Relations and Political Inquiries* (London, 1784)

de Lumbres, A. *Relations de Lumbres Antoine ambassadeur en Pologne et en Allemagne touchant ses négotiations et ambassades* ed. Lhomel, G. (Paris, 1912)

des Noyers, P. *Lettres de Pierre des Noyers, secrétaire de la reine de Pologne Marie-Louise de Gonzague ... (à Ismael Bouillaud) pour servir à l'histoire de Pologne et du Suède de 1655 à 1659* ed. Rykaczewski, E. (Berlin, 1859)

Dogiel, M. (ed.) *Codex diplomaticus Regni Poloniae et Magni Ducatus Lithuaniae* (Wilno, 1758–64)

Fredro, A.M. *Scriptorum seu Togae et Bellum Notationum Fragmenta. Accesserunt Peristromata Regum Symbolis Expressa* (Danzig, 1660)

Grabowski, A. (ed.) *Ojczyste spominki w pismach do dziejów dawnej Polski. Diaryusze, relacye, pamiętniki, i.t.p., służyć mogące do dojaśnienia dziejów krajowych i tudzież listy historyczne do panowania królów Jana Kazimierza i Michała Korybuta, oraz listy Jana Sobieskiego marszałka i hetmana koronnego* (Cracow, 1845)

Jemiołowski, M. *Pamiętnik Mikołaja Jemiołowskiego, towarzysza lekkiej chorągwi, ziemianina*

Bibliography

województwa bełzkiego, obejmujący dzieje Polski od roku 1648 do 1679 współcześnie, porządkiem lat opowiadziane ed. Bielowski, A. (Lwów, 1850)

Jerlicz, J. *Latopisiec albo kroniczka Joachima Jerlicza* ed.Wójcicki, K. (Warsaw, 1853)

Kluczycki, F. (ed.) *Pisma do wieku i sprawa Jana Sobieskiego.* Acta Historica Res Gestas Poloniae Illustrantia I (Cracow, 1880)

Kochowski, W. *Annalium Poloniae climacter secundus bella Sueticum, Transylvanicum, Moschoviticum, aliasque res gestas ab Anno 1655 ad Annum 1661 inclusive continens* (Cracow, 1688)

Konopczyński, W. and Lepszy, K., (eds.) 'Akta ugody kiejdańskiej 1655 roku' *Ateneum Wileński* 10 (1935)

Lauda sejmików ziemi dobrzyńskiej Acta Historica Res Gestas Poloniae Illustrantia X, ed. Kluczycki, F. (Cracow, 1887)

Levinson, A. (ed.) *Die Nuntiaturberichte des Petrus Vidonis über den ersten nordischen Krieg aus den Jahren 1655–1658* Archiv für österreichische Geschichte XCV (Vienna, 1906)

Lubomirski, J.S. *Jawnej niewinności manifest. Boga, światu, oyczyźnie przez Jaśnie Wielmożnego Jego Mci Pana, P. Ierzego Sebastiana Hrabia na Wiśniu y Jarosławiu Lubomirskiego ... Podany z przydaniem perspektiwy na proces, responsa na informatia, discursu ziemianina y inszych rzeczy wiadomości godnych* (1666)

Łoś, W. *Pamiętniki Łosia, towarzysza chorągwi pancernej Władysława Margrabi Myszkowskiego, obejmujące wydarzenia od roku 1646 do 1667, z rękopisma współczesnego, dochowanego w zamku podhoreckim* ed. Żegota, P. (Cracow, 1858)

Medeksza, S.F. *Stefana Franciszka z Proszcza Medekszy, sekretarza Jana Kazimierza, sędziego ziemskiego kowieńskiego, księga pamiętnicza wydarzeń zasłych na Litwie 1654–1668* Scriptores Rerum Polonicarum III, ed. Seredyński, W. (Cracow, 1875)

Michałowski, J. *Księga pamiętnicza – Jakuba Michałowskiego wojskiego lubelskiego a później kasztelana bieckiego księga pamiętnicza z dawnego rękopisma będącego własnością Ludwika Hr. Morsztyna* ed. Helcel, A. (Cracow, 1864)

Moerner, T. (ed.) *Kurbrandenburgs Staatsverträge v. 1600–1700* (Berlin, 1867)

Pasek, J. *Memoirs of the Polish Baroque* ed. Leach, R. (Berkeley, Los Angeles, 1976)

Poczobut-Odlanicki, J.W. *Pamiętnik* ed. Rachuba, A. (Warsaw, 1987)

Pollak, R. et al. (eds.) *Listy Krzysztofa Opalińskiego do brata Łukasza, 1641–1653* (Warsaw, 1957)

Polonicae ex Archivo Regni Daniae III, VI Elementa ad Fontium Editiones XX, XXXIII, ed. Lanckorońska, C. and Steen Jensen, G. (Rome, 1969, 1974)

Pribram, A.F. (ed.) *Die Berichte des kaiserlichen Gesandten Franz von Lisola aus den Jahren 1655–1660* Archiv für österreichische Geschichte LXX (Vienna, 1887)

Przyboś, A. (ed.) *Dwa pamiętniki z XVII wieku Jana Cedrowskiego i Jana Floriana Drobysza Tuszyńskiego* (Wrocław, Cracow, 1954)

Pufendorf, S. *De rebus a Carolo Gustavo Sueciae Rege gestis commentariorum libri septem* (Nuremberg, 1729)

De rebus gestis Friderici Wilhelmi Magni, Electoris Brandenburgici, commentariorum libri novendecim (Berlin, 1695)

Querelae universi Cleri in Maiori Polonia et diocesi Posnaniensi super Barbara Austriaci Militis Insolentia in Ordinem Ecclesiasticum et Christi Patrimonium Exercita ad Sacram Regiam Maiestatem Hungariae et Bohemiae etc. (Poznań, 1658)

Raczyński, E. (ed.) *Portfolio królowej Maryi Ludwiki, czyli zbiór listów, aktów urzędowych i*

Bibliography

innych dokumentów, ściągających się do pobytu tej monarchini w Polsce (Poznań, 1844)
Radziwiłł, A.S. *Memoriale Rerum Gestarum in Poloniae* Polska Akademia Nauk, Oddział w Krakowie. Materiały Komisji Nauk Historycznych XXV, ed. Przyboś, A. and Żelewski, R. (Wrocław, Warsaw, Cracow, 1968–75)
Radziwiłł, B. *Autobiografia* ed. Wasilewski, T. (Warsaw, 1979)
Repertorium Rerum Polonicarum ex Archivo Orsini in Archivo Capitolino Elementa ad Fontium Editiones III, VII, ed. Wychowska-de Andreis (Rome, 1961, 1962)
Roberts, M. (ed.) *Swedish Diplomats at Cromwell's Court, 1655–1656* Camden Fourth Series XXXVI (London, 1988)
Rudawski, W.J. *Historiarum Poloniae ab excessu Vladislai IV ad pacem Olivensem usque libri IX seu Annales regnante Joane Casimiro Poloniarum Sueciaeque rege ab anno 1648 usque ad annum 1660* (Warsaw, Leipzig, 1755)
Rykaczewski, E. (ed.) *Relacye nuncyuszów apostolskich i innych osób o Polsce od roku 1548 do 1690* (Paris, 1864)
Szilágyi, S. (ed.) *Transsylvania et Bellum Boreo-Orientale. Acta et documenta* (Budapest, 1890–1)
Temberski, S. *Roczniki, 1647–1656* Scriptores Rerum Polonicarum XVI, ed. Czermak, W. (Cracow, 1897)
Theatrum Europeum (Ireno-polemographia, sive Theatri Europaei septenniam) ed. Schledenus, J.G. (Frankfurt-am-Main, 1684)
Theiner, A. (ed.) *Vetera monumenta Poloniae et Lithuaniae gentiumque finitimarum historiarum illustrantia maximam partem nondum edita ex tabulariis vaticanis* III (Rome, 1863)
Urkunden und Aktenstücke zur Geschichte des Kurfürsten Friedrich Wilhelm von Brandenburg (Berlin, 1865–84)
Volumina Legum (Prawa, konstytucye y przywileie Królestwa Polskiego, y Wielkiego Xięstwa Litewskiego, y wsystkich prowincyi należących: Na walnych sejmiech koronnych od Seymu Wiślickiego roku pańskiego 1347 az do ostatniego seymu uchwalone ed. Konarski, S. (Warsaw, 1732–82)
Wójcicki, K. (ed.) *Biblioteka starożytna pisarzy polskich* (Warsaw, 1854)
Wójcik, Z. (ed.) 'Akta poselstw Morstina oraz Leszczyńskiego i Naruszewicza do Szwecji w 1655 roku' *Teki Archiwalne* 5 (1957)
Traktaty polsko-austriackie z drugiej połowy XVII wieku (Warsaw, 1985)
Wydżga, J.S. *Pamiętnik ... spisany podczas wojny szwedzkiej w roku 1655 do 1660* ed. Wójcicki, K. (Warsaw, 1852)
Zherela do istorii Ukrainy-Rusy V Fontes Historiae Ukraino-Russicae XII, ed. Korduba, M. (Lwów, 1911)

SECONDARY WORKS

Adamus, J. 'Nowe badania nad dziejami sejmu polskiego i geneza liberum veto' *Czasopismo Prawno-Historyczne* 13 (1961)
Allen, W.E.D. *The Ukraine* (Cambridge, 1940)
Attman, A. *Swedish Aspirations and the Russian Market during the Seventeenth Century* Acta Regiae Societatis Scientiarum et Litterarum Gothoburgensis: Humaniora XXIV (Gothenburg, 1985)
The Russian and Polish Markets in International Trade, 1500–1650 Publications of the

Bibliography

Institute of Economic History of Gothenburg University (Gothenburg, 1973)
Augustyniak, U. and Sokolowski, W. 'Spisek orleański' w latach 1626–1628 (Warsaw, 1990)
Babiński, L. Trybunał skarbowy radomski (Warsaw, 1923)
Backus, O.P. 'The problem of unity in the Polish–Lithuanian state' Slavic Review 22 (1963)
Balzer, O. Zarys historii ustroju Polski (Lwów, 1935)
Z zagadnień ustrojowych Polski. Studia nad historią prawa polskiego (Lwów, 1917)
Baranowski, B. 'Geneza sojuszu kozacko-tatarskiego z roku 1648' Przegląd Historyczny 37 (1948)
'Organizacja regularnego wojska polskiego w latach 1655–1660' Studia i Materiały do Historii Sztuki Wojennej 2 (1956)
Organizacja wojsku polskiego w latach trzydziestych i czterdziestych XVII wieku (Warsaw, 1957)
'Problematyki stosunków polsko-rosyjskich w XVII wieku' Zeszyty naukowe Uniwersytetu Łódzkiego Ser. 1: Nauki humanystyczno-społeczne II (1958)
'Skład społeczny wojska polskiego w połowie XVII wieku' Bellona 1 (1945)
Baranowski, B. and Libiszowska, Z. (eds.) Walka narodu polskiego z najazdem szwedzkim (Warsaw, 1952)
Bardach, J. 'Czy istniało obywatelstwo w szlacheckiej Rzeczypospolitej?' Czasopismo Prawno-Historyczne 17 (1965)
Deputés à la diète en Pologne d'Ancien Régime' Acta Poloniae Historica 39 (1979)
'L'Election des deputés à l'ancienne diète polonaise, fin XVe–XVIIIe siècle' Parliaments, Estates and Representation 5 (1985)
'L'Union de Lublin: ses origines et son rôle historique' Acta Poloniae Historica 27 (1973)
'Sejm dawnej Rzeczypospolitej jako najwyższy organ representacyjny' Czasopismo Prawno-Historyczne 35 (1983)
'Sejm szlachecki doby oligarchii' Kwartalnik Historyczny 75 (1967)
Studia z ustroju i prawa Wielkiego Księstwa Litewskiego XIV–XVIIIw. (Warsaw, 1970)
'W 300 rocznice wojny z najazdem szwedzkim' Nowe Drogi 12 (1955)
Basarab, J. Pereiaslav 1654: A Historiographical Study (Edmonton, 1982)
Bąkowa, J. Szlachta województwa krakowskiego wobec opozycji Jerzego Lubomirskiego w latach 1661–1667 Prace Krakowskiego Oddziału Polskiego Towarzystwa Historycznego XII (Cracow, 1974)
Biskup, M. and Zernack, K. (eds.) Schichtung und Entwicklung der Gesellschaft in Polen und Deutschland im 16. und 17. Jahrhundert. Parallelen, Verknüpfungen, Vergleiche Vierteljahrschrift für Sozial- und Wirtschaftsgeschichte LXXIV (Wiesbaden, 1983)
Bobrzyński, M. Dzieje Polski w zarysie ed. Serejski, M. and Grabski, A. (Warsaw, 1974)
Carlson, F. Geschichte Schwedens IV (Gotha, 1855)
Castellani, G. 'Giovanni Casimiro di Polonia. Tra la porpora e la corona' La Civiltà Cattolica 102 (1951)
Chéruel, P. 'Le Baron Charles d'Avaugour, ambassadeur de France en Suède' Revue d'histoire diplomatique 3 (1889)
Chłapowski, K. 'Alienacja dóbr królewskich w latach 1578–1668' Przegląd Historyczny 69 (1978)
Realizacja reform egzekucji dóbr 1563–1665. Sprawa zastawów królewszczyzn małopolskich (Warsaw, 1984)
Choulgine, A. 'Le Traité de Péréyaslav et l'union de l'Ukraine avec la Moscovie' Revue

Bibliography

historique 222 (1959)

Chynczewska-Hennel, T. '*Świadomość narodowa szlachty ukraińskiej i kozaczyzny od schyłku XVI do połowy XVIIw.* (Warsaw, 1985)
 'The national consciousness of Ukrainian nobles and Cossacks from the end of the sixteenth to the mid-seventeenth century' *Harvard Ukrainian Studies* 10 (1986)

Ciara, S. *Kariera rodu Weiherów 1560–1657* (Warsaw, 1980)

Codello, A. 'Konfederacja wojskowa na Litwie w latach 1659–1663' *SMHW* 6 (1960)
 'Pacowie wobec opozycji Jerzego Lubomirskiego (1660–1667)' *Przegląd Historyczny* 49 (1958)
 'Rywalizacja Paców i Radziwiłłów w latach 1666–1669' *Kwartalnik Historyczny* 71 (1964)
 'Wydarzenia wojenne na Żmudzi i w Kurlandii, 1656–1660' *Przegląd Historyczny* 57 (1966)

Cynarski, S. 'The shape of Sarmatian ideology in Poland' *Acta Poloniae Historica* 12 (1968)

Czaplewski, P. 'Senatorowie szwieccy, podskarbiowie i starostowie Prus Królewskich, 1454–1792' *Roczniki Towarzystwa Naukowego w Toruniu* XXVI-XXVIII (1919–21)

Czapliński, W. 'Blaski i cienie kościoła katolickiego w Polsce w okresie potrydenckim' *Odrodzenie i Reformacja w Polsce* 14 (1969)
 Dwa Sejmy w roku 1652. Studium z dziejów rozkładu Rzeczypospolitej w XVIIw. (Wrocław, 1955)
 Dzieje Danii nowożytnej, 1500–1795 (Warsaw, 1982)
 'Emigracja polska na Śląsku, 1655–1660' *Sobótka* 10 (1955)
 'Ideologia polityczna "Satyry" Krzysztofa Opalińskiego' *Przegląd Historyczny* 47 (1956)
 'Le Problème Baltique aux XVIe et XVIIe siècles' in *XI Congrès International des sciences historiques. Rapports* IV (Gothenburg, Stockholm, Uppsala, 1960)
 'Licht- und Schattenseiten der polnischen Adelsrepublik' *Österreichische Osthefte* 13 (1971)
 O Polsce siedemnastowiecznej (Warsaw, 1966)
 Opozycja wielkopolska po krwawym potopie (1660–1668) Prace Krakowskiego Oddziału Polskiego Towarzystwo Historycznego VIII (Cracow, 1930)
 'Pierwszy pobyt Jerzego Lubomirskiego na Śląsku (1664–1665)' *Sobótka* 1 (1946)
 'Polacy z Czarnieckim w Danii, 1658–1659' *Rocznik Gdański* 9–10 (1935–6)
 'Polityka Rzeczypospolitej polskiej w latach 1570–1648' *Pamiętnik VIII Powszechnego Zjazdu Historyków Polskich w Krakowie, 14–17 września 1958* III (Warsaw, 1960)
 Polska a Bałtyk w latach 1632–1648. Dzieje floty i polityki morskiej (Wrocław, 1952)
 'Projekt utworzenia floty kaperskiej w casie "potopu" szwedzkiego' *Rocznik Gdański* 12 (1938)
 'Przełomowe znaczenie XVIIw. w dziejach Polski' in *Pierwsza Konferencja Metodologiczna Historyków Polskich* (Warsaw, 1953)
 'Rola sejmów XVII wieku w kształtowaniu sie kultury politycznej w Polsce' in Gierowski (ed.) *Dzieje kultury politycznej w Polsce* (Warsaw, 1977)
 'Rządy oligarchii w Polsce nowożytnej' *Przegląd Historyczny* 52 (1958)
 'Senat za Władysława IV' in *Studia historyczne ku czci Stanisława Kutrzeby* I (Cracow, 1938)
 'Sprzedawanie urzędów w Polsce w połowie XVII wieku' *Przegląd Historyczny* 50 (1959)
 (ed.) *The Polish parliament at the summit of its development (sixteenth to seventeenth centuries)* (Wrocław, 1985)

Bibliography

(ed.) *Uchwalenie konstytucji na sejmach w XVI–XVII wieku* (Wrocław, 1979)
Walka pierwszych Wazów polskich ze stanami Acta Universitatis Wratislaviensis no. 504, Historia XXXIV (Wrocław, 1981)
Władysław IV i jego czasy 2nd edition (Warsaw, 1976)
Władysław IV wobec wojny 30-letniej Polska Akademia Umiejetności: Rozprawy Wydziału Historyczno-Filozoficznego Seria 2, XLV (Ogólnego zbioru LXX) (Cracow, 1937)
'Władysław Konopczyński jako historyk XVI i XVIIw.' *Studia Historyczne* 22 (1979)
'Wyprawa Czarnieckiego na Pomorze, 1657' *Roczniki Historyczne* 18 (1949)
'Wyprawa Wielkopolan na Nową Marchię w r.1656 i układ w Sulęcinie' *Roczniki Historyczne* 23 (1957)
'Z problematyki Sejmu polskiego w pierwszej połowie XVIIw.' *Kwartalnik Historyczny* 72 (1970)
Czapliński, W. and Długosz, J. *Życie codzienne magnaterii polskiej w XVIIw.* (Warsaw, 1982)
Czapliński, W. and Filipczak-Kocur, A. 'Udział senatorów w pracach sejmowych za Zygmunta III i Władysława IV' *Przegląd Historyczny* 69 (1979)
Czapliński, W. and Kersten, A. (eds.) *Magnateria polska jako warstwa społeczna* Referaty z sympozjów XI Powszechnego Zjazdu Historyków Polskich w Toruniu, wrzesien 1974 (Torun, 1974)
Czermak, W. 'Jan Kazimierz; próba charakterystyki' *Kwartalnik Historyczny* 3 (1889)
Ostatnie lata Jana Kazimierza (Kersten, A., ed.) (Warsaw, 1972)
Plany wojny tureckiej Władysława IV (Cracow, 1895)
'Próba naprawy Rzeczypospolitej za Jana Kazimierza' *Biblioteka Warszawska* 51 (1891)
Studya Historyczne (Cracow, 1901)
Częścik, L. *Sejm warszawski w 1649/1650 roku* (Wrocław, 1978)
Damus, R. *Der erste nordische Krieg bis zur Schlacht bei Warschau, aus Danziger Quellen* Zeitschrift des Westpreussischen Geschichtsvereins XII (Danzig, 1884)
Davies, I.N.R. *God's Playground. A History of Poland* (Oxford, 1981)
Dembkowski, H. *The Union of Lublin: Polish Federalism in the Golden Age* East European Monographs CXVI (Boulder, Colorado, 1982)
Dembski, K. 'Wojska nadworne magnatów polskich w XVI i XVIIw.' *Zeszyt naukowy Uniwersytetu im. A.Mickiewicza* no.3 Historia XXI (Poznań, 1956)
Dobrzycki, S. 'Program naprawy Rzeczypospolitej w XVIIw.' *Ateneum* 3 (1897)
Droysen, J.G. 'Die Schlacht von Warschau 1656' *Abhandlungen der philologisch-historischen Classe der Königl. Sächsischen Gesellschaft der Wissenschaft* 4 (1864)
Dubiecki, M. 'Tsar Aleksy Michałowicz na Litwie. Fragment dziejowy z XVII stulecia' *Przegląd Powszechny* 33 (1892)
Dworzaczek, W. *Genealogia* (Warsaw, 1959)
'Kto w Polsce dzierżył buławy' *Przegląd Historyczny* 39 (1949)
'La Mobilité sociale de la noblesse polonaise aux XVIe-XVIIIe siècles' *Acta Poloniae Historica* 36 (1977)
'Perméabilité des barrières sociales dans la Pologne du XVIe siècle' *Acta Poloniae Historica* 24 (1971)
'Skład społeczny wielkopolskiej reprezentacji sejmowej w latach 1572–1655' *Roczniki Historyczne* 23 (1957)
Dzieduszycki, I. *Polityka brandenburska podczas wojny polsko-szwedzkiej w latach 1655–1657* (Cracow, 1879)

Bibliography

Dziewanowski, M. 'Dualism or trialism? Polish federal tradition' *Slavonic and East European Review* 41 (1963)

Fabiani, B. *Warszawski dwór Ludwiki Marii* (Warsaw, 1976)

Federowicz, J.K. (ed.) *A Republic of Nobles: Studies in Polish History to 1864* (Cambridge, 1982)

Filipczak-Kocur, A. 'Materiały do dziejów skarby koronnego za Władysława IV' *Przegląd Historyczny* 77 (1986)

'Problemy podatkowo-wojskowe na sejmie w roku 1628' *Zeszyty naukowe Wyższej Szkoły Pedagogicznej im. Pówstancow Śląskich w Opolu* Seria A: Historia XVI (Opole, 1979)

Sejm zwyczajny z roku 1629 (Wrocław, 1979)

Filipczak-Kocur, A. and Seredyka, J. 'Senatorowie na sejmach okresu wojny pruskiej ze Szwecją, 1626–1629' *Sprawozdania Opolskiego Towarzystwa Przyjaciół Nauk* Wydział 1: Nauk historyczno-społecznych XVII (1980) (Opole, 1981)

Forstreutter, K. *Preussen und Russland von den Anfängen des deutschen Ordens bis zu Peter dem Grossen* Göttinger Bausteine zur Geschichtswissenschaft 23 (Göttingen, 1955)

Frost, R.I. '*Initium Calamitatis Regni*? John Casimir and monarchical power in Poland–Lithuania, 1648–1668' *European History Quarterly* 16 (1986)

'Liberty without licence? The failure of Polish democratic thought in the seventeenth century' in Biskupski, M.B. and Pula, J.S. (eds.) *Polish Democratic Thought from the Renaissance to the Great Emigration: Essays and Documents* East European Monographs CCLXXXIX (Boulder, Colorado, 1990)

Gawlik, M. 'Projekt unii rosyjsko-polskiej w drugiej połowie XVIIw.' *Kwartalnik Historyczny* 23 (1909)

Gierowski, J. (ed.) *Dzieje kultury politycznej w Polsce* Prace XI Powszechnego Zjazdu Historyków Polskich III (Warsaw, 1977)

Historia Polski, 1505–1764 (Warsaw, 1979)

'L'Europe centrale au XVIIe siècle et ses principes tendences politiques' *XIIIe Congrès International des Sciences Historiques* (Moscow, 1970)

(ed.) *O naprawę Rzeczypospolitej XVII–XVIII w. Prace ofiarowane Władysławowi Czaplińskiemu w 60 rocznice urodzin* (Warsaw, 1965)

'Rzeczpospolita szlachecka wobec absolutystycznej Europy' *Pamiętnik X Powszechnego Zjazdu Historyków Polskich* III (Warsaw, 1971)

Sejmik generalny Księstwa Mazowieckiego na tle ustroju sejmikowego Mazowsza Prace Wrocławskiego Towarzystwa Nauk Serja A, XXIV (Wrocław, 1948)

Górski, K. *Problematyki dziejów Prus Królewskich, 1466–1772* (Toruń, 1963)

Grauert, W. 'Über die Thronentsagung des Königs Johann Casimir von Polen und die Wahl seines Nachfolgers' *Sitzungsberichte der philosophisch-historischen Classe der Kaiserlichen Akademie der Wissenschaften* VI (Vienna, 1851)

Grodziski, S. 'Les Devoirs et les droits politiques de la noblesse polonaise' *Acta Poloniae Historica* 36 (1977)

Obywatelstwo w szlacheckiej Rzeczypospolitej (Cracow, 1963)

'Sejm dawnej Rzeczypospolitej jako najwyższy organ ustawodawczy. Konstytucje sejmowe – pojęcie i próba systematyki' *Czasopismo Prawno-Historyczne* 35 (1983)

Grönebaum, F. *Frankreich in Ost- und Nordeuropa. Die französisch-russischen Beziehungen von 1648–1689* Quellen und Studien zur Geschichte des östlichen Europa II (Wiesbaden, 1968)

Gronski, P. 'Le Traité lituano-suédois de Keidany (18 août 1655)' *Revue historique* 159 (1928)

Bibliography

Grzybowski, K. *Teoria reprezentacji w Polsce epoki Odrodzenia* (Warsaw, 1959)
Halecki, O. *Dzieje unii jagiellońskiej* (Cracow, 1919–20)
'La Pologne et la question d'Orient de Casimir le Grand à Jean Sobieski' *La Pologne au VIIe Congrès international des sciences historiques* (Warsaw, 1933)
'Why was Poland partitioned?' *Slavic Review* 22 (1963)
Haller, J. 'Franz von Lisola, ein österreichischer Staatsmann des 17. Jahrhunderts' *Preussische Jahrbücher* 69 (1892)
Hassenkamp, R. 'Die Bewerbung des Pfalzgrafen Philipp Wilhelm von Neuburg um die polnische Krönung' *Zeitschrift der Historischen Gesellschaft für die Provinz Posen* 11 (1896)
'Der Ehebund der polnischen Prinzessin Anna Catherina Constantia mit Philipp Wilhelm v. Pfalz-Neuburg und seine politischen Folgen' *Zeitschrift der Historischen Gesellschaft für die Provinz Posen* 9 (1894)
Haumont, E. *La Guerre du nord et la Paix d'Oliva, 1655–1660* (Paris, 1893)
Hellie, R. *Enserfment and Military Change in Muscovy* (Chicago, 1971)
Hirsch, F. 'Der österreichische Diplomat Franz v. Lisola und seine Thätigkeit während des nordischen Krieges in den Jahren 1655–1660' *Historische Zeitschrift* 60 (1888)
Hoszowski, K. *O znakomitych zasługach w kraju rodziny Korycińskich* (Cracow, 1862)
Hubert, W. *Wojny bałtyckie* (Bydgoszcz, 1938)
Hudita, I. *Histoire des rélations entre la France et la Transylvanie au XVIIe siècle* (Paris, 1927)
Jadwisieńczak, M. 'Projekt elekcji "vivente rege" z r.1655 (Mikołaja Prażmowskiego)' *Studia Historyczne* 22 (1979)
Jakštas, J. 'How firm was the Polish–Lithuanian federation?' *Slavic Review* 22 (1963)
Jarochowski, K. 'Przejście województw wielkopolskich do szwedów pod Ujściem r. 1655' *Przyjaciel Ludu* 6 (1840)
Wielkopolska w czasie pierwszej wojnie szwedzkiej od roku 1655 do 1657 (Poznań, 1864)
Jasnowski, J. 'England and Poland in the sixteenth and seventeenth centuries (political relations)' *Polish Science and Learning* 7 (1948)
Jones, G. *The Diplomatic Relations between Cromwell and Charles X Gustavus of Sweden* (Lincoln, Nebraska, 1897)
Kaczmarczyk, Z. 'Oligarchia magnacka w Polsce jako forma państwa' *Pamiętnik VIII Powszechnego Zjazdu Historyków Polskich w Krakowie* I (Warsaw, 1958)
'Typ i forma państwa demokracji szlacheckiej' *Odrodzenie w Polsce* 1 (1955)
Kaczmarczyk, Z. and Leśniorodski, B. *Historia państwa i prawa polskiego* II (Warsaw, 1957)
Kalicki, B. *Bogusław Radziwiłł* (Cracow, 1878)
Zarysy historyczne (Lwów, 1869)
Kalinka, W. 'Negocyacye ze Szwecyą o pokój 1651–1653. Przyczynek do historyi wojen szwedzkich' *Czas. Dodatek Miesięczny* 2 (1857)
Kamińska, A. *Brandenburg–Prussia and Poland: a Study in Diplomatic History (1669–1672)* Marburger Ostforschungen XLI (Marburg-Lahn, 1983)
Kamińska–Linderska, A. 'Lenno Lębork i Bytów na tle stosunków polsko-brandenburskich 1657–1670' *Studia i Materiały do Dziejów Wielkopolski i Pomorza* 6 (1960)
Między Polską a Brandenburgią (Wrocław, 1966)
Kamiński, A. 'The Cossack experiment in szlachta democracy in the Polish–Lithuanian Commonwealth. The Hadiach (Hadziacz) Union' *Harvard Ukrainian Studies* 1 (1977)
'The Polish–Lithuanian Commonwealth and its citizens: was the Commonwealth a

Bibliography

stepmother for Cossacks and Ruthenians?' in Potichnyi, P. (ed.) *Poland and the Ukraine, Past and Present* (Edmonton and Toronto, 1980)

'The szlachta of the Polish–Lithuanian Commonwealth and their government' in Banac, I. and Bushkovitch, P. (eds.) *The Nobility of Russia and Eastern Europe* (New Haven, Conn., 1983)

Kamiński, J. *Urzędy hetmańskie w dawnej Polsce* (Lwów, 1939)

Karbownik, H. *Ciężary stanu duchownego w Polsce na rzecz państwa od roku 1381 do połowy XVII wieku* (Lublin, 1980)

Kentrschynskyj, B. 'Karl X Gustav inför krisen i öster 1654–1655' *Karolinska Förbundets Årsbok* (1966)

Kersten, A. *Chłopi polscy w walce z najazdem szwedzkim* (Warsaw, 1958)

Hieronim Radziejowski. Studium władzy i opozycji (Warsaw, 1988)

'Les Magnats – élite de la société nobiliaire' *Acta Poloniae Historica* 36 (1977)

Na tropach Napierskiego. W kręgu mitów i faktów (Warsaw, 1970)

Problem władzy w Rzeczypospolitej czasu Wazów' in Gierowski, J. (ed.) *O naprawę Rzeczypospolitej XVII–XVIII w. Prace ofiarowane Władysławowi Czaplińskiemu w 60 rocznice urodzin* (Warsaw, 1965)

Sienkiewicz – potop – historia (Warsaw, 1974)

Stefan Czarniecki, 1599–1665 (Warsaw, 1963)

Szwedzi pod Jasną Górą 1655 (Warsaw, 1975)

'Walka o pieczęć' *Sobótka* 30 (1975)

'Warstwa magnacka: kryterium przynależności' in Czapliński and Kersten (eds.) *Magnateria polska jako warstwo społeczna. Referaty z sympozjów XI Powszechnego Zjazdu Historyków Polskich w Toruniu, wrzesień 1974* (Toruń, 1974)

'Z badań nad Konfederacją Tyszowiecką' *Rocznik Lubelski* 1 (1958)

Kiereś, Z. *Szlachta i magnateria Rzeczypospolitej wobec Francji w latach 1573–1660* (Wrocław, 1985)

Kijas, A. 'Diplomatyczna działalność Atanazego Ordina-Naszczokina. Przyczynek do stosunków polsko-rosyjskich w drugiej połowy XVIIw.' in Czubiński, A. (ed.) *Polska, Niemcy, Europa* (Poznań, 1977)

Kirby, D. *Northern Europe in the Early Modern Period. The Baltic World 1492–1772* (London, 1990)

Klaczewski, W. *W przededniu wojny domowej w Polsce. Walka sejmowa lat 1664–1665* (Lublin, 1984)

Koch, F. 'Der Bromberger Staatsvertrag zwischen dem Kurfürsten Friedrich Wilhelm von Brandenburg und dem König Johann Kasimir von Polen im Jahre 1657' *Zeitschrift der Historischen Gesellschaft für die Provinz Posen* 21 (1906)

Kolberg, A. 'Ermland als churbrandenburgisches Fürstenthum in den Jahren 1656 und 1657' *Zeitschrift für die Geschichte und Alterthumskunde des Ermlands* 12 (1897)

Konarski, K. 'Charakterystyka stanowiska międzynarodowego Polski na przełomie XVI i XVII wieku' *Przegląd Historyczny* 20 (1916)

Konopczyński, W. *Chronologia sejmów polskich* Polska Akademia Umiejętności. Archiwum Komisji Historycznej Ser.2, IV (ogólnego zbioru XVI) (Cracow, 1948)

Dzieje Polski nowożytnej 2nd Edition (Warsaw, 1986)

Kwestia bałtycka (Gdańsk, 1947)

Le Liberum veto. Etude sur le développement du principe majoritaire (Paris, 1930)

Bibliography

Liberum veto. Studium porównawczo-historyczne (Cracow, 1918)
'O wojnie szwedzkiej i brandenburskiej, 1655–1657' *Kwartalnik Historyczny* 32 (1918)
Polska a Szwecja od pokoju oliwskiego do upadku Rzeczypospolitej, 1660–1795 (Warsaw, 1924)
'Polska polityka bałtycka' *Roczniki Historyczne* 3 (1927)
'Udział Korony i Litwy w tworzeniu wspólnej polityki zagranicznej (1569–1795)' *Pamiętnik VI Zjazdu Historyków Polskich w Wilnie* I (Lwów, 1935)
Korzon, T. *Dola i niedola Jana Sobieskiego, 1629–1674* (Cracow, 1898)
Kosman, M. *Reformacja i kontrreformacja w Wielkim Księstwie Litewskim w świetle propagandy wyznaniowej* (Wrocław, 1973)
'Sytuacja prawno-polityczna kalwinizmu litewskiego w drugiej połowie XVII wieku' *Odrodzenie i Reformacja w Polsce* 20 (1975)
Kot, S. *Jerzy Niemirycz w 300-lecie Ugody Hadziackiej* (Paris, 1960)
'Świadomość narodowa w Polsce w XV–XVIIw.' *Kwartalnik Historyczny* 52 (1938)
Kotłubaj, E. *Galeria nieświeżka portretów radziwiłłowskich* (Wilno, 1857)
Życie Janusza Radziwiłła (Wilno, 1859)
Krebs, O. 'Vorgeschichte und Ausgang der polnischen Königswahl im Jahre 1669. Nach den Berichten der pfalzgräffisch-neuburgischen Gesandten im kgl. Bayer. Geh. Staatsarchiv zu München' *Zeitschrift der Historischen Gesellschaft für die Provinz Posen* 3 (1888)
Kubala, L. 'Drugie Liberum Veto' *Biblioteka Warszawska* 65 (1905)
Szkice historyczne Seria 1–2 (Lwów, 1923)
Wojna brandenburska i najazd Rakoczego w roku 1656 i 1657 (Lwów and Warsaw, 1917)
Wojny duńskie i pokój oliwijski, 1657–1660 (Lwów, 1922)
Wojna moskiewska r.1654–1655 Szkice Historyczne Serja 3 (Warsaw and Cracow, 1910)
Wojna szwecka w roku 1655 i 1656 Szkice historyczne Serja 4 (Lwów, 1913)
Kuchowicz, Z. and Spieralski, Z. *W walce z najazdem szwedzkim, 1655–1660* (Warsaw, 1956)
Kukiel, M. *Zarys dziejów wojskowości polskiej do roku 1864* (Warsaw, 1965–6)
Kurzon, T. *Dzieje wojen i wojskowości w Polsce* 2nd edition (Lwów and Warsaw, 1923)
Kutrzeba, S. *Historia ustroju Polski w zarysie* I (Korona) 7th edition (Cracow, 1931) II (Litwa) 2nd edition (Lwów, 1921)
Unia Polski z Litwą (Cracow, 1914)
Lappo, I.I. 'Litovsko-Russkoe gosudarstvo v sostave Rechi Pospolitoi' *Vědečke Práce Ruské Lidové University v Praže* II (Prague, 1929)
Laska, J. 'Stosunek Gdańska do elektora brandenburskiego w początkowym okresie "potopu" szwedzkiego' *Rocznik Gdański* 27 (1968)
Leitsch, W. *Moskau und die Politik des Kaiserhofes im XVII. Jahrhundert* (Graz and Cologne, 1960)
Lepszy, K. (ed.) *Polska w okresie drugiej wojny północnej* (Warsaw, 1957)
Leszczyński, J. 'Agenci Chmielnickiego i Rakoczego na Morawach i na Śląsku' *Sobótka* 10 (1955)
'Dwa ostatnie sejmy przed potopem szwedzkim w oczach dyplomaty cesarskiego' *Sobótka* 30 (1975)
Lewitter, L. 'Poland, the Ukraine and Muscovy in the seventeenth century' *Slavonic and East European Review* 27 (1948–9)
'The Russo-Polish treaty of 1686 and its antecedents' *Slavonic and East European Review* 9 (1964)

Bibliography

Libiszowska, Z. *Certains aspects des rapports entre la France et la Pologne au XVIIe siècle* (Warsaw, 1964)

'Ludwika Maria w Berlinie (28.VI-3.VII.1658)' in Matwijowski, K. and Wójcik, Z. (eds.) *Studia z dziejów Rzeczypospolitej szlacheckiej* (Wrocław, 1988)

'Pierwsza gazeta polska Merkuriusz Polski i jej rola w walce o reformę ustroju w połowie XVIIw.' *Prace Polonistyczne* 12 (1955)

Żona dwóch Wazów (Warsaw, 1963)

Lileyko, J. *Życie codzienne w Warszawie za Wazów* (Warsaw, 1984)

Lisk, J. *The Struggle for Supremacy in the Baltic, 1600–1725* (London, 1967)

Litwin, H. 'Catholicisation among the Ruthenian nobility and assimilation processes in the Ukraine during the years 1569–1648' *Acta Poloniae Historica* 55 (1987)

'Magnateria polska 1454–1648. Kształtowanie się stanu' *Przegląd Historyczny* 74 (1983)

Litwin, H. and Maciak, D. *Sejm polski w połowie XVII wieku* (Warsaw, 1983)

Lityński, A. 'Sejmiki dawnej Rzeczypospolitej' *Przegląd Historyczny* 66 (1975)

'Sejmiki ziemskie koronne Rzeczypospolitej w okresie oligarchii' *Czasopismo Prawno-Historyczne* 35 (1983)

Szlachecki samorząd gospodarczy w Małopolsce (1616–1717) Prace naukowe Uniwersytetu Śląskiego w Katowicach 53 (Katowice, 1974)

Longworth, P. *Alexis, Tsar of all the Russias* (London, 1984)

Ludtke, F. 'Der Nuntius P. Vidoni als Gegenreformator in Posen' *Zeitschrift der Historischen Gesellschaft für die Provinz Posen* 19 (1915)

Lukowski, J.T. *Liberty's Folly: the Polish-Lithuanian Commonwealth in the Eighteenth Century* (London, 1991)

Lulewicz, H. 'Skład wyznaniowy senatorów świeckich Wielkiego Księstwa Litewskiego za panowania Wazów' *Przegląd Historyczny* 68 (1977)

Maciszewski, J. *Polska a Moskwa 1603–1618* (Warsaw, 1968)

Szlachta polska i jej państwo (Warsaw, 1969)

Wojna domowa w Polsce (1606–1609) (Wrocław, 1960)

'W sprawie kultury szlacheckiej' *Przegląd Historyczny* 53 (1962)

Maciuszko, J. 'Staropolska kategoria "stan" – Max Weber i słownictwo szlacheckie' *Przegląd Historyczny* 74 (1983)

Majewski, A. 'Les Tours canonnières et les fortifications bastionées en Pologne' *Bulletin de l'institut des châteaux historiques* 40 (1982)

Majewski, W. '1655–60: Potop' in Sikorski, J. (ed.) *Polskie tradycje wojskowe* I (Warsaw, 1990)

'Bitwa pod Mątwami' *SMHW* 7 (1961)

'Plany wojny tureckiej Władysława IV a rzekome przymierze kozacko-tatarskie z 1645r.' *Przegląd Historyczny* 64 (1973)

'Polska sztuka wojenna w okresie wojny polsko-szwedzkiej' *SMHW* 21 (1978)

Mal'tsev, A.N. *Rossiia i Belorussiia v seredine XVII veka* (Moscow, 1974)

Markiewicz, M. *Rady senatorskie Augusta II (1697–1733)* Polska Akademia Nauk: Oddział w Krakowie. Prace Komisji Historycznej L (Wrocław, Warsaw, Cracow, Gdańsk and Łódź, 1988)

'Rady senatu za Augusta III' *Zeszyty naukowe Uniwersytetu Jagiellońskiego: Prace Historyczne* LXXVII (Cracow, 1985)

Matuszewski, J. 'Sprzedawalność urzędów w Polsce szlacheckiej' *Czasopismo Prawno-*

Bibliography

Historyczne 16 (1964)

Mączak, A. 'The conclusive years: the end of the sixteenth century as the turning-point of Polish history' in Kouri, E.I. and Scott, T. (eds.) *Politics and Society in Reformation Europe. Essays for Sir Geoffrey Elton on his Sixty-Fifth Birthday* (London, 1987)

'Money and society in Poland and Lithuania in the sixteenth and seventeenth centuries' *Journal of European Economic History* 5 (1976)

Mączak, A., Samsonowicz, H. and Burke, P. (eds.) *East-central Europe in transition. From the fourteenth to the seventeenth century* (Cambridge, 1985)

Merczyng, H. *Zbory i senatorowie protestancy w dawnej Rzeczypospolitej* (Warsaw, 1904)

Meinardus, O. 'Kurfürst Friedrich Wilhelms Bemühungen um die polnischen Königsthrone' *Historische Zeitschrift* 76 (36 Neue Folge) (1894)

Michalski, J. 'Les Dietines polonaises au XVIIIe siècle' *Acta Poloniae Historica* 12 (1965) (ed.) *Historia Sejmu polskiego* I (Warsaw, 1984)

Mienicki, R. 'Utrata Smoleńska w r.1654 i sprawa Obuchowicza' *Kwartalnik Litewski* 1 (1910)

Miniewicz, J. *Bastejowe fortifikcje w Polsce* (Wrocław, 1975)

Morzy, J. *Kryzys demograficzny na Litwie i Białorusi w drugiej połowie XVII wieku* (Poznań, 1965)

Myciński, J. 'Ladislas IV Vasa et les Cosaques. L'échec des deux dernières tentatives du militarisme royal en Pologne' unpublished doctoral thesis, State University of Lille (1970)

Nagielski, M. 'Opinia szlachecka o gwardii królewskiej w latach 1632–1668' *Kwartalnik Historyczny* 92 (1985)

Neuber, A. *Der schwedisch-polnische Krieg und die österreichische Politik (1655–1660)* Prager Studien aus dem Gebiete der Geschichtswissenschaft XVII (Prague, 1915)

Nowak, T. 'Arsenały artylerii koronnej w latach 1632–1655' *SMHW* 14 (1968)

'Kampania wielkopolska Czarnieckiego i Lubomirskiego w roku 1656' *Rocznik Gdański* 2 (1937)

Oblężenie Torunia w roku 1658 Roczniki Towarzystwa Naukowego w Toruniu XLIII (Toruń, 1936)

Nowak, T. and Wimmer, J. (eds.) *Dzieje oręża polskiego do roku 1793* (Warsaw, 1968)

O'Brien, C.B. *Muscovy and the Ukraine. From the Pereiaslav agreement to the Truce of Andrusovo, 1654–1667* (Berkeley, 1963)

Ochmann, S. 'Anonimowy projekt reformy skarbowej z 1657 roku' *Sobótka* 30 (1975)

'Działalność polityczna Jana Andrzeja Morsztyna w latach 1660–1661' *Kwartalnik Historyczny* 86 (1979)

'Plans for parliamentary reform in the Commonwealth in the middle of the seventeenth century' in Czapliński, W. (ed.) *The Polish Parliament at the Summit of its Development (Sixteenth to Seventeenth Centuries)* (Wrocław, 1985)

'Postawa polityczna i moralna posła w świetle praktyce parlamentarnej lat 1661–62' *Sobótka* 31 (1976)

Sejmy lat 1661–1662. Przegrana batalia o reformę ustroju Rzeczypospolitej (Wrocław, 1977)

Sejm koronacyjny Jana Kazimierza w 1649r. Acta Universitatis Wratislaviensis 705 Historia XLV (Wrocław, 1985)

'Sprawa hetmańska w latach 1661–1662' *Kwartalnik Historyczny* 84 (1977)

Bibliography

Ochmański, J. *Historia Litwy* 2nd edition (Wrocław, Warsaw, Cracow, Gdańsk and Łódź, 1982)
'The national idea in Lithuania from the sixteenth to the first half of the nineteenth century: the problem of cultural-linguistic differentiation' *Harvard Ukrainian Studies* 10 (1986)
Odyniec, W. *Dzieje Prus Królewskich, 1454–1772* (Warsaw, 1972)
Polskie Dominium Maris Baltici. (Zagadnienia geograficzne, ekonomiczne i społeczne X–XVIIIw.) (Warsaw, 1982)
Ogonowski, Z. 'W obronie liberum veto. Nad pismami Andrzeja Maksymiliana Fredry' *Człowiek i Światopogląd* 14 (1975)
Olszewski, H. 'Funkcjonowanie Sejmu w dawnej Rzeczypospolitej' *Czasopismo Prawno-Historyczne* 35 (1983)
'Praktyka limitowania sejmików' *Czasopismo Prawno-Historyczne* 13 (1961)
Sejm Rzeczypospolitej epokii oligarchii: prawo-praktyka-teoria-programy, 1652–1763 (Poznań, 1966)
'The essence and legal foundations of the magnate oligarchy in Poland' *Acta Poloniae Historica* 56 (1987)
Opaliński, E. 'Elekcje wazowskie w Polsce. Stosunek szlachty do instytucji okresu bezkrólewia' *Kwartalnik Historyczny* 92 (1985)
Elita władzy w województwach poznańskim i kaliskim za Zygmunta III (Poznań, 1981)
'Great Poland's power élite under Sigismund III, 1587–1632' *Acta Poloniae Historica* 42 (1980)
'Postawa szlachty polskiej wobec osoby królewskiej jako instytucji w latach 1587–1648. Próba postawienia problematyki' *Kwartalnik Historyczny* 90 (1983)
Opgenoorth, E. *Friedrich Wilhelm der Grosse Kurfürst von Brandenburg. Eine politische Biographie* (Frankfurt and Zurich, 1971)
Opitz, E. *Österreich und Brandenburg im schwedisch-polnischen Krieg, 1655–1660* (Boppard-am-Rhein, 1969)
Pałucki, W. *Drogi i bezdroża skarbowości polskiej XVI i pierwszej połowy XVII wieku* (Wrocław, 1974)
Parrott, D. 'Strategy and tactics in the Thirty Years War: the "Military Revolution"' *Militärgeschichtliche Mitteilungen* 38, no. 2 (1985)
Pawiński, A. *Skarbowość w Polsce i jej dzieje za Stefana Batorego* (Warsaw, 1881)
Rządy sejmikowe w Polsce, 1572–1795, na tle stosunków województw kujawskich 2nd edition (Warsaw, 1978)
Pernal, A.B. 'The expenditure of the Crown Treasury for the financing of diplomacy between Poland and the Ukraine during the reign of Jan Kazimierz' *Harvard Ukrainian Studies* 5 (1981)
'The Polish Commonwealth and the Ukraine: Diplomatic relations 1648–1659' unpublished Ph.D. thesis, (University of Ottawa, 1977)
Petersen, E.L. 'From domain state to tax state' *Scandinavian Economic History Review* 23 (1975)
Piwarski, K. *Dzieje polityczne Prus Wschodnich (1621–1772)* (Gdynia, 1938)
Dzieje Prus Wschodnich w czasach nowożytnych (Gdańsk and Bydgoszcz, 1946)
'Kwestja bałtycka na Litwie w drugiej połowie XVIIw.' *Pamiętnik VI Zjazdu Historyków*

Bibliography

Polskich w Wilnie I (Lwów, 1935)

'Lithuanian participation in Poland's Baltic politics, 1650–1700' *Baltic and Scandinavian Countries* 3 (1937)

'Osłabienie znaczenia międzynarodowego Rzeczypospolitej w drugiej połowie XVII wieku' *Roczniki Historyczne* 23 (1957)

'Plan rozbioru Rzeczypospolitej w dobie "potopu". Polityka dworu Hohenzollernów wobec Szwecji i Rzeczypospolitej w latach 1655–1657' *Sprawozdania Poznańskiego Towarzystwa Przyjaciół Nauk* XIX (Poznań, 1955)

'Sytuacja międzynarodowa Rzeczypospolitej w drugiej połowie XVIIw.' *Pamiętnik VIII Powszechnego Zjazdu Historyków Polskich w Krakowie 14–17 wrzesnia 1958* III (Warsaw, 1960)

Plebański, J.K. *Commentatio historia de successoris designandi consilio vivo Joanne Casimiro Polonorum Rex* (Berlin, 1855)

Jan Kazimierz Waza. Maria Ludwika Gonzaga. Dwa obrazy historyczne (Warsaw, 1862)

Plourin, M.-L. *Marie de Gonzague, une princesse française, reine de Pologne* (Paris, 1946)

Podhorodecki, L. *Chanat krymski i jego stosunek z Polską w XV–XVIIIw.* (Warsaw, 1987)

Poraziński, J. 'Funkcje polityczne i ustrojowe rad senatu w latach 1697–1717' *Kwartalnik Historyczny* 91 (1984)

Porschnev, B.F. 'K kharakteristike mezhdunarodnoi obstanovki osvoboditel'noe voiny ukrainskogo naroda 1648–1654 godov' *Voprosy Istorii* 5 (1947)

Pośpiech, A. and Tygielski, W. 'Społeczna rola dworu magnackiego XVII–XVIII wieku' *Przegląd Historyczny* 69 (1978)

Pribram, A.F. *Franz Paul Freiherr von Lisola, 1613–1674, und die Politik seiner Zeit* (Leipzig, 1894)

Österreichische Vermittlungspolitik im polnisch-russischen Kriege, 1654–1660 Archiv für österreichische Geschichts-Quellen LXXV (1889)

'Zur auswärtigen Politik des Kurfürsten Friedrich Wilhelm von Brandenburg' *Forschungen zur Brandenburgischen und Preussischen Geschichte* 5 (1892)

Pritsak, O. 'Concerning the Union of Hadjač (1658)' *Harvard Ukrainian Studies* 2 (1978)

Prochaska, A. *Poseł królewski na sejmiki* (Lwów, 1925)

Przyboś, A. *Michał Korybut Wiśniowiecki, 1640–1673* (Cracow and Wrocław, 1984)

'Plan elekcji za życia króla, opracowany przez Kanclerza koronnego Mikołaja Prażmowskiego 1 maja 1665r.' *Studia Historyczne* 25 (1982)

'Z problematyki wojny polsko-szwedzkiej w latach 1655–1660' *Dziesięciolecie Wyższej Szkoły Pedagogicznej w Krakowie, 1946–1956* (Cracow, 1957)

Przyboś, A. and Rożek, M. *Biskup krakowski Andrzej Trzebicki. Z dziejów kultury politycznej i artystycznej w XVII stuleciu* (Cracow, 1989)

Przyboś, K. 'Prodworskie i opozycyjne stanowisko posłów krakowskich w latach 1648–1696' *Uchwalenie konstytucji na sejmach w XVI–XVIIIw.* (Wrocław, 1979)

Przyboś, K. and Waloszek, A. 'Reprezentacja sejmowa województwa krakowskiego w XVIIw.' *Studia Historyczne* 20 (1977)

Rachuba, A. *Konfederacja kmicicowska i Związek Braterski wojska litewskiego w latach 1660–1663* (Warsaw, 1989)

'Litwa wobec sądu nad Jerzym Lubomirskim' *Kwartalnik Historyczny* 93 (1987)

'Opozycja litewska wobec wyprawy Jana Kazimierza na Rosję (1663/4r.) *Kwartalnik Historyczny* 89 (1982)

Bibliography

'Paweł Sapieha wobec Szwecji i Jana Kazimierza (IX.1655–II.1656). Przyczynek do postawy magnaterii w okresie 'potopu'' *Acta Baltico-Slavica* 11 (1977)

'Zabiegi dworu i Jerzego Lubomirskiego o pozyskanie Litwy w 1664 roku' *Przegląd Historyczny* 78 (1987)

'Zabójstwo Wincentego Gosiewskiego i jego polityczne następstwa' *Przegląd Historyczny* 70 (1980)

Rafacz, J. 'Trybunał skarbowy koronny' *Kwartalnik Historyczny* 38 (1924)

Raffin, L. *Anne de Gonzague, princesse palatine 1616–1684* (Paris, 1935)

Rauch, G. von 'Moskau und die europäischen Mächte des 17. Jahrhunderts' *Historische Zeitschrift* 178 (1954)

Reddaway, W.F. (ed.) *The Cambridge History of Poland* I (Cambridge, 1951)

Redlich, O. *Weltmacht des Barock: Österreich in der Zeit Kaiser Leopolds I* 4th edition (Vienna, 1961)

Rembowski, A. *Rokosz i konfederacja w dawnym prawie polskim* (Warsaw, 1893)

Rhode, G. 'Staaten-Union und Adelsstaat: Zur Entwicklung von Staatsdenken und Staatsgestaltung in Osteuropa, vor allem in Polen/Litauen im 16. Jahrhundert' *Zeitschrift für Ostforschung* 9 (1960)

Roberts, M. *Essays in Swedish History* (London, 1967)

From Oxenstierna to Charles XII. Four Studies (Cambridge, 1991)

Roos, H. 'Der Adel der polnischen Republik im vorrevolutionären Europa' in Vierhaus, R. (ed.) *Der Adel vor der Revolution. Zur sozialen und politischen Funktion des Adels im vorrevolutionären Europa* (Göttingen, 1971)

'Ständewesen und parlamentarische Verfassung in Polen, 1501–1771' *Veröffentlichungen des Max-Planck Instituts für Geschichte* 27 (Göttingen, 1969)

Rostworowski, E. 'Ilu było w Rzeczypospolitej obywateli szlachty?' *Kwartalnik Historyczny* 94 (1987)

Rowen, H. *John de Witt, Grand Pensionary of Holland, 1625–1672* (Princeton, 1978)

Russocki, S. 'Le Système représentatif de la république nobiliaire de Pologne' in Bosl, K. (ed.) *Der moderne Parlamentarismus und seine Grundlagen in der ständischen Repräsentation* (Berlin, 1977)

Rybarski, R. 'Podatek akcyzy za czasów Jana Kazimierza i Michała Korybuta' *Studia ku czci Stanisława Kutrzeby* (Cracow, 1938)

Skarb i pieniądz za Jana Kazimierza, Michała Korybuta i Jana III (Warsaw, 1939)

Sadowski, Z. *Pieniądz a początki upadku Rzeczypospolitej w XVIIw.* (Warsaw, 1964)

Sajkowski, A. *Krzysztof Opaliński: wojewoda poznański* (Poznań, 1960)

Od Sierotki do Rybeńki. W kręgu radziwiłłowskiego mecenatu (Poznań, 1965)

Salzer, E. *Der Übertritt des Grossen Kurfürsten von der schwedischen auf die polnische Seite während des ersten nordischen Krieges in Pufendorfs "Carl Gustav" und "Friedrich Wilhelm"* Heidelberger Abhandlungen zur Mittleren und Neueren Geschichte VI (Heidelberg, 1904)

Sauter, W. *Krzysztof Żegocki; pierwszy partyzant Rzeczypospolitej, 1618–1673* (Poznań, 1981)

Sawczyński, H. 'Sprawa reformy sejmowania za Jana Kazimierza (1658–1661)' *Kwartalnik Historyczny* 7 (1893)

Schevill, F. *The Great Elector* (Chicago, 1947)

Schmidt, H. *Philipp Wilhelm von Pfalz-Neuburg (1615–1690) als Gestalt der deutschen und*

Bibliography

europäischen Politik des 17. Jahrhunderts I (Dusseldorf, 1973)

Schottmüller, K. 'Brandenburgische Kämpfe und Unterhandlungen mit dem Posener Adel im schwedischen Kriege' *Historische Monatsblätter für die Provinz Posen* 9 (1908)

Serczyk, W. 'The Commonwealth and the Cossacks in the Ukraine in the first quarter of the seventeenth century' *Harvard Ukrainian Studies* 2 (1978)

Serczyk, W. *Na dalekiej Ukrainie: dzieje Kozaczyzny do 1648 roku* (Cracow, 1984)

Seredyka, J. 'Aktywność senatorów wielkopolskich na sejmach drugiej połowy panowania Zygmunta III Wazy (1611–1632)' *Pamiętnik Biblioteki Kórnickiej* 18 (1981)

'Senatorowie Rzeczypospolitej na sejmach 1629–1632' *Zeszyty naukowe Wyższej Szkoły Pedagogicznej w Opolu* Historia XVI (Opole, 1979)

Seredyński, W. 'Sprawa obioru następcy na tron za panowania i po abdykacyi Jana Kazimierza' *Rocznik Cesarsko-Królewskiego Towarzystwa Naukowego Krakowskiego* IX (ogólnego zbioru XXXII) (Cracow, 1864)

Serwański, M. *Francja wobec Polski w dobie wojny trzydziestoletniej (1618–1648)* (Poznań, 1986)

'Znajomość ustroju i państwa francuskiego w Polsce w XVII wieku' in Czubiński, A. (ed.) *Polska – Niemcy – Europa. Studia z dziejów myśli politycznej i stosunków międzynarodowych* (Poznań, 1977)

Siemieński, J. 'Jednomyslność' *Pamiętnik IV Powszechnego Zjazdu Historyków Polskich w Poznaniu* (Lwów, 1925)

Sikora, L. *Szwedzi i Siedmiogrodziani w Krakowie* (Cracow, 1908)

Śladowski, W. *Skład społeczny, wyznaniowy i ideologia sejmiku lubelskiego* Annales Universitatis Mariae Curie Składowska Sectio F: Nauki filozoficzne i humanistyczne XII (1957) (Lublin, 1960)

Sobieski, W. 'Bałtycka polityka Mazarina i wywołania nią opozycja we Francja (1655–1660)' in Sobieski, W. *Trybun ludu szlacheckiego. Pisma historyczne* ed. Grzybowski, S. (Warsaw, 1978)

'Der Kampf um die Ostsee von den ältesten Zeiten bis zur Gegenwart' *Schriften des Baltischen Instituts* (Leipzig, 1933)

'Za kim opowiadziały sie Prusy Królewskich w r.1655?' *Pamiętnik V Zjazdu Historyków Polskich* I (Lwów, 1930)

Sobociński, W. *Pacta konwenta. Studium z historii prawa polskiego* (Cracow, 1939)

Socha, Z. *Hiberna. Studium z dziejów skarbowości w dawnej Polsce* (Lwów, 1937)

Spielman, J.P. *Leopold I of Austria* (London, 1977)

Śreniowski, S. 'Z zagadnień ideologii prawno-ustrojowej w Polsce XVIIw.' *Czasopismo Prawno-Historyczne* 6 (1955)

Stade, A. 'Geneza decyzji Karola X Gustawa o wojnie z Polská w 1655r.' *SMHW* 19 (1973) (ed.) *Carl X Gustafs Armé* Carl X Gustaf-Studier VIII (Stockholm, 1979)

Stadtmüller, G. 'Das Mächtesystem Osteuropas bis zum Ende des 17. Jahrhunderts' *Saeculum Weltgeschichte* 6 (Freiburg-im-Breisgau, 1971)

Stankiewicz, J. 'System fortyfikacyjny Gdańska i okolicy w czasie wojny 1655–1660r.' *SMHW* 20 (1974)

Subtelny, O. *Ukraine: A History* (Toronto, 1988)

Sucheni-Grabowska, A. 'Losy egzekucji dóbr w Koronie w latach 1574–1650' *Kwartalnik Historyczny* 80 (1973)

'Próby aukcji dochodów z dóbr domeny królewskiej w świetle lustracji z lat 1615–1620'

Bibliography

Przegląd Historyczny 58 (1967)
'Walka o wymiar i przeznaczenie kwarty w końcu XVIw. i na początku XVIIw.' *Przegląd Historyczny* 54 (1965)
Sysyn, F.E. 'Adam Kysil and the synods of 1629: An attempt at Orthodox-Uniate accommodation in the reign of Sigismund III' *Harvard Ukrainian Studies* 3–4 (1979–80)
Between Poland and the Ukraine: The Dilemma of Adam Kysil, 1600–1653 (Cambridge, Mass., 1985)
'Concepts of nationhood in Ukrainian history writing 1620–1690' *Harvard Ukrainian Studies* 10 (1986)
'The problem of nobilities in the Ukrainian past: the Polish period, 1569–1648' in Rudnytsky, I.L. (ed.) *Rethinking Ukrainian History* (Edmonton, 1981)
'Regionalism and political thought in seventeenth-century Ukraine: the nobility's grievances at the Diet of 1641' *Harvard Ukrainian Studies* 6 (1981)
'Ukrainian–Polish relations in the seventeenth century: the role of national consciousness and national conflict in the Khmelnytsky movement' in Potichnyi, P.J. (ed.) *Poland and Ukraine, Past and Present* (Edmonton, Toronto, 1980)
Szajnocha, K. 'Hieronim i Elżbieta Radziejowscy' in Szajnocha, K. *Szkice Historyczne* seria I-II (Warsaw, 1876)
Szcząska, Z. 'Sąd sejmowy w Polsce od końca XVI do końca XVIIIw.' *Czasopismo Prawno-Historyczne* 20 (1968)
Szczotka, S. *Chłopi obrońcami niepodległości Polski* (Warsaw, 1946)
Udział chłopów w walce z potopem szwedzkim (Lwów, 1939)
Szelągowski, A. 'Próby reform skarbowych w Polsce za Zygmunta III' *Ekonomista* 4 (1904)
'Sprawa reformy elekcji za Zygmunta III' *Sprawozdanie Dyrekcji c.k. Gimnazjum we Lwowie za rok szkolny 1912* (Lwów, 1912)
'Upadek waluty w Polsce za Jana Kazimierza' *Kwartalnik Historyczny* 15 (1901)
Szilágyi, S. 'Siebenbürgen und der Krieg im Nordosten 1654–1655' *Ungarische Revue* 12 (1892)
Targosz, K. *Hieronim Pinocci; studium z dziejów kultury naukowej w Polsce w XVII wieku* (Wrocław, Warsaw and Cracow, 1967)
La Cour savante de Louise-Marie de Gonzague et ses liens scientifiques avec la France, 1645–1667 (Wrocław, 1982)
Tazbir, J. 'Diariusz Stanisława Lubienieckiego (młodszego)' *Odrodzenie i Reformacja w Polsce* 5 (1960)
'Die Polonisierungprozesse in der Adelsrepublik' *Acta Poloniae Historica* 55 (1987)
'Poland and the concept of Europe in the sixteenth to eighteenth centuries' *European Studies Review* 7 (1977)
'Polish national consciousness in the sixteenth to the eighteenth centuries' *Harvard Ukrainian Studies* 10 (1986)
(ed.) *Polska XVII wieku. Państwo, społeczeństwo, kultura* (Warsaw, 1969)
'Prawdziwe oblicze Jerzego Niemirycza' *Przegląd Historyczny* 51 (1960)
'Recherches sur la conscience nationale en Pologne au XVIe siècle' *Acta Poloniae Historica* 14 (1966)
'Rol' protestantov v politicheskikh sviaziakh Pol'shi s Transil'vanii v XVIIv.' in Rybakov, B.A. (ed.) *Rossiia, Pol'sha i prichernomor'e v XVI–XVIIIvv.* (Moscow, 1979)
Rzeczpospolita i świat (Wrocław, Warsaw, Cracow and Gdańsk, 1971)

Bibliography

Stanisław Lubieniecki. *Przywódca ariańskiej emigracji* (Warsaw, 1961)
'The political reversals of Jurij Nemyryč' *Harvard Ukrainian Studies* 5 (1981)
Teodorczyk, J. 'Polskie wojsko i sztuka wojenna pierwszej połowy XVII wieku' *SMHW* 21 (1978)
Termesden, L. 'Carl X Gustafs Armé 1654–1657. Styrka och dislokation' in Stade, A. (ed.) *Carl X Gustafs Armé* Carl X Gustaf-Studier VIII (Stockholm, 1979)
'Karola X Gustava plan kampanii polskiej 1655 roku. Powstanie planu i jego przeprowadzenie' *SMHW* 19 (1973)
Tomkiewicz, W. 'Czasy Władysława IV i Jana Kazimierza w historiografii ostatnich lat dwudziestu' *Przegląd Historyczny* 34 (1937)
Jarema Wiśniowiecki (1612–1651) (Warsaw, 1933)
'Ograniczenie swobód kozackich w roku 1638' *Kwartalnik Historyczny* 44 (1930)
'Unia hadziacka' *Sprawy Narodowościowe* 11 (1937)
Toscan, R. *Marie de Gonzague, princesse nivernaise et reine de Pologne* (Paris, 1930)
Trumpa, V. 'The disintegration of the Polish–Lithuanian Commonwealth: a commentary' *Lituanus* 10 (1964)
Ulewicz, T. 'Il problema di sarmatismo' *Ricerche Slavistiche* 8 (1960)
Sarmacja: studium z problematyki słowiańskiej XV i XVI wieku (Cracow, 1950)
'Ustęp z wojen szwedzkich. Polityka możnych panów w XVII wieku. Z niedrukowanego rękopisu wyjął L.P.' *Dziennik Literacki* 18 (1863)
Vainshtein, O. 'Russko-shvedskaia voina 1655–1660 godov. (Istoriograficheskii obgor)' *Voprosy Istorii* 3 (1947)
Vetulani, A. 'Nowe spojrzenie na dzieje państwa i prawa dawnej Rzeczypospolitej' *Czasopismo Prawno-Historyczne* 10 (1958)
Polskie wpływy polityczne w Prusiech Książęcych (Gdynia, 1939)
Waddington, A. *Le Grand Electeur Frédéric-Guillaume de Brandebourg. Sa politique extérieure* (Paris, 1905)
Walewski, A. *Geschichte der hl. Ligue und Leopolds I. vom Umschwung im Gleichgewichtssystem des Westens durch den schwedisch-polnisch-österreichischen Krieg, bis zur Verwicklung der orientalischen Frage durch August II 1657–1700* (Cracow, 1857–61)
Historia wyzwolenia Polski za panowania Jana Kazimierza, 1655–1660 (Cracow, 1866–8)
Historia wyzwolenia Rzeczypospolitej wpadającej pod jarzmo domowe za panowania Jana Kazimierza (1655–1660) (Cracow, 1870)
Waliszewski, K. *Polsko-francuskie stosunki w XVII wieku, 1644–1667. Opowiadania i źródła historyczne ze zbiorów archiwalnych francuskich publicznych i prywatnych* (Cracow, 1889)
Wasilewski, T. *Jan Kazimierz* (Warsaw, 1985)
Jan Kazimierz: ostatni Waza na polskim tronie (Katowice, 1984)
'Zdrada Janusza Radziwiłła w 1655r. i jej wyznaniowe motywy' *Odrodzenie i Reformacja w Polsce* 18 (1973)
Wegner, J. *Szwedzi w Warszawie, 1655–1657* (Warsaw, 1936)
Warszawa w latach potopu szwedzkiego, 1655–1657 (Wrocław, 1957)
Wimmer, J. *Historia piechoty polskiej do roku 1864* (Warsaw, 1978)
'Nowe szwedzkie prace dotyczące przygotowań do wojny z Polską, 1655–1660' *SMHW* 17 (1971)
(ed.) *Wojna polsko-szwedzka, 1655–1660* (Warsaw, 1973)
'Wojsko i skarb Rzeczypospolitej u schyłku XVI i w pierwszej połowie XVIIw.' *SMHW*

Bibliography

14 (1968)
Wojsko polskie w drugiej połowie XVIIw. (Warsaw, 1965)
Wisner, H. 'Działalność wojskowa Janusza Radziwiłła, 1648-1655' *Rocznik Białystocki* 13 (1976)
'Litwa i plany wojny tureckiej Władysława IV. Rok 1646' *Kwartalnik Historyczny* 85 (1978)
'Litwa i projekt reformy elekcji 1629-1631' *Przegląd Historyczny* 64 (1973)
Najaśniejsza Rzeczpospolita. Szkice z dziejów Polski szlacheckiej XVI-XVII wieku (Warsaw, 1978)
'Rok 1655 na Litwie: pertraktacje ze Szwecją i kwestia wyznaniowa' *Odrodzenie i Reformacja w Polsce* 16 (1981)
Rozróżnieni w wierze. Szkice z dziejów Rzeczypospolitej schyłku XVI i połowy XVII wieku (Warsaw, 1982)
Unia. Sceny z przeszłości Polski i Litwy (Warsaw, 1988)
'Wielkie Księstwo Litewskie – Korona – Rzeczpospolita' *Przegląd Historyczny* 67 (1976)
'Wojsko litewskie 1 połowy XVII wieku' *SMHW* 19 (1973), 20 (1976), 21 (1978)
'Wojsko w społeczeństwie litewskim pierwszej połowy XVII wieku' *Przegląd Historyczny* 66 (1975)
Wiślocki, J. 'Walka z najazdem szwedzkim w Wielkopolsce w latach 1655-56' *Studia i Materiały do dziejów Wielkopolski i Pomorza* 2 (1956)
Witusik, A. 'Elekcja Jana Kazimierza w 1648 roku' Annales Universitatis Maria Curie-Składowska 17 (1962) (Lublin, 1965)
Włodarczyk, J. *Sejmiki łęczyckie* (Łódź, 1973)
Wojciechowski, Z. 'Les Eléments médievaux dans l'organisation de l'état polonais du XVI au XVIIIe siècles' *Czasopismo Prawno-Historyczne* 1 (1948)
Wolff, J. *Pacowie. Senatorowie i kniaziowie litewscy* (St Petersburg, 1885)
Senatorowie i dygnitarze Wielkiego Księstwa Litewskiego, 1386-1795 (Cracow, 1885)
Woliński, S. 'Urzędy hetmańskie w świetle ustawodawstwa polskiego' *Przegląd Historyczno-Wojskowy* 6 (1935)
Wójcik, Z. *Dzikie pola w ogniu: o kozaczyźnie w dawnej Rzeczypospolitej* 3rd edition (Warsaw, 1968)
'Feudalna Rzeczpospolita wobec umowy w Perejasławiu' *Kwartalnik Historyczny* 61 (1954)
'Financial aspects of the Polish-Tatar alliance, 1654-1666' *Acta Poloniae Historica* 13 (1966)
'From the Peace of Oliva to the Truce of Bakhchisarai; international relations in Eastern Europe, 1660-1681' *Acta Poloniae Historica* 34 (1976)
(ed.) *Historia dyplomacji polskiej* II (Warsaw, 1982)
Jan Sobieski, 1629-1696 (Warsaw, 1983)
'Poland and Russia in the seventeenth century. Problems of internal development' *Poland at the Fourteenth Congress of Historical Sciences in San Francisco* (Wrocław, 1975)
(ed.) *Polska służba dyplomatyczna, XVI-XVIII wieku* (Warsaw, 1966)
'Poselstwo Andrzeja Olszewskiego do Wiednia w roku 1658/59' *Sobótka* 31 (1976)
'Rywalizacja polsko-tatarska o Ukrainę na przełomie lat 1660-1661' *Przegląd Historyczny* 45 (1954)
'Rzeczpospolita na arenie międzynarodowej w XVIIw. Wybrane zagadnienia dyskusyjne'

Bibliography

Pamiętnik X Powszechnego Zjazdu Historyków Polskich w Lublinie I (Warsaw, 1969)
'Some problems of Polish-Tatar relations in the seventeenth century' *Acta Poloniae Historica* 13 (1966)
'Stosunki polsko-austriackie w drugiej połowie XVII wieku' *Sobótka* 38 (1983)
'The early period of Pavlo Teterja's hetmancy in the right-bank Ukraine (1661–1663)' *Harvard Ukrainian Studies* 3–4 (1979–80)
Traktat andruszowski i jego geneza (Warsaw, 1959)
'W sprawie sytuacji międzynarodowej Rzeczypospolitej w XVII wieku' *Kwartalnik Historyczny* 79 (1972)
'Zmiana w układzie sił politycznych w Europie środkowo-wschodniej w drugiej połowie XVII wieku' *Kwartalnik Historyczny* 67 (1960)
'Znaczenia wieku XVII w historii stosunki polsko-rosyjskich' *Prace na V Międzynarodowy Kongres Slawistów w Sofii 1963* (Warsaw, 1963)
Wyczański, A. (ed.) *Polska w epoce Odrodzenia: państwo, społeczeństwo, kultura* (Warsaw, 1970)
Polska – Rzeczą Pospolitą szlachecką (Warsaw, 1965)
'Le Revenu national en Pologne au 16e siècle' *Annales E.S.C.* 21 (1971)
(ed.) *Społeczeństwo staropolskie. Studia i szkice* I–III (Warsaw, 1976–83)
'La Structure de la noblesse polonaise aux XVIe–XVIIIe siècles; remarques méthodiques' *Acta Poloniae Historica* 36 (1977)
Wyczawski, H. *Biskup Piotr Gembicki* (Cracow, 1957)
Zaborovskii, L.V. 'Politika Shvetsii nakanune pervoi severnoi voiny (vtoraia polovina 1654 – seredina 1655g.' *Voprosy Istoriografii i Istochnikovedeniia Slaviano-germanskikh Otnoshenii* (Moscow, 1973)
'Russko-litovskie peregovory vo vtoroi polovine 1655g.' *Slaviane v epokhu feodalizma: k stoletiiu Akademika V.I.Pichety* (Moscow, 1978)
'Russkaia diplomatiia i nachalo pervoi severnoi voiny (ianvar'–oktiabr' 1655g.)' *Sovetskoe Slavianovedenie* 48 (1973)
Załuski, J.K. *Uwagi nad projektem obioru księcia Ludwika Kondeusza na tron Polski, tudzież nad elekcyą i panowaniem króla Michała Wiśniowieckiego* (Jasło, 1857)
Zarzycki, S. 'Stosunek księcia siedmiogrodzkiego Jerzego II Rakoczego do Rzeczypospolitej polskiej od początku wojny szwedzkiej do wyprawy tegoż na Polskę w roku 1657' *Sprawozdanie dyrekcjyi C.K. Wyższego Gimnazyum w Kołomyi za rok szkolny 1889* (Kołomija, 1889)
'Stosunek księcia siedmiogrodzkiego Jerzego II Rakoczego do Rzeczypospolitej polskiej od wyprawy tegoż na Polskę w r.1657 do końca wojny szwedzkiej w 1660r.' *Sprawozdanie dyrekcjyi C.K. Wyższego Gimnazyum w Kołomyi za rok szkolny 1890* (Kołomija, 1890)
Zarzycki, W. *Dyplomacja hetmanów w dawnej Polsce* (Warsaw and Poznań, 1976)
Zielińska, T. *Magnateria polska epoki saskiej. Funkcje urzędów i królewszczyzn w procesie przeobrażen warstwy społecznej* (Wrocław, 1977)
Žmuidzinas, J. *Commonwealth polono-lithuanien ou l'Union de Lublin* (Paris, the Hague and New York, 1978)

Index

Adersbach, Andreas, Brandenburg resident in Warsaw, 35
Adriano, Polish diplomatic agent, 56–7
Alexander VII, pope, 95, 119, 124
Alexis, tsar of Muscovy, 1, 2, 32, 48–50, 72–4, 76–7, 80, 82–3, 86, 89–91, 93–6, 101–2, 110, 123, 126, 128, 149, 153–4, 156–8, 161–4, 168
Allegretti, Allegretto di, Austrian diplomat, 73
Allenstein, 100
Alsace, 125
Altmark, truce of (1629), 17, 23, 37
Anderson, P., 4, 14
Andrusovo, treaty of (1667), 3, 170
Anjou, Philippe, duc d', 108, 160
Anna Jagiellońka, queen of Poland, wife of Stefan Batory, 16
Anne Henriette of the Palatinate, niece of Louise Marie, 68, 88, 96, 107, 166–7, 170, 173, 176
Avaugour, Charles d', French diplomat, 37, 71, 109
Auersberg, Johann Weikhard von, Austrian privy councillor, 57, 109
Augustus III, king of Poland, 15
Austria, 55, 65, 94, 98, 100, 104, 114, 153–4, 161, 164–5; army, 5, 117–20, 122, 125, 155–6, 160, 164–5; and Polish throne, 57, 72–3, 76, 107, 110, 169, 177–8; unpopularity in Poland, 78, 80, 84, 89, 106–7, 109, 112, 118–19, 121, 155–6, 159, 161; reluctance to prosecute war actively, 106, 109; more positive approach (1658), 125, 128

Bąkowa, J., 116, 122
Bąkowski, Jan Ignacy, 36, 89
Baltic trade, 7, 18
Berestechko, battle of (1651), 29, 32, 37
Berlin, 109, 113, 116–17, 126, 129–30, 154
Berlin, treaty of (9 February 1658), 117, 120, 126, 159
Białobłocki, Paweł, 32, 136, 174
Bila Tserkva, treaty of (1651), 29
Blondel, François, French diplomat, 109, 130
Bochnia, 95, 176

Bogislav XIV, duke of Pomerania, 100
Boguski, Jan, catellan of Czechów, 59
Bohemia, kingdom of, 111, 125
Bouillaud, Ismaël, 64
Brandenburg, electorate of, 4–5, 55, 65, 77–9, 83, 97–8, 100, 109, 114, 122, 127, 153–4, 159, 161, 164
Branecki, Jan, suffragan bishop of Poznań, 53
Bratslav, palatinate of, 157
Braunsberg, 100, 105
Bremen, 39
Brest (Litovsk), 89
Brest, union of, 9
Bromberg, 104, 130
Brömsebro, treaty of (1645), 95
Brzostowski, Cyprian Paweł, 162
Butler, Gotard Wilhelm, 35
Buturlin, Vasilii, Muscovite general, 32
Bütow, 100, 104–5
Bye, Nicholas de, Polish diplomatic agent, 55

Canasilles, Henri de, secretary and diplomatic agent of John Casimir, 37–9, 55
Casimir the Great, king of Poland, 10
Catherine Jagiellońka, queen of Sweden, wife of John III, 16
Charles IV, duke of Lorraine, 176
Charles X, king of Sweden, 1–2, 34, 38–9, 49, 51–2, 53, 62, 65, 67, 69, 71–2, 76–7, 79, 85–6, 94–5, 102, 108–9, 112, 116, 125–30, 139, 153–5, 157, 159–60, 164, 177
Charles XI, king of Sweden, 140, 164
Chernigov, palatinate of, 3, 12, 157, 170
Chodkiewicz, Jan Karol, 12, 17
Chojnice, 77
Christina, queen of Sweden, 1, 37
Cieciszewski, Wojciech, S.J., Polish diplomat, 88, 91, 121–2, 155
Condé, Louis II de Bourbon, prince de, 54, 124, 165, 167
Constance, queen of Poland, wife of Sigismund III, 26
Copenhagen, 95, 107, 125, 159; treaty of (28 July 1657), 95, 107, 153; treaty of (6 June 1660),

203

Index

Copenhagen (*cont.*)
164
Cossacks, 8, 13, 17–18, 32, 35, 41–2, 55, 66, 74, 85, 120, 126, 146, 154, 157–8, 170–1
Courland, duchy of, 98
Courland, duke of; *see* Kettler, Jacob
Coxe, archdeacon William, 12–14
Cracow, 52–3, 57, 69, 76, 95–6, 110, 132, 144, 176; palatinate of, 155–6, 177
Cromwell, Oliver, 55, 80
Czapliński, W. 16, 18, 133–4, 137, 147
Czarniecki, Stefan, castellan of Kiev (1655), palatine of Ruthenia (1657), xvii, 67, 69, 90, 92, 106, 112, 118, 122
Czartoryski, Florian Kazimierz, bishop of Cujavia, 57, 63, 94, 105, 124, 158, 172
Czartoryski, Mikołaj Jerzy, palatine of Volhynia, 59
Czersk, 173
Częstochowa, 85, 87
Częstochowa, convocation of (March 1656), 85–6, 88–92, 99, 115, 130, 144, 147–8, 177
Czorstyn, 58

Danzig, 5, 12, 46, 53, 71–2, 75–81, 84, 86–8, 100, 141
Danzig, treaty of (1526), 101
Denmark, 4, 55, 65, 83, 95, 98, 106, 112, 116, 121, 125–6, 129, 140, 153, 157, 159–60, 164, 178
des Noyers, Pierre, secretary to Louise Marie, 25, 28, 61–2, 64, 66, 109, 117, 130–1, 137–8, 147, 160, 175
diets (individual): *1562–3* ('execution diet'), 19; *1563–4*, 19; *1567*, 19; *1627*, (2), 23; *1652* (1), 14; *1654* (1), 32; *1654* (2), 33; *1655*, 41–6; *1658*, 130, 132, 134, 142, 145, 149–51, 153–9; *1659*, 135, 170; *1661*, 168–9; *1662*, 170; *1664–5*, 170–1, 174–5; *1665*, 170; *1666* (1), 170; *1666* (2), 170; *1668* (1), 170
Draheim, 104–5
Drucki-Sokoliński, Samuel, 48
Dünaburg, 48
Działyński, Michał Ezram, bishop of Kamianiets, 158

Edward of the Palatinate, 68
Elbing, 46, 69, 76, 96, 100, 104–5
Elizabeth Charlotte, electress of Brandenburg, 102
Enghein, Henri Jules, duc d', 23, 165–71, 176–7, 179
England, 55, 164
Este, Alfonso d', duke of Modena, 166
Este, Almerico d', 166
Execution movement, 18–20

Ferdinand II, grand duke of Tuscany, 63–4
Ferdinand III, Holy Roman Emperor, 28, 34, 41–2, 56–8, 63, 72, 76, 84, 89–91, 108
Ferdinand IV, king of the Romans, 56
Ferdinand-Maria, elector of Bavaria, 63, 65, 165–6
Fleury, François de, confessor to Louise Marie, 35
Florence, 63–4
France, 55, 65–6, 71, 83, 94, 108, 112, 127, 129, 154, 159, 164; and election campaign, 130, 160, 164–5, 167–70
Fragstein, Johann Christoph von, Austrian diplomat, 37, 42
Frankfurt-am-Main, 121–2, 125, 127, 129, 158
Frederick II, king of Prussia, 5
Frederick III, king of Denmark, 55, 79, 95, 121, 140
Frederick, V, elector of the Palatinate (Pfalz), 68
Frederick William, elector of Brandenburg, 4, 38–9, 46, 55, 65–6, 69–70, 72, 77–9, 85–6, 90, 109, 115–116, 122–3, 125–6, 156, 163; and Polish succession, 62, 124; attitude in 1655, 62–3; discussions with Poland 1657, 97–105; attitude towards alliance after 1657, 106; and French candidature, 113; and Pomeranian campaign, 125–30, 160
Fredro, Andrzej Maksymilian, castellan of Lwów, 14, 23, 172

Galiński, Piotr, 72–4, 81
Gardie, Magnus de la, 2, 49, 51
Gawlik, M., 82
Gembicki, Jan, bishop of Płock, 59
Gembicki, Krzysztof, castellan of Danzig, 169
Gembicki, Paweł, castellan of Międzyrzecz, 47
Gembicki, Piotr, bishop of Cracow, 58, 88, 121
Golz, Joachim Rüdiger von der, Brandenburg colonel, 126–7
Gonzaga, Anne, sister of Louise Marie, 68, 167
Gonzaga, Charles, duke of Nevers and Mantua, 27–8
Gosiewski, Wincenty Korwin, Lithuanian field hetman, Lithuanian treasurer, xvii, 33, 45, 48–9, 72, 77–9, 98–103, 111; and France, 112, 118, 122, 124–5, 127; and Muscovy, 123, 127, 161–3
Great Britain, 178
Great Northern War (1700–21), 3, 13
Great Poland, 46, 85, 93, 98–100, 106–7, 118, 155
Grodno, 33
Grudziński, Andrzej, palatine of Kalisz, 47
Grunwald, battle of (1410), 5
Gustavus Adolphus, king of Sweden, 12, 17

Index

Habsburg, archduke Charles Joseph, 88–9, 91–4, 96, 107–8, 110, 124, 167
Habsburg, archduke Ferdinand Charles, 56
Habsburg, archduke Leopold William, 58, 66, 87, 94
Habsburg, archduke Maximilian, 58
Habsburg, archduke Sigismund Francis, 56
Habsburg, house of, 57–8, 85–6, 88–9, 91, 93–5, 102, 108, 110–11, 113, 164–5, 169–70
Hadiach, treaty of (16 September 1658), 2, 157, 170
Hague, first concert of the (May 1659), 164
Halicz, 156, 173
Henrician articles, 10, 15
Henry III, king of France and Poland, 11, 16, 123
Hlebowicz, Jerzy Karol, starosta of Samogitia, 50
Holstein, duchy of, 120, 125–6
Holy Roman Empire, 56, 66, 102, 106, 150; election diet (Frankfurt, 1658), 121–2, 125, 158
Horodło, union of (1413), 5
Hoverbeck, Johann von, Brandenburg privy councillor and diplomat, 44, 79, 98, 101, 122, 148, 156
Hungary, kingdom of, 111

Ingria, 102
Istanbul, 107
Ivan IV, tsar of Muscovy, 5, 32

Jewłaszewski, Kazimierz Ludwik, castellan of Smolensk (1656), 172
John Casimir, king of Poland, 1, 9, 13, 14, 17, 29–32, 35–6, 42–3, 48, 51–2, 53–5, 59, 61, 70–1, 74, 76–9, 87–8, 95, 107–10, 117, 122, 126–7, 129, 131–2, 153, 156–8, 163–4; historical reputation, 23–4, 28; character and early career, 26–8; relationship with Louise Marie, 27–8, 115–16; attitude to Sweden, 37–8, 40, 54, 116; calls for abdication, 57, 59; attitude to Transylvanian candidature, 61–3, 66–9; attitude to Austria, 63–6, 92, 114, 120–1, 154–5, 161, 176; opposition to peace with Sweden, 80–1, 128; and treaty of Wilno, 82–4, 86, 89–90; conduct of talks with Brandenburg, 1657, 97–105; attitude to France, 115–17, 119, 135, 154–5, 160–1, 164; and political reform, 135–45, 152, 171–9; and French election campaign, 168–71; abdication, 170
John III, king of Sweden, 16
John III Sobieski, king of Poland, 13, 53, 177

Kalinowski, Marcin, Crown field hetman, xvii, 26, 30
Kalisz, 77, 81, 98–9
Kalisz, palatinate of, 2, 100
Kamińska-(Linderska), A., 97
Karlowitz, treaty of (1699), 3
Karwat, Seweryn, S.J., 44, 156
Kentrshynskyj, B., 39
Kersten, A., 35, 41, 92, 133, 137–8
Kettler, Jacob, duke of Courland, 34, 124
Khmelnytskyi, Bohdan, Cossack hetman, 1, 2, 17, 27, 29, 33, 43, 55, 74, 80, 157
Khmelnytskyi, Iurii, Cossack hetman, 157
Khotyn, battle of (1621), 12, 13; (1673), 13
Kiejdany, 49–50; treaty of (17 August 1655), 2, 34, 49–52, 54
Kierdej, Eustachy, castellan of Samogitia, 50
Kiev, 3, 8, 170; palatinate of, 22, 157, 173
Kircholm, battle of (1605), 12, 17
Kiszka, Janusz, Lithuanian grand hetman, xvii, 31–2
Klaczewski, W., 171
Klushino, battle of (1610), 12
Kock, Johan, Swedish agent, 39
Koniecpolski, Aleksander, palatine of Sandomierz, 53, 157
Königsberg, 55, 107; treaty of (17 January 1656), 63
Korsør, 159
Korsun, 157; battle of (26 May 1648), 18, 26
Koryciński, Stefan, Crown grand chancellor (1652), xvii, 30–1, 41–2, 56, 61, 68, 90–1, 96, 114–15, 121, 132, 138, 143, 154; opposition to Muscovite election, 74–7, 89; suport for peace with Sweden, 80, 87; angers Lithuanians, 81, 83; complains at French dishonesty, 86; opposition to Austrian alliance, 87; opposition to Brandenburg alliance, 99, 101, 104; attitude to France, 112
Korzon, T., 82
Kościan, 100
Košice, privileges of (1374), 10
Krasiński, Jan Kazimierz, palatine of Płock (1650), Crown treasurer (1658), xvii, 89, 160
Krosno, 65
Kubala, L., 24, 73, 108, 111–13, 15, 117, 119, 129, 135

Labiau, treaty of (20 November 1656), 79, 85
Łacki, Teodor, Lithuanian marshal of the court, xvii, 89
Lanckoroński, Stanisław, palatine of Ruthenia, Crown field hetman, xvii, 52, 92
Lauenberg, 100, 104–5
Łęczyca, 77

Index

Łęczyca, palatinate of, 100, 155
Lelewel, J., 174
Leopold I, king of Hungary (1654), Holy Roman Emperor (1658), 56, 91, 93, 96, 101, 105, 108–9, 117, 119, 123–5, 128–30, 154, 158, 167, 176; reluctance to prosecute war actively, 106–7, 126
Leszczyński, Andrzej, archbishop of Gniezno, xvii, 30, 36, 42, 56–8, 60–1, 63, 65–7, 71, 75, 80, 83, 87, 90, 105, 109, 115, 118–21, 124
Leszczyński, Bogusław, Crown treasurer (1650), Crown vice-chancellor (1658), xvii, 20, 40, 88, 144, 166; Vienna mission (1657), 90–1, 93, 108; attitude to France, 112, 115, 118, 160
Leszczyński, Jan, Bishop of Chełmno, 56–8, 64–5
Leszczyński, Jan, palatine of Łęczyca (1653), palatine of Poznań, (1656), xvii, 35–6, 38–40, 49, 68, 76, 79–80, 90–1, 98, 106, 111, 113, 117, 135, 143, 148, 177; mission to Sweden (1655), 41; mission to Vienna (1655–6), 62–3, 72, 84; attitude to Austria, 87–8, 95, 117, 121, 155; and Brandenburg negotiations, 1657, 100–1, 103; and France, 122; opposition to French election, 169
Leszczyński, Wacław, bishop of Warmia (1644), archbishop of Gniezno (1658), 40, 98, 100, 103, 124, 160
Lewitter, L., 82
Liberum veto, 12, 14–15, 23, 131–2, 136–8, 150–1, 168
Libiszowska, Z., 129
Likhariev, V.N., Muscovite diplomat, 50
Lilienthal, Meyer von, Swedish agent, 39
Lisola, Franz von, Austrian diplomat, 25, 57, 78, 86, 92–3, 97, 99, 102–5, 109, 117, 119–22, 125, 130, 159–60, 163, 167
Lithuania, grand duchy of, 1, 2, 5, 8–9, 32, 85, 146, 161; relations with Poland, 43–5, 80–1, 86; relations with Muscovy, 80, 94, 123, 154, 161–4; union called into question, 81, 94, 98, 146, 154, 157–8, 161; and election campaign, 164, 172–3
Little Poland, 20, 85, 93, 176–7
Livonia, 5, 12, 17, 18, 23, 38–40, 62, 69, 72, 94, 102, 160, 163–4
Longueville, Anne Geneviève, duchesse de, 29
Longueville, Henri d'Orléans, duc de, 124, 165, 167
Longueville, Charles-Paris d'Orléans, duc de, 124, 160, 166–7
Lorbach, Theodor, Austrian diplomat, 73
Louis of Anjou, king of Poland, 10
Louis XIII, king of France, 27

Louis XIV, king of France, 66, 93, 123
Louise Henriette of Orange, electress of Brandenburg, 79
Louise Marie, queen of Poland, 24, 31, 52, 63–4, 68, 79–81, 83, 85, 87, 89–90, 96, 129, 153–4, 156, 162, 170, 177; early career, 27; relationship with John Casimir, 27, 115–16; historical reputation, 27–8; and French candidature, 64, 110–13, 160–1, 164–7, 168–9; attitude to Austria, 93, 107, 109–10, 119, 122; attitude to France, 93, 107–9, 114–16, 118, 122–5, 127–30, 159–60; attitude to Brandenburg, 102, 109, 113–14, 126–7, 129–30; and political reform, 131, 135, 137–8, 144
Lubau, 61–2
Lübeck, 37
Lubieniecki, Władysław, 59
Lublin, 71, 77, 80
Lublin, union of (1569), 6–7, 9, 19, 142
Lubomirski, Jerzy Sebastian, Crown grand marshal, Crown field hetman (1657), xvii, 31, 35, 56, 69, 80, 83, 85, 105, 111–13, 115, 118, 122, 131, 152, 156–7, 161, 165; and Transylvania, 34, 59–62, 67–9, 173; contacts with Sweden, 53, 117; attitude to Austria, 58–9, 88, 90, 92–3, 110–11, 176; and throne, 60, 176–7; appointment as field hetman, 92–3; and French candidature, 112, 169–70, 176; impeachment, 170, 172, 174–5
Lubomirski's *rokosz*, 170
Lubomirski, Sebastian, palatine of Cracow, 31
Lubowiecki, Jan Franciszek, castellan of Chełmno, 169, 172
Lumbres, Antoine de, French diplomat, 25, 71–2, 75–7, 83–6, 93–6, 102, 107–16, 118, 120–2, 124, 127–8, 130, 137, 154, 160, 165, 167
Lwów, 1, 52, 73

Mal'tsev, A.N., 48
Mantua, duchy of, 28
Maria Casimira d'Arquien, queen of Poland, wife of John III Sobieski, 177
Marienburg, 46, 48, 53, 76
Marienburg, treaty of (25 June 1656), 69, 85
Martinozzi, Laura, 166
Mątwy, battle of (1666), 170
Maximilian Philip of Bavaria, 165–6
Mazarin, cardinal Jules, 28, 37, 71, 76, 86, 108, 110, 112–14, 116, 128, 165–7
Mazovia, 171
Medeksza, Franciszek, 45, 101, 123, 127, 162
Medici, Mattia de', 63–5, 68, 76, 124, 165, 167
Mehmet IV, sultan of Turkey, 83, 94

206

Index

Merkuriusz Polski, 168, 178
Miaskowski, Maksymilian, castellan of Krzywiń, 47
Michael Korybut Wiśniowiecki, king of Poland, 105, 170, 177
Międzyrzecz, 99
Mikes, Mihály, Transylvanian diplomat, 61–2, 132
Minsk, 48
Mogilev, 32
Moldavia, 74
Montecuccoli, Raimondo, Austrian general, 125, 132
Morsztyn, Jan Andrzej, 38–41, 111, 115, 126, 160
Moscow, 72–4, 89, 107
Muscovy, grand duchy of, 54–5, 72–4, 77, 79, 87, 91, 98, 100, 123, 127–8, 153, 168, 170, 178; army, 5, 32; 'Time of Troubles', 3, 17; policy in Ukraine, 55, 157; and Polish throne, 102, 104, 128, 145, 154, 156–8, 161, 177–8

Naruszewicz, Aleksander, Lithuanian vice-chancellor (1658), xvii, 41, 172
Neuburg, duke of; *see* Philip William, duke of Neuburg
Nevers, 28
Niemież, 82
Nieszawa, privileges of (1454), 10, 19
Nikon, patriarch of Moscow, 95
Nowak, T., 35
Nowiejski, Wojciech, canon of Warmia, 98

Oberglogau, Silesia, 2
Obuchowicz, Filip, 44
Ochmann, S., 132, 134, 140
Okhmativ, battle of (1644), 18
Oliva, treaty of (3 May 1660), 2–3, 164, 167–8, 178
Olszowski, Andrzej, bishop of Chełmno, (1661), 172
Opaliński, Jan Poitr, palatine of Podlasie, 47, 107
Opaliński, Krzysztof, palatine of Poznań, 2, 13, 33–5, 46, 53–4, 61, 139, 174, 177
Opaliński, Łukasz, Crown marshal of the Court, xvii, 35, 132–3, 145, 147, 169, 172
Oppeln, 59–60, 131, 138
Oppeln, duchy of, 109
Orléans, Gaston, duc d', 34
Orsza, battle of (1514), 5
Ossoliński, Jerzy, Crown grand chancellor, xvii, 27, 30
Ottoman empire, 156

Pac, Claire Isabelle Eugénie, (de Mailly-Lascaris), wife of Krzysztof, 115
Pac, Krzysztof, Lithuanian grand chancellor (1658), xvii, 50, 78, 80–1, 83–4, 89–90 109, 114–15, 154, 156, 160, 177; attitude to France, 112, 122, 162–4; and French election, 169, 172
Pac, Michał Kazimierz, xvii, 172
Pac, Mikołaj Stefan, palatine of Troki, 81
Parczewski, Piotr, bishop of Samogitia, 40
Paris, 170
Pasek, Jan Chryzostom, 28
Pereiaslav, treaty of (18 January 1654), 1, 157
Philip William, duke of Neuburg, 63–5, 68, 166
Philipowo, battle of (22 October 1656), 78
Pinocci, Hieronim, 168
Piotrków, privileges of (1493), 10
Piotrków Czarniecki, 100
Piquet, French diplomat, 37
Piwarski, K., 78, 97, 99, 102, 104–5
Podlasie, palatinate of, 7
Podolia, palatinate of, 22
Pokłoński, Konstanty, 48
Poland-Lithuania, Commonwealth of: army, 5, 12–13, 17–18, 29, 54, 77, 80, 92; political structure, 5–6, 9–12, 14–16, 18–23, 29; international position, 12, 17; nobility, 6, 10, 11, 20–3; political reform, 13, 14, 23–4, 29–30, 131–51, 171–9; senate council, 15–16, 33, 54, 137–9, 142–5, 148–50, 152; position of monarchy, 18–23; taxation, 18, 22–3, 144–5, 147–50, 159; relations with Sweden, 37–41; election campaign, 164–7, 172
Polotsk, 32
Pomerania, duchy of, 55
Pomerania, Swedish, 98, 106, 113–14, 116–17, 120, 123, 125–6, 130, 155–6, 160–1, 164
Potocki, Mikołaj, Crown grand hetman, 26, 30
Potocki, Stanisław 'Rewera', Crown grand hetman, xvii, 32, 42, 96
Poznań, 69, 95–6, 99, 104, 106, 123, 125–6, 128–30; diocese of, 118; palatine of, 2, 100
Prażmowski, Mikołaj, Crown grand-chancellor (1658), xvii, 67–9, 111, 115, 122
Preussisch-Holland, 86
Prostken, battle of (8 October 1656), 77
Proszowice, 174
Prussia, Ducal, 4, 12, 55, 62, 69, 72, 77, 79, 97, 100–5, 126, 160
Prussia, Royal, 1, 5, 8, 10, 12, 40, 42, 53, 55, 62, 69, 71, 79, 85, 88, 93, 112, 126–8, 141, 153, 155, 160, 173
Putzig, 53
Pyliavtsi, battle of (23 September 1648), 18, 26
Pyrenees, peace of the (1659), 167

Index

Radnot, treaty of (6 December 1656), 85
Radom, 72, 74
Radziejowski, Hieronim, Crown vice-chancellor, xvii, 30–1, 33, 35, 47, 152, 172
Radziwiłł, Albrycht Stanisław, Lithuanian grand chancellor, xvii, 16, 25, 81
Radziwiłł, Bogusław, 50–1, 77–8, 156
Radziwiłł, Janusz, palatine of Wilno, Lithuanian grand hetman, xvii, 2, 13, 35, 40, 43–5, 47, 53–4, 61, 139, 152, 161–2, 174, 177; contacts with foreign princes, 34, 36; disputes with John Casimir, 32–3, 45; dealings with Sweden, 1655, 48–51
Radziwiłł, Krzysztof, palatine of Wilno, Lithuanian grand hetman, 34
Rákóczi, George I, prince of Transylvania, 26–7, 34
Rákóczi, George II, prince of Transylvania, 34, 36, 55, 59, 61–4, 66–9, 74, 80, 83, 85–9, 91–2, 95–6, 98–9, 106, 113, 132, 143, 165, 169, 176
Rákóczi, Sigismund, 26–7, 30, 34
Ratibor, duchy of, 109
Rawa, 19
Rey, Władysław, chancellor to Louise Marie, 121–2, 129
Riga, 72, 83
Rinsk, treaty of (12 November 1655), 62, 101
Romanov, tsarevich Alexis, 77, 82–3
Roskilde, treaty of (26 February 1658), 125–7, 135, 159, 164
Rozrażewski, Jakub, palatine of Inowrocław, 47
Rudawski, Wawrzyniec Jan, 27–8, 60, 116–18, 121, 129
Russia; see Muscovy, grand duchy of
Ruthenia, duchy of, 146, 157; palatinate of, 22, 144

St Germain-des-Prés, abbey of, 170
Sajkowski, A., 35, 36, 47
Samogitia, 71, 163
Sapieha, Kazimierz Leon, Lithuanian vice-chancellor, xvii, 40, 45, 81
Sapieha, Paweł, Lithuanian grand hetman (1656), xvii, 51, 73, 89, 99, 123, 142, 156, 162–3, 168, 172
Schlippenbach, Christoph Carl, count von, Swedish diplomat, 116
Schönhoff, Austrian diplomat, 56
Schwerin, Otto von, Brandenburg privy councillor, 79, 116, 126
Siciński, Władysław, 14–15, 36
Sielski, Aleksander, castellan of Gniezno (1659), 169
Siena, 63
Sieradz, palatinate of, 155, 173

Sigismund I, king of Poland, 19
Sigismund II Augustus, king of Poland, 5–6, 10, 16, 19
Sigismund III, king of Poland, 9, 16–17, 20–3, 26, 31, 33, 41, 61, 71, 169, 175
Silesia, 114, 120, 138, 160, 170
Smolensk, 3, 5, 12, 32, 73, 170
Sobieski, John; see John III Sobieski, king of Poland
Sobota, 62
Souches, Charles Louis, comte de, Austrian general, 155, 161
Środa, 173–4
Stanisław Augustus Poniatowski, king of Poland, 13, 179
Stefan Batory, prince of Transylvania and king of Poland, 11, 16–17, 42, 60–1
Stettin, 55, 96
Stockholm, 37
Stuart, house of, 55
Stuart, James, duke of York, 165–6
Stuhmsdorf, truce of (1635), 37
Sweden, 4, 17, 37–41, 53, 55, 62, 71, 74, 77, 87, 96, 109–10, 112, 114, 123, 127, 140, 153, 158–9, 161, 164
Szumowski, Jan, Polish diplomatic agent, 61

Tannenberg, battle of; see Grunwald
Tański, Jan, 62
Tarło, Jan, palatine of Lublin, 59
Tarnowski, Jan, archbishop of Lwów, 158
Tatars, 8, 41, 46, 55, 66, 72, 74, 78–9, 85, 96, 120, 126, 156
Telefus, Piotr, 175
Teutonic knights, 5
Thorn, 69, 72, 76, 96, 155, 176
Tolibowski, Wojciech, bishop of Poznań, 118–19, 158–9
Transylvania, 34, 55, 126
Trzebicki, Andrzej, Crown vice-chancellor, bishop of Cracow (1658), xvii, 30–1, 36, 40, 56–8, 63, 71, 74, 80–2, 90, 96, 105, 115, 117, 120–2, 144, 158–9, 169, 176
Tuscany, grand duchy of, 63, 66
Tyszkiewicz, Jerzy, bishop of Wilno, 49–50
Tyszowce, confederation of (29 December 1655), 54

Ujejski, Tomasz, bishop of Kiev, (1656), 158, 169
Ujście, treaty of (25 July 1655), 2, 34, 46–7, 51, 54
Ukraine, 1, 6–9, 32, 46, 85, 97, 128, 132, 146, 157, 170
Umiastowski, Jan Kazimierz, 42
Uniate (Greek Catholic) church, 9, 146, 154, 158

Index

United Provinces, 55, 65, 71, 79, 98, 159, 164

Vasa, house of (Poland), 17
Vasa, Anne Catherine, 63, 65
Vasa, Charles Ferdinand bishop of Płock and Breslau, 17, 26, 27, 30–1, 39, 56, 65
Vasa, John Adolf, brother of Charles X, 69
Vasa, John Albert, bishop of Cracow, 26
Vidoni, Pietro, 25, 57, 61, 63–5, 67, 71, 76, 80–1, 84, 87, 89–92, 94–5, 100, 105, 110, 117–22, 124, 127, 131, 135–7, 153, 158, 165–6, 177
Vienna, 77, 80, 88, 93; battle of (1683), 13; treaty of (1 December 1656), 84–5, 87–8; treaty of (27 May 1657), 95–6, 98, 102, 106–7, 111–12, 119, 144, 153, 155–6, 159, 176
Vitebsk, 32
Volhynia, palatinate of, 7, 22
Vyhovskyi, Ivan, Cossack hetman, 157

Waldeck, Georg Friedrich von, Brandenburg privy councillor, 79
Walewski, A., 90, 117, 119
Wallachia, 74
Warka, battle of (April 1656), 69
Warmia, bishopric of, 100, 104
Warsaw, 51, 54, 56, 70–1, 74–5, 90, 119, 122, 130, 159, 162–3; battle of (28–30 July 1656), 5, 70–1; confederation of (1573), 9–10; convocation of (March 1658), 115–20, 122, 124, 127–8, 130, 132–3, 135, 144–9, 159
Wawel, royal castle (Cracow), 155
Wehlau, 115
Wehlau–Bromberg, treaty of (19 September and 6 November 1657), 97, 104–6, 126, 153, 156
Weiher, Jakub, palatine of Marienburg, 53, 98
Weiher, Ludwik, palatine of Pomerania, 53
Wiemann, Daniel, Brandenburg diplomat, 126
Westphalia, treaty of (1648), 126, 158
Wieliczka, 31, 95, 176
Wielopolski, Jan, castellan of Wójnicz, 59, 67, 72, 111, 142, 169
Wieluń, county of, 100, 173
Wierzbołów, armistice of (October 1656), 78, 98; confederation of (23 August 1655), 51
Wilno, 1, 30, 48–9, 72–3, 76, 82, 123, 139, 163; treaty of (3 November 1656), 82–7, 89–90, 92–4, 98, 103, 127–8, 132, 142, 146, 151, 153, 156–8, 161–2
Wisner, H., 41, 44
Wiśniowiecki, Jarema, palatine of Ruthenia, 18, 29, 31, 170, 177
Wiśniowiecki, Michael Korybut; see Michael Korybut Wiśniowiecki, king of Poland
Wittenberg, Arvid, Swedish field marshal, 1–2, 46
Wizna, 173
Władysław Jagiełło, king of Poland, grand duke of Lithuania, 8
Władysław IV, king of Poland, 9, 15–17, 25–7, 29, 39, 41, 63, 76, 169, 175
Wójcik, Z., 73, 82
Wolmar, 163
Wreich, Christoph Sigismund von, Brandenburg diplomat, 99
Wydżga, Jan Stefan, bishop of Lutsk, 111, 158

Zakroczym, 173
Zamoyski, Jan, Crown grand chancellor, Crown grand hetman, 60
Zamoyski, Jan, palatine of Kiev (1658), palatine of Sandomierz (1659), 59, 177
Zaporozhian Sich, 8
Żarnów, battle of (16 September 1655), 52
Zasławski, Władysław Dominik, palatine of Cracow, 59
Zawisza, Jerzy Dowgaiłło, bishop of Wilno (1656), 75, 89, 127, 158
Zawisza, Krzysztof, grand marshal of Lithuania, xvii, 30
Zbąszyn, 98
Zboriv, treaty of (1649), 29
Zealand, 159
Zebrzydowski, Mikołaj, palatine of Cracow, 22, 34
Zebrzydowski's *rokosz*, 34
Zhovti Vody, battle of (11–16 May 1648), 18, 26
Zielenzig, truce of (December 1656), 98–100
Zips, 59
Zolotarenko, Vasyl, Cossack commander, 32, 48
Żytkiewicz, Daniel, Crown prosecutor, 31
Żytomierz, 173

CAMBRIDGE STUDIES IN EARLY MODERN HISTORY

The Old World and the New*
　　J.H. ELLIOTT
The Army of Flanders and the Spanish Road, 1567–1659: The Logistics of Spanish Victory and Defeat in the Low Countries Wars*
　　GEOFFREY PARKER
Neostoicism and the Early Modern State
　　GERHARD OESTREICH
Prussian Society and the German Order: An Aristrocratic Corporation in Crisis
c.1410–1466
　　MICHAEL BURLEIGH
Richelieu and Olivares*
　　J.H. ELLIOTT
Society and Religious Toleration in Hamburg 1529–1819
　　JOACHIM WHALEY
Absolutism and Society in Seventeenth-Century France: State Power and Provincial Aristocracy in Languedoc*
　　WILLIAM BEIK
Turning Swiss: Cities and Empire 1450–1550
　　THOMAS A BRADY JR
The Duke of Anjou and the Politique Struggle during the Wars of Religion
　　MACK P. HOLT
Neighbourhood and Community in Paris
　　DAVID GARRIOCH
Renaissance and Revolt: Essays in the Intellectual and Social History of Modern France
　　J.H.M. SALMON
Louis XIV and the Origins of the Dutch War
　　PAUL SONNINO
The Princes of Orange: The Stadholders in the Dutch Republic*
　　HERBERT H. ROWEN
The Changing Face of Empire: Charles V, Philip II and Habsburg Authority, 1551–1559
　　M.J. RODRIGUEZ-SALGADO
Frontiers of Heresy: The Spanish Inquisition from the Basque Lands to Sicily
　　WILLIAM MONTER
Rome in the Age of Enlightenment: The Post-Tridentine Syndrome and the Ancien Regime
　　HANNS GROSS
The Cost of Empire: The Finances of the Kingdom of Naples during the period of Spanish Rule
　　ANTONIO CALABRIA
Lille and the Dutch Revolt: Urban Stability in an Era of Revolution
　　ROBERT S. DUPLESSIS

The Armada of Flanders: Spanish Maritime Policy and European War, 1568–1668
R.A. STRADLING
The Continuity of Feudal Power: the Caracciolo di Brienza in Spanish Naples
TOMMASO ASTARITA
After the Deluge: Poland–Lithuania and the Second Northern War 1655–1660
ROBERT I. FROST

*Titles available in paperback marked with an asterisk**

The following titles are now out of print

French Finances, 1770–1795: From Business to Bureaucracy
J.F. BOSHER
Chronicle into History: An Essay on the Interpretation of History in Florentine Fourteenth-Century Chronicles
LOUIS GREEN
France and the Estates General of 1614
J. MICHAEL HAYDEN
Reform and Revolution in Mainz, 1743–1803
T.C.W. BLANNING
Altopascio: A Study in Tuscan Society 1587–1784
FRANK MCARDLE
Gunpowder and Galleys: Changing Technology and Mediterranean Warfare at Sea in the Sixteenth Century
JOHN FRANCIS GUILMARTIN JR
The State, War and Peace: Spanish Political Thought in the Renaissance 1516–1559
J.A. FERNANDEZ-SANTAMARIA
Calvinist Preaching and Iconoclasm in the Netherlands, 1544–1569
PHYLLIS MACK CREW
The Kingdom of Valencia in the Seventeenth Century
JAMES CASEY
Filoppo Strozzi and the Medici: Favour and Finance in Sixteenth-Century Florence and Rome
MELISSA MERIAM BULLARD
Rouen during the Wars of Religion
PHILIP BENEDICT
The Emperor and his Chancellor: A Study of the Imperial Chancellery under Gattinara
JOHN M. HEADLEY
The Military Organisation of a Renaissance State: Venice c.1400–1617
M.E. MALLETT and J.R. HALE

Printed in Great Britain
by Amazon